Praise for *Pinkerton's Gr...*

"A suspenseful page-turner pivoting around the enigmatic life of Pinkerton detective James McParlan, later McParland . . . Riffenburgh writes smooth and compelling prose, and McParland is a fascinating character. Any fan of American crime stories or Westerns will revel in Riffenburgh's vivid narratives of crimes McParland had a part in investigating, including the bank robberies of the Hole-in-the-Wall gang." —*Chicago Tribune*

"Locating the real James McParland amid the invective, acclaim, and invention (including his own) is no easy task, and Beau Riffenburgh, author of *Shackleton's Forgotten Expedition*, has made good use of the recently released Pinkerton archives. . . . McParland was the prototype of a character that has become an adored part of America's cultural landscape, the hard-boiled gumshoe, the lone sleuth in search of justice." —Ben McIntyre, *The New York Times*

"A measured, thought-provoking tale . . . Riffenburgh has unearthed a trove of collateral information that allows him to create a credible if flawed human hero at the center of [a] dark maelstrom." —*American History*

"McParland was neither a demon nor a saint. This is no cop out. The man belonged to an age ravaged by violence and conflict, and his job as he understood it was to capture the guilty. . . . He was not always in the right, but he broke with the right less often and less deliberately than the criminals he hunted. That is as much heroism as Riffenburgh, a great detective in his own right, has managed to find in this alien, tumultuous time." —*The Christian Science Monitor*

"Riffenburgh navigates . . . [a] moral quagmire deftly, contextualizing McParland and his far more violent time, while simultaneously deconstructing the image of the 'Great Detective.'" —*The Daily Beast*

"An illuminating look at a fascinating life with a nuanced analysis of how Pinkerton's agency functioned in the context of the labor movement in nineteenth-century America." —*The Columbus Dispatch*

"Energetic . . . Riffenburgh brings a forgotten rough-and-tumble world to life." —*Publishers Weekly*

PENGUIN BOOKS

PINKERTON'S GREAT DETECTIVE

Beau Riffenburgh has a PhD in history from the University of Cambridge, where he was a member of the academic staff. He is the author of numerous books on exploration, including *Nimrod*, about Ernest Shackleton's first Antarctic expedition, and *Racing with Death*, about Douglas Mawson's Australasian Antarctic Expedition. He lives in Llanarthne, Carmarthen, Wales.

PINKERTON'S
GREAT DETECTIVE

The Rough-and-Tumble Career of

James McParland, America's

Sherlock Holmes

BEAU RIFFENBURGH

PENGUIN BOOKS

PENGUIN BOOKS

Published by the Penguin Group
Penguin Group (USA) LLC
375 Hudson Street
New York, New York 10014

USA | Canada | UK | Ireland | Australia | New Zealand | India | South Africa | China
penguin.com
A Penguin Random House Company

First published in the United States of America by Viking Penguin,
a member of Penguin Group (USA) LLC, 2013
Published in Penguin Books 2014

PHOTOGRAPH CREDITS
Page 1, 2, 3, 5 (bottom), 7 (middle), 8 (middle), 9, 11, 12, (bottom): Library of Congress; 4 (top), 7 (top):
Author's collection; 4 (bottom): Franklin B. Gowen, *List of Outrages in Schuylkill and Shamokin Regions*
(1875); 5 (top), 6 (bottom): Allan Pinkerton, *The Mollie Maguires and the Detectives* (1880); 7 (bottom),
8 (top, bottom), 15: Charles A. Siringo, *A Texas Cow Boy* (1886); 10 (top, bottom), 12 (top): Albert E.
Horsley, *Confessions and Autobiography of Harry Orchard* (1907); 10 (middle): *The Idaho Daily Statesman;*
13 (top), 14: *Current Literature*, July 1907; 13 (bottom right): James H. Hawley, *History of Idaho:
The Gem of the Mountains*, Volume 2 (1920); 16: Courtesy Annette Fujita

THE LIBRARY OF CONGRESS HAS CATALOGED THE HARDCOVER EDITION AS FOLLOWS:
Riffenburgh, Beau.
Pinkerton's great detective : the amazing life and times of James McParland / Beau Riffenburgh.
pages cm
Includes index.
ISBN 978-0-670-02546-6 (hc.)
ISBN 978-0-14-312607-2 (pbk.)
1. McParland, James P. 2. Pinkerton's National Detective Agency—Biography.
3. Private investigators—United States—Biography. I. Title.
HV7911.M3884R54 2013
363.28'9092—dc23
[B]
2013017204

Printed in the United States of America
1 3 5 7 9 10 8 6 4 2

Designed by Nancy Resnick

In loving memory of my Mother,
Angelyn Kelley Riffenburgh

CONTENTS

PREFACE

McKenna knew his life could end at any moment. Each day that passed pieces of the puzzle were being put together, and soon the inevitable conclusion would be reached by the "bodymasters"—and they knew all too well how to eliminate problems. He realized that his every move was being watched, his actions scrutinized, and that he might soon be given the "black spot," marking him for murder.

No one understood better than the rough brawler known throughout the less salubrious parts of Schuylkill County as Jim McKenna how easy it was to kill a man. His life could be snuffed out at home in the dead of night, or in the street on a dark evening, or even in a crowded, well-lit place that had seemed secure until it was too late. McKenna would not go easily—he was well armed and could hold his own with a pistol, knife, lead pipe, or his fists—but he could feel Death looking over his shoulder.

The premonition had started a week or so before, in mid-February 1876, when Mary Ann Higgins, whom he was courting, told him about the rumor that he was an informer—accused of being behind the arrests of several men from the Ancient Order of Hibernians (AOH), an Irish fraternal society with a large local membership. McKenna was convinced that the AOH was actually more than that. He believed it was essentially the same as the Molly Maguires, a shadowy and brutal Irish American brotherhood responsible for sabotage, beatings, and at least sixteen murders—some said more than fifty—in the Pennsylvania coalfields.[1]

But it was not the notion of killing and violence that aroused Mary Ann's disgust; it was the thought that McKenna might be a spy. For in a region heavily populated by immigrants from the turbulent northern counties of Ireland, few were detested more than informers. And few could expect shorter life spans.

McKenna's friend Frank McAndrew and a friendly Pottsville saloon keeper, Danny Hughes, soon added to his worries.[2] Each indicated that John Kehoe, a handsome, charismatic, steely eyed Irishman who ran a tavern in Girardville and was the Schuylkill County delegate of the AOH, had sent a warning for "every one to beware of me [McKenna]; that I was a detective; that such was the report, and that he, John Kehoe, had it from responsible sources."[3]

Outwardly incensed that after two years as an officer of the AOH he should be accused, McKenna went to Kehoe to protest his innocence, and to demand an opportunity to prove his case. Kehoe agreed to set a "trial" for early March, near McKenna's lodgings in Shenandoah, a grimy little mining town in the anthracite coal region about twelve miles north of Pottsville, the Schuylkill County seat. In fact, so convincing had McKenna's protests been that he was allowed to spend the night in Kehoe's house. But in the ensuing days, away from his smooth talking, Kehoe's suspicions returned.

Kehoe saw McKenna in Pottsville on the day before the scheduled trial and urged him to accompany him on the train back to Shenandoah that evening. McKenna agreed, but when he boarded it, there was no trace of Kehoe. Mrs. Kehoe was there, but she said that her husband had left in the afternoon. "The suspicion struck me, then, just at that time, that all was not right," McKenna later testified. "I began to see then where I stood."[4]

Concerned that trouble might be waiting at the little crossing where he usually jumped off because it was close to his boardinghouse, McKenna stayed on the train. He was glad he had when he saw several suspicious figures in the shadows around the usually deserted track.

After disembarking at the main station, he made his way toward McAndrew's house through dark streets encrusted with oft-thawed and refrozen mud and snow. He exchanged greetings with a few friends and was alarmed when one pointedly ignored him. When he popped into a tavern, another offered him a drink, but the man's hands shook so violently that he could barely pull the stopper from the bottle. McKenna wryly asked if he had the ague, although he knew the man was simply terrified to be with him.

A fellow named Edward Sweeney fell into step with him after he left the tavern, and McKenna innately sensed danger: "I got him to walk in front of me. I said my eyes were bad, and I could not see; that the pavements had holes in them. . . . I got him ahead of me, and I made up my mind to keep him there."[5]

At McAndrew's house, McKenna was unable to prise any information from his friend, so he waited until several others who were there left, and then, listening intently for sounds of pursuit, slipped out again. He ignored the direct route to his boardinghouse and crept through the edges of a swamp to avoid an ambush. Once inside his tiny bedroom he laid out his weapons and sat awake through the long, freezing night, keeping anxious watch between the tattered curtains into the moonlight for the men he was certain planned to kill him.

Early the next morning, his hand tucked inside his old brown coat gripping the cold butt of a .36 caliber Colt Navy revolver, McKenna entered a smoky Shenandoah saloon with McAndrew. "My God, man, don't you know why you've been summoned here?" an acquaintance blurted before hurrying away.

McKenna did know. Only a couple of bodymasters—the heads of the AOH lodges—had arrived, and it was obvious that judgment had already been passed: There would be no hearing. McAndrew, the only person now willing to be seen with him, suggested they go for a ride in a "cutter," a lightweight, open sleigh. Following them in another cutter were two AOH men. Once they were racing across the deep snow, McAndrew informed McKenna that one of them had been charged to kill him. "Have you got your pistols?" he asked.

McKenna answered in the affirmative, and McAndrew continued, "So have I, and I will lose my life for you. I do not know whether you are a detective or not, but I do not know anything against you. I always knew you were doing right, and I will stand by you. Why don't they try you fair?"[6] McAndrew then informed McKenna that he had saved his life the night before.

"He told me that John Kehoe had came to Shenandoah upon the afternoon previous, and that he had assembled . . . all the Mollies who were in town," McKenna stated, "and that he told him, McAndrew, for God's sake to have me killed that night or I would hang half the people in Schuylkill County; and McAndrew said that he consented, and Kehoe and the men were satisfied, and they assembled just a little below the depot, twelve or fourteen of them."[7]

But the men had been flummoxed when McKenna failed to alight at his usual location. They had been armed with iron bars, axes, and tomahawks, because shooting him would make too much noise and bring the police. "If you had stepped off the train, at that place, you would surely have been killed, cast into a wagon, which was in waiting for the purpose, and then tossed down a deserted shaft."[8]

Frightened himself, McAndrew paused to calm his voice. "You were in queer company then, and you will find you are in queer company now," he said. "What will you do?"

"I do not give a cent," spat McKenna, furious and indignant. "I am going down to Kehoe's."[9]

It was four miles from Shenandoah to the rough-and-tumble borough of Girardville, where Kehoe ran the Hibernian House. Six feet two inches tall in his stocking feet, with "jet black, curly hair, bushy eyebrows, and bright blue, piercing eyes,"[10] Kehoe was an intimidating figure. As well as being a publican, he also served as the town's high constable. But McKenna was satisfied that Kehoe was something more—he was also the kingpin of the Molly Maguires.

McKenna knew that entering Hibernian House was akin to walking into a lion's den, but he felt that he had no choice but to brazen out the situation—because, despite all his denials, he actually *was* an undercover detective.

NOTES, REFERENCES, APPENDICES, BIBLIOGRAPHY, AND MAPS

The full Notes and References, two Appendices, the Bibliography, and a selection of maps and more material about the Molly Maguires and other parts of James McParland's career can be easily accessed on the websites below:

www.susannagregory.com/beauriffenburgh/pinkertons-great-detective

and

www.penguin.com/PinkertonsGreatDetective

INTRODUCTION

The gravestone stands in an open area, unprotected by trees and exposed to the blustery snow flurries and frigid winds that regularly rake north-central Colorado. Near the top of this granite marker is a single name: McParland. Below is a record of the supposed birth and death dates of a man once so widely recognized that when his admirers referred to him as the "Great Detective" others instantly knew of whom they spoke. But James McParland surely would have chuckled at the dates on his tombstone, for throughout his life this master of evasion, obfuscation, and, at times, outright deceit maintained that he did not know when he had been born. So was this the long-hidden truth finally appearing? Had his widow ordered this particular date for reasons of her own? Or was it another instance of the elusiveness and ambiguity that marked McParland's entire life?

Any could be the answer, because it is impossible to be sure about McParland, who relished being a man of mystery. Confusion even surrounds his name: Originally it was McParlan, and he only added the "d" midway through life, while other spellings and aliases were also used at times. Throughout his career he delighted, even when under oath, in evading questions and offering only vague, and sometimes contradictory, information. According to one attorney he was "the most skillful, cunning man, the most unfair witness that I ever saw on the stand."[1]

Because of the uncertainty he engendered as a witness, aspersions cast about his behavior and morals during investigations, his creation and perpetuation of myths about himself, and that few of his reports or letters have survived, it has proven difficult through the years to make a full assessment of McParland. But what *is* certain is that few people have undergone such a dramatic fall from grace after death—such a change from idol to villain.

There is—and long has been—little middle ground about McParland. He has been perceived as a great American hero: "[I]f there ever was a man to whom the people of this county should erect a monument, it is James McParlan," said one contemporary.[2] Others have reviled him as the worst kind of scoundrel, a perjurer who twisted testimony to send innocent men to the gallows, a man with "the bearing of a brute and the visage of a vulture, his hands befouled with blood, venomous as a viper, a beastly snarl on his forbidding lips, he stalks the streets a thing unclean, hated by all."[3] Widely varying depictions still abound in books and film even a century after his death—many making up for a lack of depth, balance, and accuracy with emotive language and unsubstantiated allegations. So who *was* the real man behind the contrary portraits—courageous hero or contemptible rogue?

Throughout his career, McParland was a controversial figure for the equally contentious Pinkerton's National Detective Agency. In fact, a significant part of that company's reputation—good and bad—was based on his triumphs and failures. McParland first gained fame for his undercover role in the breaking of the Molly Maguires in the Pennsylvania coalfields in the 1870s, a tale that concluded with twenty men being hanged. He returned to center stage three decades later for his role in the attempt to convict a trio of leaders of the Western Federation of Miners (WFM) for the assassination of former Idaho governor Frank Steunenberg.

Between those cases he rose steadily in the Pinkerton's hierarchy, eventually managing the agency's operations west of the Mississippi River. He was a key figure in the investigation of the first-known "murder by mail" and helped solve the theft of $280,000 of gold from a San Francisco smelting works. He oversaw the efforts of legends such as the charismatic "cowboy detective" Charlie Siringo, the incorruptible lawman "Doc" Shores, and the cold-blooded killer Tom Horn. He supervised operations to catch murderers, train robbers, and con men, including swindlers who targeted the lord mayor of London, a band accused of attempting to murder New Mexico politicians, and the Wild Bunch led by Butch Cassidy. He also played a key role in Pinkerton's much criticized use of undercover agents to infiltrate and destroy miners' unions.

But more than anything else it was McParland's role in the Molly Maguire saga that earned him enduring status as a man of exceptional evil or good. The Molly Maguires—Irish miners and tavern owners accused of violent crimes— have been depicted during the past 150 years as everything from thugs and murderers to innocent martyrs in the cause of workers' rights. Interpretations have changed dramatically as accounts of their actions, fate, and motives have been manipulated to justify different political, social, or legal agendas. McParland's role in their convictions has been similarly shaped to validate ideological positions.

One classic article stated that "the ambiguity surrounding the episode is such that it permits the construction of a plausible justification for *any* stance on the issues as well as . . . guilt or innocence."[4] Thus, it is possible to arrive at widely differing assessments of almost any event, decision, or individual in the narrative of the Molly Maguires.

After years being hailed as a savior, more recently the appraisals of McParland have tended to be highly critical. He has been labeled a perjurer, an agent provocateur, and even a murderer. The accuracy of these conflicting judgments is at the heart of the mystery this book is trying to unravel. That is in part because, rather than using established facts as building blocks for a final evaluation, many previous assessments have been derived from preexisting assumptions and display a reckless disregard for actual evidence. Moreover, those making such assessments have overlooked the fact that social norms, societal and ethnic attitudes, and law enforcement and the justice system were far different a century and more ago than they are today.

When also colored by the age-old Irish loathing of the informer, the traditional American support for the "little man," and a long espoused view of Pinkerton's as an archenemy of the labor movement, many recent works have been one-dimensional narratives that, when not supported by the facts, use conjecture and innuendo. They justify the violence of the Molly Maguires, portraying them as innocent and oppressed while demonizing those who opposed them, the legal system of the time, and especially McParland, whom they pronounce an unscrupulous liar and informer who betrayed his fellow Irish Catholics for money.[5]

This is a far cry from other portrayals of McParland as a benefactor of the honest people of Schuylkill County and Pennsylvania.[6] Thus, there is a clear need for a reassessment of the Great Detective. Only through thorough study can a deeper understanding be gained of a man whose public persona was so divergent that he was once said to have "performed one of the greatest services that has ever been rendered to the Catholic Church" but at another time to be the "most horrible Gorgon of this monster-bearing age."[7]

The genesis of this book can be traced back more than four decades to when, still in high school, I first saw the movie *Butch Cassidy and the Sundance Kid*. As the mysterious posse thundered after the characters portrayed by Paul

Newman and Robert Redford, I was gripped by the outlaws' oft-repeated question, "Who are those guys?" I found myself wondering if "Mr. E. H. Harriman of the Union Pacific Railroad" really did send an all-star team of lawmen after them. Forty years ago there were few books about the Wild Bunch,[8] but I hunted them down in an effort to learn more not only about the outlaws, but about the grim, determined men on their trail.

What I discovered, late in James D. Horan's classic account *Desperate Men*, was that the hunt was organized not by the Union Pacific but by a man "feared by the post-Civil War thugs and confidence men as a relentless, dogged type of detective,"—the superintendent of Pinkerton's Denver office, "J.P. McPharland."[9]

Coincidentally, it was only the next year that, interested because of his roles as James Bond, I went to see Sean Connery in a movie named *The Molly Maguires*. But it wasn't Connery's portrayal of John Kehoe that struck me—it was that of Richard Harris as the Pinkerton's operative James McParlan. Surely, I thought, despite the difference in spelling, this *must* be the same man who later led the hunt for the Wild Bunch. So again I headed for the library to read about the Molly Maguires. Afterward I felt confident that he was the same man, but I found myself with many more questions because of the different images presented of him.

Several years later, while working on a paper for a college course on the American West, I was directed by a friendly librarian to a well-written, highly intelligent, and thought-provoking account of the 1907 trial of several union leaders for the assassination of the former governor of Idaho.[10] And to my amazement, the Pinkerton operative heading the investigation was none other than James McParland. The man seemingly would just not leave me alone.

As the years passed I witnessed the ebb and flow of many reputations. As new materials became available, the images of people changed, including those of the lord protector Oliver Cromwell; the Antarctic explorer Robert Falcon Scott and his African counterpart Henry Morton Stanley; the South African political activist and statesman Nelson Mandela; and, most recently, Penn State football coach Joe Paterno. Throughout these reassessments I kept returning to the question of who James McParland really was, not least because the books in which he was mentioned failed to tell his full story or to address his historic milieu, and therefore they became little more than crude caricatures.

Finally, tiring of waiting for someone to conduct the research and write the definitive account of this most mysterious and complex individual, I decided to tackle it myself. It was obvious from the beginning that finding the real James McParland would not be easy. Nor would it be simple to place him in the context of his times, cultural background, and chosen profession. But little did I know just how difficult or lengthy the process would actually be.

I started my investigation from scratch, with no particular preconceptions and no agenda other than to tell McParland's story, based on the evidence. As before, my initial research raised more questions than answers. Could McParland's role in the Molly Maguire story be separated from what are considered the unfair aspects of the trials? How unusual were those trials compared to others of the time? How different was McParland's behavior throughout his career from that of members of other law-enforcement agencies of his time, or of today? What could be learned about him during the years between his two most famous cases? Had his personal moral code, and therefore his behavior, changed after he submersed himself in deceptive tactics? Given that his testimony under oath was so widely different from one trial to another, could anything he ever said be believed? Did he have his own distinctive code of honor that explains his actions? Was he a nice man, or had his undercover work soiled him irretrievably? Would I want to have dinner with him, or invite him into my home?

I had high hopes of finding an abundance of materials, as the Library of Congress had recently opened the Pinkerton's archives, which had been closed to most researchers for more than eighty years. Unfortunately, although the holdings are massive, there is precious little in the McParland files—and virtually nothing from the Denver office, of which he was in charge. The papers had been culled by Pinkerton's many years before.[11] However, I was successful in finding material elsewhere, as his trail took me to archives and libraries in Pennsylvania, Delaware, Rhode Island, Connecticut, New York, Massachusetts, New Hampshire, Virginia, Minnesota, Wisconsin, Illinois, Kansas, Colorado, Idaho, Utah, Montana, Wyoming, New Mexico, California, Nevada, Texas, Oklahoma, Canada, the United Kingdom, Ireland, and New Zealand.

As I familiarized myself more with the man and his period, McParland—and the ethos of Pinkerton's—slipped seamlessly into the mentality of his time, one far different from today. Life was not gentle in the anthracite region of Pennsylvania in the 1870s, and it was just as tough in the American West in the decades thereafter. And in both places it was cheap. Violence was an accepted part of day-to-day existence to many men who worked the mines: They were hard drinking, short tempered, unwilling to back down, and unafraid to die. They came to the taverns with knives, handguns, and a passionate hatred for foreigners, those of other religions, or strangers.[12] McParland testified in one Molly Maguire trial that he met some of the defendants "on the main street of Mahanoy City, a little east of the dead line."[13] Such was the mentality of the time that few thought it odd that there should be a dead line—a boundary marking an ethnic divide beyond which it was unsafe for the inhabitants of one side to pass to the other at night.

During his career, McParland experienced many more places where there was a fine line between going home and going to the morgue. Criminals and lawmen alike were quick to drink, quick to draw, and quick to take offense; rule breaking and rule enforcing could be so closely intertwined as to be nearly indistinguishable. To deal with such men one had to be just as rough and mean as they were, and perhaps that is why it is difficult to tell the heroes from the villains. This was not a society in which Robert Redford and Katharine Ross were made into lovely sepia prints, but one that was vicious, dirty, and cruel. This was highlighted in the struggles between the men who owned the railroads, mines, and ranches and those who worked them.

And yet understanding McParland still remained as slippery a proposition as grabbing an eel. It was not only the basic difficulty in getting to know a long-dead individual. Nor was it just the challenge thrown out by defense attorney Lin Bartholomew in his final summation at the trial of four alleged Molly Maguires: "Whenever you undertake to analyze the motives of men, when you undertake to go behind the shirt bosom and get into the heart, whenever you undertake to analyze the workings of the mind, that moment you are at sea."[14]

No, despite Pinkerton's culling policy, it began to feel as though someone had covered this particular detective's tracks. Not only could almost no copies of his original reports from the Molly Maguire investigation be found, even the edited versions for many of the most significant dates were missing. Similarly, most of the records about his operations in Kansas, Colorado, and Minnesota had disappeared without trace.[15] McParland remained an enigma.

Oh, there are lots of stories about him—many probably first told by McParland himself. A few might even be true. Historian Kevin Kenny once damned the book *Lament for the Molly Maguires*—upon which the Sean Connery movie was based—as "a peculiarly misleading mixture of speculation, invented dialogue, interviews, and documented, undocumented and mis-documented historical 'facts.'"[16] The book contains numerous tales of McParland's adventures that appear nowhere else, all supposedly confided by

McParland to a friend and passed down through the friend's family. Yet, while Kenny rightly regarded the stories as inaccurate, that doesn't mean they were *not* told by McParland. In his later years the Great Detective loved to brag and fantasize about his exploits, sometimes telling contradictory stories. One of his most outrageous anecdotes was repeated shortly after his death:

> While the Civil War was on, Secretary [of War Edwin] Stanton visited the head of the Pinkerton detectives and asked for a man to go to England to find whether the English people were not building ships for the Confederates. McParland, a boy of 18, was chosen. He was called into conference at the White House with President Lincoln, Secretary [of State William H.] Seward and Secretary Stanton. Stanton wished him to take passage on the best boat he could get. McParland said he intended to go over on a tramp steamer. Stanton was rather nettled that a mere boy should question the wisdom of his course, but Lincoln, rising to his seven feet height, said: "Perhaps the boy is right." McParland went over on a tramp steamer, secured work in a shipyard, and got positive proof of England's duplicity, on which the Alabama claim was later based.[17]

Never let it be said that McParland—a youth still living in Ireland when this incident was supposed to have occurred—let the facts get in the way of a good story. And realizing that is one of the keys to understanding him and judging his testimony through the years. Other important traits were that he was extraordinarily quick-witted and had a natural aptitude for the necessities of undercover work. For example, he showed the ability to charm, to form instant friendships, and to gain the trust of those from whom he might prize information. And despite being bespectacled and not large of stature, he was a man's man who could drink, brawl, and intimidate with the best of them, and he was able to impose his will on those not as clever, cunning, or forceful as he was.

It is also important to bear in mind the difference in McParland between when he began to conduct his investigations in Schuylkill County at the age of twenty-nine and when he was hunting the heads of the Western Federation of Miners, as a portly man in his sixties who walked with a cane. A darker character had appeared by the end of his career, one who perhaps drank too much and was inclined more than ever to exaggerate and fabricate, a believer in his own infallibility, disliking intensely anyone who challenged him, and a follower of Allan Pinkerton's notion that "the ends being the accomplishment of justice, they justify the means used."[18] All these traits had been accentuated by McParland's long involvement in undercover operations and labor espionage.

Not that this was unique to McParland. The life of an undercover agent or spy is rarely easy or glamorous, and the pressure and psychological demands can be overwhelming both mentally and physically (as McParland experienced in Pennsylvania, when his hair fell out and he was bedridden with a gamut of stress-related illnesses). The moral ambiguity of betraying one's friends is exacerbated by the incongruity of attempting "to do good by doing bad—preventing crime or apprehending criminals by resorting to lies, deceit, trickery; preventing crime by facilitating it; seeking to reduce crime by unintentionally increasing it; preventing harm at a cost of uncertainty about whether it would in fact have occurred . . . seeing criminal informers act as police."[19]

These experiences ultimately tend to make even the most good-natured, amiable men sour.[20] And this lifestyle has turned some men away from the righteousness with which they began or, as Samuel Johnson put it: "Where secrecy or mystery begins, vice or roguery is not far off."[21]

For such reasons there has always been hostility and repugnance toward men who report on the activities of others, whether they are called undercover agents, spies, or informers. For some, this antipathy was leavened by fascination and curiosity, and by an acknowledgment that such unsavory tasks are a necessary evil in society. There were also those who justified undercover techniques, and not just because, as the seventeenth-century "intelligencer" Dudley Bradstreet noted, there is a little of the spy in everyone.[22] Just as there has always been the tendency to damn the enemy spy for his duplicity and perfidy, the spy on the home side is a hero working for justice and the greater good. Moreover, to many, even negative practices or personal attributes of such investigators were long accepted, because "you cannot expect a detective to be an angel of light. . . . [I]f our detectives only associated with merchants . . . they would not be in a position to detect lawbreakers and bring them to justice."[23]

Despite such justifications, McParland was so despised that one socialist journalist wrote of how he followed him for days in order to murder him.[24] Yet his adventures so intrigued Sir Arthur Conan Doyle that in 1914 the author gave the detective the highest of compliments by having him meet Sherlock Holmes in one of his novels.[25] To much of the hero-worshipping public it was apparent that the greatest fictional detective had met his even greater living counterpart.

Thus, the story of the Great Detective is marked by widely varying opinion, belief, interpretation, and assessment, yet it is one that has never been told before in all its component pieces. What follows here is that tale—one of paradoxes, ambiguity, and mystery. It can be seen as a story of duplicity or honor, of good or evil, of morality or treachery, of a hero or a villainous brute. It is the story of the conundrum that was James McParland.

CHAPTER 1

✦

THE MAKINGS OF A DETECTIVE

There was little about his birth or formative years to suggest that the man baptized as James McParlan would become a celebrated detective.[1] But his earliest days did start with what he would love throughout his life: a murky mystery. He was born in the rural townland of Drumachee, Mullaghbrack Parish, County Armagh, in the northern Irish province of Ulster—but without the date being officially recorded.[2] Throughout his career McParlan claimed that he did not know his exact birth date—he usually said he thought it was 1844, although he once declared it as early as 1839.[3] Yet his tombstone gives it as March 22, 1844. So, *was* that the date? Did he actually know all along but simply refuse to acknowledge it?

To add to the uncertainty, the parish register at the Catholic Church of St. James in Mullaghbrack shows that his baptism took place on April 6, 1845, more than a year after the birth date on his grave. At a time of very high infant mortality, would a Catholic family have risked denying a son "the priceless grace of becoming a child of God were they not to confer Baptism shortly after birth"?[4]

The answer, as for so many other questions about McParlan, remains elusive. According to historian Eugenio Biagini of the University of Cambridge: "It is quite plausible that a person of that period might grow up without knowing his birth date," and without his family making any record of it. "Furthermore, although more surprising, it would not be altogether implausible for the family to postpone the child's baptism."[5] On such inconclusive evidence are mysteries built.

One thing that *is* well-known, however, is that McParlan was still an infant when a disaster overtook not only his family but all of Ireland. The funguslike oomycota microorganism *Phytophthora infestans*, having spread from Mexico to North America to Europe,[6] severely damaged the Irish potato crop of 1845 and devastated it in the following years. With at least one third of the population of Ireland almost entirely dependent on the potato for food, a catastrophic period of mass starvation and accompanying disease ensued, the effects of which were exacerbated by political, social, and economic decisions and indecision. About a million people are estimated to have died as a result of the Great Famine, and between one and two million to have emigrated as a consequence of it.[7] Despite living in an area that lost about a quarter of its population in the 1840s,[8] the family of Eneas and Mary McParlan continued to grow, with James the fifth son and seventh child of a throng that eventually numbered eight boys and four girls.[9] Although originally tenant farmers on lands owned by the Earl of Charlemont, the rich soil of their holdings meant the family was better off than average, and Eneas eventually left the two sons who stayed on the farm with him—Patrick, the eldest, and Henry, the youngest—three ample pieces of arable land in his will.[10]

The McParlans were Catholics in a heavily Protestant area, and with no Catholic school nearby, James and his brothers went to a Presbyterian one. There they were given the basic elements of an education. James also was taught many passages from the Bible, which allowed him, in behavior more representative of Presbyterians than Catholics of the time, to quote freely from it for the rest of his life.[11] Despite the Protestant influence, family members later stated that McParlan was, from his earliest days, an active and dutiful member of the Catholic Church, and that in times of trouble it was his faith in God and his devotion to the Church that sustained him.

In October 1863, by then a young man hoping for a future better than being a junior member of a large farming family, McParlan left for new opportunities in England. Walking the first twenty-one miles to the rail station in Lisburn in order to save on the fare, he took a train to Belfast, from where he crossed the Irish Sea to Whitehaven in Cumberland. Thence, with one companion, he made his way to Carlisle, tramped thirteen miles to Low Row Station on the old Newcastle and Carlisle Railway, and caught a train to the bleak industrial city of Gateshead on the south bank of the River Tyne, opposite Newcastle.

McParlan lived in Gateshead for about a year and a half and was employed by C. Allhusen and Sons, soap and alkali manufacturers at the site known as the Tyne Chemical Works, making "chloride of lime—bleaching powder, in other words—not a very pleasant occupation either."[12] Tiring of this job, he worked briefly at the Jarrow Chemical Company before moving north to Wallsend—the easternmost point of Hadrian's Wall—for a position with the

Carville Chemical Works. However, it proved similar to the previou.
and within a year he was back in Gateshead with yet another chemical fi.

According to one account, McParlan then briefly toured with a traveling
circus—for which he worked as a roustabout, gambling shill, and barker. "I
took on all comers for two bits, if I didn't throw them with both shoulders on
the mat in less than two minutes," he supposedly said. "I can tell you we didn't
pay out many quarters!"[13] Sadly, this colorful story does not ring true: There
were no quarters in the British currency, the term "two bits" was distinctly
American, and, most important, he testified in court that his only employment in England was with chemical companies.

In September 1866, after almost three years of working with powerful,
reeking, dangerous chemicals, McParlan returned home. There was still little
draw for him on the farm, however, and after a few weeks he took a position
as a stockkeeper at the wholesale linen warehouse of William Kirk and Sons
in Belfast. But what appears from even the beginning to have been a restless
personality made him unsuited for such a sedentary job. So before long, the
United States—with its seemingly unlimited possibilities of entrepreneurial
success—began to beckon to McParlan, as it did to so many young Irishmen
at the time, and he started saving to purchase a passage to a new life.

The next June he boarded the Inman Line's immigrant transatlantic
steamer *City of London*, in which he joined 1,002 other steerage passengers—
mainly Swedish, Irish, and English—and headed to New York. The stories of
his voyage vary from helping a priest aboard give communion, to preparing
meals for young mothers too ill to cook, to beating the stuffing out of a ham-
fisted bully that picked a fight. Regardless, the passage ended on July 8, 1867,
when—with his name incorrectly registered as James McPharland and his
occupation listed as laborer—he landed at Castle Garden in New York City,
America's first official immigrant reception center, in a brutally sweltering
summer.[14]

Typically, even for something so straightforward as that voyage, McParlan
seemingly was driven to muddy the waters relating to his background. His
trial testimony in the 1870s matched the official records about the Atlantic
crossing, but years later he stated that he had first come to America in 1857—
after spending thirteen years as a sailor. If one believes his usual claim of being
born in 1844, this story would mean that he must have been stolen from his
parents and taken to serve before the mast before he was a year old![15]

Upon his arrival, New York was not particularly welcoming. He was fronted with the anti-Irish attitude so blatantly expressed in in *The New York Herald*, the largest newspaper in the United WANTED—To do general housework ... any country or except Irish." Or, as the New York weekly *Frank Leslie's Il- ...paper* commented: "The real American hates the Irishman, very often without denying he is useful, because he is weary of his rowdy, noisy, anarchical ways."[16]

Such sentiments made it difficult for immigrants to find jobs and meant that many drifted into the city's crime-infested tenements and dirty side streets and alleys, particularly in Manhattan's infamous Five Points slum, which had become, according to one Methodist reformer, "the synonym for ignorance the most entire, for misery the most abject, for crime of the darkest dye, for degradation so deep that human nature cannot sink below it."[17] Despite having a volatile streak, McParlan was not of such an ilk, however, and he proved to be single-minded about bettering his situation. Thus, it was not long before he landed a position working behind the counter and making deliveries for McDonald and Boas, a retail grocery at the corner of Ninth Avenue and West Thirty-sixth Street in what became Manhattan's Garment District.

But McParlan hoped for something still better, and before long he was offered a post through the New York agents of his old Belfast employers, William Kirk and Sons. Promised twenty-five dollars a month plus board, he seemed to be already moving up in the world, as he traveled to the village of Medina, on the Erie Canal in upstate New York. He soon learned, however, that the clerks had not been paid for two months, and that the owner thought he was just another "gullible Mick" like the others. McParlan saw things differently: "I wanted my pay and I could not get it, and I kind of concluded that one month's pay was enough to lose."[18] So he headed to Buffalo, and, finding nothing in the offing there, continued west a few days later.

By the autumn of 1867, McParlan had reached Chicago, a city with its own rough reputation but where hard physical labor allowed him to make ends meet. He first worked as a teamster, paving and grading streets for DeGolyer & McClelland, and then at the same job for John Anderson and Company. He next drove a meat wagon for a slaughterhouse, and then served as a deckhand on the steamer *J.J. Truesdell*, which traded on Lake Michigan between Chicago and Grand Haven, Muskegon, Sheboygan, and Manitowoc. During the heartless winter he trudged through deep snow to chop timber in the forests of Berrien County, Michigan. After a job as a laborer in H.W. Holden

Brothers' hardwood lumberyard back in Chicago, and a second stop with John Anderson and Company, he was hired as a coachman by John Alston of the firm Alston, Devoe & Company, a wholesale paint, oil, and glass store, a position he kept for about four months.

But McParlan was ambitious and clearly wanted something more exciting, more challenging, and with more of a future than short-term jobs as a manual laborer. To find such a position he turned in July 1868 to W.S. Beaubien and Company, one of Chicago's early private detective agencies. It is intriguing that he had apparently not attempted to join the police force in New York, which featured an uncommonly high percentage of Irish immigrants, because once he was hired as a merchant or preventive policeman, he proved a natural for a job usually populated by rough, rollicking, hard-drinking men, of which he had become one. He later claimed that he stayed with Beaubien for more than two years, carrying out a variety of duties in Illinois and Ohio, including walking a beat, guarding business premises, and investigating crimes—serving "in the capacity of private policeman, and as detective just as required."[19]

From Beaubien it was but a short step to the then-expanding Chicago Police Department, as many of the duties were similar to those of the private police, including making visible patrols, arresting drunks and beggars, controlling public disorder, regulating saloons, and suppressing vice. To be effective, a policeman needed to be physically fit and willing to step straight into the fray, as he had to face challenges from rowdy and drunken men and young delinquents, race after criminals, and push, drag, or carry unwilling offenders to the station house.[20] One can well imagine that McParlan—like many policemen of the time—settled his fair share of arguments, disorder, and petty crimes on his own terms, with fists or police truncheon.

Despite the many ways that law enforcement seemed to fit McParlan's temperament, it did not pay well—which was perhaps part of the reason why the Chicago force became so notably corrupt—so, with his eye still on more lucrative opportunities, he left it for a job as a traveling salesman for the wholesale liquor suppliers Dodge and Brothers in downtown Chicago. McParlan's outgoing disposition, sense of humor, inherent garrulousness, and enjoyment of drinking made him a natural for interacting with a hard-swilling clientele. Therefore, after what he stated was seven or eight months, he embarked on a venture "upon my own hook," using his savings—and some assistance from Dodge and Brothers as well as John Alston—to start his own liquor store at 349 South Canal Street, in the heart of Chicago. It was a resounding success, and he soon opened a saloon at Twelfth Street and Centre Avenue, which also thrived.²¹ McParlan's future looked secure as long as people continued to drink.

Then suddenly, over the course of a day and a half, everything changed for both McParlan and the city of Chicago. On the night of October 8, 1871, according to disputed legend a cow kicked over a lantern in a small barn behind De Koven Street, and what became known as the Great Chicago Fire was whipped by strong winds through the parched wood buildings of the city.²² The flames eventually destroyed an area of approximately four square miles, including some 17,500 buildings, while making 30 percent of the city's inhabitants homeless. One of the buildings incinerated was McParlan's liquor store, including its entire stock, which represented virtually his entire monetary worth.

In the months following the fire, Chicago's population had little money to spend on alcohol, and McParlan's income decreased dramatically. The saloon became insolvent, and in March 1872 he sold out. McParlan once again had to start his career from scratch. But he now had experience in police and investigative work—which he had discovered suited his nature—so he decided his best option was to return to that. But rather than go back to Beaubien, in April 1872 he joined a bigger and better known company—Pinkerton's National Detective Agency.

Allan Pinkerton, who personally interviewed and hired McParlan, probably saw something of himself in the young man struggling to make a career in a new country.²³ Born in 1819 in the Gorbals, a rough slum of Glasgow, Pinkerton's schooling was interrupted at age twelve, when his father died. He initially worked for a harness maker, but then apprenticed as a cooper. When he was nineteen—the same age as McParlan when he left home—Pinkerton began a four-year journey through Scotland and northern England, making barrels wherever he could find work.

When he returned to Glasgow, the normally taciturn Scot was caught up by the emergence of Chartism, a political effort to broaden suffrage to working-class men and to make Parliament more representative of the masses. He became an active campaigner, and later asserted that he had participated in the Newport Rising of November 1839, when several thousand Chartist sympathizers marched into the Monmouthshire town to free some imprisoned comrades, only to be driven back, with many killed in a fiercely contested battle against soldiers and constables.²⁴

Legend has it that Pinkerton left Scotland a step ahead of the police, by whom he was wanted for participation in other Chartist riots. The story may or may not be true, but what *is* certain is that he reached Montreal in May 1842 with his new bride, but only after their ship had foundered on the reefs off of Sable Island, some two hundred miles southeast of Halifax, following which they were robbed by unscrupulous locals before being rescued by another ship.[25]

As it turned out, the couple was not in Montreal many months before an invitation from a friend who had also emigrated from Scotland led them to the frontier town of Chicago, on the shore of Lake Michigan. It proved to be a raw, nasty place, and it was not long before Pinkerton moved to Dundee, a heavily Scottish settlement about forty miles northwest of Chicago. As the only cooper in the area, Pinkerton quickly built up a business employing eight men.

In 1846 or 1847, while cutting timber on an island up the Fox River, Pinkerton stumbled upon a camp of counterfeiters. He led the sheriff back to arrest the men, and in the aftermath, in which Pinkerton became a bit of a local celebrity, two merchants convinced him to help end the fast-growing problem of distribution of fake currency. His audacious tactics quickly proved effective—when a man named John Craig arrived in Dundee, Pinkerton sought him out and asked to buy some counterfeit money. Craig produced the notes, and after arrangements were made for a larger exchange, Pinkerton arrested him.[26]

That Pinkerton had the right to take Craig into custody might seem odd, but the system of arrest for crimes was significantly different in the first half of the nineteenth century than today. The first police department in the United States—New York City's, patterned roughly after the London Metropolitan Police—had only been established in 1844, there were essentially no state law-enforcement organizations, and local constables had more civil than criminal duties.[27] Members of the public not only had broad law-enforcement powers, it was considered their *duty* to aid in the arrest of criminals.[28] When a crime was committed, citizens were expected to arm themselves and pursue the suspect, and "not faintly and with lagging steps, but honestly and bravely and with whatever implements and facilities convenient and at hand."[29]

Similarly, the investigation of crimes was considered the province of the private citizen, not the government.[30] However, although individuals inquired into crimes affecting them personally, it was not commonplace for a private individual to probe numerous unrelated offenses. But when his role in the Craig case became known, Pinkerton began to be sought out for other enquiries.

Finding that such work appealed to him a great deal more than building barrels, Pinkerton moved back to Chicago, where he was appointed a deputy sheriff of Cook County. In 1850 or 1852—he indicated each at different times—he formed Pinkerton and Company, although he continued to handle most of his cases personally. At the time, with few investigative means at their disposal, it was common for government agencies to hire private individuals as investigators, and in those early years the U.S. Treasury Department used Pinkerton to fight counterfeiting in Illinois. Then, in 1854, working for the Michigan Southern and Northern Indiana Railroad—while still holding down his Cook County position—Pinkerton arrested a man for attempting to destroy lines and derail cars.[31]

February 1855 marked a major turning point in Pinkerton's career. His agency agreed to a contract with six railroad companies, for which it would police the burgeoning network in the regions surrounding Chicago.[32] Pinkerton and Chicago attorney Edward A. Rucker expanded the company into the North West Police Agency. Its primary tasks were to provide protection for the passengers from armed robberies and for the railroad companies from hooliganism along rural routes and from theft by employees. Pinkerton quickly began hiring operatives to work the train lines.[33]

That spring, Pinkerton arrested a station manager who was stealing from freight cars in Oak Ridge, Illinois.[34] But an even bigger concern for railroad companies was conductors embezzling money by pocketing the fares they were paid. Determined to end the practice, as well as that of conductors sleeping on the job and letting friends travel free, Pinkerton developed what he called a "testing program," in which agents checked the honesty of employees by posing as travelers. Before long, Oscar Caldwell, a conductor for the Chicago Burlington and Quincy line, was caught pocketing money from onboard ticket sales. In a showcase trial, he was found guilty and sentenced to prison, providing an incredible boon of publicity for Pinkerton.[35]

At the same time, the Chicago Post Office hired Pinkerton as a special agent, tasked to investigate a series of postal thefts and to check the honesty of its employees. He went undercover in the sorting section, and by sending a decoy letter that appeared to contain large sums of money was able to nab Perry Denniston—who worked as a "piler," arranging letters so that the addresses could be read easily—in the act of stealing it. Four months later he arrested Denniston's brother Theodore after finding four thousand dollars stuck to the backs of pictures at his home.[36]

Pinkerton also had success protecting the post office from external crime. When the owner of a lottery business accused post office employees of stealing payments coming to him, Pinkerton sent another decoy letter, which led to the arrest and confession of an employee of the lottery company.[37] The success of these cases made Pinkerton believe wholeheartedly in what he called "discreet or covert surveillance" and promoted his agency's long-term involvement in spying on workers.[38]

Rucker left the company after about a year, and under Pinkerton's sole control, it soon began a meteoric rise. In 1856, he hired George H. Bangs, who had previously been a reporter for *The Era* and a New York City policeman, serving on the squad detailed to New York's Crystal Palace. Bangs proved to be a better administrator than an operative, and eventually became the agency's general superintendent.[39] The year after that Pinkerton made an even more important professional contact, when the Illinois Central hired as its chief engineer the former U.S. Army officer George B. McClellan. He and Pinkerton respected each other, and they remained in contact after McClellan was promoted to vice president of the Illinois Central, and then, in 1860, left to become president of the Ohio and Mississippi Railroad's Eastern Division.[40]

Another acquaintance was the head of the firm serving as the legal consultant for the Illinois Central—Abraham Lincoln. The two again came into contact in early 1861, when—while investigating threats by Southern sympathizers against the Philadelphia, Wilmington & Baltimore Railroad—Pinkerton became aware of a plot to assassinate the president-elect en route to his inauguration. Pinkerton contacted several of Lincoln's advisers, and with their help persuaded Lincoln to alter his travel plans. Hard proof of a conspiracy never surfaced, however, and it was later claimed that Pinkerton invented the plot to gain attention for his agency. The truth has never been determined with certainty.[41]

At the beginning of the Civil War, McClellan was appointed commander of the Department of the Ohio and asked Pinkerton to head an intelligence-gathering system. When later given command of the Army of the Potomac, McClellan instructed Pinkerton to form a secret service for that army. While serving as Major E. J. Allen, Pinkerton provided reports of troop strengths determined both personally and by his operatives.[42] Concurrently, his work included counterespionage, the exposure of corrupt contractors, interrogation of deserters and prisoners, and efforts against black-market racketeers. After

McClellan was dismissed in 1862, Pinkerton resigned and returned to criminal investigations with his renamed Pinkerton's National Detective Agency.

Pinkerton's organization expanded rapidly following the Civil War, and an office was opened in New York in November 1865 under Bangs, and in Philadelphia the following May. At the same time, the agency was establishing a broad reputation for success. Part of this was due to results, but part was also due to excellent self-promotion, such as the wide distribution of a picture of Pinkerton with Lincoln and Major General John McClernand at Antietam and the company's famous motto "We Never Sleep," shown under an unblinking eye—the origin of the term "private eye."[43]

The agency also gained respect, in some quarters, for the practices, ethics, and code of conduct to which its owner insisted his employees abide. Corrupt behavior had long given police, particularly detectives, a shady reputation, and to combat this Pinkerton decided that his staff would use the term "operative" rather than "detective" and that he himself would be known as the "principal." More important, he launched a plan to create a favorable public image of the private detective while at the same time professionalizing the occupation. To do this he began producing pamphlets that would teach his employees his philosophy and also provide a positive representation to the public.[44]

The most significant of these was the 1867 pamphlet *General Principles and Rules*, in which he established company guidelines. "The profession of the Detective is a high and honorable calling," he wrote. "Few professions excel it. He is an officer of justice and must himself be pure and above reproach. The public . . . have a right to know that their lives and property are to be guarded by persons . . . of whose integrity there can be no question." Further, he outlined a set of principles governing what kind of cases would be accepted by the agency: "Only such business will be undertaken as is strictly legitimate and right, and then only for the purpose of furthering the ends of justice and bringing Criminals to punishment."[45] This meant that Pinkerton's would not: investigate public officials in the performance of their duties; accept employment from one political party against another; shadow jurors; investigate the morals of women nor handle cases of divorce or a scandalous nature; or accept contingent fees, gratuities, or rewards.

What Pinkerton's *did* take on were high-profile cases brought about by an upsurge in lawlessness following the Civil War. Key among these were attempts to curb the new breed of train and bank robbers that sprang from groups of raiding irregulars, such as the Reno and James-Younger gangs. The agency also continued to receive work from the federal government, including conducting an investigation into any potential breach of neutrality or military interventionism by American citizens supporting the Cuban struggle for independence from Spain, in what became known as the Ten Years' War (1868–78).[46]

Pinkerton's reputation continued to rise at the beginning of the new decade, by which time the agency employed more than twenty operatives and about sixty members of Pinkerton's Protective Patrol, a uniformed private police force created in 1858 and used primarily to guard warehouses and plants.[47] In 1871, the year after the founding of the Department of Justice, the U.S. Congress appropriated fifty thousand dollars so the department could establish a unit devoted to "the detection and prosecution of those guilty of violating federal law." However, discovering that the fund was insufficient to found a new investigative unit, it was decided to contract out the services to Pinkerton's.[48]

Despite such work, Pinkerton's struggled financially, and the Philadelphia office went into the red, draining the other centers' reserves. Pinkerton's older son, William, at that time a rising executive in the Chicago office, suggested the Philadelphia branch be closed, but instead the principal moved some of its operatives to New York and sent others out to hustle business. In 1871, depressed about his lack of success, George Smith, the Philadelphia superintendent, resigned.[49] But that was nothing compared to the devastating setback that Pinkerton—like McParlan—suffered later that year when the Chicago fire gutted the agency's main premises. Included in the materials destroyed were approximately four hundred volumes of criminal records and the only copy in existence of the complete records of the Secret Service of the Army of the Potomac, which the government had already offered to purchase for thirty thousand dollars, which would have eliminated Pinkerton's economic problems.[50]

In the next year, business worsened considerably. Pinkerton hired Benjamin Franklin, the former chief of detectives of the Philadelphia police, as that office's superintendent, and the new operative began using his connections to pull in jobs.[51] But by August 1872, Pinkerton was facing a critical shortage of cash. "We are in great want of money," he wrote to one of his Chicago operatives. "On every hand I am in debt, yet I cannot get any person to help me, but everyone whom I owe a shilling to are calling me on it."[52]

The financial situation became progressively more troubled, and two months later Pinkerton wrote to Bangs in New York, telling him to: "collect all your Bills without one moment's delay, as things are coming right on us. Let business stand for the moment—go to work and collect Bills, sacrifice everything to get money, discount at any price. . . . [A]ny day whatever there may be a crash around us that we little suspect."[53]

In November 1872, Pinkerton was forced to take a loan from his employees, and then to mortgage personal property. The total carried the company into the next year but was not enough to turn the corner, and hopes for improvement appeared doomed. In fact, it would not be long before Pinkerton's prediction about a crash proved accurate, as the depression known as the Panic of 1873 set in following the collapse of Jay Cooke and Company, one of the chief financiers of the Union war effort.[54] The Cooke debacle set off a chain reaction of bank failures and the closing of the New York stock market. Pinkerton lost even more in the latter event, as the value of his railroad stocks plummeted.

On May 18, 1873, Pinkerton admitted his worries to Bangs: "I can scarcely tell which way to go, and many a time I am perfectly bewildered what to do. . . . I am afraid." Desperate, he continued: "go to Franklin Gowan [sic]. . . . Suggest some things to Mr Gowan about one thing and another which would be feasible and I have no doubt he will give us work."[55]

The timing of the suggestion proved extremely fortunate. Gowen, the president of the Philadelphia and Reading Railroad (commonly referred to as the Reading) and its subsidiary, the Philadelphia and Reading Coal and Iron Company, was indeed receptive to the help Pinkerton could offer. Gowen was a man of great ambition and determination, and one unwilling to let anything interfere with the successful attainment of his objectives. And at that moment there were several obstacles in the way of his economic and political goals—organizations that would therefore have to be subdued or eliminated. One of these—notorious in the press for having engaged in murder, mayhem, and destruction—was popularly known as the Molly Maguires.[56]

Franklin Benjamin Gowen was still relatively young in 1873, but he had already proven to be a formidable and resourceful figure in Pennsylvania business and politics.[57] Born in 1836 in Mount Airy, then a community on the edge of Philadelphia, he was the fifth child of an Irish Episcopalian immigrant who had become wealthy as a grocer and wine merchant before retiring to be a gentleman agriculturalist. At the age of nine young Gowen was sent to the elite John Beck's Boys' Academy in the Moravian village of Lititz, Pennsylvania, where he rubbed shoulders with the patrician classes while receiving the advanced elements of a nineteenth-century education—astronomy, chemistry, algebra, German, natural philosophy, and etiquette. However, at thirteen he was taken out of school and apprenticed to Thomas Baumgardner, a dry-goods merchant in Lancaster County. Three years later Baumgardner and his brother sold their business and entered the coal trade, taking Gowen with them.

At the age of twenty-one, with his unrelenting father demanding he become a successful businessman, Gowen and a partner signed a ten-year lease for two collieries at Mount Laffee, just north of Pottsville. He and his young bride became a part of Pottsville's expanding social scene, and Gowen organized a literary society. But things were not as positive on the business front—within a year one of the mines had to be flooded to put out a fire, and the owners had to pay to pump out the water. Their funds quickly disappeared, and in October 1859 the company's property was auctioned to pay its debts.

Gowen now turned to law, in which two of his brothers had preceded him. He studied throughout the winter and spring in the office of a Pottsville attorney, and in May 1860 was admitted to the Schuylkill County bar. He quickly showed a natural oratorical eloquence, sprinkling his speeches with flowery images and classical references and demonstrating techniques that allowed him to guide his listeners down any path he chose. When combined with his good looks, remarkable memory, and personal magnetism, his speeches proved spellbinding.

Building on these talents, in 1862 he was elected the county's district attorney. His tenure encompassed a period in which riots and other violent antiwar activities coincided with an upsurge of labor troubles—murder, beatings, and vandalism popularly attributed to the Molly Maguires. Although Gowen has been lambasted for doing little to prosecute these crimes, such arguments tend to show a lack of understanding of the American legal system of the time.

For much of the period before the Civil War, criminal or civil prosecutions were carried out by private prosecutors. Victims of crime could either take their complaint to a magistrate, who could issue a bench warrant for the defendant's arrest, or they could go directly to a grand jury, which, after investigating, might issue a presentment or an indictment. Under either of these scenarios the victim or his representative could then prosecute an individual before a petit jury, at the victim's expense.[58]

The primary difference between a civil and criminal prosecution was that the latter theoretically involved the public interest, and not just that of the victim. For that reason, a state attorney general could either prosecute the case or assign the task to a local attorney, typically at the expense of the State.[59] In Pennsylvania, the position of county district attorney was created in 1850 in order to have a public official who could prosecute criminal cases as opposed to private lawyers. However, as with most states, Pennsylvania provided inadequate funds for public prosecutors, and for more than twenty years did not allow them to hire outside investigators.[60]

Under these restrictions it is easy to see that Gowen did not necessarily lack diligence; without any funding or investigative assistance, he simply could not prove an individual had the motive, intent, and opportunity to commit murder or other crimes. Obtaining convictions was made even more difficult, since Schuylkill County was well-known as a place in which committing perjury to provide alibis was essentially a way of life. In the long run, this last point would prove of huge significance, because the "ease with which the alibis were produced convinced . . . Gowen of the existence of a criminally oriented power elite in Schuylkill County."[61]

After two frustrating and undistinguished years in public service, Gowen resigned to concentrate on his private practice, which in 1864 had made him the second-highest-paid lawyer in the county.[62] While in public office, he had cultivated influential friends who helped in his appointment as Pottsville counsel for the Philadelphia and Reading Railroad. Gowen's reputation within the company soared after he won an important case before the Pennsylvania Supreme Court, and in 1867 he became the Reading's general counsel. He moved back to Philadelphia, where he showed a brilliant grasp of the railroad's legal issues, an in-depth understanding of company finances, and, most important, the ability to impress the directors of McCalmont Brothers and Company, of London, the Reading's majority stockholders. In 1869, when company president Charles E. Smith took leave for health reasons, Gowen was named acting president. The following year, with Smith unable to return, Gowen was elected president in his own right.

At the age of only thirty-three Gowen now had day-to-day control of a powerful corporation that owned 706 miles of double-track, 1,385 miles of single-track, some two hundred locomotives, and more than twenty-two thousand train cars that hauled approximately 180,000 tons of coal each week.[63] But he envisioned something much larger, richer, and more powerful—a railroad that "owns its own traffic, is not dependent upon the public and is absolutely free from the danger of competition from rival lines."[64] As time passed, he convinced McCalmont Brothers of the soundness of his plan to win complete control over the Schuylkill County anthracite coal industry, including its production, transportation to point of sale, and distribution. To do this he would need to eliminate any competition from other entities that had desires to oversee aspects of the industry: the small, independent mining operators; the few companies offering alternative means of transport out of the region; the middlemen who controlled coal marketing in Philadelphia; and the union representing the mine workers. He believed that with appropriate financial backing he could control or crush the first three of those sets of competitors.

That left only the union—the Workingmen's Benevolent Association (WBA)[65]—which hoped to control the amount of coal mined and therefore its distribution and, ultimately, price, which would mean long-term, stable pay for the miners. The WBA had already led a series of strikes in the Schuylkill County coalfields, and although Gowen had triumphed over each, he had realized that it would take more than simple economic repression to break the union. So at some point in early 1871—after what he considered to be a breach of faith by the WBA—he decided on an additional method that would, in conjunction with forceful economic measures, bring the miners to heel. His chosen course was to make an implicit connection between the union and the Molly Maguires. Gowen hoped that by tarring the WBA with the Molly Maguire brush—that is, by establishing in the minds of others that the two were related and intertwined—he might deal the union a setback from which it would never recover.

It is possible that the letter from George Bangs in May 1873 helped make clear to Gowen just how the final steps of his plan could be carried out a great deal more forcefully than even he had previously imagined. In the preceding two years he had taken control of virtually all aspects of the mining operation in Schuylkill County. However, the early months of 1873 had seen a dramatic increase in violence—with attacks on mine superintendents, fires at collieries, and derailment of railroad cars—actions publicly attributed to the Molly Maguires. If its members could be caught and convicted, and Gowen could link them to the WBA, it would do more than weaken the union—it might destroy it once and for all. Pinkerton's was noted for its undercover work in a variety of settings, and what better way to obtain the proof needed, Gowen must have thought, than to have Pinkerton's insert agents directly into the organizations under investigation.

In his *General Principles* pamphlet, Pinkerton had addressed the ethics of such a situation, stating that devious or seemingly underhanded means could legitimately be used in the enforcement of justice. Indeed, secrecy was a prime condition for a detective's success. "It frequently becomes necessary for the Detective, when brought in contact with Criminals, to pretend to be a

Criminal," he had written, because "the Detective has to act his part, and in order to do so, he has, at times, to depart from the strict line of truth, and to resort to deception."[66]

Inherent in this concept was the befriending of suspects as a means of gaining information to implicate them in crimes. "Moralists may question whether this be strictly right," Pinkerton wrote, but then noted that although the technique was distasteful, "it is a necessity in the detection of Crime, and it is held by the Agency that the ends being the accomplishment of justice, they justify the means used."[67]

Thus, Pinkerton's had the necessary ethos to institute Gowen's plan. In fact, its operatives had been employed as early as 1863 by the Reading to spy on conductors. Gowen himself had hired them for similar work in January 1870 after receiving a letter from a passenger who complained that he had been cheated by a conductor. Riding the line anonymously, Pinkerton's men had uncovered numerous instances of conductors stealing fares or failing to collect them from acquaintances.[68]

So now Gowen again brought in Pinkerton's. A number of operatives— generally referred to in reports only by their initials—invaded the mining region, where they gathered information while keeping watch on trains and switch and signal boxes.

Several incidents occurred in September 1873 in the vicinity of Glen Carbon—a mining settlement about nine miles northwest of Pottsville— culminating in the burning of a large coal tipple. Benjamin Franklin of Pinkerton's Philadelphia office therefore decided to concentrate his operatives in that area. And it was from there that a report on October 9 first linked Gowen's target to the ongoing trouble: "The operatives report the rumored existence at Glen Carbon of an organization known as the 'Molly Maguires,' a band of roughs joined together for the purpose of instituting revenge against any one of whom they may take a dislike. The operatives have been unable to learn who any of the members are."[69]

In the following weeks the operatives remained as stumped as a local man they had interviewed: "He could give no particulars in regard to the society, or who belonged to it. He said he had been trying to find out the leading members, but had failed."[70]

Meanwhile, spurred on by the damage to Reading property, Gowen met Pinkerton and Franklin at the Reading's plush Philadelphia offices. No reliable record of the meeting exists, but, according to Pinkerton's undoubtedly embellished account, Gowen instigated the meeting because "The coal regions are infested by a most desperate class of men, banded together for the worst purposes—called, by some, the Buckshots, by others the Mollie Maguires—and they are making sad havoc with the country."[71]

Gowen was concerned that at trial a perjured alibi would free the guilty parties. Therefore, he wanted Pinkerton "to investigate this mysterious order, find out its interior workings, expose its evil transactions, and see if the just laws of the State cannot again be made effective in bringing criminals to justice."

This initial conversation was strictly about the suppression of crime and the protection of industry and had nothing to do with union matters, according to Pinkerton. So, after some consideration, he agreed, replying, "I will enter upon the business, but it will require time, sharp work, and plenty of both!" But, realizing that his current operatives were not accomplishing what needed to be done for a successful conclusion, he decided he would have to bring an entirely new man into the operation, this time as a deep-cover operative.

It would not be easy, but eventually he would find just the man for the job—and that man would be James McParlan.

CHAPTER 2

THE MOLLY MAGUIRES

Franklin Gowen was not the first person to hope that the outrages attributed to the Molly Maguires could be suppressed by the full force of the law. He was, however, the most determined opponent a society branded with that name had yet faced. And there had been more than one group called that in the previous decades.

The name "Molly Maguires" first appeared in the 1840s in the countryside of northern Ireland, ascribed to a secret society engaged in agrarian violence—threats, beatings, burnings, property damage, and occasionally murder—against English landlords, their agents, and other Irish engaging in land practices considered by the Mollys to be unjust. It was not the first such underground organization in Ireland but was rather part of a lineage of secret societies that existed as far back as the 1760s.[1] That decade saw the advent of a movement known as the Whiteboys, because of their practice of wearing white shirts or frocks over their clothes and white bands around their hats while making nighttime raids expressing their opposition to rack rents, evictions of tenant farmers, and tithe collections. The British government attempted to repress the Whiteboys by outlawing them and using military intervention, but the illegal behaviors only increased. Eventually, the expression "Whiteboyism" was applied not just to the original organization but as a generic term for rural violence.

The Whiteboys were succeeded by other kindred groups, such as the Defenders and the Threshers. Early in the nineteenth century the Society of Ribbonmen, a secret Catholic brotherhood named for the green ribbon worn by its members, was established in opposition to the Protestant Orange Order and as an ongoing protest against landlords, land agents, and tithes to the Protestant Church. As with Whiteboyism, the term "Ribbonism" became a catchall for different movements espousing agrarian aggression.

The Molly Maguires had appeared by the mid-1840s in north Leinster, north Connacht, and Ulster. The identity of the original Molly Maguire remains a topic of debate, and stories and legends abound about whence the organization's name sprang, although they tend to be more folkloric than historical.[2] One tale states that she was a destitute old widow evicted from her house by armed bailiffs; another that she was the owner of an illegal tavern in which the society's members met; and a third that she was a woman of such phenomenal strength and charisma that she led nighttime raids herself. One theory places the origins of the movement in the Irish Rebellion of 1641, in honor of Connor Maguire, Second Baron of Enniskillen, who was executed for high treason after the failed attempt by Catholic gentry to seize power in Ireland.[3] Thomas Foster, an English journalist and lawyer who produced newspaper articles and a book about his travels in Ireland in 1845–46, indicated that the movement had its beginnings in 1835 with the eviction of Catholics living on the Ballinamuck estate of Lord Lorton in County Longford. Another mid-nineteenth-century recorder of Irish life, land agent W. Steuart Trench, wrote that it developed on the Shirley estate at Carrickmacross in County Monaghan in 1843.[4]

What *is* certain is that some members of the society marauded while dressed in women's clothing, which was seen either as honoring the concept of Molly Maguire or as representing the Irish mother begging bread for her children.[5] As Trench wrote: "These 'Molly Maguires' were generally stout active young men, dressed up in women's clothes, with faces blackened or otherwise disguised; sometimes they wore crape over their countenances, sometimes they smeared themselves in the most fantastic manner with burnt cork about their eyes, mouths, and cheeks. In this state they used suddenly to surprise the unfortunate grippers, keepers, or process-servers, and either duck them in bogholes, or beat them in the most unmerciful manner."[6]

Actually, men of a much wider range of professions were attacked: landlords' agents, peasant farmers who settled on land from which previous tenants had been evicted, and shopkeepers and merchants who charged rates that were considered too high. Crops and fences were damaged, grazing animals driven off or killed, and small plots and buildings burned. It was widely accepted in the past that such actions had nationalist or religious undertones, but a more recent assessment suggests that these attacks were attempts to resist changes to traditional patterns of land use due to agrarian modernization. The violence, therefore, could be interpreted as a means "to correct transgressions against traditional moral and social codes."[7]

But how did that translate to the New World—who were the *American*

Molly Maguires and how were they related to their Irish counterparts? For decades it was accepted that both were parts of a single, well organized, conspiratorial society driven by ethnic and religious issues, suggesting that the Molly Maguires transferred either directly from Ireland to Pennsylvania, or with a stop in Britain en route.[8] But it appears more likely that the pattern of outrages in Pennsylvania's anthracite coal area was a result of the demographics of immigration; that is, the high number of immigrants who settled there from northwest and north-central Ireland—particularly Donegal—brought with them that region's distinctive mode of direct, violent action in pursuit of what they deemed justice.[9] And because "Molly Maguires" was an accepted term in the north of Ireland, it is likely that those in Pennsylvania took the same name due to familiarity with it.[10]

To the average citizen of Schuylkill County, unaware of this historic background, the name Molly Maguires first appeared in October 1857, introduced by Benjamin Bannan, the intensely anti-Irish editor of *The Miners' Journal and Pottsville General Advertiser*, the region's leading Republican newspaper. Bannan—who tended to be supportive of mine owners and operators, unsympathetic to workers, and vitriolic toward Roman Catholicism and Irish immigrants[11]—reported that fifty-five fraud indictments had been passed down by a Philadelphia grand jury against inspectors for the 1856 presidential election. "Every one of these inspectors were Irishmen," he wrote, "belonging no doubt to the order of 'Molly Maguires,' a secret Roman Catholic association which the Democracy is using for political purposes."[12]

Throughout his forty-four-year tenure as editor (1829–73), Bannan, a devout Presbyterian with an extreme nativist agenda, regularly castigated Irish immigrants for the standard stereotypes—drunkenness, laziness, turpitude, ignorance, and criminality. After that initial article, the Molly Maguires and the Buckshots—a name sometimes applied as an alternative to Molly Maguires and at other points to an entirely different organization—began taking a regular battering in his columns. So did the Irish fraternal organization the Ancient Order of Hibernians and its series of lodges scattered across northeast Pennsylvania. As in that initial article, Bannan's early charges against such organizations concentrated on political corruption rather than violence.[13] However, that changed during the Civil War, when the anthracite coalfields—already among the most important economic regions in the Union—also became some of the most troublesome.

The special significance of the region was that it contained approximately

95 percent of the western hemisphere's known supply—estimated at sixteen billion tons—of one of nature's most prized gifts: anthracite, also called "hard coal" or "black coal." Anthracite is purer, harder, and of a higher carbon content than other grades of coal, and it therefore burns longer, slower, and cleaner. In 1808, Jesse Fell developed an L-shaped, open-air grate that allowed it to be kept in a state of continuous combustion with a steady flow of air. Then, in the 1820s and 1830s, new types of stoves made it possible to use anthracite for "luxury heating" in hearths, kitchens, and public buildings much more cheaply than wood, and it was soon being used for steam engines and became the coal of choice for powering blast furnaces for smelting iron ores.[14]

The anthracite region, covering approximately 485 square miles and parts of seven counties, was a wild area split asunder by a series of rugged mountains interspaced with valleys.[15] Although there was some arable land, the steep, heavily wooded hills and rocky outcrops made widespread agriculture difficult. Instead, the region's economic mainstay was based around its four vast coal beds. Two of these —the Northern Field, running through the district of Wilkes-Barre and Scranton and the Lehigh or Eastern Middle Field centering around Hazelton—were located in what was called the northern or upper anthracite region.

The other two fields—in the lower or southern region—were the centers for the Molly Maguire saga. The Southern Field was some fifty miles long by up to eight miles wide and extended from Lebanon and Dauphin counties across central Schuylkill County and into Carbon County, the seat of which was Mauch Chunk (since renamed Jim Thorpe). North of this—nestled between Broad Mountain and Mahanoy Mountain—was the Western Middle, or Mahanoy, Field, about thirty-six miles long and including Girardville, Shenandoah, and Mahanoy City, the districts where James McParlan would become known as Jim McKenna.

Although Pottsville, the Schuylkill County seat, was only about ten miles from Shenandoah in a straight line, they were in isolated valleys separated by untamed intervening mountain ridges. Travel in the region was extremely difficult, as the train lines tended to run along individual valleys and only crossed between them at occasional gaps. Therefore it was much easier to travel within a valley than between them, which led the Pottsville residents to refer to Shenandoah, in what they thought of as the distant northern part of the county, as "over the mountain." Even Mahanoy City was separated from Shenandoah by the five-hundred-foot-high Bear Ridge. This isolation of towns, and their even more remote satellite hamlets, or "patches," could be so complete that individuals who lived only five miles from a settlement might be total strangers there, a fact that played a key role in the way the Molly Maguires functioned.

More than hills and forests separated the northern and southern anthracite regions, however. The entire economic structure of the two areas was a series of contrasts. In the north, the fields were largely controlled by major transportation companies—such as the Lehigh Valley Railroad and the Delaware, Lackawanna and Western Railroad—that had expanded into the coal industry and shipped the anthracite to New York City.[16] The southerly fields, on the other hand, had numerous small, independent operators. In 1853, no fewer than 86 different mining operations were located in Schuylkill County, running 115 collieries.[17] Due to the links by river, canal, and railroad, it was natural for these companies to send coal south to Philadelphia. Thus, in the southern anthracite region, rather than large companies managing every aspect of extraction, transportation, and sales, such tasks were controlled by separate operators. As a result, the southern fields were considerably less economically secure than their northern counterparts. In the southern region, for example, miners' pay was often only 80 percent that of their northern colleagues, and many southern companies collapsed after only a few years.

Following a brief economic downturn at the beginning of the Civil War—due to the enlistment of thousands of miners—the demands for anthracite by suppliers of war materials caused a boom that drove up companies' profits and miners' wages. Seeing the possibilities of financial windfalls, the Reading Railroad began to buy out smaller transport companies to consolidate its position as Schuylkill County's primary coal carrier.

However, the anthracite region—and particularly Schuylkill County—proved highly unstable. Great numbers of laborers throughout the country were against the Civil War, seeing it as "a rich man's war and a poor man's fight." Nowhere was this feeling stronger than in the coalfields, where Irish immigrants replaced many of those who had enlisted and filled the new jobs created by the increase in demand. Among these workers, who tended to occupy the lower-grade positions, there was a great deal of sympathy for the South, as well as anxiety about freed slaves replacing them in the mines.[18] Therefore, much of the violence that initially brought widespread attention to the region was related not just to labor issues but to political protest—specifically, draft resistance.

In mid-June 1862, in Audenried, Carbon County, the first murder occurred that would later be legally attributed to the Molly Maguires. At a meeting of some two hundred people preparing for Fourth of July celebrations, mine fore-man Frank W. Langdon denounced a group of unruly Irish miners who had displayed antiwar sentiments. Among that group was John Kehoe, who reput-edly wrapped an American flag around his hand and struck Langdon in the face, following which he spit upon another flag hanging on a porch. Shortly thereafter, having left the meeting, Langdon was given such a severe beating with large stones that he died three days later. Langdon had worked as a "ticket boss" in the mines, which entailed checking cars of coal to assess how much of it was waste, for which the miners would not be paid.[19] Such a position was naturally unpopular, and revenge was a likely motive for the murder. In fact, Kehoe had allegedly threatened Langdon only three weeks previously, saying: "You son of a bitch, I'll kill you before long," and had been part of the group of men that Langdon denounced and from which the comment was thereupon heard: "If we had the son of a bitch down here, we would kill him."[20] But al-though arrests quickly followed, the grand jury failed to bring charges, and the crime officially remained unsolved for more than fourteen years.

Trouble erupted numerous times in Schuylkill and Carbon counties in the next year and a half, showing significant differences from that of the prewar period. The Buckshots had traditionally chosen not to kill their victims, "but to discipline them by bodily punishment that ceased just short of murder," including the use of a weapon known as "Donolan's cat."[21] But as the Civil War progressed, not only did more weapons—particularly revolvers—become readily available, but life seemed cheaper in the face of the massive slaughter; consequently, attacks in the anthracite region became progressively more deadly.

The violence escalated to such an extent that when lists of conscripts were announced in October 1862 in response to the Militia Act—which required states to supply men for the Union army—military force was required to sup-press the resistance in the heavily Irish and Democratic community of Cass Township in central Schuylkill County.[22] It appeared there would be no way to meet the required numbers without sustained trouble, because, according to the officer in charge of the quota: "In several of the mining districts there were positive indications of revolutionary disloyalty, and it was especially manifested in Schuylkill, where the Molly Maguires were in the zenith of their power."[23]

Hoping to avoid riots and the resultant military intervention that might damage the conscription program, President Lincoln essentially agreed to turn a blind eye to exempting Schuylkill County from the draft as long as the pretense of carrying it out had been fulfilled. Benjamin Bannan, the county's draft commissioner, presented a series of fictitious affidavits showing that the quota of Cass Township had been filled by volunteers, and the authorities released the area from having to supply conscripts, temporarily steering clear of trouble.[24]

Not for long, however. Serious confrontations threatened to erupt again when the Enrollment Act of March 1863 established a federal draft due to a shortfall in state-run conscription. Antagonism toward the act was fostered by a provision under which a payment of three hundred dollars allowed an individual to evade military service. Although this was more than a year's wages for most working in the mines, it was easily affordable for the wealthy, such as Franklin Gowen, who paid the fee and avoided serving.[25] In response to the Enrollment Act, between three thousand and ten thousand draft resisters reportedly organized in Schuylkill County, creating the threat of armed rebellion. Troops were again sent in, with the understanding that "if the miners resist the law forcibly, I hope you will make a severe example among them."[26]

The resulting military crackdown kept the area relatively quiet through the end of the draft. However, the underlying hostility remained, as was apparent to Charles Albright, a lawyer who had practiced in Mauch Chunk before joining the Union army, in which he rose to brigadier general. In a letter to President Lincoln, Albright noted that a powerful group had been terrorizing the anthracite region. "They dictate the prices for their work, and if their employers don't accede they destroy and burn coal breakers, houses, and prevent those disposed from working. . . . The life of no Union man is secure among them, and the murder of such a citizen is almost a nightly occurrence. . . . These men are mostly Irish and call themselves Buckshots."[27]

It was not until after the war that the name Buckshots was consistently replaced in the press by Molly Maguires. Meanwhile, killings continued to bring the organizations into the spotlight. On January 2, 1863—the day after Lincoln signed the Emancipation Proclamation—James Bergen, a mine manager from Coal Castle, a patch five miles from Pottsville, was murdered by five strangers who knocked on his door. Gowen, then district attorney, found himself without the evidence for a prosecution. On November 5 that same year, a similar murder occurred, this time near Audenried, when mine owner George K. Smith was brutally murdered at home in full view of his family by a party of about twenty-five men with blackened faces. *The New-York Times* described the killers as a "riotous crowd of Irishmen, who, under the names of

Buckshots and Molly Maguires, have disciplined themselves into an organization, in but few instances dissimilar to the Indian Thug."[28]

The Smith killing, the fourth near Audenreid in five weeks, showed the
classic hallmarks of Molly Maguire vengeance in more than just disguise.
Smith fit the victim profile of having violated his killers' moral code by enter-
taining soldiers who were in the area to enforce the draft, to whom he was
"suspected of giving certain information as to the domicile of drafted men."
Once again, no one was tried for the murder due to a lack of evidence and an
abundance of alibis for all suspects. In fact, several men who *were* taken into
custody were forcibly released by a mob of antidraft miners, and were never
arrested again.[29]

Benjamin Bannan was not the only one to view the murders, labor activ-
ism, and attempts to subvert coal production as related elements of a picture
that included a terrorist, conspiratorial organization at its center. By the end
of the war the Molly Maguires were being blamed for almost any labor action
or social violence in the region. However, although it was widely anticipated
that the conclusion of the conflict would end these activities, such optimism
soon proved misplaced.

The years following the end of the Civil War saw a high level of social unrest
and crime throughout the reunited country, including in the industrial North,
the rebuilding South, and the expanding West. However, in few places was the
extent of disorder greater than in the anthracite region. This instability was
exacerbated by a downturn in coal prices and workers' wages, the return of
thousands of now-unemployed soldiers, the continuing influx of job-seeking
immigrants, a growing militancy in the labor movement, and a broad public
antilabor sentiment to which the famed clergyman Henry Ward Beecher put
a voice in 1877 when he stated, "Laborers' unions are the worst form of despotism and tyranny in the history of Christendom."[30]

In the anthracite region, violence soon became commonplace. In August
1865, David Muir, the Scottish-born superintendent of a colliery near Cass
Township, was murdered in broad daylight. Less than five months later, Henry
Dunne, an Irish Protestant mine superintendent, was killed on the road between Pottsville and Heckscherville. Both murders were blamed on the Molly
Maguires, but this was only the tip of the iceberg according to *The Miners'
Journal*, which reported that beatings, robberies, and destruction of property
in Schuylkill County were overshadowed only by the fourteen murders in 1863,
fourteen in 1864, a dozen in 1865, and six in 1866.[31]

Other newspapers also sounded the alarm. "There is probably no district or county of the same dimension, within the United States, that harbors so many vile and desperate characters as portions of Schuylkill County," editorialized the *Lebanon Courier*, from the county immediately southwest of Schuylkill. "And the law seems to be inoperative there, or unable to arrest crime or punish criminals."[32]

That was reemphasized in March 1867, when William Littlehales, superintendent for the Glen Carbon Coal Company, who often carried the company payroll with him, was murdered on the road between Pottsville and Cass Township. Another such attack again resulted in murder in October 1868, when Alexander Rea, the general superintendent of the Locust Mountain Coal and Iron Company, was shot six times at close range on a lonely four-mile stretch of highway between Centralia and Mount Carmel, just north of Schuylkill County.[33] Neither crime resulted in a successful prosecution at the time.

In the midst of this period, in a desperate attempt to restore order, big business struck back. In February 1865, the Pennsylvania Legislature—acknowledging the lack of law-enforcement organizations in the state—empowered railroad companies to create private police forces with virtually full police powers and consisting of individuals granted a commission by the governor to serve as law officers. In April a year later, an extension was passed to "embrace all corporations, firms, or individuals, owning, leasing, or being in possession of any colliery, furnace, or rolling-mill within this Commonwealth." Thus were born the private police forces jointly called the "Coal and Iron Police."[34]

Although the violence subsided, this was less to do with the new forms of law and order than with the growth of an organization many owners would have expected to be the last thing to restrain workers: a union. Earlier efforts to form a local miners' union had achieved little, but that changed in 1868 when the Workingmen's Benevolent Association (WBA) was founded in St. Clair, two miles north of Pottsville.[35] The formation of the union came in the midst of a strike at the Eagle Colliery, which ended successfully and peacefully when the mine operator rescinded a 10 percent pay cut.

Within a year, the WBA had expanded to include approximately thirty thousand of the thirty-five thousand mine workers in the region, men with a diversity of tasks in the mines and a variety of national backgrounds: Irish, Welsh, English, German, Scots, and American. Part of this success was because from its beginning the WBA had clear aims that could be supported by all grades of mine workers—safer working conditions and higher wages. The union also created a comprehensive program to achieve welfare for sick or incapacitated members, to build a hospital that would provide medical care for workers suffering from mining-related diseases, and to establish an eight-hour workday.

But it was safety that was an ever-present concern to the men who descended far below the surface of the earth to a grim, black hell, where they faced a constant risk of death, injury, and exposure to hazards that would produce long-term debilitating disorders.[36] The most obvious danger was a large fall of rock or coal that could crush men on the spot or block off their exit passage and shut out the air. Their only warnings might be the sudden eerie departure of thousands of rats that lived in the mines or the horrible creak of the pillars—sounds known as "squeezes"—shortly before they buckled under the thousands of tons of rock.

The miners also faced the threat of flooding should there be a collapse near a river or the boring suddenly reach an unknown body of water. Fire, propelled by noxious gases trapped underground, and sometimes set off by the regular gunpowder explosions, not only burned men to a cinder but asphyxiated whole shifts of workers. Even without fire, many gases killed silently, including "blackdamp" (a mixture of carbon dioxide and nitrogen), "stinkdamp" (hydrogen sulfide), "whitedamp" (carbon monoxide), and "afterdamp," a deadly combination of carbon monoxide, carbon dioxide, and nitrogen that formed after an explosion, threatening rescue parties.

In addition to constant dangers in the mines themselves, the workers faced a variety of fatal pulmonary disorders—called "miners' asthma," "miners' consumption," or "black lung disease"—caused by the inhalation of coal and rock dust, smoke, gunpowder, and underground gases.

Although the WBA's program for fighting such conditions and to raise pay for those who faced them was a key factor in its success, virtually as significant was its leadership, particularly in the person of John Siney.[37]

Born in 1831 in Queen's County (now County Laois) in the heart of Ireland, Siney was only four when his father, a tenant farmer, was evicted from his small holding after a periodic failure of the potato crop (one of many in parts of Ireland prior to the devastating blight that launched the Great Famine). Shortly thereafter his family moved to the industrial town of Wigan in Lancashire, England. Three of Siney's brothers worked in local coal mines, while at the age of seven John began working as a bobbin boy in a cotton mill, bringing the reels to the women running the looms and collecting the full bobbins of spun cotton or wool thread. He remained at the mills for nine years until, at the age of sixteen, he was discharged for refusing to accept a pay cut.

Thereafter apprenticed to a brickmaker, in the ensuing years he advanced to the position of journeyman while being exposed to the radical economic and social ideas of the Chartist movement. Despite being illiterate, he helped organize the Wigan Brickmakers' Association, for which he served as president for seven years. In 1863—a year after he was widowed—he experienced the severe economic downturn in Lancashire brought about by the cessation of cotton shipments from the Confederacy. He thereupon emigrated, joining several former Lancashire colleagues in St. Clair, where he gained work at the Eagle Colliery. Siney began as a laborer and within a year rose to the position of contract miner while simultaneously learning to read and write.

Siney and his friends from Lancashire were the key leaders in the founding of the WBA in 1868, and the new organization reflected their beliefs in the revolutionary unionism they had experienced in Wigan. The quiet, moderate Siney proved the most influential voice in the union's founding and early development. His strategy—and the policy of the WBA—was to use gradual, systematic, and peaceful means to improve the lot of the mine workers. This meant establishing a conciliatory position and using persuasion, arbitration, and joint agreements rather than the rough talk and violent actions of the Molly Maguires—acts that the union publicly forbade under threat of expulsion. But Siney's willingness to work closely and openly with owners and operators did not mean he lacked courage or conviction. With his own followers he could be a strict disciplinarian, and once, when threatened personally by Molly Maguires, he bluntly resisted them and their demands.[38]

Ultimately, Siney's and the union's efforts returned to the goals of safety and higher wages. Siney wanted to establish control over the production, and therefore the distribution, of coal, because he believed limiting the supply would maintain it at a high price. As wages were essentially set by the market, it followed that restricting production would keep wages high, while at the same time making a profit for the operators. The best way of limiting production was through lengthy strikes or suspensions from work involving the majority of the mining workforce—which occurred each year between 1868 and 1873. As the WBA newspaper, *The Anthracite Monitor*, explained: "[T]he reduction or depletion of the surplus of coal already in the market, together with the preventing, if possible, of the enormous over-supply that was going to the market" would stabilize the market, increase wages, and empower the WBA and its miners.[39] It was a powerful and logical strategy, but, unfortunately for Siney, mere months after the local unions joined the WBA in 1869, a new opponent appeared with a very different goal—and that man was Franklin Gowen.

Like Siney, Gowen hoped to control the production and distribution of coal coming from the southern anthracite region. But rather than keeping prices up by limiting production, his strategy was to ship and sell as much as possible, thereby making the largest profit for his railroad: the exact opposite of Siney's strategy. However, it was not just Gowen's goals that differed from those of Siney; so did his tactics. When negotiation was not successful, Gowen was willing to crush the opposition, economically or otherwise. To do this the Reading not only had to buy or lease the lines of the competing railroads that transported coal to market, but also had to take over the operations of the retailers in Philadelphia and the independent mining operators in Schuylkill County, as well as to eliminate any unwanted interference from the trade union. This would require time, capital, political clout, and merciless business ethics. Gowen had each in abundance.

When Franklin Gowen became acting president of the Reading in 1869, he was, in one sense, an outsider to the labor issues in Schuylkill County. The Reading did not own any coal lands and was prohibited from doing so under its charter. However, it made substantial profits hauling coal to Philadelphia, and one of Gowen's initial goals was to take over all such transport. In his first year as president he began leasing lines from other railroads to open new targets for the Reading, eventually connecting to Norristown, Danville, Williamsport, Chester, and Allentown. He also coveted the Schuylkill Canal, which ran 108 miles from Port Carbon—the southern region's main distribution center—to Philadelphia. In 1870, he leased it to prevent competition, and two years later he leased the Susquehanna Canal to open a route to Baltimore.[40]

Meanwhile, intending the Reading to become a major force in the coal industry, Gowen took an active interest in the skirmishes between the WBA and the operators. Strikes were called in both 1868 and 1869, but both were undermined by the unwillingness of the miners in the northern anthracite region to honor the general work suspension. In the lead-up to the resumption of work in June 1869, the union leaders proposed a package consisting of a minimum wage tied to a sliding scale.[41] Each region conducted negotiations separately, but in Schuylkill County, the minimum, or "basis," was tied to the price of coal at Port Carbon. When coal sold there for $3 a ton, workers would receive their base pay, which varied according to the level of the job and whether the individual was employed as a wage worker or an independent contract miner. Outside laborers on a regular wage, for example, would receive $11 per week, inside laborers $12, and miners $14, with an increase of 5 percent for every rise of 25¢ in the price of coal. The minimum would still be paid if the price of coal fell below $3 a ton.

After six months of harmony, in December 1869 the recently formed Anthracite Board of Trade (ABT), the operators' association in the lower region, became concerned that coal was then selling for under $3 a ton—meaning it was *their* profits that were being lost, as the miners were receiving the same pay as at the $3 rate. The ABT therefore proposed a new basis of $2 per ton, with the mine workers having a 25 to 40 percent base pay cut depending on their position. This decrease was immediately rejected, as was a compromise offer of $2.50, and the union demanded that the 1869 pay scales remain in place. The operators then gave the union an ultimatum: accept the compromise or face a suspension on April 2. When the union refused to budge, the southern operators shut down the fields, causing both privation and extreme bitterness among the miners. It was not a coincidence that on April 15, Patrick Burns, a foreman at Silver Creek Colliery in Tuscarora, was killed, the first murder since the nonviolent WBA had been formed.

Throughout the closure, Gowen nervously watched the Reading's coal cars remain idle while the northern operators made inroads into supplying anthracite to Philadelphia. In July, with more than a little self-interest, he offered his services as a mediator, and he soon won Siney over to what became known as the Gowen Compromise.[42] Gowen's plan set the new basis at $2 a ton, but for each 25¢ rise in the price, the wage workers would receive an increase of 8.25 percent (instead of 5 percent). This meant that if coal prices held at $3, those on wages would make essentially the same as in 1869; contract miners were also offered a better package. As coal was then selling for more than $2.75 per ton and the union hoped it would return to $3, this was extremely attractive to its members. However, the danger of the compromise to the miners was that if prices dropped, the wages would go down the same 8.25 percent per 25¢ until coal reached $2. Thus, the gamble for the miners was that if coal prices would remain high, so would their wages, but if the prices dropped to $2 they could lose up to 33 percent of that potential higher wage.

Siney enthusiastically supported the compromise and, trusting Gowen's assurances about the future, advised his union members that Gowen was, in fact, working on their behalf. The operators were considerably more hesitant, but they eventually accepted the agreement and the mines reopened. By late 1871, however, it was the miners who were dissatisfied, as the price of anthracite had dropped substantially, and their wages had decreased by 24.75 percent.

In November, representatives of the WBA and ABT met to determine the basis for the Schuylkill area for the following year. An accord was reached, but before it could take affect the miners from the northern region announced a strike. Despite the northern miners having broken faith by not supporting past southern strikes, the Schuylkill County workers ignored Siney's recommendations to honor their agreement with the ABT and resolved to suspend operations in support of the northern miners. The strike began in January 1871, and shortly afterward the Schuylkill miners took an even more radical step by voting to hold out for the 1869 basis.[43]

This backtracking had a profound impact on how Gowen thereafter proceeded in his efforts to gain control.[44] Frustrated by the failure of negotiation and compromise, he replaced those conciliatory strategies with a straightforward effort to break both the operators and the union.

The first to feel the force of Gowen's new mission were several operators who, fearing bankruptcy due to a third consecutive year marred by strike, agreed to concede to the 1869 basis. Gowen quickly crushed the attempt by unveiling new freight charges that doubled (and then tripled) the cost of transporting coal from Port Carbon to Philadelphia, establishing a price so prohibitive that it terminated any attempt to continue mining operations in Schuylkill County.[45] The WBA leaders were incensed but, knowing they were beaten, approached the ABT to accept the rate previously offered. But with Gowen now pulling the strings, their offer was not accepted, and the head of the ABT insisted that he was not authorized to deal with them.[46]

In short order, Gowen's highhandedness and exorbitant charges launched a wave of protest. The *State Journal* of Harrisburg warned that "the precedent, if established, will be one of the most dangerous infringements on personal rights ever inflicted on the people of this State. . . . If a railroad company can advance and lower its charges for transportation at will, then there is not an industrial operation in the State that may not be destroyed in a month."[47] Governor John White Geary felt the full force of the media and public opinion and called for a legislative investigation.

On March 8, 1871, the hearing opened, but union hopes were quickly shattered. Gowen was the first witness, and, using his considerable skills, he convinced the legislative committee that much more important than the specific legal issues at stake were the reasons and conditions behind the series of strikes that he insisted threatened the entire industry. Once accepted, this assumption allowed him to dismiss the legal questions and to follow with the claim that the Reading had the right to charge whatever it wished, as the rate increases were not to restrain trade but to cover operating costs. Following a series of denials about the way he took control of the negotiations between the operators and the union—contradicting all known facts—he plied his charismatic eloquence to turn the proceedings into an indictment of the WBA. The union, he insisted, was dominated by a small group of secret conspirators who twisted it into a lawless organization that prevented men from working, forced them into poverty, led the honest majority astray, and singlehandedly caused the depressed conditions in the industry.[48]

But Gowen's skillful denunciation of the WBA and its leadership did not end there. "There has never been, in the most despotic government in the world, such a tyranny," he declared, "before which the poor laboring man has to crouch like a whipped spaniel before the lash." Then, without mentioning the Molly Maguires by name or making a direct accusation, he intimated that the WBA was actually either the same as that secret society or overlapped it to such an extent that the distinction was irrelevant:

> I do not charge this Workingmen's Benevolent Association with it, but I say there is an association which votes in secret, at night, that men's lives shall be taken, and that they shall be shot before their wives, murdered in cold blood, for daring to work against the order. . . . *I do not blame this association*, but I blame another association for doing it; and it happens that the only men who are shot are the men who disobey the mandates of the Workingmen's Benevolent Association. [emphasis in the original][49]

By the time Gowen was done, all Siney and the other stunned WBA leaders could do was try to defend themselves and their organization against having been "stigmatized as a band of assassins."[50] Any hope of a real investigation into Gowen's actions or the powers of the Reading vanished once Gowen linked violence in the coalfields and the role of the WBA in an overriding conspiracy. It was a huge and shocking loss for the WBA. At the end of the hearings the increased rail rates remained, the union's reputation had been tarnished, and Gowen was unhindered in his march toward total control of the Schuylkill anthracite fields.

After the legislative investigation was concluded, the operators and union agreed to settle their standoff by arbitration, in which the basis was set at $2.75. Although this might have seemed like a victory for the WBA, it was actually just another in a string of triumphs for Gowen, as the pay rate still decreased as the cost of coal dropped below the basis.

One of Gowen's most public successes was the full-throated support given to his assertions about the WBA by Bannan, who in 1869 had added a daily newspaper to his weekly. When *The New York Herald*, the largest newspaper in America, ran a story about a series of shootings in Schuylkill County, Bannan took exception. "He [*The Herald* correspondent] says that the Molly Maguires do not belong to the WBA," he wrote. "This is not true; they all belong, because they could not get any work whatever if they did not."[51] This public assertion of Gowen's key strategy for undermining the union was a crucial victory.

In late March, Gowen's political allies submitted a bill to the legislature to obtain a charter for a new corporation—the Laurel Run Improvement Company. Deep in the document's obscure language were clauses indicating that the company would be a coal-owning subsidiary of the Reading. Gowen had tried the same strategy only six weeks previously, but the charter for his proposed Franklin Coal Company had been defeated by Senator Esaias Billingfelt—a lifelong opponent of monopolies. Once again, the senator saw through the ruse and argued persuasively against the Reading obtaining such power; by a vote of 17 to 15, the clause granting coal-mining rights was deleted. But at the lunch break, Gowen showed his covert political skills. When the Senate reconvened in the afternoon, a motion was introduced to reinstate the clause and, with three of those voting against it suddenly absent and one changing his vote, the bill passed with the clause restored. The Reading now had the power not only to buy its own coal land but, due to the passage of another measure, to borrow an unlimited sum of capital needed for the purchases.[52]

Gowen wasted no time in accumulating these lands. By the end of the year his shell company—renamed the Philadelphia and Reading Coal and Iron Company—had purchased 65,605 acres. By 1874, the Reading owned more than 100,000 acres of coal land—double that of any other organization—and controlled more than one hundred collieries.[53] Although eventually this rapid-fire series of investments would lead to economic disaster, for the time being it meant Gowen controlled one more phase of the mining operation.

As Gowen gobbled up coal land, he also moved to take over marketing and distribution. He first aimed at the coal "factors"—the men who retailed it in Philadelphia at a profit of 25¢ per ton, a return so large that Gowen characterized them as "sitting at the water's edge like leeches, sucking the lifeblood of a healthy trade."[54] He established large retailing centers in Philadelphia, where the coal was sold directly to the public at a rate below that set by the factors. He then brought the remaining independent operators in the southern region in with him by selling their coal at a fee of only 10¢ per ton. Thus undercut, the factors went out of business.[55]

Gowen's next major step was to determine, in conjunction with the corporations selling coal to New York, the volume that could be distributed to the entire market, because unless the total volume was controlled, producers and shippers from any one region could undercut the others. In early 1873, Gowen met with a group of railroad and coal company presidents, who jointly agreed to fix the New York price of coal at $5 per ton wholesale. This cartel's price-fixing arrangement—the first industrywide case in American history and "the first attempt to revise the old law of laissez-faire to meet the conditions of a new industrial world"[56]—was followed by an agreement to limit the tonnage that each company could ship to a percentage of an agreed total. Under this arrangement, the Reading was to have 25.85 percent of the market, the Delaware and Hudson 18.37 percent, the Jersey Central 16.15 percent, the Lehigh Valley 15.98, the Delaware, Lackawanna, and Hudson 13.80 percent, and the Pennsylvania Coal Company 9.85 percent.[57]

The establishment of the shipping quota left Gowen only one major stumbling block: organized labor. The WBA's position had been weakened at the legislative hearings, it had meekly agreed to a drop in the basis from $2.75 per ton in 1871 to $2.50 in 1872, and Gowen had tried to undercut one of its platforms by establishing his own scheme of company benefits and welfare.[58] But Siney and his organization still remained thorns in Gowen's side, and eliminating them would allow Gowen to consolidate his control and impose his desired order over the lower anthracite region. So when, for the first time in several years, rumblings of activities by the Molly Maguires surfaced again in 1873, Gowen determined to destroy both organizations, which could best be accomplished by proving they were a single entity.

Gowen's active opposition to the WBA at a time when Molly Maguire violence was on the rise seems contradictory. The union was clearly opposed to such outrages and helped keep them in check. The period between the founding of the WBA in 1868 and the beginning of 1873 had been notable for the cessation of most crime and for peaceful interactions with the owners. Robberies and assaults had decreased, and only two murders officially attributed to the Molly Maguires had occurred: Patrick Burns, foreman at the Silver Creek Colliery in Tuscarora, in 1870, following the closing of the southern fields, and Morgan Powell, a Welshman who had risen through the ranks to become a superintendent for the Lehigh Coal and Navigation Company (see Appendix A for the list of murders recognized by the State as being by Molly Maguires; the appendix can be found at www.penguin.com/PinkertonsGreat Detective or www.susannagregory.com/beauriffenburgh/pinkertons-great -detective). Powell had been shot in the chest at about 7:00 P.M. on December 2, 1871, as he left a store in Summit Hill, Carbon County. Immediately thereafter, numerous newspapers, including the WBA's *The Anthracite Monitor*, roundly criticized the assassins, who were said to be Molly Maguires.[59]

With disorder again reigning in Schuylkill County, Gowen saw the opportunity to condemn all labor activists as terrorists, murderers, arsonists, robbers, and politically corrupt, whether Molly Maguires or leaders of the WBA. So, despite the longtime peaceful stance of the union, he determined to move ahead with his master plan. He would need help to link the two groups and, more important, help to destroy them both. He believed that he could not rely on local law enforcement: "Municipal detectives, employed by the police authorities of cities, who operate only for rewards, are the last persons to whom you could trust an enterprise such as this."[60] So he must have been relieved and pleased following his meeting with Allan Pinkerton, knowing he had found an agency capable of seeing the task through to its successful conclusion.

CHAPTER 3

✦⟶⟵✦

A NEW IDENTITY

Allan Pinkerton had a problem. He had received a commission from Franklin Gowen, but, try as he might, he could not settle on an operative who fit the requirements for the job. "It is no ordinary man that I need in this matter," he remarked to Gowen. "He must be an Irishman, and a Catholic, as only this class of persons can find admission to the Mollie Maguires. . . . He should be hardy, tough, and capable of laboring, in season and out of season."[1]

More than that, Pinkerton's agent had to be sociable, charming, discreet—and therefore able to hold his liquor—and definitely a bachelor, as Pinkerton would not allow a man to take the job who, if killed, would "leave his mate and their helpless innocents to the cold charity of an unfeeling world." He also needed a man who, despite being initiated into an "oath-bound brotherhood, would yet remain true to me; who could make almost a new man of himself, take his life in his hands, and enter upon a work which was apparently against those bound to him by close ties of nationality, if not of blood and kindred; and for months, perhaps for years, place himself in antagonism with and rebellion against the dictates of his church."[2]

As an Irishman the operative would come from a culture in which, because of the long history of Irish insurrection being riddled with those in the pay of the British, few were despised more than informers. As a Catholic he would be concerned that the Church had threatened to excommunicate the Molly Maguires because of their violence and for belonging to a secret society. And by the very nature of his work and the people with whom he would associate, he would acquire a reputation for evil that might follow him even after his tasks were completed. Robert Pinkerton, the founder's younger son and later one of the agency's two principals, recognized that these conditions meant the agent had to have an extraordinary sense of mission.

"It required something more than mere pecuniary reward to secure the right sort of person for this task," he wrote. "The man had to feel that he was serving his church, his race and his country; otherwise it would be impossible to get anyone to undertake a work which invited death by assassination."[3]

Initially, these exacting requirements made the search seem fruitless—one of the agency's operatives who would otherwise have been perfect had several small children; another was soon to be married; and yet others had not been with the company long enough to engender Pinkerton's total trust. But on October 8, 1873, Pinkerton boarded a streetcar on the west side of Chicago, and there, serving as the conductor, was James McParlan, an undercover agent assigned to determine if cable car employees were pocketing fares. As Pinkerton considered the man, his hopes soared. McParlan, then twenty-nine years old, fit the physical requirements. He was about five feet eight and a half inches tall, with a wiry but muscular build and slightly stooped shoulders, auburn hair with a somewhat darker mustache and beard, a ruddy complexion, and hazel-colored eyes over which he wore glasses, because he was extremely nearsighted.[4] There was nothing special about his looks—not a bad thing for a detective trying to remain inconspicuous. He was also able to mingle easily with people he did not know, and had a sharp sense of humor, a cordial manner, and the ability to tell a story in his slight brogue, dance a jig, or sing a fetching song. Now Pinkerton had only to determine if he was "mentally correct,"[5] so when he reached his office he sent a message to the operative, directing him to come to the agency after work.

McParlan must have been nervous when he was ordered to meet with the principal, because the company was struggling financially and he had not demonstrated the total loyalty Pinkerton so valued and required. He had been hired a year and a half before, in April 1872, and his early days likely consisted of testing—undercover work exposing dishonest railroad employees—as such investigations provided Pinkerton's with the bulk of its business at the time. He must have distinguished himself in some way, because later that year, when the agency felt the crunch of the economic downturn, he was not released, as some other operatives were. Then, in November, Pinkerton's entire testing program was jeopardized and severely scaled back.[6]

At the same time, further financial belt-tightening was implemented throughout Pinkerton's, and McParlan's pay almost certainly decreased to less than that of a Chicago policeman. He also likely was pulled from other duties and sent out to collect bills, not a task that, despite his ability to use strong-arm tactics, he would have found stimulating. Therefore, in January 1873, McParlan left for a position as a conductor on Chicago streetcars until he found a better business opportunity. It had not materialized, and in August he went back to Pinkerton hat in hand to apply for reinstatement. Taken on again, he was sent straight back to the streetcars to observe his coworkers for illicit behavior.[7] Thus, when Pinkerton considered him for the task of investigating the Molly Maguires, McParlan had already been engaged in an assignment that required him to report on his colleagues.

Now, to McParlan's amazement, Pinkerton talked confidentially and at great length to him about a major assignment. Before any details were settled, however, Pinkerton sent him home to write a report about everything he knew regarding Irish secret societies and the Molly Maguires.

On October 10, McParlan submitted a tightly spaced, seven-page report, showing a spidery scrawl and a weak grasp of punctuation, grammar, and spelling.[8] Its substance was more striking than its form, however, as it laid out a surprisingly comprehensive history of the Irish societies, particularly those in the north. The Whiteboys, Threshers, and Ribbonmen had been formed in opposition to the Orangemen, he wrote, and "being secret & having no other object in view But the breeding of di[s]cord were streniously opposed by the Catholic Clergy & to the Credit of the Irish people it may be said few or none of the educated or Respectable Catholics ever belonged to the last named Societies it was principally composed of the poor & Ignorant classes with a few agitators who duped them into it for political or other purposes."

When the Famine devastated the country, McParlan continued, the Molly Maguires were organized to "take from those who had abundance & give to the poor who were then dying by Hundreth with hunger." Sadly, this Robin Hood attitude did not last long, and "Instead of performing the simple Acts of taking from the rich & giving to the poor the[y] commenced hostilities something after the fashion of the Ku Klux Klahn [*sic*] . . . but, as the[y] had no Negroes to kill the[y] commenced by shooting down Landlord's Agents Bailiffs or any unoffending neighbour who might not coincide with their views." Eventually, due to government action, the Ribbonmen emigrated to England or Scotland and thence to the United States. As "the name Ribbonman or Molly McGuire was now considered treason this Society assumed a new name which was called the Ancient Order of Hibernians."

McParlan's letter showed he was familiar with the various organizations and their actions in the old country. Not surprisingly, as an Ulster Catholic, his view of Irish secret societies concentrated on religious affiliation—the Orange movement and Catholic opposition to it. Even more important in the long run was an issue mentioned near the end—the connection of the Molly

Maguires and the Ancient Order of Hibernians. Before he ever went to the anthracite region, McParlan believed the two organizations were identical. This was not uncommon: The Catholic Church—most notably in the person of Bishop James Wood of Philadelphia—condemned the AOH both because it required its members to swear a secret oath of loyalty, and due to the assumption that it was a cover for the Molly Maguires. In addition, many newspapers equated the two.[9] But McParlan's belief would prove more significant, because it would guide the early investigation, and his view of the link between the AOH and the Molly Maguires would influence the way the members of those organizations would eventually be prosecuted.

Impressed with McParlan's report, Pinkerton decided that he had found his man. He offered McParlan an assignment "For the purpose of investigating and finding out as to who belonged to a supposed organization called Mollie Maguires; to see what kind of outrages they committed, and who committed them."[10] Acknowledging the many dangers that would face him in the field, Pinkerton told McParlan that although he would be disappointed if he did not take on the task, he would not hold the decision against him. With little hesitation, McParlan accepted the mission.

One has to wonder what swayed McParlan to accept an assignment so riddled with perils. It could not have been the standard detective's salary of "$12 a week and found," although he could save his entire income because "found" included "board, railroad fares, all expenses, clothing, if I needed it, washing, and everything else."[11] However, this was plainly not a large enough sum to explain his decision on the basis of mere greed. Although it has been speculated that he was promised much larger payments or promotion, not only would payments based on results go against everything that Pinkerton always practiced, there is simply no hard evidence to indicate either of these were true.[12]

It is likely, however, that one of several reasons motivating him to take the assignment was that success might open a door to a brighter future with Pinkerton's, a common notion to spies, as historically it is evident that many have wanted to prove their skills as a way to promotion.[13] McParlan's characteristic drive for excitement also probably meant he viewed it as a chance to engage in something less monotonous than working on the streetcars. Certainly undertaking an adventurous mission in an undercover role would bring thrills to an otherwise humdrum daily life, and McParlan would not be unique in feeling this way.[14]

His strong religious beliefs almost certainly caused McParlan to also look upon the assignment as a chance to strike a blow on behalf of the Catholic Church, or he might even have seen it as an opportunity to altruistically help the Irish-Catholic mining community. Some cynics have scoffed at such concepts, but reasons of religious fervor, the perceived betterment of a part of society, or the triumph of one political or social view over another have been major motivations throughout the history of undercover operations.[15]

Finally, as has been the case with many men through the centuries, McParlan might have found the idea of spying upon others appealing because it gave him some form of psychological gratification. It is clear that, historically, "it was part of human nature to be thrilled by the possession of secret knowledge, and to be involved in secret activities, for it brought with it a form of secret power, and pandered to a form of vanity and a sense of self-importance not available to most men."[16] Indeed, collecting and reporting information about others is found at virtually every level, from governments to corporations to families. As the Irish agent Dudley Bradstreet noted, there is no "plainer proof that this business is the universal and natural propensity of humankind [than] if we consider how neighbours and friends watch each other, the pleasure they take upon the least hint given them in mangling the reputation or interest of those they professed a friendship for before, and all these without the least expectation of fee or reward."[17] That McParlan's penchant for storytelling indulged the same elements of ego and narcissism only increases the likelihood of this explanation.

Regardless of his exact reasons, McParlan's acceptance of such a dangerous assignment suggests he had courage and confidence in his skills. He would need them, for he would be living by his wits on a day-to-day basis.

From the start the operation was to be conducted with the greatest secrecy, and McParlan was assured that only Pinkerton and his sons, Bangs in New York, and Franklin in Philadelphia would know any details. Even Gowen would not be privy to the agent's true identity, as just his initials would be used (although that did not take long to change; on March 25, 1874, Franklin wrote to Gowen, enclosing "our report relative to Jas McParlan's operations among the Molly Maguires"[18]). Pinkerton and Gowen also agreed that there could be no mention of the agency until the case was resolved, and that—significantly— neither McParlan nor any other member of Pinkerton's would have to testify in court. To accommodate these requirements for secrecy, shortly before McParlan went to Philadelphia to meet with Franklin, who would be his supervisor, he mentioned to the company's Chicago cashier that he was being sent to Europe "for the betterment of my health, an' to look after the King Bee of all the forgers."[19]

For the next two weeks in Philadelphia, McParlan worked with Franklin to develop a new identity: James McKenna. His details and name had to be changed because: "I lived in Chicago and kept a liquor store pretty much opposite the Alton and St Louis depot, and that is a kind of direct communication between the coal fields of Pennsylvania and the coal fields of Indiana and Illinois; and it might very possibly be that some of those parties going back and forth knew me, or had seen my sign out and seen the name."[20]

Although McParlan had much less experience than his new superior in such operations, he clearly had an innate understanding of what was required for such work, and he actively joined Franklin in developing key details of the new persona. For example, James McKenna had been the name of McParlan's older sister Rose's first sponsor for baptism in 1835.[21]

McParlan's new character was not a nice man. He supposedly had come to the coal region to hide from the police after murdering a man in a grain elevator in Buffalo. But this was not to be "disclosed" to just anyone—his initial story was to be that he had worked in the silver mines of Colorado, where jobs had become scarce. His "true" tale—designed specifically to make him seem to be a particularly "tough customer," and therefore to earn acceptance by the criminal elements—was to be reserved for those likely to be members of the Molly Maguires, or at least rough enough to be hanging around the fringes.

An additional element of his fictional past—created to account for the money he would spend in bars and taverns plying the locals with alcohol to make them drop their guard—was that he had fraudulently gained a U.S. Navy pension by swearing that he had been wounded in action during the destruction of the Confederacy's Mississippi River fleet and the capture of Memphis by the Union squadron under Charles Davis in 1862.[22] More of his financial resources supposedly came from "shoving the queer"[23]—passing counterfeit money. That pretext could also be used to facilitate clandestine meetings with Franklin—when he needed to travel to Philadelphia or some other rendezvous point, one of his reasons could be that he was going to gather more queer cash.

Before he went into the field, McParlan spent several days loitering around the city docks, particularly those areas where the mule-hauled coal barges from the Schuylkill Canal were unloaded. He didn't speak much, but he listened and watched, gathering knowledge of local habits, interests, and figures of speech. Most important, he learned to reply when someone called him "McKenna": Such a response needed to be automatic if he wanted to stay alive.

On October 27, 1873, McParlan left Philadelphia by train, dressed to fit his unwholesome new role, and looking every bit the itinerant tramp. He wore baggy brown pantaloons, a collarless gray wool shirt, and a faded black vest under a coarse, ragged gray coat. He topped the outfit off with a dirt-colored slouch hat with a band for his cutty-pipe—a short pipe popular with smokers at the time—and a pair of heavy, high-topped, hob-nailed boots. His battered valise and carpetbag held a dark suit for church, shirts, underclothes, two Navy revolvers, and enough ink, writing paper, envelopes, and postage stamps to allow him to send regular reports.²⁴

Late that day McParlan reached Port Clinton, near the border of Schuylkill and Berks counties, where a bellicose German innkeeper chased him out of a tavern into an equally inhospitable rainstorm. Fortunately, a friendly Irish family put him up, and then, after a day exploring the environs, he traveled five miles to Auburn. He found nothing of much interest there, so he continued up the rail line to Schuylkill Haven, which was strategically located near the head of the Schuylkill Canal and the junction of a branch line with the main Reading Railroad service. He stayed there for four days, watching the workers on the boats and railroads, visiting the company store, wandering into the surrounding countryside, and making "myself acquainted with the country and the nature of the people; [so] when I would move to another quarter that I could refer them to places I had been and describe the places so they would think I had been an old resident of the county."²⁵

Over the next two weeks McParlan rode the rail lines into the remote western reaches of the Southern Field, to settlements with names like Swatara, Tremont, Rausch Creek, and Donaldson, before doubling back to Minersville. Everywhere he went he asked for work—knowing full well that collieries were laying off laborers. Consistently receiving the negative reply he expected, he would thereafter sit in the weak lamplight that penetrated the smoky haze of the taverns, downing drinks with the locals, smoking incessantly, playing cards, gossiping, and listening. Day after day he continued, always traveling, making acquaintances, and hearing stories in the inns and "shebeens," the illicit bars in private houses that sold home-brewed liquor and gave a chance for a chin-wag, a couple of songs, and the opportunity to take note of rumors.

The Molly Maguires rarely frequented this area, McParlan learned, but their reputation was there, as he first confirmed with a man named Fitzgibbons, a watchman at the train crossing opposite the hotel in Tremont.[26] Under normal circumstances, raising their name might have aroused suspicion, but luck was with him, because a short while before, *The Pilot*—the newspaper of the Catholic diocese of Boston—reprinted a long letter from *The Boston Daily Globe* about "the reign of terror of the Molly Maguires." A rejoinder then stated, "If, therefore, you wish to know all about the 'Molly Maguires' you must look to the 'Ancient Order of Hibernians,' for in that Society you will find everything of 'Molly Maguireism' that has made the coal regions so famous for lawlessness."[27]

McParlan found the first letter still the subject of talk. And the chatter told him that there were some members of that mysterious order in Pottsville, although the heaviest concentration—"the ground where the boys are true"[28]—was "over the mountain," in the wild region running from Girardville to Shenandoah and on to Mahanoy City.

McParlan now had a number of leads, so he returned to Philadelphia to consult Franklin. His supervisor determined that for the time being he should make his headquarters in Pottsville, the county's seat and largest city, with about thirteen thousand inhabitants. By late November McParlan had moved into Mary O'Reagan's boardinghouse on East Norwegian Street, where a young lodger named Jennings almost immediately offered to show him the sights of the city.

While on their tour, the pair walked down Center Street, which divided the town between the working-class section that ran gently downhill down to the Schuylkill Canal and the wealthier areas on the higher hillsides, where the homes belonged to the likes of Bannan; David Yuengling, the founder of America's oldest brewery; Judge Cyrus Pershing, who would be the Democratic nominee for governor in 1875; and, in previous years, Franklin Gowen. Spotting a lively looking tavern named Sheridan House, with a sign announcing that the proprietor was Pat Dormer, McParlan headed for its door, only to be stopped by his companion, who begged him not to go in, saying nervously under his breath: "Dormer is a captain of the Sleepers!" And the Sleepers, he continued in response to McParlan's questions, "are the Mollie Maguires!"[29]

That night, after ditching Jennings, McParlan returned to Sheridan House prepared to give a virtuoso performance.[30] Walking in the front door, he immediately recognized the old fiddler's jig "The Devil's Dream," and he moved to the middle of the floor and started an energetic dance that quickly gained the attention of all inside, including Dormer, a giant of a man at six feet four inches. The effort was roundly applauded and earned him a free shot of whiskey, following which he launched into a rendition of a famous Donegal ballad of Molly Maguire.[31] By the end of it he had won his audience, but to make certain he ordered a round for everyone.

So impressed was Dormer by the newcomer that he invited him into the back room to play the popular card game euchre. As Dormer and McParlan began to lose regularly to the other pair of players—a fellow introduced as Daniel Kelly, alias "Kelly the Bum," and a scowling, heavyset man named Frazer, who was nicknamed "the Pottsville Bully"—McParlan noticed that Frazer was dealing himself extra cards. He leaned over suddenly and grabbed the man's hand, proving to the others that Frazer had been cheating. The Bully responded by challenging him to a fight, and, with the crowd in the bar forming a square, the two went at it. Despite being knocked down early, McParlan battered his opponent through six rounds, until, punch-drunk and with his right eye swollen closed and the left nearly as bad, Frazer refused to continue and slunk away. To celebrate, McParlan bought everyone in the bar another drink.

Dormer, Kelly, and another fellow now joined McParlan at a quiet table. Knowing he was on a winning streak, the detective tried his luck again, raising his glass of gin to "the power that makes English landlords tremble," a toast he had heard several weeks before in Tremont, and that he had assumed had a special meaning to members of a secret society. From the glances that passed between the others, he knew he had guessed correctly.

During the following weeks, McParlan became a regular at Dormer's place, which was part hotel, part saloon, part bowling alley, and part family residence. There he told select others a little about his supposed background: "Sometimes, I told them that I was a counterfeiter, and had been found out; and sometimes, I told them I killed a man or two there [Buffalo]; and several other things; according to the company I was in. The more desperate the company, the more desperate the crime I committed, and the more I was thought of."[32]

Certainly the men he confided in were impressed by the quality of the "bad money" he showed them—which was not surprising, considering it was actually legitimate government tender. Meanwhile, he subtly indicated that he had been a member of the Ancient Order of Hibernians back in Ireland, and occasionally dropped a hint about a lodge in New York or Buffalo. But before anyone could check, he made sure they knew that any request for information might alert the police that he was in Schuylkill County and result in his arrest.

It was a dangerous game McParlan was playing, because despite having mentioned the AOH in his report to Pinkerton, he was not familiar with the branch in the United States and did not understand its organization or function. The American version had been founded in May 1836, as a peaceful fraternal organization to aid new Irish immigrants, help the poor, and protect Irish women and the Catholic faith. According to its original constitution, "[A]ll members must be Roman Catholics, and Irish or of Irish descent, and of good and moral character, and none of your members shall join in any secret societies contrary to the laws of the Catholic Church, and at all times and at all places your motto shall be: 'Friendship, Unity, and True Christian Charity.'"[33] It was therefore not dissimilar to other fraternal organizations such as the Masons, Knights of Pythias, and Odd Fellows, which used initiation rites, secret passwords, toasts, and signals of recognition (and had likewise been pronounced forbidden societies by the Catholic Church[34]).

However, the locus of power in the AOH—at least in Schuylkill County—did not reside in a central body but rather in the local lodge or its leader, the bodymaster. This meant that some Schuylkill County lodges served as virtual adjuncts to the Democratic Party, which, outsiders said, paid handsomely in cash or favors for political support. In other lodges some members used the organization as a front to plan violence and acts of sabotage against the mining and railroad companies. So although the AOH and the Molly Maguires were not the same, the overlap in the anthracite fields could, depending on the lodge, make the differences hard to distinguish.

One evening in December, McParlan's cover was almost blown. Michael Cooney, an old miner from Wadesville, became highly skeptical about McParlan having been an AOH member in the old country—as had Cooney himself. He stalked over to the detective and instead of testing him with current recognition signals—McParlan had quickly learned to say he didn't know the modern secret signs—gave him some very old ones. Recognizing he was out of his depth, McParlan, who had already been acting very drunk, knocked back a large glass of gin and pretended to pass out. Unable to rouse him, Cooney told Dormer that he had a mind to kick McParlan all the way out onto the street, but the innkeeper insisted that McParlan's claims were legitimate, and Cooney was persuaded to leave the prostrate detective alone.[35]

Dormer had taken quite a shine to McParlan, but unfortunately for both of them, the innkeeper found himself in trouble with the AOH after someone accused him of joining the Odd Fellows. While that problem simmered, Dormer could not push his new friend for membership in the society. Instead, seeing that McParlan had been unable to find a job, Dormer suggested he go over the mountain to Shenandoah, where Michael Lawler, the bodymaster, would look after him. This suited McParlan perfectly, and he set out eagerly. But first he made a quick stop at the St. Clair post office, where instructions from Franklin ordered him to Girardville instead.

Even the scenery on the other side of Broad Mountain—the region of the Western Middle Field—must have brought home to McParlan how dangerous his business truly was. He had portrayed himself as a wild Irish lad accustomed to danger and now entered a territory even wilder than he could have imagined. Sir Arthur Conan Doyle described it in *The Valley of Fear* as the "gloomy land of black crag and tangled forest. Above the dark and often scarcely penetrable woods upon their flanks, the high, bare crowns of the mountains, white snow, and jagged rock towered upon each flank, leaving a long, winding, tortuous valley in the center."[36] In fact, McParlan was about to visit what would prove to be the most dangerous place in Schuylkill County: John Kehoe's Hibernian House.

Born in July 1837 in County Wicklow in the east of Ireland, Kehoe had come to America with his parents, brothers, and sisters at the age of thirteen, at a point late in the Great Famine.[37] The family lived in several parts of Schuylkill County, including Tuscarora and Middleport, where Kehoe early on followed his father into the mines, first as a common laborer and later rising to a position as a miner. In the late 1850s Kehoe took a job at a colliery run by J. B. McCreary & Company near Audenreid, and he had a stable position at a point when new immigrants began to take the jobs that had been left open by the departure of miners for the Union army. An antiwar Democrat, Kehoe's politics kept him from serving in the army, and, according to later testimony, were potentially part of the reason that he was supposedly involved in the fatal beating of mine boss Frank Langdon in Audenreid in 1862.

In the mid-1860s the Kehoe family moved to Mahanoy City, where John's father, Joseph, was elected constable and later magistrate. In 1867, while still working as a miner, John Kehoe married Mary Ann O'Donnell, who had immigrated with her family from Donegal. Three years later he took his wife and children to Shenandoah and, while continuing to work as a gangway miner at the Plank Ridge Colliery, opened a tavern. Not long thereafter he sold up and moved to Girardville, where he opened another tavern, Hibernian House, which became highly successful—having as many as sixteen paying boarders at a time—allowing Kehoe to give up mining once and for all and still provide for his five children.

Intelligent, driven, and uncommonly successful for an Irish immigrant miner—he reportedly purchased Hibernian House for the large sum of $3,500—Kehoe soon became a leader of the Irish community in Girardville, where he was twice elected high constable, was the bodymaster for the local lodge of the AOH, and in 1874 was elected the AOH's Schuylkill County delegate. Thus, this was no small-time, provincial publican whom McParlan met when he pretended to wander into Hibernian House but a smooth, shrewd, and perceptive operator who was every bit the intellectual equal of the wily detective.

Little is known of the first meeting between McParlan and Kehoe, because, although Pinkerton gave an account of it, his record of the incident was suspiciously similar to what occurred several days later in McDermot's—a Mahanoy City saloon—according to the earliest existing set of McParlan's reports.[38] It is likely that, for literary effect, Pinkerton simply transferred the events at McDermot's to an otherwise uneventful meeting with Kehoe. In fact, there appears to have been no reason for McParlan to remain in Girardville, as shortly thereafter he got on a train heading to Shenandoah, hoping to meet Lawler. After overhearing in the smoking carriage that Lawler had gone to Pottsville, he continued to Mahanoy City. There he found a large number of "true bred Molly Maguires."[39]

On January 3, 1874, McParlan walked into McDermot's, hopeful that his friendship with Dormer would mean he was not immediately set upon, as strangers often were. He wasn't, but his lack of knowledge about the AOH once again almost caused trouble. One of the men in the tavern gave him a sign: placing his right forefinger to his right ear. McParlan smiled and slowly shook his head, saying only that he "had seen the day." When asked what that meant, he enigmatically responded that he "knew as much as the doctor." Surprised that that seemed to do the trick—despite some curious looks—he "entertained the crowd with anecdotes & songs . . . interspersed with a few fights."[40]

Several days of bad weather convinced McParlan that Mahanoy City was "a God-forsaken place—the most miserable so far visited."[41] So he moved on to Tamaqua, where he discovered that Daniel Kelly's real name was Manus Cull and that he had simultaneously been cited on nine arrest warrants. McParlan also went to Columbia House, a tavern he would later make his base in the town. Heading five miles east to Storm Hill—now a section of Lansford—he visited a tavern run by Alexander Campbell, whom he was told was "a 'Boss' in the MMs of that vicinity."[42]

McParlan returned to Pottsville, and spent much of his time drinking at Sheridan House and hoping to hear something more concrete than barroom bragging. But he still needed an entrée to the AOH for his investigation to move ahead. Finally, on January 21, Dormer introduced him to Lawler, who was down from Shenandoah. Lawler was in his forties and usually known as Muff due to his passion for breeding and training fighting gamecocks (or "muffs"), which he matched in his basement against those of other men. He was "above medium height, heavily but not clumsily built . . . with black hair and heavy side whiskers of the same color, the chin being shaven,"[43] all below a bald crown. Like Dormer and Kehoe, he ran a tavern, but he also still worked occasionally as a contractor in the mines, and he offered to help McParlan get a job there. That was, in reality, the last thing McParlan wanted, but he realized that Lawler was also his best route into the AOH, so on January 30 he said good-bye to his Pottsville friends and headed to Shenandoah, little knowing it would be his home for more than two years.

CHAPTER 4

ON THE INSIDE

McParlan would have been quite happy if Lawler sponsored him for membership in the AOH but never found him a job. But within twenty-four hours it had worked the other way around, and he had been offered a position loading wagons inside the mine at the Davies Colliery, which was owned by the Philadelphia and Reading Coal and Iron Company.[1] Due to unexpected cutbacks, the original start date was then pushed back almost two weeks, during which time McParlan learned much about the hard lives of the miners.

Many of the mine workers lived in shabby homes in the overcrowded and poorly built hamlets, called patches, where most of the houses were owned by the companies.[2] The dwellings usually had one room downstairs, two above, and no cellars. Living conditions were crude, even primitive, with unfilled cracks in the walls; no sanitary facilities; scant, tatty furniture and only occasional carpets; and cooking and heating sometimes based on a stove but just as often simply on open coal grates. The front door led directly onto a dirt road, with no porch front or back, but perhaps a small vegetable garden attached. The houses were covered inside and out with coal dust and other pollutants of the mining process, ultimately damaging the lungs, eyes, and nasal passages of every family member, including those children too young to have yet gone to pick slate out of the breakers—and they frequently started there when only seven or eight years old.

The miners not only had to pay unreasonable rents for their squalid accommodations, but often faced extortionate measures requiring them to use the company store, where prices were 10 to 50 percent higher than in independent shops. The mining operation Joseph Walton & Company, for example, announced that: "from this time henceforth we shall take particular notice who deals at the store and who does not. And as the time is near at hand when we shall reduce the number of our men, just such men as have no account at the store will be dropped, and those who have shown the sense to deal justly will be retained."[3]

Once in the store, they were overcharged for work and dress clothes, shoes, soap, candles, picks, shovels, blasting powder, lamps, sugar, coffee, potatoes, rice, pork, flour, tobacco, and many more items. After these costs were deducted from a miner's wages, he might find that he had no money for anything else and had to use credit to buy his drinks—and most miners drank hard to make the monotony and sufferings of life disappear. Then, if he lost his job, his house was immediately repossessed, and he had absolutely nothing in reserve to fall back on.

McParlan discovered all this while visiting taverns and joining the locals at cockfights—a favored blood sport, as it had been in Ireland—dogfights, which were the scene of heavy betting and heavier drinking, and street fights, which spilled over from the former two kinds of entertainment, as well as footraces, card games, and bars. In anticipation of such "fun," men regularly carried billy clubs, knives, and even revolvers to anywhere crowds might form. One of the most violent such men was Ed Lawler, the nephew of McParlan's friend. Young Lawler was "a very hard case," McParlan wrote, and "seems to be much feared by every one—is reported to have shot and maimed some 4 or 5 men although he is only 21 years old—carries steel knuckles all the time. . . . He said he would as soon shoot some of the boys as he would a dog."[4]

Having decided that this "locality is full of MMs" and that he was "on the right track though it will take some time yet,"[5] McParlan did his best to build his relationship with Muff Lawler by helping the tavern keeper train his gamecocks for the ring. The first step involved clipping the spurs off the poor creatures, then fitting steel gaffs, or artificial spurs, in their place. The men daily went through a repetitive process to build the cocks' endurance and encourage their aggression.[6] The success in the matches—viewed by upward of two hundred people—against a set of cocks from Girardville helped earn McParlan an invitation to move in with Lawler, his wife, their six children, and Mrs. Lawler's brother. Despite having to share a bed with the brother, McParlan quickly accepted, little dreaming of the problems it would cause when preparing his reports. Previously he had been able to write them each night in the seclusion of his room; now it became dangerous, because writing regularly might make his bedmate suspicious. Often he stayed up until everyone had left the bar and Lawler turned in. Then, writing by candlelight in the kitchen, he recorded the day's events before sneaking to a post office in a nearby town, so as not to be recognized. Alternatively, having learned the schedule of the mail train, he threw a report on its floor when it was at a standstill, knowing it would be delivered despite the unusual posting technique.[7]

McParlan also had other difficulties to overcome. He could not leave postage stamps in his luggage, lest it was searched, and he could not take them with him into a wet mine. So he cut a small cavity in the lining of the boots he left on the surface and hid them there. Ink proved a problem as well, because it froze in Lawler's house. McParlan was reduced to making his own from water and chimney soot. Then one day Lawler asked him to write a letter for him, and thereafter he allowed McParlan to make ink with the laundry blueing.[8]

Finally, on Thursday, February 12, McParlan went to work in the mine, loading coal into wagons. Not only did he feel queasy due to the length of time he had to stay in the dark, claustrophobic environment, it was also "the hardest work he ever did—his hands at the end of the day being well blistered."[9] And he received a stiff lesson about the realities of coal mining.

Two techniques were commonly used to extract anthracite in Schuylkill County. Where the coal lay in relatively horizontal or gently descending seams not far below the surface, "breast and pillar" operations were employed. Gangways ten to fifteen yards wide and between a few hundred and a few thousand yards long ran along the sides of the coal bed, and breasts, or chambers twelve to thirty yards wide, were driven into the coal, separated by pillars ten to twenty-five yards wide, which were left standing to support the overlying strata. The depth of the breasts was determined by their inclination, because that controlled how far wagons could proceed in.[10]

In areas where much of the coal lay in sharply descending seams, the method of choice was usually chute mining. A gangway was driven down to the bottom of the seam, from where a chute braced with timber rose to the coal face. Narrow manways allowed the miners to reach the face and air to circulate. When the angle of the chute was around thirty degrees, the coal blasted or cut off slid down to the gangway under the force of gravity. If the chute was not this steep, the coal was pushed down by hand. If the chute was steeper, platforms were built to hold the coal at locations from where it could be released by the laborers below, who either directed it into waiting cars or shoveled it in—the latter being McParlan's job. The cars were then pushed by hand or hauled by mules or engine power to the shaft.[11]

McParlan's position was in the middle of the mining hierarchy. At the top of the workingmen—below mine bosses, bosses of the breakers (where the coal was broken into useful sizes and the slate and other impurities removed from it), engineers, and mechanics—were skilled miners, who established the supports for safety, drilled or blasted the coal from the face, were in charge of the underground operation, and determined the length of their own working day. The belowground, or first-class, laborers were next in the social pecking order and pay scale but far enough below the miners to cause dissatisfaction. As one Welsh miner wrote that same winter:

> Look again at the unfairness of the system to the laborer who has to fill from six to seven cars a day with coal and he gets but one third of the wages of the miner. . . . The miner and laborer go to work at seven o'clock in the morning and probably the miner will cut enough coal by ten or twelve o'clock. Then he will go out leaving the poor laborer up to his waist in water and he will have to pile the lumps and fill three or four cars with coal after the gentleman has left. . . . Between five and six, the laborer, poor thing arrives home wet as a fish.[12]

The aboveground, or second-class, laborers were next in the hierarchy. At the bottom were the young boys, three quarters of whom were pickers and sorters, separating slate from coal in the breakers, while the other quarter tended to be in charge of the mules and ventilation underground.[13]

As McParlan discovered, these divisions mirrored the region's ethnic tensions. Many of the Welsh, Scots, English, and some Germans were miners, whereas most of the Irish were laborers. Although this reflected the fact that many Welsh and English were more experienced—having worked in the anthracite fields of South Wales—it left some Irish feeling maltreated. This was most apparent in immigrants from Donegal and other northern Irish regions, who not only tended to be the least skilled, but—due to regional connections— the most likely to become Molly Maguires. Such feelings of discrimination played out in factional conflict between the Irish and Welsh, which included beatings, street fights, and murders.[14]

Other hardships of life in the mines were brought home to McParlan only five days after he began, when he "got his hands jammed by a fall of coal and was seriously injured."[15] It was a comparatively small price to pay when confronting the daily hazards of injury and death deep in the earth, where the miners continually breathed in coal dust, powder smoke, "chokedamp" (carbon monoxide), and other gases; were overwhelmed by the deafening noise of blasting, shoveling, and hauling of anthracite; and had an underground fatality rate as high as 7.8 percent during a career due to ceiling collapses, "firedamp" (methane) explosions, and accidents when being hoisted up the shaft to the surface.[16]

Despite losing the nails on his fingers, within a week McParlan was back at work. There he learned that, although he was surrounded by discrimination, not all Molly Maguire activity was based on national or religious considerations. When a Molly was killed in Centralia, a patch four miles west of Girardville, Lawler said that the members of the Chain Gang who killed him would suffer in return. The Chain Gang (also known as the Sheet Irons) mainly comprised Irish immigrants who been hired as skilled miners due to their experience in the coal mines of County Kilkenny. Their economic and social position made them more natural allies of the Welsh than of other Irish, and therefore a rival faction to the Molly Maguires.[17]

As he again settled into his subterranean job, McParlan continued to pay attention to men he identified as Molly Maguires. One was Frank McAndrew, who was employed at the same colliery and with whom McParlan quickly became fast friends. A twenty-six-year-old immigrant from Ireland, McAndrew was a good-looking man with blue eyes, straight teeth, wavy auburn hair that was kept nicely cut, and a sandy-colored mustache. He was more presentable than the average miner, married, and the father of a young child.[18]

Early in March, McParlan and others were released from the mine, but eight days later he and McAndrew were hired at the West Shenandoah Colliery, where McParlan "turned the shutes and headings." That ended about a week later when "the operative met with a slight accident . . . a piece of coal fell against his ankle and bruised it so that he is unable to wear his mining boots."[19] Once again McParlan was out of work, but this time he would not try to find more.

When Mrs. Lawler became ill, in order not to inconvenience the family, McParlan instead took a room at the home of Fenton Cooney on Coal Street, where he was often on his own but shared at times with Michael Doyle, a member of the Shenandoah branch of the AOH. Discovering that McParlan would write a letter for him if asked, Cooney thereafter allowed him to use the kitchen, where the ink would not freeze, and he could write his reports safely.

Not long after his second accident, McParlan's schmoozing of Muff Lawler began to pay off. Lawler told him how the signs and passwords of the AOH were "manufactured in Dublin Ireland and sent here . . . by a man named Murphy who is steward on one of the steamship lines."[20] The next day, Lawler spilled even more, telling McParlan how "coffin notices" were sent to frighten men into changing their behavior or leaving the area. "A Welshman—who was a boss—discharged all the Irish under him," Lawler said, and "a few days after that a letter was handed this boss—and upon asking the bearer where it came from was answered, 'from Hell.' The letter notified him to leave at a stated time—this he neglected doing & the consequence was that his house was entered by a party, his furniture all smashed & he beaten almost dead."[21]

These disclosures encouraged McParlan's hope that he would get an invitation "into the ring," that is, the Shenandoah lodge of the AOH.[22] On April 14, his efforts were rewarded when he, Lawler, McAndrew, and three other miners met at Lawler's house, where, after a conference, the others called him upstairs. There he took an oath administered by Lawler, paid a $3 initiation fee, and was given "the goods," the recognition signs and passwords that were changed each quarter of a year. They all returned to the bar, where McParlan treated his new "brothers" to several rounds. Then, beginning the following morning, he and Lawler spent the day "baptizing his initiation in all the saloons of the place and meeting the congratulations of the gang."[23] He was one of them; he was on the inside; he was a Molly Maguire.

If McParlan thought that his initiation into the Shenandoah lodge of the AOH was a "final triumph,"[24] he was soon disabused of the hope that his investigation was almost over. Five days later he attended his first lodge meeting to find that just seven other members were there, and that the most pressing business was finding nine dollars to send Barney Dolan, the county delegate to state and national conventions.[25]

However, he now was in possession of "the goods" for that quarter, so he could at least ask subtle questions of those whom it would not have previously been safe to approach.[26] To introduce himself to these men, he "put the tip of the little finger of the right hand to the corner of the right eye." Their response was "to catch the lappel of the coat with the little finger and thumb of the right hand." Similarly, if wanting to identify members of the AOH in a crowded tavern, he could use the "drinking toast," which was "The Emperor of France & Don Carlos of Spain may they unite together." The answer from a fellow member was: "And the Pope's rights maintain." Or, if outside in the dark and uncertain whom he was running into, he could say: "The nights are very dark" and be assured that it was a member of the AOH if the other man replied: "I hope they will soon mend."

Before long, being on the inside began to pay dividends. Two weeks after his initiation McParlan was able to provide Franklin with a list of ten Schuylkill County bodymasters. Two days later he explained how Molly Maguire violence was planned without the knowledge of the majority of the members:

> [W]hen there is a "job" to be done (man to be beaten or murdered) the question or matter is never brought up in open Lodge— but the Bodymaster receives the grievance and complaint and appoints the man or men privately and secretly notifies them of what they are required to do, and then the "job" is done, and the very members of the Lodge are never made aware of the transaction or who the "avengers" are, which must be kept a profound secret by the principals lest they might be given away. That if any member is caught in a fuss and arrested, he can always prove an alibi.[27]

This was the first written indication by McParlan that perhaps the Molly Maguires and the AOH were *not* synonymous. Rather, he now understood that the bodymasters and a limited number of other members formed an "inner circle" that acted without general knowledge or approval to mete out justice. It was not the membership but this inner circle that formed the Molly Maguires and that McParlan referred to when he wrote: "[T]hey are held in such terror that all the office holders and politicians are on their side, and they can always command both money & influence."[28]

The next stage of McParlan's plan therefore was to infiltrate the upper echelons of the AOH, from where the corruption, violence, and murder stemmed. It didn't take long to impress the foot soldiers, from whom he was hoping for introductions to the local officers. "I told them I was a counterfeiter, from the fact that I always had money, and did not seem to work any," he testified later. "[I]t had come from some other source; and from the fact of being able to kill a man; a man that was able to do that, and get away with it, seemed to be a man highly prized by those parties that I associated with; and they thought more of me, the more crimes I had committed and got away with."[29]

As a result, only days after his initiation he had gained such acceptance that the "boys all swear by him & say that they would like to see anyone come there to follow him."[30]

Little did McParlan know that while he was associating with these rough elements, Gowen and Pinkerton decided to expand their undercover

operation by infiltrating the WBA. In February 1874, Pinkerton selected for
this task P. M. Cummings, a Scottish immigrant who had once served in the
Dublin police. Cummings had moved to Dundee, Illinois, in the 1850s, gained
mining experience, and was "in good standing with the National Union
Working-Mens Association in Illinois."[31]

After entering the anthracite region, Cummings went directly to St. Clair,
where he found John Siney at a cockfight. As he walked with Siney on his way
home, he explained that he had been victimized in Illinois for his union activities and was looking for a new job.[32] In the previous few months Siney had
helped found the Cleveland-based Miners' National Association, of which he
had been elected president, but he concurrently continued for six months as
president of the WBA. He tried unsuccessfully during this time to amalgam-
ate the WBA with the national union, which already had effectively organized
bituminous (soft-coal) miners and gained a solid footing in the northern parts
of the anthracite region.[33]

Siney took an immediate liking to Cummings and was only too willing to
help him find work. During the next year and a half they developed a close
relationship—at just the time when Siney was becoming progressively less
popular with the members of the WBA. Many of them disagreed with Siney's
growing reluctance to use strikes during negotiations, as he came to believe
that harmony, in the form of arbitration, was more productive than conflict.
Other WBA members simply believed he had abandoned them for a more
powerful role with the national union.[34] Nevertheless, Siney earned the respect of Cummings, who eventually was elected vice president of the WBA's
St. Clair local, and whose reports noted the union's leaders were unbendingly
opposed to violence and were working toward amicable agreement with
Gowen. He did not give extensive information about the Molly Maguires,
because, he wrote, in St. Clair they "were kept down by the secret society
known as the 'Chain Gang,'" and he had been warned that it "would be foolish to go up the mountain where nobody knew him—and he being a total
stranger it would be almost certain death."[35]

As McParlan discovered, it could be dangerous even if one were *not* a
stranger. One warm spring day he traveled to Big Mine Run with Lawler to
get the new quarterly "goods." Stopping on their return for a drink with Hugh
Mulligan—"once a great M.M."—they were just settling in when a man
named Dick Flynn "came in with a carving knife in one hand and a revolver—
full cocked—in the other" to kill Lawler. McParlan jumped up and grappled
with him while Lawler escaped out the window. Once Lawler was gone,

McParlan convinced Flynn to put down his weapons and have a drink. Flynn agreed, but after tossing down a shot of whiskey, announced that he would kill McParlan instead, and reached for his pistol. However, "the operative placed his revolver full cocked close to the ear of the man and remarked that ... if he dare move his hand or feet, he would blow his brains out. The party then begged like a child for mercy."[36]

In the following months, despite regular carousing with AOH members and an investigative trip into the upper anthracite region, McParlan made little headway. In June, he met Franklin in Philadelphia, where he produced a list of those he had discovered to be Molly Maguires. However, his health took a downward spiral after he caught a bad cold at an initiation "on the mountain" on an unusually frigid night. Combined with heavy drinking, lack of sleep, general dissipation, and the heavy mental strain he was under, it led to ague and lethargy, and he spent increasingly frequent periods in bed, too weak to leave his room. Moreover, his hair began to thin noticeably, and he was described as looking "thin and cadaverous."

The summer saw a number of struggles within the AOH, and in July McAndrew replaced Lawler as bodymaster in Shenandoah. Because McAndrew was virtually illiterate, McParlan was immediately appointed secretary in order to deal with correspondence. Shortly thereafter, county delegate Barney Dolan was removed from his position and dismissed from the order for misappropriating funds. He was replaced following a vote of Schuylkill County bodymasters by the region's rising star—John Kehoe.

Kehoe's ascendance coincided with more troublesome times. McParlan's reports—which had earlier told of weddings, dances, and boisterous drinking sessions—became heavy with crime as the summer neared its end. In August, several brutal fights broke out between Welsh and Irish miners, with Germans entering the brawls on the side of the Welsh. One man was killed and several others severely injured. Then a riot at Ringtown Park ended in the stoning of a constable by drunken ruffians.[37]

In September, James McHugh, a Shenandoah AOH member, became blazingly drunk, following which he attempted to shoot first an innkeeper and then a liquor dealer. Two days later McAndrew, normally relatively controlled, caught a man who had thrown two stones through his window and beat him over the head with his revolver; several of McAndrew's friends then trounced the man until he was at death's door.[38]

A few days further on, Lawler himself was set upon and seriously beaten by members of the Shenandoah AOH. Lawler's offense was a failure to respond quickly or aggressively enough. In August 1873, Edward Cosgrove, a member of the AOH, had been killed in Shenandoah. A tough Welsh miner, Gomer James, was tried for the crime but acquitted.[39] It was not simply the verdict—helped, some said, by brazen lies—that infuriated the Molly Maguires, but James's blasé attitude, which led the judge to reprimand him: "The next time you are on trial for your life, take a little interest in it."[40] James became a marked man, and pressure was put on Lawler to have him killed. Lawler seemed to prevaricate for months—although he told McParlan he had assigned Cosgrove's cousin to do it, only for the man to back out.[41] Finally, though he was no longer bodymaster, a few members decided to teach Lawler a lesson about being decisive.

Later that month McParlan had his own scare, when he was told by a post office clerk that a letter from Philadelphia addressed to James McParlan appeared to be written in the same hand as those that "McKenna" regularly received. McParlan "thought of ten thousand things at once,"[42] particularly what might happen if his cover story was blown. Nevertheless, keeping his voice casual, he responded that McParlan was a friend in Wilkes-Barre, and that he would take the letter to him; the unsuspecting clerk handed it over.

The rise in violence throughout the autumn incited a serious backlash from a disapproving Catholic Church.[43] As far back as 1862, when he intervened in the conscription troubles in Cass Township, Bishop James Frederic Wood of Philadelphia had opposed the Molly Maguires. Two years later he composed a pastoral letter condemning secret societies, which he required to be read in every church of his diocese.[44] Other Catholic bishops in Pennsylvania had not been as openly opposed to the Molly Maguires—Wood's diocese included the coalfields where most of the violence was occurring—but they were beginning to follow his lead.

In October 1874, Daniel McDermott, the priest at New Philadelphia, a patch east of Pottsville, delivered and then published a diatribe against secret societies. Father McDermott noted particularly the AOH and the Emerald Brotherhood of America, which he declared "evil of their very nature" and "a conspiracy against the souls of men, against our neighbor, against our country, against religion, against Christ." A week later a follow-up article by seven priests in the region condemned the AOH as run by "men of notoriously infamous character," engaging in "works forbidden by the Commandment thou shalt not kill."[45] These were significant declarations—as AOH members were concerned about being named publicly from the pulpit or, worse, excommunicated. Yet even such potential perils could not stop the outrages.

The next major incident occurred that same month. Seven miles east of Shenandoah, the rapidly growing town of Mahanoy City was a center of rival gangs. The heavily immigrant town was divided down the middle by Main Street, and for an individual to "cross the dead line" and enter the section controlled by a rival ethnic group was asking for a severe beating or worse. Not only did the Molly Maguires engage in frequent altercations with the Welsh gang known as the Modocs, they also did battle with the Kilkenny miners who formed the Chain Gang.

A fire in town was a frequent occasion for a clash between the rival groups. Each side of the town had a volunteer fire company that served its own section, but when a fire broke out in the center, both crews inevitably arrived ready for a fire and a fight. In fact, some blazes were set just to bring the opponents together. Cummings wrote in one of his reports that "another fire will be gotten up by the Sheet Iron gang, at which they will go around and clean the MMs out."[46]

On the night of Saturday, October 31, a fire started in a stable just east of Main Street. Both fire companies showed up, and it was not long before a serious brawl developed. George Major, the thirty-three-year-old chief burgess (the equivalent of the mayor) and foreman of the Citizens Fire Company, tried to get the situation under control. As he stepped into the street with his two brothers, he shot a dog that was adding to the general confusion, in the hope of getting people's attention. But in the chaos that followed, more shots were fired, and Major was hit in the chest while shooting twice himself. At the same time, Daniel Dougherty, a member of the Mahanoy City AOH, was struck under the left ear by a bullet. Major died on Tuesday, following which Dougherty was arrested on the assumption that Major had hit him while returning fire.

The situation quickly became a cause célèbre. Robert Ramsey, who had succeeded Bannan as editor of *The Miners' Journal*, attacked the Molly Maguires as the cause of the "carnival of crime" in Schuylkill County. He noted an easy solution to such problems: "One good, wholesome hanging, gently but firmly administered, will cure a great deal of bad blood, and save a great many lives in this community."[47] Meanwhile, the members of the AOH lined up behind Dougherty, insisting that he was being persecuted for political and ethnic reasons.

The following Monday, having been directed by Franklin to investigate, McParlan traveled to Mahanoy City, where he tracked down an Irishman named John McCann. In the confusion following Major's first shot, McCann admitted, he had struggled to wrest the gun from the chief burgess, but instead it went off and shot Major. When Major died, McCann made himself scarce, taking with him Dougherty's alibi. And for reasons that would not be explained for almost two years, McParlan was not about to tell what he had just learned.[48] He did by all accounts file a report with Franklin, but unfortunately his reports from the time are missing. Meanwhile, Franklin, like McParlan, chose not to advise the Schuylkill County authorities that they had arrested the wrong man. So Dougherty stayed in jail for the time being while the local lodges of the AOH raised more than six hundred dollars for his defense.[49]

Major's death brought the Molly Maguires back into the limelight to a greater degree than any time since 1868, as both *The New York Herald* and *The World* published articles about unrestrained violence in Schuylkill County.[50] In the meantime, the ugliness continued, and in late November a clash between "a party of roughs" from Jackson's Patch and the Modocs culminated in shots being fired into the Mahanoy City Catholic Church.[51] Then, on December 18, fifty-seven-year-old Frederick Hesser, the night watchman at the Hickory Swamp Colliery near Shamokin in Northumberland County, was beaten to death with a machinist's hammer and a four-foot wooden club.[52] Although the motive for the murder was unknown, it was widely attributed—as was much of the other carnage—to the Molly Maguires.

CHAPTER 5

THE LONG STRIKE

As the outrages in the anthracite region reached new heights, so did Gowen's determination to crush any opposition—starting with the union. At the beginning of 1874, the WBA and the Anthracite Board of Trade had agreed to hold wages at essentially the same level as the previous year. But before they met again, Gowen prepared for a showdown. He organized the remaining independent operators into the Schuylkill Coal Exchange, which, under his direction, limited coal production and shipped an agreed quota, thereby crushing the union's last hopes of controlling those functions. Then, during the autumn, the Reading and other operators built up stocks so they could continue supplying customers through the winter regardless of production.

With Gowen pulling the strings, the operators then issued harsh wage offers for 1875. In Schuylkill County, miners' pay was reduced 20 percent and laborers' 10 percent. The minimum basis was abolished and a 1 percent cut in wages instituted for each 3¢ coal dropped below $2.50 per ton. The operators refused to negotiate with the union, maintaining that the individual miner could accept the offer or lose his job. As there was no doubt the union would advise its members to reject the offer, a strike was inevitable. This was just what Gowen wanted, for he believed that a protracted strike would break the union.[1]

As expected, the miners in the two southern fields voted to strike, and throughout December 1874, mines shut down, initiating what became known as the Long Strike. But the miners in the Northern Field—most of whom did not belong to the WBA—accepted the cuts and continued to work, once again reducing the chances of a union victory.

Meanwhile, new Pinkerton's operatives infiltrated the union. William McCowan became an officer in the Shamokin branch in Northumberland County, while an agent identified as "WRH" was based in Frackville. Gowen was also served by H. B. Hanmore, a reporter who offered to pass information to the Reading president—for a price.[2] Several months later, when a new legislative investigation was launched into the Reading's dealings in the railroad and coal industries, Pinkerton's supplied three more detectives to investigate those bringing the charges.[3]

During this time McParlan charted shifting viewpoints meticulously, noting in February, for example, that the operators were "nearly all willing to sign the basis, but were afraid of the Reading Rail Road Company." Three weeks later, "The men . . . declared that the P&R treated them a great deal better" than the independent operators. But in late March, he stated to Gowen that "all classes of people in the coal region are very much embittered toward your Company and openly denounce the course you have pursued" and that "when the Miners . . . committed their first depredation, they were censured for it by all classes of people, but now . . . they are universally praised for the actions."[4]

Early in the strike, McParlan also regularly noted that the miners felt confident and showed high spirits.[5] But as it dragged on for months, with its attendant hardships, homelessness, and hunger, the optimism disappeared, and with that came an increase in violence by what *The Pottsville Standard* termed the "turbulent" minority.[6]

Throughout the spring of 1875, Schuylkill County proved a dangerous place. In a four-day period, McParlan reported that a man named Dixon was shot and killed in Mine Hill Gap, that a Sheet Iron Gang member aiming for a Molly Maguire hit a young woman instead, and that a man named McAneeny was shot by a Welshman, "Bully Bill" Thomas, in Mahanoy City.[7] At the same time, the violence began shifting from random and diffuse to direct and targeted—particularly at operators. In February there was a fire in the shaft of the Reading's East Norwegian Colliery, followed shortly by another in the shaft of the West Norwegian Colliery. The next month watchmen at several collieries were beaten and robbed, coal was dumped on the tracks, a telegraph office was burned down, train crews were stoned, toolhouses were robbed, and a train with about one hundred loaded cars was released down the grade near Excelsior.[8]

Many of these and other "outrages" were blamed on the Molly Maguires, although McParlan attributed some to local conflicts and at least a couple to union members, and also noted that widespread opinion about the shaft fires was that they had been set by the Reading "to prejudice the public against the men who are now on a strike."[9] Regardless, the increasing violence played into the hands of Gowen, as local newspapers regularly identified the WBA, AOH,

and Molly Maguires as the same entity—an assessment that McParlan rein-
forced with a report stating that of "about four hundred fifty Molly Maguires
in Schuylkill County . . . about four hundred of them belong to the W.B. Association."[10] The newspapers thus implied that both the union and the AOH
were terrorist organizations, and that the Molly Maguires, rather than being
a small group of malcontents, were actually part of a conspiracy with an insti-
tutional basis in two associations.[11]

Meanwhile, the Catholic Church took symbolic action against the AOH.
In February 1875, Father Charles McFadden of Mahanoy City refused a request to allow members of the order to enter the church in full regalia following the upcoming St. Patrick's Day parade. Three days before the parade
Father Henry O'Reilly of Shenandoah said that "God's curse, and his curse
rest on all the Molly Maguires, and their families, and on every one who went
to Mahanoy City to see them parade." And on the Sunday following the parade O'Reilly read a list of names of AOH members who had been in the
parade—"all the cut throats in the County"—and asked for the congregation
to pray for their lost souls.[12] A dedicated Catholic, McParlan would have been
horrified to hear "James McKenna" near the top of that list.

Even concern for one's immortal soul did not stop the violence. In fact, it increased as the strike continued into its fourth month and beyond and the
WBA proved unable to gain concessions. The closer to starvation the miners'
families became—in the spring, with mounting bills, many stores began refusing credit—the more the pacifist union leaders lost control of those who favored action and retribution. In late April, the WBA submitted a proposal for
arbitration to the Schuylkill Coal Exchange. The operators, aware that the
longer they waited, the closer the union would be to collapse, did not respond
for weeks. The WBA effectively disintegrated before it could make another
meaningful representation.

At the same time, the union lost its ability to hold back the shootings,
beatings, and arson. There was also a proliferation of coffin notices, the anon-
ymous, crude drawings of coffins or pistols or other weapons, with threats to
officials, foremen, or "blacklegs"—workers refusing to join the strike. One, for
example, stated: "Mr. John Taylor—Please leave Glen Carbon, or if you dont
you will suffer; by the order of the B.S.H. WE will give you one week to go
but if you are alive on next Saturday you will die."[13]

Meanwhile, McParlan was drawn into a variety of conspiracies for which
he would later be accused of being an agent provocateur, although according

to him he trod a fine line to avoid becoming a participant. For example, at the beginning of April he spoke to a man named Brennan and a pair of brothers called Welch who planned to burn the high trestle bridge near Ringtown on the Catawissa Branch of the Reading, a key point in the route for shipping coal from the upper anthracite fields to Philadelphia, a process that started when the southern operators' excess coal ran out despite their earlier stock-piling.

The men were strangers but approached McParlan, he related, because he was a well-known Molly Maguire. Deciding that the best way to thwart the effort was to delay it until he could warn Franklin, he invited them to discuss the plan at a meeting at Number 3 Hill outside Shenandoah. He then per-suaded McAndrew that they "want us to commit this outrage, and then in-form upon us and leave us all in the penitentiary." When the appointed night came, fourteen men of the Shenandoah lodge met on the cold, windswept hill, and McAndrew "used the argument just as I had used to him, only that he used it as though it originally came from himself." Combined with Brennan not showing up, McAndrew's argument killed the plan.[14]

But that was only one potential violent act; there were many more to come. The next week a car loaded with iron was let loose from a siding at Heckshers Breakers and raced downhill on the main track. Fortunately, officials hap-pened to spot it, and telegraphed to Mahanoy Plain to delay a passenger train that would otherwise have been in its path, with a result that "the loss of life and property might have been fearful." The railway workers then safely di-verted the runaway car. McParlan had little doubt "as to the party who com-mitted the depredation," and less than a week later one of the perpetrators confessed and named his accomplice.[15]

So McParlan had solved his first crime—but what could be done about it? He and McAndrew could expel the men from the lodge, but the Reading had no legal recourse. McParlan had been promised that he would not have to give evidence, as doing so would destroy his cover and any chance of future pros-ecutions of more important criminals. Even if he did testify, it would be his word against the inevitable false alibis, and he realized now how weak his position was without anyone else who could reach the site of a crime to sub-stantiate his charges. Of course, his discoveries meant "now that we know who the parties are [we could] get the evidence from another source," but that tac-tic did not guarantee success.[16] It was suddenly obvious that Pinkerton's re-quired another true field agent who would shorten his lines of communication and have the flexibility to conduct investigations, assist McParlan, make arrests when the time came, and corroborate any testimony.

In April 1875, McParlan traveled to Philadelphia to explain his needs to Pinkerton and Franklin.[17] When the operative returned to his duties, the agency's leaders proposed a solution to Gowen.[18] The Reading president was receptive to anything that would help stop the outrages, as less than a month before he had received a worrisome letter from General Henry Pleasants, the head of the Coal and Iron Police. Pleasants—once the mastermind of the plan to blow a gap in the Confederate lines at Petersburg by exploding a tunnel full of explosives under the defenders—had warned Gowen of potential assassination attempts, because the Molly Maguires "know full well that if the master spirit who planned & is carrying out the great projects of the Reading Company is removed now, that it is impossible to replace him, that these projects will be paralysed by his removal, and that the Company would probably abandon coal mining."[19]

The three men quickly agreed to the formation of a "flying squadron" consisting of half a dozen Pinkerton's men and the same number of specially chosen Coal and Iron Police. Such a combination was important, because the Coal and Iron Police could not go undercover, as they were required to wear uniforms, and the regular Pinkerton operatives did not have the power of long-term detention. The new group—eliminating the weaknesses of both—would be tasked "to arrest all parties found committing outrages." The Pinkerton agent in charge would have direct contact with McParlan, and therefore his unit could be warned in advance. This would permit them to apprehend those committing crimes at the very point they were doing so, ensuring a conviction, while McParlan would supposedly escape each time, allowing them to repeat the process. Therefore, Franklin claimed, "there would be but little difficulty in breaking up this association, and when the arrest of a gang was made, the names and localities of all the known M.M. in the county should be published, and thus strike terror in their midst."[20]

There was only one man Pinkerton trusted to lead this special unit: Robert J. Linden, then a forty-year-old assistant superintendent at the Chicago office.[21] Standing six feet four inches tall, "powerful in frame and physical organization, with black, close-curling hair, whiskers and mustache of the same texture and color, blue eyes,"[22] Linden had joined the agency shortly after serving in the U.S. Navy overseeing shipbuilding during the Civil War. A Brooklyn-born Episcopalian, he worked under George Smith in Philadelphia before being transferred to Chicago. In the immediate aftermath of the Great Fire, while a lieutenant in Pinkerton's Protective Patrol, he played an important role in the agency's efforts to prevent looting. Before long his organizational talents, energy, and obsessive drive led to a promotion, and those same traits now meant that he wasted no time in taking on the assignment and traveling to Schuylkill Haven. There, on May 3, over whiskey and cigars, he met with McParlan and the two astute operatives made detailed plans regarding their future rendezvous sites and methods of contact.[23] Shortly thereafter, Linden and his men were officially inducted into the Coal and Iron Police and headed to their new base in Ashland, four miles west of Girardville.

Regular and frequent communications between McParlan and Linden now began, and they enabled Linden to deploy his men to prevent a series of planned attempts to derail trains, burn breakers, or blow up stations. For some reason, however, the criminals failed to appear each time, and Linden and his flying squadron returned empty-handed.[24]

In the same week as the decision to create the flying squadron was made, Daniel Dougherty finally went to trial for the murder of George Major. The prosecution produced a lengthy list of witnesses, all of whom swore fervently that they had seen Dougherty shoot Major. The defense responded with an equally large and impassioned set, each claiming to have seen Major shot by John McCann—who had since returned to Ireland. It was so blindingly obvious that most were committing perjury that the *Lebanon Courier* commented, "[I]f this is the character of testimony that prevails in the Schuylkill County courts, we do not wonder that there are no convictions."[25]

The defense argued that Dougherty had been shot by Major's brother William, who let off an indiscriminate volley in the midst of the melee. Eventually it became apparent that the defense's best course was to prove that the bullet that hit Dougherty was *not* from Major's pistol, and therefore the dead man had not shot his attacker, as the prosecution contended. The difficulty was that the bullet was still in Dougherty's head, because doctors felt it too dangerous to extract it. Now the surgery went ahead, and the bullet was proved to be the wrong caliber for George Major's gun. The jury was convinced, and Dougherty was acquitted.

At no point did McParlan inform the authorities that McCann had already admitted that *he* had shot Major. In later trials this omission was raised to show that McParlan was unethical. At one point, defense attorney Martin

L'Velle asked him: "You knew he was in prison charged with that murder, you also knew that he was on trial for his life, charged with murder, and yet remained silent?"

McParlan responded: "I also knew Dan Dougherty was apprised where John McCann was, and could get out at any time. The idea was that Dougherty was innocent, and knew where McCann was, and he would be tried, knowing he could be cleared, and meanwhile McCann could escape."[26]

Although L'Velle—and others since—used this to discredit McParlan, the flip side is that had the detective testified, it would have undermined his position and eliminated the chance for more important prosecutions. For the sake of an individual whom McParlan believed could clear himself, the risk was simply not worth it. But an intriguing question is what McParlan or his superiors would have done had Dougherty been convicted. Would the pending execution of a man known to be not guilty have provoked a different response? It is impossible to know, but what *is* apparent from McParlan's silence is that he, Pinkerton, and Gowen had determined that to succeed they needed to be, like their enemies, "cold-blooded and heartless."

Heartless is exactly what McParlan has been accused of being when he went to Northumberland County shortly after the trial, apparently to avoid taking part in a planned crime. McParlan first visited Dennis Canning, the AOH county delegate, before spending the night at a tavern run by Patrick Hester at Locust Gap Junction. A successful local Democratic politician and former bodymaster, Hester had been arrested in 1868 for the murder of Alexander Rea, although the charges never came to trial. At the time of McParlan's visit, he was not long out of prison on a separate charge.[27]

While at Hester's place, according to Pinkerton, McParlan played euchre through the night while flirting with Hester's fair younger daughter, Maria.[28] This interlude has been cited to criticize McParlan for dealing with the emotions of vulnerable young women in an ungallant way while using them as steppingstones to achieve his goals. However, although he demonstrated such behavior at other times, this was not an example of it. Maria was neither as young nor as vulnerable as Pinkerton indicated; in fact, she was already married to Martin Dooley, a known Molly Maguire.[29]

Although McParlan had hoped to steer clear of criminal activity, he was thrust into the middle of it shortly after his return to Shenandoah, when McAndrew's departure for a job in the northern fields effectively left McParlan in charge of that lodge. John Gibbons and Thomas Hurley—two of the most impulsive men McParlan had met—immediately proposed that they execute Gomer James, a marked man ever since his acquittal for killing Edward Cosgrove. McAndrew had long supported the murder of James, particularly after he and the Welshman exchanged shots in a drunken brawl earlier in the year. At that point McAndrew had told McParlan that "as soon as the Collierys resumed work, two men must be brought from away, somewhere, and put an end to James, as it was a disgrace to the Molly Maguires to let him live as long as they have done."[30]

Now, with the bodymaster out of the county, Gibbons, Hurley, and others argued so vehemently for the killing that McParlan could not but outwardly agree. Although the situation was perhaps not as desperate as Pinkerton made it seem—"to show cowardice or hesitation, under the circumstances, would prove sure if not immediate death"[31]—the detective could not put a stop to the assassination without losing face and, perhaps, trust. He therefore agreed to go to the bodymaster in Mahanoy Plane to recruit men to shoot James, who was serving as a watchman at the Kohinoor Colliery near Shenandoah. Concerned, however, that something might happen before he could see Linden, he bought a round of drinks and had several extras himself before falling into a feigned drunken stupor, thus postponing the mission (a strategy that he had also successfully used only a few weeks before in stopping three Shenandoah men from leaving to kill the blacklegs at a local colliery[32]). The next morning he met Linden in Port Clinton, who in turn consulted Franklin and saw to it that James was temporarily relieved of his position, leaving Hurley to wait in vain to ambush him.[33]

Although McParlan had managed to prevent several men from being killed, there was nothing that could be done about saving the WBA from its death throes. In late May, with the blessing of Gowen, the operators began to reopen the mines and provide employment—and protection—to anyone who would agree to the 1874 basis. Men who had not been paid for six months quickly returned to their jobs, although the most radical workers—from the Shenandoah and Mahanoy City areas—continued to hold out.

On June 1, the Reading's massive West Shenandoah colliery opened, and McParlan informed Linden that there would be trouble the next day if the strikers could not persuade the blacklegs to leave. Linden and Captain Joseph Heisler, his counterpart commanding the Coal and Iron Police of the flying squadron, took a squad of heavily armed men to protect the colliery. Late that night, hundreds of out-of-work miners drank heavily on Number 3 Hill, and the next morning "their drums were beating as early as 5 am, but they were not in sight until 7 am."[34] Heisler left to get reinforcements, while Linden formed his twenty-five men in front of the colliery "on a piece of ground about 100 ft square."

When the throng of shouting, drum-beating miners appeared, Linden counted 613 men. Among those at the front was McParlan, "hair flying wildly in the breeze, a long, patched, gray coat, with two revolvers in his belt, beside a big hickory club which he carried in his hand. . . . By the side of the detective was a sleek bull-terrier . . . trained ready for the pit, its tongue protruding, and showing the white teeth appearing fully as murderous and ugly as his master."[35]

The mob surged forward, and Linden ordered his men to level their sixteen-shot Winchester rifles. There was a moment of hesitation, as the miners wondered if Linden would actually tell his men to fire. In that instant McParlan shouted that "twenty times sixteen wor three hundred an' twenty, an' that was the number that must fall before them Winchesters were exhausted!"[36]

The strikers retreated but regrouped and headed for Mahanoy City where, their number swollen to two thousand, more trouble broke out. When the sheriff, police, and a volunteer posse ordered them back to their homes, a riot ensued. Shots were fired and at least eight rioters wounded, as were four of the posse, including William Enke, a member of the recently formed Silliman Guards, who was shot in the head. Fortunately, the arrival of the state militia signaled an end to the outbreak.[37] By the next day virtually all of the region's collieries had been reopened.

After a week of desperate negotiations, hoping to keep their organization alive, WBA leaders announced that they would make a direct appeal to Gowen for a compromise settlement. However, realizing that doing nothing was the most powerful option, Gowen squashed any such hopes. "I am not a member of the committee of the Coal Exchange," he wrote to new union president John F. Welsh, "appointed to take charge of the subject of wages, and therefore I cannot consent to have any conference whatever with your Association."[38]

Within days of Gowen's response, the WBA had authorized a full return to work "under protest," and Gowen knew he had effectively killed the union. Virtually all of the mine workers in Schuylkill County returned to their jobs, on average receiving wages at 26.5 percent below those of 1869.[39] It was no surprise that under these conditions the trouble not only continued, it escalated.

Even before the humiliating end of the Long Strike, acts of violence had set in motion key sequences of events. On a sultry evening in early May, the week after his acquittal, Daniel Dougherty was shot at in Mahanoy City by one of Major's brothers.[40] Toward the end of the month, another attempt on his life came so close to success that, although unscathed, Dougherty could show the bullet holes in his coat.[41]

In response, John Kehoe, now the Schuylkill County delegate, called a convention of AOH bodymasters to determine how to take retribution. With McAndrew still in the north, McParlan was directed to represent the Shenandoah lodge. The convention, and the plan that came out of it, would prove to be central to several of the most sensational Molly Maguire trials.[42]

According to McParlan, he first found out about the meeting when he visited Kehoe on May 26. Two days later he was told by Michael O'Brien, the Mahanoy City bodymaster, that Kehoe wanted "to get about six good men, armed with navy revolvers, and he would send a man around with those men, and this man would point out to those strangers who would come who he wanted shot, and that they could do it all in one night."[43]

Kehoe's attitude had changed little by the time the meeting was held at Michael Clarke's Emerald House on Centre Street in Mahanoy City on June 1. Present were nine lodge or county AOH officials: Kehoe, O'Brien, Northumberland County delegate Dennis Canning, Schuylkill County treasurer Chris Donnelly, Schuylkill County secretary William Gavin, Coaldale bodymaster James Roarity,[44] Tuscarora bodymaster John "Yellow Jack" Donahue, McParlan representing Shenandoah, and Mahanoy City secretary Frank McHugh, who was called upon to keep the minutes. Dougherty was brought in to show the bullet holes in his coat and reported that he believed the Majors and their friend "Bully Bill" Thomas were still planning to kill him.

The response of those present was simple. As the Majors were then working at an isolated mine near Tuscarora, Donahue and Donnelly agreed "to take care of their side of the mountain" if McParlan, O'Brien, and Roarity would dispose of Thomas.[45] Canning asked if they wanted any men from Northumberland County who would not be recognized, but Donnelly stated that "the job was but a light one"—meaning the seclusion of the site would prevent such problems—so they could easily do it themselves.[46]

As for Thomas, Kehoe—according to McParlan—stated that "the best plan was to get a couple of men well armed, and go right up to him on the street and shoot him down in daylight."[47] However, O'Brien objected to this, so McParlan and Roarity were ordered to find men for the job. McParlan notified four of the roughest he knew—Hurley, Gibbons, Michael Doyle, and Ned Monaghan—and at a lodge meeting on the side of Ringtown Mountain a few days later the first three agreed to carry out the murder the next day. When they invited McParlan to accompany them, he had no choice but to accept, lest he rouse suspicion. "I had been appointed to go, and, if I refused, I would not have lived," because "once a deed of that kind has to be committed, any party trying to make inducements for to prevent them from doing it, they are not only expelled from the organization, but the probabilities are, in a hundred cases to one, that they shall lose their lives afterwards."[48]

With the plan moving forward, McParlan contacted Franklin that night—he did not know Linden's location—reporting that "I was satisfied that I could postpone it until perfect arrangements were made to catch them all in the trap." After all, "[w]e wanted to catch these men right in their tracks. We could not arrest them for what we knew they were going to do, unless they did it, and we wanted to take them right in the act."[49]

The next day, in Mahanoy City, he managed to postpone it, telling the others that "it was impossible to shoot Thomas, being that the military, and Coal and Iron Police was stationed all around the neighborhood; and, of course, we would be arrested. This had the desired effect."[50]

McAndrew reappeared in the following days, and responsibility for overseeing the operation passed back to him. Concurrently, McParlan became ill, as he had been off and on throughout the year.[51] This time, however, it was much more severe, and the doctors initially thought he might be suffering from typhoid fever. He was confined to his bed, where he was delirious for several days, and, even when better, he was ordered to stay in his house for a period of weeks in order not to tire himself.[52] Being unwell did not stop him from receiving information, however, and one evening in late June, as he sat in the front stoop of his boardinghouse, McAndrew, the three intended murderers, and a mine worker named John Morris visited to let him know that Thomas would be killed in the morning. Around 9:30 P.M., after Hurley had borrowed McParlan's coat, the men left.

Now should have been McParlan's chance to get a message to Linden—but, he claimed, he couldn't. Not only was he still very sick, but Michael Carey, who was scheduled to replace Doyle at work the next day, stayed until almost midnight, indicating that the doctor had not wanted McParlan left on his own. There was no way to sneak out. "I was ill at the time," he later testified, "and even if I had been well I would not have done it, as it was as much as my life was worth to have communicated the facts to Captain Linden."[53]

Early the next morning, Doyle arrived when McParlan was finishing a report to Franklin. He insisted that no matter how ill he was, McParlan had to accompany him to Ringtown Mountain. As it was right behind the boarding-house and an easy walk of no more than three hundred yards, McParlan left home for the first time in days, and slowly ambled up to where Morris, Gibbons, and Hurley were waiting. They excitedly told him how they had lain in wait for Thomas at a stables, and when he came in to saddle his horse, first Hurley and then the others each shot him a couple of times. When he fell under one of the horses, they had escaped. The job was done—Bully Bill was dead![54] After retelling the story to McAndrew, the men went their separate ways, thinking that was the end of "a clean job." But they were wrong—because, although seriously wounded, Thomas was clinging to life, and he would recover to see most of them in court.

CHAPTER 6

+⟩————⟨+

THREE DEAD MEN

By the second half of 1875 Franklin Gowen was the virtual ruler of the mining industry in the lower anthracite region. The Philadelphia and Reading Coal and Iron Company owned or leased the majority of collieries in Schuylkill County and dominated the others, the mother company controlled the shipping of coal, power was asserted by a private police force, and the Reading had significant influence over the Pennsylvania legislature. With the union in a state of final collapse, the mine workers faced diminishing wage packages, an increase to a ten-hour day, and new regulations that the Reading strictly enforced.[1]

Gowen realized that the only things standing in the way of achieving his vision of Schuylkill County as a stable entrepot were the unlikely revival of the WBA or actions by what McParlan had shown to be a violent subset of the Ancient Order of Hibernians.[2] Neither was likely to impact the Reading's control, but they could potentially affect the secure social order he envisioned.[3] Gowen's goal now therefore became to firmly connect the Molly Maguires to the AOH—as he had previously linked them to the union—since doing so would likely eliminate any power wielded by the order.

In July 1875, a month after the end of the Long Strike, a joint committee of the state legislature began a second inquiry into the affairs of Gowen's empire. Once again, his masterful oration aided him, as he linked the union leadership—"a class of agitators, a few men trained in the school of the Manchester cotton-spinner, men brought here for no other purpose than to create confusion, to undermine confidence, and to stir up dissension"—to terrorist activities enumerated in a ten-page "List of Outrages" that he had created. The primary goal of the murders, assaults, arson, and property destruction, he told the legislators, was not to damage the employers' assets, but "to intimidate the workingmen themselves and to prevent them from going to work."[4]

Thus, his own purpose, Gowen proclaimed, was to serve "as the champion of the rights of labor—as the advocate of those who desire to work."[5] He wanted to help those workers who faced "a tyranny and a despotism such as neither khan nor caliph ever exercised, and such as in the wildest dream of power was ne'er conceived by sultan or by czar," one that "rewards submission by starvation, and which punishes disobedience by a ghastly and a horrible death."[6] By the time Gowen had concluded speaking of this "tyranny which holds thousands of men in subjection, and which I ask you to do your utmost to destroy,"[7] there were few listeners who would not agree that the only way to protect the labor force and achieve peace was to bring the conspirators linking the WBA, AOH, and Molly Maguires to swift and final justice.

Gowen's arguments were legitimized to the public by a rampage of violence in the months following the end of the Long Strike. In the most deadly period yet, at least six killings were attributed to the Molly Maguires. For a while this was perceived as opposition to the owners, and it made the organization popular. "Applications from men to join the association are very numerous," McParlan wrote, adding that "men who last winter would not notice a 'Molly Maguire' are now glad to take them by the hand and make much of them. If the bosses exercise tyranny over the men they appear to look to the association for help."[8]

The growing troubles actually indicated exactly the opposite of what Gowen implied: The WBA was a key force in preventing such violence and was a strong opponent of the Molly Maguires. However, this point did not sink in with many, although it was clear to McParlan: "Now you can see yourself, how this is, and what I predicted at the time of the suspension—'that if the Union would fail there would be rough times.' . . . [T]here was very little killing a doing whilst Union stood, but now it is quite the reverse."[9]

The first of those killings occured within a week of the botched assassination of Bully Bill Thomas. The Fourth of July was a Sunday, and with many AOH members seriously liquored, McParlan—who was still recovering his health—heard about a plan to murder a mine boss named Fresythe, who had discharged a miner called Patrick Garvey. Remarkably, even Tom Hurley, one of the most vicious of the bunch, felt this was a step too far, saying that Fresythe had fired Garvey for insolence, and that if he had been boss he would have done the same. That did not satisfy several others, however, and the next day at a picnic held to celebrate the national holiday that fell on Monday the fifth, McParlan was told that "if the boys in Shenandoah were willing, they were going to <u>finish</u> Fresythe that night after the dance." McParlan quickly made an excuse to leave and went to notify Linden, who saw to it that Fresythe disappeared.

A few hours later—very early on the morning of July 6—Benjamin Yost, a thirty-four-year-old policeman in Tamaqua, fifteen miles east of Shenandoah, was not so lucky. Born in Schuylkill County of German parents, Yost had been appointed to his position only two years before, but his no-nonsense approach and his ethnic background quickly earned him the intense dislike of several Irish miners, particularly Jimmy "Powderkeg" Kerrigan, the tiny but volatile bodymaster in Tamaqua. Yost had arrested Kerrigan for drunkenness several times, at least once beating him with his baton for resisting being taken into custody. Such events led to threats against Yost, but being a hardened war veteran, he dismissed any attempted intimidation.

One of the duties Yost and his Irish police partner, Barney McCarron, carried out before retiring each night was extinguishing the town's gas streetlamps. At two in the morning Yost was climbing a ladder to put out the last one—outside his own home, from where his wife was watching him through the window—when two men approached through the shadows and shot him twice. The thinly clad Mrs. Yost raced out to her husband who, blood spurting from his chest, could only faintly mumble, "Sis, give me a kiss! I'm shot and I have to die!"[11]

Meanwhile, McCarron, who had wandered down the street the other way, came running back to give chase. He fired at the assassins, but they managed to escape in the dark. Carried into his home, Yost died in agony about seven hours later, after indicating that he thought his assailants were two men he and McCarron had seen earlier that night when they stopped by Union House, a tavern run by James Carroll, the secretary of the Tamaqua AOH. When asked, both Yost and McCarron were certain that Kerrigan, who had joined them for a drink, was not one of the killers, because his height—five feet at a push—made him easily identifiable.

The murder of Yost did not immediately send McParlan into action, because he had not heard a single word about an attempt on the policeman's life and had no idea that the Molly Maguires might be involved. Moreover, the next day he was sent to Pottsville for what Franklin initially thought a much more significant assignment. The members of the legislative committee hearing testimony about the Reading had decided to spend several days there, and Gowen accompanied them. McParlan's orders were to pass on a warning if any of the Molly Maguires mentioned plans to attack Gowen or the other participants.

For most of his three and a half days there, McParlan found considerable grumbling but little concerted action from the men he was supposed to monitor, so he spent much of the period with Linden, smoking and planning future contacts.[12] But then he noticed a suspicious-looking man who more than once appeared near Gowen. McParlan put him under surveillance, and followed the man to several drinking establishments frequented by Molly Maguires, including Dormer's tavern and that of Danny Hughes. The man finally left his last bar after ten that night, scurrying along and looking about in such an apprehensive manner that McParlan had no doubt that the time for mischief had arrived. He tailed the man to a small house, followed him over a garden fence, and looked through the kitchen window when the man entered the house. Able to see and hear everything, McParlan was shocked to find that the man was, in fact, only carrying on a relationship with the cook in the back apartment of the house!

Uncertain if he needed to wait any longer, McParlan crossed the street to sit briefly under a large tree, but within moments he heard someone coming up behind him. Taking off his boot and fiddling with it as if it had a hole, McParlan hoped whoever it was would pass by. But the newcomer turned out to be a rather drunken policeman, who told the detective to get on the move. As McParlan pulled on his boot, the man suddenly cracked him over the head with a heavy blow from his club. A second stroke went wide, and McParlan managed to escape down the street before the policeman could take further action.[13]

McParlan's bruised and broken forehead was only just healing when he received an unexpected order to investigate Yost's murder. The decision came on the heels of Franklin receiving a commission from the policeman's close friends Michael Beard and Daniel Shepp—the latter also Yost's brother-in-law—who were on a borough council committee formed to ensure the killers did not escape.[14] McParlan, who had long used a fictitious sister as one of his reasons to explain his traveling to Philadelphia to meet Franklin, now told McAndrew that he had to disappear, because she had warned him that detectives from Buffalo would be searching for him in Shenandoah.

If McParlan had truly wanted to lie low, he went about it the wrong way, as he made a boisterous entrance into Tamaqua on July 15 by spending large sums treating AOH members to prodigious amounts of alcohol, first at Carroll's tavern—where he said he was out on "a bit of a spree"—then five miles on, at the liquor store of Alexander Campbell, the treasurer at Storm Hill in

Carbon County, and finally the saloons of Patrick McKenna, the Summit Hill bodymaster, and Thomas Fisher, the former Carbon County delegate for the AOH. One of McParlan's most effective methods of gathering intelligence was encouraging his targets to drink so much that they finally lost any inhibitions about passing on information they might otherwise have kept to themselves. Meanwhile, he had developed a sophisticated technique of staying relatively sober, by claiming he preferred to switch his drinks back and forth between whiskey and gin, and then swapping the gin with the water inevitably also sitting on the counter, deftly throwing the liquor out the door, and imbibing large quantities of the water. This trip was a clear example of how alcohol was a key component of his investigation, as his costs for "treating" to whiskey (at a nickel a glass) were $6.85 on the fifteenth and $5.20 two days later.[15]

Whether due to the drink or not, his investigation moved ahead quickly. First, Carroll acknowledged that it was "a clean job well done" and then Campbell "walked with me from his own house at Storm Hill to Summit Hill [just south of Lansford] and on our way we talked of this murder. . . . He said it was a very clean job. He guessed they would not have bothered with it but it was done on a trade."[16]

The previous year McParlan had reported about the way lodges exchanged men to carry out beatings and murder, thus avoiding being identified. This was clearly such a case, but who was the other target? The next day he visited McKenna's saloon in Storm Hill and took the landlord's son Mike into an adjacent vacant lot to talk. Having primed the younger man with stories of his own involvement in crime, McParlan was told in return the basic background of the Yost murder, which had been carried out by two men from Summit Hill—Hugh McGehan and James Boyle—in an exchange of killings. In the following days and weeks, McParlan conducted one of his most successful investigations, discovering the stunning details of how such an operation actually worked.[17]

Apparently Yost had made deadly enemies of Kerrigan and Thomas Duffy, another member of the Tamaqua AOH, the previous winter. While breaking up a fight between Kerrigan and a man named Flynn, McCarron had tried to restrain Kerrigan, who was then stabbed by Flynn. When a drunken Duffy became involved in the scuffle, Yost and McCarron proceeded to knock him about before taking him to jail. After Duffy had paid a fine to be released, he and Kerrigan shared a bottle with Carroll, who—Kerrigan later testified—said: "Never mind, we will make Yost pay for this. We will make his head softer than his arse for what he done to you."[18]

Kerrigan and Duffy thereafter asked James Roarity, the bodymaster in Coaldale, if he would kill Yost, offering him "$10.00 for his trouble—there is always a little trouble when a house is burned, or a man is shot."[19] Roarity promised to either do the deed himself or find others who would. After some delay, on the night of July 5, Kerrigan, Duffy, and the two men selected by Roarity—McGehan and Boyle—met at Carroll's saloon. Roarity had initially accompanied them, but had returned home when he received a message that his wife was ill. McGehan took Roarity's revolver, and Carroll handed a one-shot pistol to Boyle but recommended that they postpone the killing, because the policemen had stopped by the tavern together, and it would be too danger-ous if they were working in tandem. McGehan, however, declared that his feet were sore and that "they come three times to Tamaqua to do the job and they were disappointed and by their God, they would not go home that night until they did do it."[20]

Kerrigan led McGehan and Boyle to the cemetery, where they could watch the streetlamp until Yost and McCarron approached, while Duffy remained at Carroll's, where he would spend the night so he would have an alibi.[21] Ker-rigan then went home to set up his own alibi, and later met the Summit Hill men at the cemetery. At that point he said he "wanted to have a hand in the play, and stated that he would take two rocks after Yost fell, and he would knock his brains out."[22] But McGehan objected, so Kerrigan went to the tav-ern, where he had a drink with McCarron and bought a cigar for Yost. Then, from a distance of about seventy yards, he watched the two men approach Yost when McCarron wandered off and saw the flashes from the gun as they shot him at point-blank range. Kerrigan met up with them after they fled and guided them on a circuitous route to the White Bear tavern, where he left them at the road that led straight to Summit Hill. Despite their efforts to avoid anyone else up late that night, the killers did happen to meet a former member of the AOH on the road home, although they attempted to dismiss his surprised reaction by saying they were returning from a holiday ball.[23]

A payment, in the form of another murder, was now due, but before it could be made, Campbell—whom McParlan had determined was one of the most influential Molly Maguires—brokered a new deal. McGehan and miner Tom Mulhall had sworn revenge against a Welsh "inside boss" named John P. Jones, who they said had blacklisted them with the Lehigh and Wilkes-Barre Coal Company.[24] Campbell, according to McParlan, insisted on the murder of Jones in exchange for that of Yost, but he wanted things to "remain quiet for the present" before securing his murderers.[25]

McParlan was stunned by the ease with which he had discovered the essence of the story, and, although still far from knowing all the details, he sent a report to Franklin mentioning the threat to Jones, although there was some confusion as to whether the man's name was Jones or Jennings.[26] Shortly thereafter, he was introduced to McGehan at Campbell's saloon, and described him as "About 5 ft 9 inches high—straight and well built, probably weighs from 165 to 175 lbs, about twenty three years of age, rather light complexion, face clean shaved." The same afternoon, McParlan's hot streak regarding confessions continued, as Roarity implicated himself with the admission that the murder had been "a clean job."[27]

McParlan left town, and for several anxious days performed tasks for Kehoe and his other AOH colleagues in Shenandoah and Pottsville while trying to get as much rest as possible to avoid becoming ill again. All the while he eagerly anticipated going back to Tamaqua to obtain corroborating testimony and find the murder weapons, but he worried constantly about giving his game away. His mind was set at rest at his first stop back, when Carroll warned him to be careful, as the town had been "swarming with detectives ever since the murder," although the taverner proudly commented that he had seen through their disguises. But to his brother in the AOH, Carroll readily admitted that he had provided the single-shot pistol used for the murder.[28]

McParlan's combination of luck and skilful manipulation resumed its remarkable run only two days later, when the string of confessions continued during a visit to Kerrigan. Coincidentally, Kerrigan and a couple other men had initially been scheduled to kill Jones the night McParlan called, but since Campbell had put the murder on hold, Kerrigan was there when the detective arrived.[29] It did not take long for McParlan to get the egotistical bodymaster to open up. Pulling out a .32 caliber revolver he had been given by Linden, the detective bragged that he had stolen it. In a game of one-upmanship, Kerrigan himself produced a gun, Roarity's he said, which "Fixed Yost." When McParlan feigned disbelief, Kerrigan not only admitted he had planned the murder and had been there when it was carried out, but also divulged new details, including that Yost had "hollered like a panther."[30] McParlan had received a direct admission of guilt.

But McParlan had more than the confession to think about that night, for while drinking with Kerrigan he was reintroduced to the bodymaster's sister-in-law, Mary Ann Higgins. McParlan was immediately attracted to the blue-eyed lass, whom he had met briefly many months earlier at a Polish wedding. Now, however, he realized that she would provide a brilliant cover for his investigation, so he promptly began "sparking"—courting—her, admitting later that "it was not for the sake of throwing off suspicion on Kerrigan's part that I made love to his sister-in-law, but to throw off any suspicion there might be as to my object in stopping around Tamaqua."[31]

With Mary Ann as the apparent reason, McParlan spent more and more time with Kerrigan, attempting to corroborate the confession. Several times he attempted to talk Kerrigan into going out for an evening walk near the cemetery, where Linden would be hiding behind a hedge and could hear the conversation, but the plan was never carried off.[32]

Linden did gain other information, however. "[T]he Summit Hill [Jones] assassination has been postponed until a couple of men get work, to avoid the suspicion which would naturally attach to them if they were idle," he wrote. "It is decided that the job shall be done in daylight by four men, one to point out the boss, one to keep the way for retreat clear, and two to do the shooting." He also discovered that the man was "to be shot at Ashton, on the old railroad track. I did not learn the boss's name."[33]

At the same time, McParlan also made headway. In early August he had eye-opening conversations with Carroll, Kerrigan, and Campbell, the last revealing the reasons behind the murder of Yost and indicating "that he calculated for to start McGehan in a saloon for the clean job that he had done at Tamaqua." Campbell also confirmed that he had stopped Kerrigan's scheduled murder the week before, because "[w]hat he wanted was to get McGehan settled in his saloon and Mulhall at work and then they would try to get the men to murder Jones."[34]

That same evening, Carroll not only confirmed what Campbell had said, but provided fuller details about the next target.[35] "Jones is the boss who is to be assassinated," Linden wrote confidently the day after McParlan had gained the information, "but it has been postponed until the last of the month, and after the Molly Maguire convention which is to be held at Tamaqua on the 25th."[36] Nevertheless, Franklin reported the information to Beard and the committee, as well as to Jones's employers, while also ordering Linden and several of his men to stay in Tamaqua and shadow any Molly Maguires involved, so that when the attempt was made he could "surround them if they went to Summit Hill, and ambush them, if necessary, and shoot them down if they undertook it."[37]

Further measures were evidently also taken to protect Jones. After discussions with Charles Parrish, the head of the Lehigh and Wilkes-Barre Coal Company, and William Zehner, general superintendent of the company's

Lansford mines, Captain T. C. Williams of the Coal and Iron Police detailed two officers to guard Jones at his home each night. For several weeks, however, Jones actually slept under guard at Zehner's house, since he also was considered a target.[38]

Meanwhile, McParlan and Linden traveled to Mauch Chunk to meet Franklin and a Pinkerton's operative named Spittall. They traveled out to the beautiful hills of Glen Onoko, where they discussed putting Spittall undercover in Summit Hill to be ready for action. The plan was ultimately abandoned due to the risk of sending a stranger there.[39]

On their return to Mauch Chunk, the four split up, with McParlan and Linden continuing their conversation over a drink at the American Hotel. Upon exiting they saw a group of men across the street at the courthouse, among them Campbell, McGehan, and Barney Philips, the county recorder. Ditching Linden, whom he claimed was a drunk who had asked directions, McParlan joined the others for a beer, and in the ensuing conversation Campbell stated that he "had got a license for McGehan to start his saloon . . . for he considered McGehan was the best man in the County on account of the clean job he had done in Tamaqua. Now, all that was to be done was to get Jones out of the way."[40]

With a license in his pocket, Campbell as his liquor distributor, and an $8-a-month lease on a basement room at the corner of Ludlow and Oak streets in Summit Hill, McGehan was ready to open his saloon, and the date was scheduled for Thursday, August 12. McParlan arrived on the day to find that, due to difficulties with the occupier of the other part of the house, the opening had been postponed. Welcomed to spend a couple of nights at Campbell's house, McParlan later testified that on the next evening, Campbell "described to me the house where John P. Jones lived as near as he could describe it and informed me that he left his house . . . somewhere before seven o'clock, and taking an old railroad track to the mines . . . he stated 'this is the place to have the men placed to shoot him just as he comes out in the morning and goes to his work.'"[41]

Two days late, on a raucous Saturday evening, McGehan's saloon finally opened. Following Linden's instructions, McParlan approached the new taverner and quietly asked if he had cartridges for a .32 caliber revolver. McGehan took him into a side room, where he said, "I have no cartridges, Mac, that will fit that pistol. James Roarity has, and I guess you can get a few from him." He continued confidentially: "Roarity is kind of cautious about purchasing any cartridges to fit his pistol, on account of it being the weapon I used to shoot officer Yost."[42] McGehan then gave the detective a firsthand account of the murder. The next morning, while attending church with Roarity, McParlan invited him to have a drink at McGehan's. There he used the same subterfuge, and while in the company of both Roarity and McGehan, the former admitted to owning the gun, and both confessed their roles in the crime.[43]

McParlan felt inwardly triumphant at having so fully cracked the case, and was buoyed up for his further investigations by the knowledge that no longer would murderers feel safe after their crimes. Little did he know that all hell was breaking loose across the major towns of the area that very night, including two more sensational murders.

So widespread were the troubles that the headline in the next *Weekly Miners' Journal* read "A Bloody Night North of the Mountain."[44] In Girardville, armed gangs drinking and shooting guns in the air wandered the streets "absolutely rampant and defiant of lawful restraints." In Jacob Wendel's bar, a man named Hoary assaulted another patron, and when the latter went to the house of Squire Thomas Gwyther, a justice of the peace, to demand his arrest, Hoary's friend Billy Love barged in. Gwyther ejected Love from his house, but when the justice began to step out of his door, a pistol was leveled at him. As his daughter screamed for the gunman not to hurt her father, Gwyther was shot down on the porch. John Kehoe, as high constable, quickly arrested Thomas Love, only to release him when the murderer transpired to be his brother, who in the interim had fled, never to be caught.[45]

Meanwhile, in Mahanoy City, Bully Bill Thomas, already back on the prowl, was wounded by a bullet in the face when he engaged in a shoot-out with Irishman James Dugan. As the lead flew, a stray bullet killed Christian Brenhower, a German miner walking nearby. Thomas was arrested for assaulting Dugan, but neither man was prosecuted for shooting the bystander.

But it was at Glover's Grove, just outside Shenandoah, that the most startling killing took place. That same night, during a picnic for the volunteer Rescue Hook and Ladder Company, Gomer James—who had remained in the area even after being removed from his job for his own safety—was drawing a beer behind the counter of an outside bar when a man strolled up, pulled out a revolver, and shot him dead. As the scene erupted in chaos, the murderer walked into the crowd and vanished.[46]

The identity of the killer was not a mystery to the members of the Shenandoah AOH, however. That night Mike Carey rushed breathlessly into their meeting and blurted out, "Tom Hurley has shot Gomer James." Two days later, having heard about the killing while in Tamaqua, McParlan returned to Shenandoah, where he was given the details by Hurley, Lawler, and John Morris. Lawler then pressed McParlan to see Kehoe about a reward for Hurley for carrying out the "long-overdue" assignment. When the detective went to Girardville the next day, Kehoe postponed any decision until the Schuylkill County AOH convention, which was scheduled to be held in a week and a half, on Wednesday, August 25.[47]

Meanwhile, the very night McParlan returned to Shenandoah, there was yet another attempted murder. James Riles, a saloonkeeper, had previously pressed charges against a Molly Maguire by the name of John Tobin—who had shot Riles earlier in the year—with the result that Tobin was sentenced to fifteen months in prison. In response, James McAllister and several other men—thought to include Tobin, who was out on bond—walked into Riles's saloon and shot him in the back.[48]

Things then quieted down, as, according to Linden, "no more murders were to be committed until after the convention of the 25th."[49] The day prior to that McParlan spent the morning tending bar for Carroll, who was at a funeral, and when Campbell came by, he "asked me to help to get men to shoot John P. Jones. . . . [H]e could not depend upon the man Kerrigan to get the men for the reason why he supposed Kerrigan would get drunk." Once again, McParlan saw no way out of the situation and felt compelled to agree.[50]

The convention held the next day—on the second floor of Carroll's house—was attended by "Sleepers here from all parts of the County," although with no general session most of them remained in the saloon while an appointed committee conducted business in the rooms upstairs. Some members were expelled, others readmitted, but it was only in the late afternoon that Hurley's claim to have killed James arose. Then, to the surprise of the men from Shenandoah, it was disputed by John McClain of Number 3 Hill, who insisted *he* had carried out the assignment. McParlan and Patrick Butler, the bodymaster at Lost Creek, were appointed to investigate and make a final determination.[51]

Then came discussions about future "actions," such as the potential murder of Amos Lamberson, a policeman who had killed an Irishman two years before.[52] No decision was made, but John Reese, a mine superintendent at the Plank Ridge Colliery, was not so fortunate and was targeted for murder.[53] Finally, Kerrigan, along with Duffy and McParlan (who volunteered at the direction of Linden), were assigned to eliminate Jones, although no specific time was set.[54]

In the days immediately following the convention, two other names were mentioned as candidates for murder, and neither made the Pinkerton's men happy. Hurley had concerns about Linden—who had been discovered to be in the Coal and Iron Police (although not yet that he was a Pinkerton's agent)— and said that if he "was spooking about anything not right they would shoot him on arrival in Shenandoah." When McParlan informed Linden, the latter returned the favor, letting McParlan know that he "was suspected by the Welsh and English of being the instigator of all the murders as it is generally supposed that he is a leader of the Molly Maguires, and they threaten to have revenge on him if any more murders are committed."[55]

For the time being, no one was safe.

CHAPTER 7

MURDER AND VIGILANTE VENGEANCE

T he murder of policeman Yost was not the only killing McParlan was unable to prevent because he had not heard enough in advance. On the morning of August 31—the week after the county convention—he woke to find Michael Doyle, with whom he shared a room, asleep next to him, and a Smith & Wesson revolver on the washstand. Knowing Doyle did not own one, McParlan woke him and asked about it. "[H]e told me he got it from Ed Monaghan," McParlan wrote, adding that Doyle, along with James McAllister and the brothers Charles and James "Friday" O'Donnell "were going down to Raven Run to shoot Sanger, the mining boss just as he went out to get dinner."[1] Doyle also asked McParlan for his gray coat, as "he would like to get one of mine to prevent detection afterward. . . . I told him to take it."[2]

McParlan and Doyle had just gone downstairs for breakfast when Hurley—who lived in the next street—arrived. Buoyed by his murder of James—with which McParlan and Butler's investigation had just credited him[3]—he gave a detailed demonstration to Doyle about how best to kill a man. Hoping for confirmation of the intended victim's name, McParlan wandered into town, where he ran into James O'Donnell, who told him that "his brother and McAllister went to work that morning, and that they were working with members of the organization and could easily slip out, and they were bound to shoot him [Sanger] at noon-time."[4]

So McParlan had only a few hours to act, but he could neither find Linden, nor get away from Hurley: "I made several excuses during the day and Hurley was always ready to go along; he did not seem to have any particular business."[5] Every effort ended in failure: "I tried to shun Hurley and despatch to you, as I do not know where L. is but I could not manage," he wrote, knowing that by the time Franklin received the report a man would have been killed.[6] But what, he asked himself, could he do, short of taking action that might expose his role?

Meanwhile, McAndrew had called a meeting for that afternoon about killing Reese, as agreed at the convention. McAndrew instructed McParlan to go to Tamaqua to meet Kerrigan and finalize the plans for the murder of Jones; Kerrigan, in turn, would find men to eliminate Reese. The meeting and its aftermath—with Hurley as a constant shadow—meant that McParlan once again did not have the opportunity to send a message about Jones, Reese, or, most urgently, Sanger. "I am in the fix," he wrote when he finally was alone. "I do not know where to find Linden, and it would cost me my life to despatch as you may also see it takes all my time to get a chance of writing, although they have no suspicion of me so far, but it dont take much to make them have one, and neither man nor woman of them will spare a man, if they get a chance on him."[7]

This report to Franklin—not previously seen for almost half a century because it is held privately—is revelatory. While many critics portray McParlan as supremely confident, too clever by half, priding himself on his ability to spin lies into a web of deceit, this shows him as one who saw his task as neither easy nor glamorous, but rather extremely unnerving and dangerous. Additionally, it reveals McParlan's growing anxiety, and perhaps guilt, as demonstrated by his need to explain his lack of action when the reasons are actually evident.

It was later questioned (in court and by subsequent writers) why McParlan did not warn Sanger that night when Hurley went home and Doyle had not yet returned. However, both Doyle and O'Donnell had said that the killing would occur by noon, when Sanger came out of the mine, and by evening, McParlan assumed the deed had been done. He had not received a definite report, but "I heard nothing to counteract the intimation I had." More important, the key reason behind his hesitation was fear: "Hurley remained with me up until it was ten o'clock and it was utterly impossible for me to give any information without endangering my own life."[8]

McParlan later tried to downplay his inaction (and perhaps to assuage his guilt) by testifying under oath in three trials that even if the target had been alive, "I did not know what colliery the boss worked at, or what was the name of the boss."[9] But his report about his discussion with Doyle clearly shows this not to be the case—he did, in fact, know Sanger's name.

Hurley reappeared early the next morning and accompanied McParlan to Lawler's saloon. Shortly before 8:00, five heavily armed and overheated men—the four who had set out together the day before plus Thomas Munley of the Gilberton lodge—showed up. "We made a clean job," announced James O'Donnell, "we killed two, we only intended to kill one."[10] First they downed whiskey as well as a pitcher of water, and after catching their breath from a hard run, they excitedly told of how, after spending the night at the home of Dennis "Bucky" Donnelly, the former bodymaster at Lost Creek, they had exchanged clothes and hats and then lurked around Heaton's Colliery—which was actually comprised of a number of small collieries in the same area, all owned by Robert Heaton—as if waiting to see if they could find work.

When Sanger, the thirty-three-year-old Cornish "inside boss," and William Uren, a young Cornish miner who had moved to the United States only three years before and boarded with his countryman, left the Sangers' house carrying their dinner cans in their hands, the assassins made their move. Charles O'Donnell, Doyle, and McAllister approached a group of men who were waiting for work to start and, "drawing revolvers said, 'clear out you sons of bitches' and fired four or five shots apparently at the crowd."[11] As the miners scattered, James O'Donnell, wielding two large revolvers, moved quickly toward Sanger. A shot rang out and the foreman "kind of fell or staggered," before running toward the back of a house. While one of the killers pursued him, Munley raced up the road and circled around behind the house from the other direction; he blocked Sanger's path and shot him just as he was going for the door of the house. Sanger fell to his hands and knees, and Munley pushed him over and fired again at close range.[12] Meanwhile, James O'Donnell shot Uren as he attempted to go to Sanger's aid, and the young man died a few hours after his friend. The fatal wound for each was in the groin, near the femoral artery.[13]

Heaton, the mine owner, heard the shots, grabbed his pistol, and ran out of his house toward where the murders were taking place, some two hundred yards away. As he reached Sanger, the fatally wounded man gasped, "Don't stop for me, Bob, but give it to them!"[14] Heaton then chased the fleeing assassins and fired five shots at them, but hit no one. The men returned fire, disappeared behind a breaker, ran through the mule yard, and escaped unscathed along a mountain path, heading northeast.[15]

Within an hour or so of the shootings, McParlan had heard the confessions of all five killers. However, he was helpless to do anything about it immediately and, moreover, was expected to travel to Tamaqua the following day with Munley, Mike Darcy, and John McGrail to eliminate Jones and bring back two men to dispatch Reese. Hoping to go ahead of the others so that he could tell Linden about both the Sanger murder and the projected one, McParlan again could not shake Hurley and McAndrew nor send out a warning about the dangers facing Jones.[16]

The next morning, Munley and Darcy joined McParlan on the train to Tamaqua, but the two had been drinking much of the night, so McParlan led them to Carroll's saloon, where Mrs. Carroll gave them a bed to sleep it off. Although this freed McParlan to find Linden, it was too late. Linden had already left town, having received a dispatch from Franklin that "a mining boss at Raven Run had been shot dead and another man mortally wounded—for me to proceed there immediately so as to ascertain the names of the witnesses and find out all the witnesses knew . . . I left there immediately on the first train . . . and that is why MacParlan never knew where I went—did not know anything at all about me."[17]

Unable to find Linden, who remained in Raven Run for two days, McParlan went to Columbia House—where he often stayed when in Tamaqua—and wrote to Franklin, recommending that Jones's house be surrounded in order to catch any would-be killers, while he would try to "hold back the murder of Jones upon some pretext until I could get Captain Linden . . . to come there and gobble up the crowd."[18] Using the excuse that Kerrigan could not be found, he sent Munley and Darcy back—although "I didn't look for Kerrigan or make any inquiries for Kerrigan. I did not want to see him that I might postpone the murder."[19] Thinking that he had gained Jones a reprieve, he went to Carroll's that night, only to be told at ten o'clock that "Kerrigan had went to Lansford some one or two days previous with two men, to shoot John P. Jones."[20]

McParlan was again in a fix. He was stunned that events were moving ahead so quickly without his knowledge, when *he* was supposed to be organizing the Jones murder. But there was nothing he could do, as he had no idea of Linden's location and no way of safely transmitting a message. He did not even know if Jones had already been killed. So, figuring that "Jones was on his guard," and being absolutely worn out by the stress of the past weeks, he "went to my hotel, and wrote out my report, and went to bed."[21]

In fact, Jones was still alive when McParlan turned in.[22] The previous day, September 1, two men from the Mount Laffee lodge, Edward Kelly and Michael J. Doyle—a different Michael Doyle than McParlan's roommate—had arrived at Carroll's saloon, where they had been sent to carry out the job. Carroll told Kerrigan to lead them to Lansford to commit the murder, after which he could guide them back to safety. Unlike Kerrigan's previous effort, this time it would prove to be anything but a "clean job."

That evening, the three made their way first to Campbell's liquor store and then to Summit Hill, the western terminus of the switchback railroad, where

McGehan's new tavern was located. After McGehan cleaned and oiled two pistols, Campbell, realizing that none of the other three had ever seen Jones and needed to be certain of his identity, "gave them a description of Jones. He said he wore a kind of black hat, and a blue blouse and pants, usually in his boots, and carried a dinner can, and no bottle."[23]

The next day, Kerrigan, Doyle, and Kelly wandered over to Jones's neighborhood, hoping to intercept him when he approached Heaton's Number 4 colliery. However, rather than walking along the tracks as they expected, Jones took the train from the Lansford depot, thereby eluding his killers. They hunted him that day, asking about him at Heaton's different collieries and waiting for an hour outside of Number 5 colliery, only to be foiled when he followed a tunnel to a different exit.[24] They had no more luck questioning his neighbors—even walking into a house they thought to be Jones's, to find they were mistaken—and returned to see Campbell, who was angry because he "thought we would see him in the morning, and have shot him in the afternoon."[25]

Coincidentally, that night, having decided that the danger had been overestimated, Jones stayed in his own house with his wife and seven children for the first time in weeks. Around 7:00 A.M., he headed down the pipeway for the Lansford depot, half a mile away. Carelessly alone and unprotected, despite numerous previous warnings, he was within one hundred yards of the depot when Kelly and Doyle approached him on the path, and he moved aside to let them pass. Instead, the two men drew their pistols and shot him, Doyle twice. Jones tried to reach the bushes to escape but was pursued, and when the wounded man fell, Doyle, using the same pistol that had dispatched policeman Yost, riddled his body with bullets. Kerrigan and the two killers then fled toward the high woods to the west.

Before long, a search was organized and accounts of the murder were telegraphed to the towns that the organizers suspected the killers might pass through. Samuel Beard, who was studying law in a local office, had just arrived on the train from Tamaqua when the murder occurred. He followed several people to where Jones was writhing in his death throes. Horrified, he returned to Tamaqua on the next train with rough descriptions of the killers, gained from men who had run toward Jones as the murderers raced off. Knots of men formed throughout the town, discussing what could be done. Beard and a friend, hearing rumors that the highly disreputable Kerrigan had been seen with two strangers at the end of town, went to the Odd Fellows' cemetery, which was located on a nearby hill, to see if they could spot anyone through a spyglass.

What they saw was Kerrigan on a mountainside across the valley, waving a handkerchief in signal to two men, who came out of the woods to meet him. Immediately suspicious, Beard raced back to the town center, where a posse was formed. Dividing in two, it advanced up the hill, surrounding Kerrigan and the two strangers—Doyle and Kelly—who were quickly captured while drinking whiskey near a mountain spring. The men were unarmed, but both Doyle and Kelly had AOH badges on their coats and when they were identified as having been in Lansford the previous day, they were assumed to be guilty of the murder. The case against them seemed quickly proven when three pistols were found secreted in leaves beneath the trees surrounding the spring. An ugly crowd formed, hoping "to get hold of the prisoners to hang them without trial . . . they would have been strung up like dogs."[26] To prevent a lynching, the three were taken across the county line to the Carbon County jail in Mauch Chunk. It would not be the last time a mob threatened to dispense its own justice.

The Jones murder and the arrests of Kerrigan, Doyle, and Kelly were the turning point in the saga of the Molly Maguires. Likewise, the nine hours prior to Jones's murder proved a key period in the development of the image of James McParlan. His failure to warn Jones of imminent danger was harped upon by the defense throughout the trials of the Molly Maguires, as were his failures to provide warnings for Thomas or Sanger. Although such arguments had little impact on the juries, they have been a primary criticism of McParlan more recently, as in Kevin Kenny's assessment: "The weight of the evidence in the Sanger, Uren, and Jones cases is that McParlan let these killings go ahead in order to accumulate evidence."[27]

In actuality, the totality of the evidence suggests otherwise. This is particularly true if McParlan's rarely consulted reports for the days prior to the Jones killing are taken into account.[28] When considering what McParlan actually knew, his instructions, and his concerns for his own safety, his decisions are not as callous as they have been made to seem.

McParlan was, after all, working in a vacuum—he did not know what steps his superiors or other agencies were taking and so could not adjust accordingly. It is clear, for example, that in July McParlan passed to both Linden and Franklin indications of a plot against an "inside boss." His next step—accomplished in early August—was confirming that the target was Jones. However, the steps of actually protecting Jones had nothing to do with

McParlan but were determined by Zehner, Charles Parrish of the Lehigh and Wilkes-Barre Coal Company, and Captain T. C. Williams of the Coal and Iron Police.[29] As far as McParlan was aware—based on information from both Linden and Franklin—Jones was being protected.

Moreover, McParlan had been successful numerous times in postponing violence, including having done so only that day, when he sent Munley and Darcy home. Therefore, he undoubtedly felt confident that he could do so again. His first task in this regard was to telegraph Linden, but, not knowing where he was, "I could not dispatch to him, and on leaving Carrolls I found I could not dispatch either to Mr Franklin. The telegraph offices were closed."[30] So he planned to send the message first thing in the morning, only to find out that Jones had already been killed.

Despite his assumptions that Jones would be protected, and that his own messages could be sent the following day, McParlan has been called to task for not attempting to warn the victim. However, he not only had no obligation to do so—he was a private detective, not a policeman—he was also unaware of Kerrigan's plans and therefore was liable to stumble into a dangerous position. Moreover, there is no indication that McParlan could have recognized Jones, nor that he knew where his house was. Asking for such information would likely not only have blown his cover, but would have been highly dangerous. This was also true of passing information to local authorities—who could not be totally trusted, as demonstrated by Shenandoah policeman Ned Monaghan, an AOH member who was eventually found guilty as an accomplice in the attempted murder of Thomas.[31] McParlan acknowledged this concern when he testified that "I do not wish to cast aspersion upon the civil officers who are good officers, but as a rule, as to detectives, we manage our own business until it comes to a focus."[32]

Such an action would also have violated every agreement that McParlan had made with Pinkerton's and their employers and might have destroyed the broader goals of the investigation. "He was expressly forbidden to communicate with anybody," Franklin later testified. "He would have been dismissed at once, and his life would have been jeopardized. He was in jeopardy whenever he spoke to Capt Linden in the coal regions. He was in jeopardy all the time."[33]

That last reason, understandably, is what most dictated McParlan's decisions. He believed that trying to walk five to six miles to Lansford late at night, in the dark, to warn Jones would likely have "given his game away" and cost him his life. As he stated in later testimony:

Q: Why did you not go over, yourself, from the Columbia House, five miles, to save the life of a man you knew was going to be assassinated?

A: My reason was that I was afraid of being assassinated myself.

Q: You would not take that risk to save the life of John P. Jones?

A: I would not run the risk of losing my life for all the men in this Court House.

Q: You were playing the part of a detective and yet you would not take that much trouble to walk five miles?

A: I would walk twenty, but it was saving my own life I was looking to. . . .

Q: You would rather see this man Jones sacrificed?

A: Than sacrifice myself? Decidedly.[34]

McParlan's statement may sound unfeeling, and it is easy for a defense attorney in court or for someone sitting safely at home to criticize him, yet were it to come to the push, many people would be unwilling to sacrifice their lives for someone they have never met. In fact, rather than showing McParlan to be a demon, these sentiments show him to be very human, for ultimately self-preservation is one of the strongest instincts. It might be overcome by love, honor, ethics, or impetuosity, but the natural human drive is to survive. And McParlan did.

Unfortunately for McParlan, however, there were those who did not want his survival, because he had played his role so well that they thought him deep in the midst of planning the outrages. Even John Reese, the mine superintendent whose life he had attempted to save, told Linden that "an Irishman named McKenna was supposed to have originated, planned, and assisted in . . . the death of John P. Jones," and that if he showed up in Tamaqua, the residents would turn out by the hundreds to hang him.[35]

For much of the public that attitude extended well beyond McParlan—to all those involved in the killings. The night after the Jones murder *The Tamaqua Courier* asked: "Who can blame the friends of the victims if they demanded an eye for an eye, a tooth for a tooth and blood for blood? Something *must* be done; that something must be *sure*, swift, and terrible."[36] Journalists throughout the district agreed, as the rash of murders set off a clamor for rough justice.[37] Almost overnight, a specter of vigilante action spread through the lower anthracite region.

Vigilance committees had already gained national notoriety, starting with a group in San Francisco—first formed in 1851 and reconstituted five years later—that hanged eight people in an effort to control crime and corruption.[38] In the next decade, the Jackson County Vigilance Committee, also called the Scarlet Mask Society, was responsible for the violent end of about a dozen members of the Reno gang, which had plagued southern Indiana for years. In four separate incidents in 1867 and 1868, masked vigilantes overpowered law officers transporting or holding gang members—some captured by Pinkerton's operatives—and hanged the criminals on the spot (one location where men were hanged from a huge beech tree is known to this day as Hangman's Crossing). In the final episode, vigilantes broke into the jail in New Albany, Indiana, where three of the Reno brothers and one of their compatriots were being held, overcame the sheriff and deputy, and hanged the four men inside the jail.[39]

Thomas Foster, the editor of the *Daily Herald* of Shenandoah—who wrote that the first time a Molly Maguire was "strung up" would "strike terror into the hearts of his cowardly associates"[40]—was not the only one who recommended such tactics. Even before the murders of Sanger, Uren, and Jones, Allan Pinkerton had advocated vigilantism to give the Molly Maguires "their just deserts." This was nothing new, because there is evidence that Pinkerton's not only cooperated with the men who lynched the Renos, but were involved in vigilante tactics to terminate the James-Younger gang.[41] Despite bad publicity from the latter affair, Pinkerton still believed in such tactics, and in a letter to George Bangs, he directed:

If Linden can get up vigilence committee that can be relied upon, do so. When M.M.'s meet, then surround and deal summarily with them. Get off quietly. All should be securely masked.... The M.M.'s are a species of Thugs.... They are bound to stick by their oath, and to carry out their revenge. He, who they think does a wrong, is marked out, and he must die. It is impossible to believe that a jury in the mining districts would not give a verdict of guilty against the M.M.'s should they be brought to trial but I believe that some one on the jury would hang on, and get the guilty men to escape. The only way then to pursue that I can see is, to treat them in the same manner as the Reno's were treated.[42]

This was all very well for Pinkerton, but the idea had to give McParlan pause, because he might well have found a rope around his neck. In the aftermath of the Jones murder, Linden informed him that people on the street "began to say to each other, 'What a shame that such a fellow (this means you, McParlan) is allowed to live! He ought to be strung up!' You need to keep a sharp lookout, wherever you are."[43]

Yet, whereas one might expect such widespread opinion to have encouraged McParlan to make his final reports and leave the anthracite region for safety, it encouraged him instead to hold fast with his investigation. "He knew that, if the excited people of the vicinity could only be aware of his true purposes, they would willingly carry him in their arms, or draw him in a carriage, shielding him from harm with their own bodies," wrote Pinkerton, "and this inward consciousness of rectitude . . . kept his head above water and steadied his nerves while he continued his professional work. He knew that, if he lived yet a little longer, the residents of Schuylkill, Carbon, Columbia, and Luzerne Counties would praise him and bless him."[44]

Such psychological support was a major factor in McParlan's determination to continue an operation that was so stressful, dangerous, and scary that even the hard-drinking, obstinate, and supremely arrogant brawler that he was became worn down and suffered extreme stress reactions. The most obvious of these was that throughout the summer—as he was drawn deeper and deeper into plots, decisions, and last-minute adjustments, and found himself worrying more and more about making a mistake that would expose his role—his hair had been coming out in clumps. This condition has since been named alopecia totalis, and is marked by a loss of all head hair, including, in McParlan's case, his eyelashes and eyebrows. Although currently considered an autoimmune disorder, it can be set off by extreme stress, such as that from which McParlan suffered.[45]

The response from others to McParlan's condition was variable. Linden, seeing it with a little levity, stated: "I called him a 'Billiard Ball' . . . [b]ecause there was no hair on his head and he has a very large head for a small man, and I remarked in a saloon in Shenandoah, that somebody would take it and use it for a billiard ball."[46] Franklin, on the other hand, not knowing what other impacts such stress can have, was concerned that the condition would leave the detective "too conspicuous" in an environment in which he was becoming increasingly at-risk from vigilante operations. Therefore, the week after the Jones murder, he met McParlan at the Exchange Hotel in Pottsville, following which he sent him to see a doctor. The physician, not surprisingly, had no cure.

From Pottsville, McParlan traveled to Philadelphia, and after four days of intensive meetings he went to New York, where he prepared a list of 348 AOH members in Schuylkill, Luzerne, Carbon, Columbia, and Northumberland counties, organized by the town or patch in which they lived.[47] This printed document was widely distributed to newspapers by Pinkerton's, but not long thereafter an even more powerful one-page handbill was released. Headed "Strictly Confidential" and offered "for the consideration of the Vigilance Committee of the Anthracite Coal Region, and all other good citizens who desire to preserve law and order," it detailed six murders attributed to the Molly Maguires since the end of the Long Strike as well as the attempted murder of Thomas, in each case naming the assailants and giving their addresses.[48] The document was, in essence, an invitation for vigilantes to act.

McParlan feared that vigilante action might be directed toward himself, and he did not stay in Schuylkill County long upon his return from New York. After meeting Linden, he took the train to Wilkes-Barre in Luzerne County, supposedly to raise money for the defense of Kelly, Doyle, and Kerrigan—for which he contributed two dollars himself, claiming it back as expenses. Pinkerton indicated, however, that his ace detective had gone to Wilkes-Barre to receive treatment from "an eminent physician."[49] McParlan's health had declined radically, this time with symptoms such as dyspepsia, tension headaches, sleep disorders, gastrointestinal problems, fatigue, and, apparently, a decreased ability of his immune system to respond—all of which can be related to chronic stress.[50] As a result, in early October McParlan was ordered to avoid taxing himself unnecessarily, only a small step in the right direction, as "his attending physician seriously objects to his going out at all."[51]

While McParlan convalesced, Linden remained actively engaged in investigating the murders. However, his inquiries were not made easier when one of his special policemen killed a man who shot at him rather than submit to questioning. The officer was held for trial, and although he was eventually absolved of any wrongdoing, the incident forced Linden to disclose that he and his men were Pinkerton's operatives.[52]

Linden also held a series of meetings, which included Foster and reporter Tom Fielders of the *Daily Herald*, that are, in light of subsequent events, quite suspicious. Linden thereafter reported that he "has visited different places in the coal regions with the view of giving necessary information to some of the leading citizens, advising them as to who the parties are who have committed the recent assassinations . . . in order to place them fully on their guard against these outlaws, but as yet there seems to be so much apathy . . . that no definite steps have been taken to make examples of the well known assassins."[53] The result of Linden's efforts were, arguably, made clear by a letter to the editor from John Kehoe, complaining that Foster and the *Daily Herald* were inventing the coffin notices that appeared in the paper and otherwise inciting violence and instigating vigilantism.[54]

It was more than newspaper attacks that made Schuylkill County so dangerous, however, as personal assaults continued unabated. Few nights were worse than October 9, when, in Shenandoah alone, Irishman Richard Finnen was shot above the right eye, fifteen bullets were fired into Muff Lawler's saloon, and Welshman James Johns was shot in the back, had his throat cut from ear to ear, and was set alight.[55]

In the midst of such unrelenting violence, McParlan traveled to Mauch Chunk for the beginning of the Jones murder trial, having already submitted reports about a series of defense witnesses scheduled to testify that they had seen Kelly and Doyle elsewhere at the time of the murder.[56] Once at court, the defense scored what seemed a victory, as, although a change of venue was denied, a delay was granted until January 1876, allowing more time for the potential intimidation of prosecution witnesses and the creation of additional alibis.

Upon his return to Shenandoah, McParlan discovered that Hurley had been arrested for his role in the attacks on Bully Bill Thomas and James Johns.[57] Although still unwell, and ordered by his doctor to stay indoors,[58] one night McParlan dragged himself to Carroll's saloon, where "the subject of a traitor among them came up. They all seem to suspicion Lawler, and all wished 'to God' that the operative had his health, as they were sure if he could work at it he could find who the traitor was, as he was sharper than most of them."[59]

Unease over the potential traitor persisted throughout the following weeks, making McParlan increasingly uncomfortable. Meanwhile, Hurley was released on bail and promptly vanished. McParlan saw him in Wilkes-Barre and gave him his bull terrier, trained for the pit, which it was rumored Hurley sold for ten dollars to help him disappear for good.[60] Not long thereafter, while at a footrace, Kehoe, who had paid attorney Martin L'Velle forty dollars to represent Hurley, told McParlan with intense annoyance that Hurley had now "jumped his bail, and he would hunt him up if he had to go to California."[61]

With such anger, suspicion, and lack of trust spreading through the AOH lodges, it appeared that tensions were close to boiling over. And on a frigid December night, they exploded.

Early on the morning of December 10, most inhabitants of the tiny hamlet of Wiggans Patch were asleep, including those in the house belonging to widow Margaret O'Donnell.[62] It was a large house, divided into a duplex by a partition wall. On one side lived the Cassidy family, on the other side that night were ten people, including, in a ground-floor room, Mrs. O'Donnell's pregnant daughter, Ellen; Ellen's husband, Charles McAllister; and their fifteen-month-old child. Upstairs were widow O'Donnell, her sons Charles and James "Friday" O'Donnell, and four lodgers: James Blair, Tom Murphy, John Purcell, and James McAllister, brother of Charles.

At three o'clock, Charles McAllister "was awakened up & heard a rush for the house, there were shots fired." Immediately thereafter, the kitchen door was broken in and a group of men in long oilskin coats and masks stormed into the house. McAllister leaped out of bed, told his wife not to move, and raced down the stairs from the bedroom to the cellar. Panicked, Ellen opened the door to the back room, where one of the vigilantes saw her white-clad outline and shot her in the chest. McAllister heard her cry that she had been hit but continued into the cellar, where he pulled two boards off the dividing wall and went into the Cassidys' side to hide.

Meanwhile, in an organized fashion, teams of men rushed to the two upstairs bedrooms. In the back room, illuminated by only the light of the moon, Margaret O'Donnell was struck with "the butt end of a pistol." Her son Friday, who shared the room, was dragged downstairs.

Six or seven masked men burst into the large, front upstairs room. Two of the invaders forced Charles O'Donnell out of bed and tied John Purcell, who was sharing it, hand and foot to the bedpost. When Thomas Murphy asked their intentions, a man said, "[P]ut your hands above the clothes or else I will blow a hole through you." But another invader with a lantern "told the man not to meddle with me, I was an old man." Meanwhile, James Blair was taken downstairs with a rope around his neck, only to be released after revealing his name. James McAllister was also dragged downstairs but managed to struggle free and ran toward the nearby woods. Although a hail of shots followed him, and he was struck in the shoulder, he disappeared into the night.

Friday O'Donnell also escaped without injury, but the same could not be said for his brother. Taken outside, Charles, too, broke loose, but this time the fusillade of bullets did not miss, and he fell, wounded. Men came up to his prostrate body and riddled him with lead. As the killers melted away a neighbor ran over to find O'Donnell "lying with his face down and his clothes burning." According to a reporter, "The head, which had received no less than fifteen bullets and was in a shockingly crushed condition, was tied up in a white cloth. From the hips to the chin the body was crisped, there being no less than the marks of ten balls to be seen, and the firearms must have been held in such close proximity that the powder had actually roasted the flesh."[63]

Shortly after sunrise, a note as rough in its writing as in its message was discovered: "You are the murderers of Uren and Sanger."[64] Within hours the coroner arrived from Mahanoy City, impaneled a jury, and, with Foster recording the statements, heard testimony in the O'Donnell house. Margaret O'Donnell was about to respond to the coroner's question about whether she recognized anyone when John Kehoe—another son-in-law—arrived and ordered her not to answer, reportedly telling the coroner: "[T]his business is going to be settled in another manner."[65]

Later that day, after talking to Mrs. O'Donnell, Kehoe brought charges against Frank Wenrich, a butcher and former burgess of Mahanoy City, for assaulting his mother-in-law, who now swore she recognized him. The butcher was taken to Pottsville, where, at a habeas corpus hearing three days later, she identified him. However, when District Attorney George Kaercher asked her if Kehoe had told her to say she recognized him, she answered, "Yes." With such murky testimony, the judge released Wenrich on bail, and, upon returning to Mahanoy City, he was met by three hundred people celebrating his freedom.[66]

Although Kehoe's efforts apparently had been thwarted, he was, according to McParlan, just biding his time. The detective reported that on the day of the habeas corpus hearing Kehoe said "he had not a doubt that Winrich was one of the men, but he did not want him prosecuted, as he knew very well it would not be a fair trial, and he would rather let the affair blow over a little . . . He also said that Winrichs little girl told the day after the murders, that her papa had his face blacked the night before."[67]

That McParlan would even be filing reports had been a major concern for his superiors. The day before the events at Wiggans Patch he had visited Danny Hughes's saloon in Pottsville. He awoke there the next morning to learn of the murders, and in what was obviously an overly emotional state driven in part by the stress of his own situation, he blasted off an indignant and, at points, inaccurate letter:

This morning at 8 AM I heard that a crowd of masked men had entered Mrs ODonnells house Wiggans Patch and had killed James ODonnell Alias Friday, Cha⁵ ODonnell & James MacAllister, also Mrs MacAllister whom they took out of the house and shot (Cha⁵ MacAllisters Wife). Now as for the ODonnells I am satisfied they got their just deservings. I reported what those men were. I give all information about them so clear that the courts could have taken hold of their case at anytime but the witnesses were too cowardly to do it. I have also in the interests of God and humanity notified you months before some of those outrages were committed. Still the authorities took no hold of the matter. Now I wake up this morning to find that I am the murderer of Mrs MacAllister. what had a woman to do in the case. did the Sleepers in their worst time shoot down women. If I was not here the Vigilant Committee would not know who was guilty and when I find them shooting women in their thirst for blood, I hereby tender my resignation to take effect as soon as this message is received. If there is any other job in the Agency that you may want me for I will accept it. If not I will go home to Chicago as I am sure I am sold anyhow by some of those men on the Committee, and it is through them the Hon James B Reilly has got his information that there is something wrong. Now no doubt but there will be man for man taken, and I do not see which side will have the Sympathizers. as for myself I will remain here until you despatch for me to go down, which I hope will be soon as this letter is received. It is not cowardice that makes me resign, but just let them have it now. I will no longer interfere as I see that one is the same as the other and I am not going to be an accessory to the murder of women and children. Direct your dispatch to the Northwestern Hotel as it is not worthwhile to leave for a boarding house at present when I am going away anyhow. At 10°° AM I got your letter and contents noted but as you see this alters the state of affairs in genl, hence there is no further use of comments. of course you may expect burning and murdering all over. Where we might have had a little quietness and now innocent men of both parties will suffer, and I am sure the Sleepers will not spare the women so long as the vigilants has shown the example.⁶⁸

This letter gives intriguing—but contentious—insights into McParlan. James Horan, who in 1949 became the first researcher to discover it, indicated that it once and for all disposed of the charges that McParlan was an agent provocateur,[69] because of his obvious horror at the killing of Ellen McAllister, his disgust at the justice system for not having pursued men he felt he had proved a case against, and his abhorrence at the forces of law and order acting like criminals. Some later writers, however, have disagreed, noting not only that McParlan seemed to feel no sympathy for the men he thought had been killed, but that he did not actively disavow any knowledge of impending vigilantism.[70] Neither of these viewpoints seems fully acceptable. Although McParlan clearly found the events at Wiggans Patch reprehensible, it does not indicate whether he did or did not engage in other unscrupulous behaviors himself. Moreover, writing at an impassioned moment that someone "got their just deservings" does not indicate that one justifies the manner in which vengeance is actually effected. Finally, it would be patently unnecessary for McParlan to disavow any previous knowledge, as the letter was written for a superior who regularly received his reports.

What *is* certain is that key figures at Pinkerton's quickly soothed and assured their operative in order to keep him in the field. When Franklin forwarded McParlan's letter to Pinkerton in Chicago, he stated: "This morning I received a report from 'Mac' of which I send you a copy, and in which he seems to be very much surprised at the shooting of these men; and he offers his resignation. I telegraphed 'Mac' to come here from Pottsville, as I am anxious to satisfy him that we have nothing to do with what has taken place in regard to these men. Of course I do not want 'Mac' to resign."[71]

McParlan did not meet with his chief immediately. But the day after he wrote his impassioned letter, Linden, who had been in Chicago and Philadelphia, returned to the anthracite region, and he would have quickly contacted his agent. McParlan spent the next week gathering information from individuals who now seemed shaken not only by the arrest of Doyle, Kelly, and Kerrigan, and the release of the details about the organization, but by the brutal actions at Wiggans Patch. "The Mollies are now confident that there is a traitor in their midst," McParlan wrote the day after the killings. Then, following Wenrich's bail, he noted that "the Molly Maguires feel 'a terrible itching' for vengeance, and think they will be sure to retaliate, but there is no telling at present when or where they will act."[72] As McParlan discovered, the reason for this hesitancy was simply a lack of definitive information about who the killers actually were. Dennis Canning, the county delegate for

Northumberland County, told him that "they must all keep quiet and they would soon find out who were the perpetrators of the outrage and then they would have a chance to see what they had better do."[73] In fact, they would *not* soon find out who the perpetrators were, and to this day it remains a question without a definitive answer.[74]

After cooling down for a week following his resignation letter, McParlan traveled to Philadelphia "for consultation." There Franklin, and perhaps even Bangs, Pinkerton, or Gowen, used any and all available arguments and promises to convince McParlan to continue his undercover role. One powerful tool had been given them just that week, when Archbishop James Frederic Wood of Philadelphia formally excommunicated the Molly Maguires. He also reissued his pastoral letter of January 1864, again condemning all secret societies, but this time adding a short but significant phrase. After "Molly Maguires," it now stated "otherwise the Ancient Order of Hibernians."[75] McParlan was extremely devout, and he had most likely initially taken on the assignment in part because it was an opportunity to fight a crusade of sorts for the Catholic Church, so another direct call to assist the Church against an outcast group would have been difficult to ignore. Additionally, he knew that he was nearly at the end of his labors, that he might well have a bright future with the company, that Pinkerton's was not responsible for the vigilante actions, and that the death of Ellen McAllister was (in today's parlance) simply regrettable collateral damage. McParlan also undoubtedly saw a chance to make a name for himself as a hero of American justice. Therefore, despite his moral and emotional qualms, he eventually agreed to proceed with his investigations.

While McParlan was still in Philadelphia, Franklin decided to address the issue of his operative being too conspicuous to vigilantes. "His hair was nearly all out—merely straggling hairs all over—bare clean down the back of his neck," Franklin later testified. The superintendent had "thought probably his hair would grow in again, but it did not, and I . . . bought a wig for him, at Dollard's Chestnut Street."[76] So on December 23, with only a chin beard of his own hair[77] but sporting a large reddish-blond wig, he once again entered the anthracite region.

CHAPTER 8

TRIALS AND TRIBULATIONS

James McParlan was not the only Catholic heavily influenced by Archbishop Wood's condemnation of secret societies. In the week before Christmas, Daniel O'Connor, the priest at Mahanoy Plane, warned his parishioners that: "Bad men are a terror anywhere, but particularly so in the coal region. Beware of the Mollie Maguires. If you have a brother among them pray for his repentance, but have nothing further to do with him, and remember that he is cut off from the Church . . . Let them fight their own battles, for you have a conscience, and they have none. They are scum and a disgrace to us as Irishmen and American citizens."[1]

Within a short period, others used a more violent approach with the Molly Maguires. Hugh McGehan, identified in the Strictly Confidential handbill as the murderer of Benjamin Yost, was shot at twice by vigilantes, once in late December and then again while walking home early in January 1876. Although he was not wounded, in an escape reminiscent of Daniel Dougherty's, he could point to bullet holes in his clothes.[2]

But ultimately, the most vigorous, orchestrated, and unrelenting response to the Molly Maguires' killing spree was initiated by Charles Parrish, the president of the Lehigh and Wilkes-Barre Coal Company, who had "determined to spare neither effort nor money to bring the murderers of John P. Jones to punishment, and to demonstrate . . . that the power and majesty of the law were supreme."[3] He was joined in his purpose by both Gowen and Asa Packer, the head of the Lehigh Valley Railroad and one of the richest men in America.[4]

Each of the three rail and coal companies assigned their leading lawyers to work with Carbon County district attorney Edward R. Siewers in the prosecution of Michael J. Doyle, Edward Kelly, and Jimmy Kerrigan for Jones's murder. Charles Albright—who had reached the rank of brevet brigadier general during the Civil War, had served as a member of the U.S. House of Representatives, and was the head of the most successful Mauch Chunk law firm, which provided legal counsel for the Lehigh and Wilkes-Barre Coal Company—was the lead lawyer for the early cases. He was joined by the Reading's Francis W. Hughes, an elder statesman of the Pennsylvania legal profession and previously a state senator, Pennsylvania's attorney general, and Schuylkill County district attorney. And from the Lehigh Valley Railroad came Allen Craig, a three-time state representative, former district attorney for Carbon County, and the railroad's chief counsel, as well as Packer's personal attorney.[5]

The defense lined up an imposing team as well, with Daniel Kalbfus and Edward Mulhearn of Mauch Chunk—the latter the only Irish Catholic member of the Carbon County bar—joined by three former Pottsville prosecutors: John W. Ryon, U.S. congressman J. B. Reilly, and Lin Bartholomew, who had successfully defended Gomer James from the charge of murdering Edward Cosgrove.

On January 16, 1876, a motion for change of venue was denied, surprisingly, with the "undue excitement" of the case and the inflammatory articles in the local newspapers. Shortly thereafter the three prisoners were granted separate trials (see Appendix B for details of each of the Molly Maguire trials; the appendix can be found at www.penguin.com/PinkertonsGreatDetective or www.susannagregory.com/beauriffenburgh/pinkertons-great-detective). Two days later, with the Mauch Chunk courthouse guarded by a large force of Coal and Iron Police, jury selection for Doyle's trial began. Officially, the choice of Doyle as the initial defendant was because he was "supposed to be the one who fired the fatal shot," but it was probably also influenced by Kelly's appearance as a fresh-faced lad, whereas Doyle "wears the countenance of a determined, villainous desperado," with a "dogged and defiant expression, and looks more like a prize-fighter or Fourth Ward rough than anything else."[6]

With fifty-two-year-old President Judge Samuel S. Dreher presiding, three days were occupied with choosing the jury. The selection process has since been condemned from a constitutional standpoint for deliberately excluding Irishmen.[7] It has been claimed that this set a precedent for subsequent Molly Maguire trials—as did a similar exclusion of Catholics—while supposedly stacking the jury with "Pennsylvania Dutch," whose native tongue was German and therefore had little understanding of English.[8] However, an examination of the different trials' voir dire—the preliminary examination of prospective jurors under oath to establish their competence and suitability—shows that, although the lack of Irish was notable, there *were* Catholics of German descent on a number of the juries. Further, the claims about the number of jurors struggling with the language in the first two trials in Carbon

County seem to have been overstated[9]—and it appears to have been the *defense* that was hopeful that any language issues would be helpful to their cause, rather than the prosecution.[10]

Once the testimony started, language became the least of the defense's concerns, as the prosecution's parade of 122 witnesses left little doubt about Doyle's involvement.[11] In the moments before the killing, Doyle was seen walking toward the site where Jones was shot, and although no one actually saw him pull the trigger, he was seen running away with a pistol in his hand. Witness after witness contributed to the overwhelming circumstantial evidence indicating that Doyle had been the shooter, while Albright—dressed daily in his full general's uniform to emphasize his allegiance to law, honor, and the United States—elicited such strong testimony that the cross-examinations (usually carried out by Bartholomew) failed to dent the prosecution's case. Whenever there was a tricky legal point, Hughes conducted the argument on behalf of the Commonwealth, usually in opposition to Ryon.

The prosecution's case was missing only a motive. McParlan had laid out the background of the trade for the murders of Jones and Yost to his employers, but he was still under cover, so his testimony could not be introduced. However, such a conspiracy was hinted at because Doyle, when arrested, had been carrying an AOH button and part of a letter from Jerry Kane, the Mount Laffee bodymaster, to Carroll, giving mysterious instructions for Doyle. And when Alexander Campbell was accused of harboring Doyle, Kelly, and Kerrigan before the murder of Jones, the implication that the AOH was at the heart of the murder gained even more credence.

Unintentionally emphasizing the prosecution's conspiracy theory, members of the AOH sat prominently in the courthouse throughout the trial. Among them was McParlan, who, it has been suggested, used his contacts to improperly pass on information about the defense tactics to the prosecution.[12] Although McParlan had certainly filed reports about potential alibis the previous October when the case first was scheduled for court, and he continued to pass on any information that he could,[13] it is highly unlikely that reputable attorneys like those for the defense would have trusted an unsavory, heavy-drinking thug like "McKenna"—who was not even their client—with their delicate trial preparations.

As it turned out, any defense preparations that *had* been made came to nothing. On January 31, two weeks after the beginning of the trial and with the courthouse still stuffed to the brim with reporters and fascinated members of the public, the Commonwealth rested its case. To the shock of those in the courtroom, the defense, which had been rumored to have almost one hundred witnesses, announced that it would rest without calling any of them. The tale immediately spread that the prosecution's case had been so thorough that all the false alibis would only bring perjury charges.[14] Regardless, Judge Dreher quickly ordered the final summations to proceed. Craig initiated the process, speaking for two and a half hours and trying to terrify the jury into a conviction by warning: "If this man goes free you will be compelled to turn your houses into castles, and go about your business girded about with pistols and knives to protect your lives. Lawlessness will reign supreme, and peace and good order give way to riot and blood shed."[15] He was followed by Hughes for the prosecution, then Bartholomew and Kalbfus for the defense—both of whom pleaded for the jurors to believe that Doyle had only been in Lansford to seek work, and to remember that the AOH was a noble organization "having for its object nothing that is bad except in the diseased eyes of the learned counsel for the Commonwealth."[16] Albright then closed the summations with a masterful call for justice.

When the judge turned the case over to the jury, he instructed them that "it is very difficult sometimes to find out the motive that impels a man to commit a crime. But, though no motive may have been proven, if the guilt of this prisoner has been proven beyond a reasonable doubt, then you will convict him."[17] And convict him they did, returning a guilty verdict at nine o'clock the next morning.

Ever since the trial had begun, the newspapers had given sensational warnings that "a band of their comrades three or four thousand strong may, on any day, march into town, attack the Court House, release the criminals, and shoot down all opponents."[18] Now, at the very moment the verdict was announced, a fierce commotion broke out and the startled audience whipped around in fear, expecting to be set upon by Molly Maguires. Instead, it was three snarling dogs fighting at the rear of the courtroom.[19]

Doyle's murder conviction—the first for a man branded a Molly Maguire—was a major triumph for the railroad and mining companies, and it encouraged Gowen to become personally involved. Even more important was that during the trial, Kerrigan—with "his shrewd, cunning eyes, his small stature and the uneasy, fidgety motion of his body"[20]—suddenly turned state's evidence.

Kerrigan was a murderer, a drunkard, a braggart, a man of low morals, and a venomous enemy, but he was not a fool, and the parade of prosecution witnesses made him realize the game was up. His actions generally were self-serving and full of bravado, but were often carefully considered, as shown by how he earned his nickname, Powderkeg—one cold day, while working as a miner, Kerrigan approached a group of his colleagues sitting around an open fire and asked them to make room for him. When no one did, he seized a nearby keg of powder and placed it in the center of the fire, causing the men to flee for safety. Kerrigan then removed the keg from the fire and sat in the choice seat to warm himself.[21]

Kerrigan's decision to turn state's evidence was also prompted by finding that lawyers had been hired for Doyle and Kelly, but "not a finger was ever moved in behalf of Jimmy Kerrigan. He was left alone. This fact he discovered and without doubt determined to punish the desertion of himself."[22] Another incident that helped push Kerrigan into the arms of the prosecution occurred late in Doyle's trial, when Alfred Brenheiser testified that while working at the jail in Mauch Chunk the previous October, he had heard a conversation between Kerrigan and Doyle. "They spoke from one cell to the other; they were just opposite each other. . . . I heard Kerrigan say, 'To-morrow they [the defense lawyers] will take our statements to Mount Laffee to get them to correspond with the witnesses. They are afraid I'll squeal.'"[23]

At that moment, "Kerrigan was unable to contain himself; he jumped up excitedly and exclaimed to the witness: 'I don't want you to get up there and swear a false lie on me; I can't stomach it.' He was pulled down to his seat, but continued: 'I don't want any man to swear my life away like that: and that's a lie, by God!'"[24]

Within the next day or so Kerrigan asked to speak to Captain Samuel Peeler of the Coal and Iron Police, to whom he blurted out a lengthy confession. The astonished officer wasted no time calling in Albright and Hughes, and Kerrigan repeated his story, giving full details of the trade for the Yost and Jones murders, the roles of the men involved, and even his own actions, although he downplayed these considerably, not knowing that the attorneys were already familiar with McParlan's tale. According to Kerrigan, the Yost murder had been instigated by Duffy after he was knocked around by Yost and McCarron. Duffy contacted Roarity, who supplied one of the guns as well as McGehan and Boyle. And Alexander Campbell was not only fully aware of the Yost plans, but arranged the murder of Jones.[25] It is unknown what exactly was promised to Kerrigan, but he became a star witness in at least fourteen trials and was never prosecuted.

With a firsthand witness other than McParlan, the authorities could now take decisive action, and three days after the Doyle verdict was announced, the

Coal and Iron Police, in conjunction with Pinkerton's, simultaneously arrested Carroll in Tamaqua, Duffy at Buckville, Roarity in Coaldale, Campbell and McGehan in Summit Hill, and Boyle in Lansford. The newspapers immediately speculated that there was an informer.[26] But was it Doyle, Kelly, or Kerrigan?

Then, after almost a week of intense conjecture, two more arrests were made: Munley and Charles McAllister, for the murders of Sanger and Uren. Neither Friday O'Donnell nor Michael Doyle was found, and the authorities did not realize that they had the wrong McAllister. These arrests were extremely alarming for any Molly Maguires, because Doyle, Kelly, and Kerrigan knew nothing about Sanger and Uren. It was apparent that there must be another informer.

Hot on the heels of this second set of arrests, the news broke that Kerrigan had turned state's evidence. On February 12, a habeas corpus hearing was held for the five accused murderers of Yost, and Kerrigan took the stand to implicate each, as well as Campbell for the Jones murder.[27] Despite the judge's ruling that nothing stated in the hearing could be divulged, both *The Daily Miners' Journal* and the *Daily Herald* immediately published details, setting in motion a remarkable plot.

This was unveiled when McParlan traveled to Tamaqua to see Mary Ann Higgins, still under the pretense of courting her. He found Mary Ann's sister Fanny, Kerrigan's wife, there as well, and was shocked to discover the entire family engaged in pinning the Yost and Jones murders on Kerrigan, whom they viewed in the worst way possible—as a squealer. McParlan learned that four days before—virtually while Kerrigan was testifying—Mrs. Kerrigan had sworn an affidavit that on July 5 he had loaded his revolver and left home, not returning until morning, when he said "that he had shot officer Yost, and if she ever spoke of it he would blow her brains out."[28]

But the plot did not end with sworn statements. Knowing that the pistol in the authorities' possession was Roarity's but intending to swear it was Kerrigan's, Mary Ann said that she would "get a few cartridges belonging to Roarity's revolver, and bring them to court on the pretense that they were found in Kerrigan's drawer," and would confirm in court that "Kerrigan told her on the 6th that he shot Yost." Moreover, Charles Mulhearn would "swear that Kerrigan bought a revolver of [*sic*] him about two years ago, and the one that shot Yost was the one."

When McParlan asked if they would visit Kerrigan in jail, both women responded venomously that they would "never go to see the little rat," and

Mrs. Kerrigan added that "she never wanted to see him either dead or alive." Already taken aback by the women's vehemence, his own danger was made still more evident when Mary Ann told McParlan that "it was rumored that he (our operative) had turned traitor by a few in Tamaqua, but that no person believed it, all saying that it was Kerrigan." It was his first indication that suspicions about him were growing, and that his time in the anthracite region might be nearing its conclusion.

A week later, McParlan found that the dangers surrounding him were multiplying rapidly. On February 23, the day Michael J. Doyle was sentenced to be hanged, a habeas corpus hearing—this time closed to the press—was held for Munley and McAllister, who were denied bail.[29]

McParlan met McAndrew at the courthouse, and learned "they were making bets . . . that I [McParlan] was a detective, and that I would go on the stand at the habeas corpus hearing."[30] Shortly thereafter, saloonkeeper Danny Hughes added that Kehoe had sent a message to beware of McParlan, because he was a detective. Things moved fast, as McParlan attempted to convince Kehoe that he was not a spy by demanding a trial. But in Pottsville a few days later, Kehoe was told by Ryon, the attorney, that detectives were at work. Whether he mentioned McParlan by name or not, Kehoe became increasingly suspicious.[31]

The final straw for Kehoe was his notification by Father O'Connor that a detective was operating in the coalfields.[32] It was at this stage, according to McParlan, that Kehoe launched his plan to have him murdered. But rather than disappearing when this failed, McParlan instead went to Girardville to confront the "King of the Mollies," who reportedly appeared stunned to see a dead man walking, particularly next to McAndrew, who was to have made sure he was a corpse. A strained conversation followed, in which Kehoe admitted that he had canceled McParlan's scheduled trial. He refused to say more, however, directing him rather to "go to Father O'Connor, and see him about it: you will find it all out."[33]

McParlan indeed headed directly to the priest's home, again accompanied by McAndrew and, as on their cutter ride, shadowed by men with ill intent. The priest was not at home, and when McParlan disappeared briefly to try to find him, three men approached McAndrew, declaring they wanted to kill his friend there and then. But McAndrew refused to countenance the act, and the trio retreated. They did not abandon their murderous plans, however, as that night several men dressed as tramps went to McParlan's boardinghouse and waited hours for his arrival, knocking on the door numerous times in unfulfilled hopes of finding him in.

Once again, McAndrew had come to the rescue. When he and McParlan reached Shenandoah, he said, "You will not go to your boarding house. . . . You will sleep with me."[34] McParlan acquiesced, and therefore stayed safely at McAndrew's home while his own was surrounded by killers.

The next day McParlan again unsuccessfully attempted to see Father O'Connor, following which he met up with Linden. "I told the Captain that I came to the conclusion that they had had a peep at my hand, and that the cards were all played."[35]

Still, he wanted one last chance to redeem the situation before conceding the game was truly over, so he asked Linden to "take means to protect me, and that he would do it in such a way that it would not be noticed around Mahanoy Plane." Linden "fetched four or five men there, and had them to keep a close shadow on me, and keep themselves as unobserved as possible, while I was in Callaghan's [tavern] and to watch me till I went to Father O'Connor's."[36]

Little did McParlan know how seriously Linden took that particular commission. "A plot has been formed to murder my Friend whom you know of," Linden wrote to Schuylkill County district attorney George Kaercher. "My Friend is to go and see the priest who is represented as being the Party who branded him a traitor if the Priest acknowledges himself wrong all may yet be well if on the contrary he proves his story correct the assassins are not only selected but have been kept at Shenandoah since last Wednesday to put him out of the way at once. . . . I will be on hand to either prevent murder or arrest the parties and if I cannot save my Friend I can easily die with him but it will cost the murderers more than one life. . . . I trust that things may turn out well but please dont blame me if someone is hurt in case shooting is begun for if my Friend is killed Jack Kehoe can say his prayers in short metre if I die for it."[37]

As it turned out, McParlan's visit confirmed the depths of Father O'Connor's knowledge, because the priest identified him as a Chicago detective working for Pinkerton's.[38] He also believed McParlan to have participated in the Molly Maguire outrages—thereby making him the worst of both worlds. Most alarming, however, O'Connor stated that other priests knew more than he did. It was time to leave. Realizing that Martin Dooley, a member of the Mahanoy Plane AOH lodge who had been following him, was listening from the next room, McParlan loudly defended the order that he might "get out of there with my life."[39] The plan worked: Dooley was impressed by the detective's stand.

But McParlan knew what he had to do, and still shadowed by Linden's men, he took the train to Pottsville, where he spent the night guarded by Linden himself. Early the next morning the two headed to Philadelphia.[40] McParlan could finally breath easily, knowing that—after two and a half years of constant danger—he would never again need to return to Schuylkill County.

The disappearance of one of the most visible and dangerous Molly Maguires produced widely differing reactions in Schuylkill County. AOH members who had been part of the plan to terminate him were undoubtedly frustrated by his escape, and the members of the public who wished to hang him—at least those who realized he was no longer there—probably had mixed feelings of disappointment that he had evaded them and relief that he was gone. His continuing absence probably convinced some that Kehoe had been right about him being the bad seed, whereas others thought it only meant that he had been the victim of a "clean job." The friend who knew most about all of this—Frank McAndrew—wasn't telling anyone anything, because he fled as well around the time of McParlan's disappearance, to Ireland.[41]

Most of the regular members of the AOH—and certainly the majority of the average folks McParlan knew in Shenandoah and other areas "over the mountain"—would probably not have thought much about him at all, particularly as the weeks passed, as they would not have known about Kehoe's concerns, and would have assumed his low profile meant he was bedridden again, or simply that he would be back, probably with queer cash and more tall tales to tell.

In reality, upon his departure from the anthracite region, McParlan debriefed with Franklin and Linden, then with Pinkerton in Chicago, before returning to Philadelphia several weeks after his hurried departure. It turned out to be a beautiful spring in Philadelphia, with moderate temperatures and pleasant weather,[42] and McParlan was given time to relax and enjoy life with no grueling cases. He was able to attend church regularly, take communion, and go to confession, the latter two for the first time since he had entered the anthracite region, because he had believed it improper to do so while acting as a member of a banned society.[43] He was also able to feel like a respectable man again, with reputable friends. And without the stress of being under cover, his physical condition improved and his hair grew back.

McParlan's respite was to be a brief one, however. Pinkerton received a request from Gowen that he reconsider allowing his operative to testify openly in court.

It wasn't as though the prosecution was struggling. About three weeks after McParlan disappeared, twenty-four-year-old Edward Kelly went on trial in Mauch Chunk. There was an expectation that Kerrigan would testify, and the defense attempted to thwart this by having him tried with Kelly. This ploy was rejected, as was the request for a change of venue based on the Lehigh and Wilkes-Barre Coal Company "spending large sums of money in the preparation of, and pressing the prosecution against him."[44]

In fact, the attorneys for the Commonwealth were so confident that they proceeded entirely without Kerrigan. The strategy worked perfectly, as essentially the same set of witnesses produced the same damning information as in Doyle's trial.[45] The defense was even less challenging, its only clever tactic being to sit Kelly's brother—who closely resembled him—near the defendant. This confused one witness into incorrectly identifying the brother as the killer, but it had no impact on the outcome. On April 6, little more than a week after the trial began, Kelly was found guilty. Shortly thereafter he was sentenced to hang.

With the second conviction, newspapers throughout the northeastern United States suddenly grabbed hold of the more sensational aspects of the trials, denounced the Molly Maguires as "red-handed assassins," and attacked those who had opposed the coal companies—and were therefore assumed to be linked with the outrages. Sadly, one of those thus attacked was John Siney, who had just returned to St. Clair a defeated man after his national union had collapsed due to financial problems and internal dissension. One of Siney's most outspoken critics had long been Robert Ramsey, the editor of *The Daily Miners' Journal*, who at the end of the Long Strike had bitterly and inaccurately written: "If ever a man deserved the penitentiary for the villainy that he has set in motion and produced—the injury he has done the miners and the laborers, and the destruction of business caused by his rascality in deceiving the miners and using them for his own purposes to advance his own interests, and to put money into his own pocket, that man is John Siney!"[46] Now Siney, who more than any other individual had kept the Molly Maguires in check via his WBA policies and tactics, found himself branded "a pettifogger who had never handled a pick in his life" and part of the "herd of ruffians" most closely affiliated with the criminals.[47]

Meanwhile, on the same day that Kelly was pronounced guilty, Kerrigan's "leaked" confession appeared widely in the press. "That is the order of the Molly Maguires and nothing else," he said about the Ancient Order of Hibernians. "The Purpose of the Molly Maguires, or AOH, is to kill people and burn down dwellings. The notion is that it is to protect workingmen, but really they are all of the most hardened villains."[48] Such comments were, needless to say, music to Gowen's ears.

Yet nothing was certain. The next trial was scheduled for Pottsville, and although District Attorney George Kaercher was joined by Albright, Hughes, and local lawyer Guy Farquhar, the challenge of proving the five men guilty of Yost's murder was tricky. They had Kerrigan's confession, but, coming from an accomplice, it might be limited by the judges. Even more difficult would be convicting the murderers of Sanger and Uren, for Kerrigan had known nothing of that arrangement. Thus, it became obvious that the key to both cases was McParlan, who had not only heard the assassins' confessions but could explain the tortuous motive linking Yost and Jones. For Gowen, McParlan's testimony was crucial.

With so much hanging in the balance, Gowen appealed to Pinkerton to allow his operative to testify. The principal declined to force him, however, leaving the decision up to McParlan, who initially refused. On April 27, only a week before the start date of the Yost murder trial, Albright wrote to Kaercher that "it looks very much as if we are not to get the testimony of the detective. It will be too bad if he fails us in this, I judge Mr Linden controls this matter."[49]

Linden did not actually hold such sway over McParlan, but he definitely encouraged the detective to testify, as apparently Pinkerton himself did, after submitting to Gowen's pressure. But it was not until the silver-tongued president of the Reading met directly with McParlan that the operative gave in. Robert A. Pinkerton, Allan's son, wrote many years later that "it was agreed by Mr Gowen, that if Mr Pinkerton would allow McParland to appear as a witness in the Mollie cases, that he (Mr Gowen) would act with the District Attorney in the prosecution."[50] There is no reason to think Gowen's participation would have swayed McParlan, and it is likely that Gowen planned on being involved regardless, but what *is* clear is that he was able to manipulate McParlan just as he could virtually anyone else.

Thus, when Gowen finished his appeal, McParlan reportedly sat thinking silently and deeply for a full five minutes. Then, perhaps somewhat reluctant but determined to make the best possible job of it, he agreed to return to Schuylkill County and testify.[51]

It was never recorded just *how* Gowen managed to convince McParlan, but there were several lines of reasoning that he likely used, in addition to his remarkable charm and persuasive power. First, he would have pointed out the advantages McParlan's participation would have for the advancement of his career with Pinkerton's were the prosecutions successful. Second, and perhaps most important—as when McParlan had accepted the assignment almost three years before—was the positive impact his testimony would have on the Catholic Church. This would have been not only because the Church had openly thrown its power against the Molly Maguires and stood to be embarrassed if its members were able to get away with their crimes, but because it was a chance to testify about his meeting with Father O'Connor, and thereby to dispel the widespread rumors that the priest had informed Kehoe that McParlan was a detective. Although it was true that O'Connor had done so, McParlan would still be able to protect the priest, avoiding further embarrassment to the Church. These were powerful arguments for McParlan.

Gowen's final contention was likely to have been that McParlan's mission had been revealed, and so there was no reason *not* to testify. As his cover was blown, there was no longer an issue either of safety or of a long-term investigation preventing him from taking the stand.[52]

These last two issues were directly related, as Gowen confirmed to Archbishop Wood not long after the trial for the Yost murder began: "It seems to me that the Lord is on our side, for if it had not been for Father O'Connor we could never have had the success we are now meeting with in our efforts to crush out this society." The detective had been promised that he would never need testify, Gowen continued, and "had it not been for Father O'Connor making his mission known we could not have used him as a witness—but when his true character was discovered there was no longer any object in secrecy & by using his testimony we have been enabled to arrest all the leaders of the organization except those who ran away when Kerrigan turned informer & we will undoubtedly be able to break up the whole society."[53]

Whatever Gowen's arguments, McParlan was convinced, and he prepared to take the stand, in public, against the men who had considered him a coconspirator, an ally, and a friend.

CHAPTER 9

❧

McPARLAN ON THE WITNESS STAND

Gowen's anticipated destruction of the Molly Maguires and the Ancient Order of Hibernians began in earnest on May 4, in front of a Pottsville courtroom jammed to capacity four hours before it officially opened.[1] A full panel of three judges presided: President Judge Cyrus L. Pershing, who had been the Democratic candidate for governor in 1875; Thomas H. Walker; and David B. Green. The four prosecution lawyers—joined by Gowen the next day—faced a defense that would, more or less, appear in most of the following trials: Bartholomew, Ryon, Kalbfus, and Martin M. L'Velle, an Irish-Catholic practicing in Pottsville.

For two days, the defendants were allowed to sit with their families while the legal teams fought over impaneling a jury. In the Mauch Chunk trials, the defense had gladly taken Pennsylvania Dutch, hoping any language difficulty would result in an acquittal. But after two guilty verdicts, the defense was now concerned about such men—while the prosecution happily accepted them. William Becker, for example, asked to have the voir dire conducted "in Dutch as I am light on English. . . . I would not understand the witnesses." Nevertheless, he was accepted for the jury, as was Levi Stein, who admitted, "I don't understand much English."[2]

Those looking for sensation were supplied it in full measure during Kaercher's opening statement: "We will produce to you the full and complete confession of James Carroll and Hugh McGehan of their part of this murder, made to James McKenna, a detective, whom they knew by that name, but whose real name was James McParlan." The effect was instantaneous: "Carroll was as if struck by lightning. He could scarcely get back the breath which seemed to be lost to him. Boyle shook like an aspen, and the other prisoners became grave as judges. A thrill of excitement and astonishment went through the audience."[3] They now knew Kehoe had been right about "McKenna" being a spy, and there had been no "clean job" resolving the problem.

Soon there was more thrilling news. Near the end of Kaercher's statement, word raced through the courtroom that a dozen or so Molly Maguires were being led to the jail in chains. It was true—indeed, it had been orchestrated for just this moment. The Coal and Iron Police had made a lightning series of early morning arrests, including Kehoe, Lawler, Northumberland County delegate Dennis Canning, Schuylkill County treasurer Chris Donnelly, and Lost Creek bodymaster Patrick Butler. The entire organization appeared to be going on trial.

That afternoon, after the initial witnesses set out the details of Yost's death, the prosecution called McParlan to the stand. As the side door to the courtroom opened, the audience pushed to the rail for a better view of "the terror of the Mollies." Accompanied by Linden and two bodyguards, who would remain with him for the next year, McParlan entered, dressed "in the height of fashion."[4] He also had a full head of short, chestnut hair, slightly darker than it had been before he lost it. He seated himself in the witness chair and, devoid of the boisterousness and rowdiness that had marked Jim McKenna, quietly, calmly, and without hesitation began a remarkable four days of testimony.

With Gowen's careful guidance, McParlan detailed the original purposes of his investigation, his early days in the anthracite region, and his inquiry into the Yost murder. He repeated the confessions that were made to him, and explained the trade of the murder of Yost for that of Jones in detail. He identified Roarity's pistol, which McGehan had used to shoot Yost, told of how Kerrigan had shown it to him, established that it had reached Doyle and had subsequently been used to kill Jones, and explained that it had been found in the bushes near the spring where the three culprits were arrested. He also described Kerrigan's role in both crimes. By the end of the day his testimony had probably already sealed the defendants' fate.

More details were revealed during McParlan's second day of riveting testimony, as Gowen took full advantage of the opportunity to place not just individuals but the entire AOH on trial. Despite defense objections, Gowen elicited how McParlan became a member of the order; how the elaborate signs, passwords, and toasts—the "goods"—were distributed quarterly; and how a mysterious Irish group known as the Board of Erin controlled the AOH on an international level, a fact known previously to only very few in the courtroom. Much more damning was McParlan's testimony that the primary function of the Schuylkill County AOH was to avenge its members. He described how men went to their bodymaster to demand vengeance, how they were

assigned to carry out such illegal tasks for others, and that the defendants were
all members of—as would regularly be stated thereafter—"the Ancient Order
of Hibernians, more commonly called the Molly Maguires."[5]

McParlan's meticulous presentation was matched only by the dramatics
and rhetoric of Gowen, and by the end of the detective's initial testimony, they
had so confirmed an overwhelming conspiracy by the Molly Maguires that
newspapers throughout the northeastern United States condemned every
member as guilty by association.[6] Such a rush to acknowledge and punish a
conspiracy had not been seen since the previous decade during the investigation and trial by military tribunal of the conspirators in the assassination of
Abraham Lincoln.[7] In the aftermath of those events, many accounts and transcripts of the trials were widely distributed, helping create a public acceptance
of the concept of conspiracies in which every member of an organization was
equally guilty of a crime as those who actually committed it.[8] This preconcep-
tion allowed Gowen's runaway attack on the AOH to be carried along as
much by precedent, the highly charged atmosphere, and a desire for vengeance
as by any underlying logic to his arguments.[9]

Realizing that McParlan was the key to the entire case, the defense attorneys did all in their power to discredit his character, impugn his testimony,
and destroy the fabric of his charges. For two grueling days they searched his
past life for evidence of wrongdoing but could only find that he had changed
jobs numerous times. They claimed his testimony was being given in exchange
for financial profit but could not show that he earned anything above his
weekly salary, which he emphasized was all that he was permitted by Pinkerton's. Bartholomew tried to lessen the detective's credibility by pointing out
that he had lied to the members of the AOH, but the wind was taken out of
the lawyer's sails when McParlan openly agreed:

Q: And these stories you told were untrue; they were all lies.
A: Certainly they were lies; I swear to that.[10]

Bartholomew also tried to catch McParlan out by confusing him about
specifics, such as dates. Initially, McParlan had checked his reports to refresh
his memory. These reports had been brought into the courthouse in a protective metal box and put in a conspicuous place in order to satisfy the jury that
McParlan's testimony was based strictly on the facts recorded at the time.[11]
Now, demanding he respond without looking at his reports, Bartholomew
grilled him about conversations at Carroll's tavern on August 4 and 24 the

previous year. McParlan refused to be confounded, and responded: "[Y]ou keep between the 24th and 4th all the time. It does not shake the evidence a bit. You cannot change dates like that."[12]

Indeed, the defense lawyers, who rode roughshod over some witnesses, discovered they would get as good as they gave from the Pinkerton's operative. "Confine yourself to answering my question," Ryon snapped when McParlan attempted to explain a point. "I *am* answering the question," the detective responded. "If you propound it in a different shape it will be answered in a different shape."[13]

Ryon also challenged McParlan on why he claimed to remember some parts of conversations but not others, but was foiled by the detective's cool, deliberate, and carefully considered responses:

Q: Then do you recollect the conversation, independent of what you have in your reports, or are you detailing to us what you have committed to memory from your reports or anything else?
A: I am detailing to you what I have been committing to memory from that day to this. I have not examined the reports about it.
Q: If you are speaking from memory, why cannot you tell me what you said as well as what Campbell and Kerrigan said?
A: I never cared to tax my memory by carrying what I said as well as what other parties said, because it was more of a burden than I believed I would be able to bear, and I left that go.[14]

The theme the defense really hoped would offset McParlan's testimony was that the detective both instigated crimes and failed to prevent others that he knew about in advance. However, although McParlan acknowledged knowing about the assault on Thomas and the murders of Sanger and Jones, he never deviated in his explanation that he did not take action because he was concerned each time about being killed himself. In addition, prior to the attempted murder of Thomas, "I had not got out of my boarding house for two days. I was sick and not able to go out." Further, that he had been told by Linden that "Jones was aware of his danger and was trying to take care of himself" and also that he was being constantly guarded. Finally, in the case of Sanger, that not only did he have Hurley with him the whole time, but "I was satisfied that the murder had been committed" and that he "[d]id not know the boss' name, as there were several collieries there, I did not know what boss."[15]

Although his report for August 31 showed that McParlan *did* know Sanger's name, that remained unknown during the trial. Meanwhile, the men in the jury—each possibly worried by the specter created in the press of a Molly Maguire uprising—could well understand being frightened for their lives. In consequence, the detective "created an ineffaceable impression." When, after four days, he left the witness box, after having maintained his evidence despite hour upon hour of intense cross-examination, reporters proclaimed, "By his coolness, deliberation, carefulness and positiveness he had proven himself the sharpest and best witness ever on the stand in that Court room."[16]

The prosecution was not finished, however, and Kerrigan soon began two days of testimony. Changing his supposed role from ringleader to pawn, he admitted involvement in the Yost and Jones murders but attributed the motive to Duffy, and he claimed that his participation had been brought about by intimidation from Carroll and Campbell. Although it was obvious that his testimony was selective—and had been adjusted from that at the habeas corpus hearings—he corroborated McParlan and stuck close enough to the perceived truth that the defense was unable to make him contradict himself. He also offset any potential damage from his wife and Mary Ann by addressing in advance the stories they had planned to tell.

Gowen also planned for such fabrications, writing to Archbishop Wood that he expected certain women to provide false alibis that "will inevitably lead to the arrest & punishment of these poor misguided women for perjury"— and therefore asking Wood to instruct the parish priests to go to the trial, as their presence might prevent the women from perjuring themselves.[17]

Gowen's plea did not fall on deaf ears. The month before, the archbishop had forwarded a list of outrages in the anthracite region—which Franklin had sent him in November 1875—to at least three Pennsylvania bishops, in order to gain their support against the Molly Maguires.[18] Now he complied with Gowen's request, and two priests appeared in court, although, Gowen wrote in a follow-up letter: "their presence has not had the effect of restraining three or four witnesses from testifying to an alibi."[19]

These women were not the only ones providing alibis. The primary defense strategy was to produce enough conflicting evidence to make the jury doubt the McParlan and Kerrigan testimony. Inexperienced witnesses were no match for Gowen, however, as shown by his victory over the defense's star storyteller, Mrs. Kerrigan. Although she told the tale that had been developed at the Higgins house, Gowen deftly drew out the admission that she had turned against her husband not after the Yost killing, but only when he turned informer. Slowly he wore her down, and as the overwhelmed woman hesitated longer before each successive answer, Gowen asked why she was pausing. Trying to think on her feet, she replied that it was heart trouble, but Gowen immediately aroused raucous laughter in the courtroom by asking, "Why is it, can you tell me, that you never get the heart disease when Mr Ryon asks you a question?"[20]

Even the opposing lawyers were no match for Gowen: When the defense objected to the way he referred to the AOH, he snatched the opportunity to assert that "enough has been proved in this case, in the Court, in the last ten days, to convict of murder in the first degree every member of that organization in this county, for every murder that has been committed in it." In fact, he continued, "every member of that organization is, not only in the court of conscience, but in the eyes of the law, guilty of every murder as an accessory before the fact and liable to be convicted and hanged by the neck until he is dead."[21]

But suddenly, with Gowen ascendant and the defense reeling, everything stopped. Levi Stein, one of the jurors, fell ill, and the trial was suspended. During the next week, his condition deteriorated, and on May 25, he died of pneumonia. To the consternation of the prosecution, the judges declared a mistrial. Clearly the Commonwealth would retry the men in the next term of court, but to some the advantage seemed to have passed to the defense, which, knowing the prosecution's strategy, might have time to devise new tactics and develop new alibis.

Such would not prove the case, however. Although no verdict had been reached, the detailed testimony of McParlan and Kerrigan and the brilliant rhetoric of Gowen had convinced the press and the public of the guilt both of the defendants and the AOH as a whole. Soon the convictions would follow one after another, because this trial had already laid the foundations for the success of the prosecution—and above those foundations would be constructed a gallows.

For the next month, while the prisoners languished in their hot jail cells, the prosecution prepared for upcoming cases in both Schuylkill and Carbon counties. Linden was "busy under the direction of District Atty Kaercher in looking up corroborative testimony in the Munley case . . . also tracing as far as possible the fugitive murderers now at large."[22] The nine most important of these featured in a list distributed by Pinkerton's: Hurley; Doyle; Friday O'Donnell; James McAllister; William Love; John Flynn, wanted for the murder of Thomas Devine in October 1875; and three men charged with conspiracy to murder: Jerry Kane, Frank Keegan, and William Gavin.[23] Hurley, whom Linden termed "No 1" because he was the highest priority, had kept in touch with McParlan until the detective disappeared. At that time Hurley had also made himself scarce. At the beginning of April he had been reported working in Carbon, Indiana, under the name of John A. Simson. The same month, a man keen on the Pinkerton's reward wrote to Kaercher: "All the birds we want are in that [Luzerne] County. . . . If left to me . . . you will have Hurley for certain and others possibly."[24] However, no one was brought in.

During the opening days of the Yost trial, Linden learned that Hurley was more deeply involved in the Raven Run murders than he'd previously realized. A man named Pat Brennan confirmed that after Doyle had "flunked" by not doing his job as one of the killers of Thomas, "five men had been drawn to kill the men at Raven Run, & that Hurley had one of them withdrawn to substitute Mike Doyle as he (Hurley) had doubts of Doyle's courage & wanted to test him & if Doyle did not stand up to his work he (Hurley) would shoot him himself." Shortly after this discovery, Hurley was seen in Harrisburg en route to Pittsburgh, and Linden telegraphed ahead for his arrest. Once again, however, he proved elusive.[25]

Linden did continue to make progress, finding that McGehan's landlady, who had previously claimed he had been home all night before the murder of Jones, had, pressured by her priest, admitted that he had "left his boarding house at 6 pm and did not return until 6 am. This kills completely McGehan's hope of an Alibi."[26] Several days later, while Linden was taking Kerrigan on the train to Mauch Chunk for Alexander Campbell's upcoming trial, the little bodymaster told him that Campbell, "Yellow Jack" Donahue, and Matt Donahue had killed Morgan Powell in 1871. Campbell "had put Powell out of the way" because he had not placed Campbell in charge of his own breast in a mine.[27] Hughes immediately recommended the arrest of Matt Donahue, but Kaercher and Albright overruled him because "for the present we must not saddle anymore on either Mac or Kerrigan, as a false step now would be fatal."[28]

In early June, Linden pulled McParlan's reports out of a Pottsville bank vault, hoping to confirm various statements. One of these reports led to a visit to Fenton Cooney, but Linden found that the wife of McParlan's erstwhile landlord disputed the operative's account by stating that Doyle did not sleep there the night before the Sanger and Uren murders. Further, she did "not remember Hurly being there talking to Doyle the morning of the day previous to the murder. Doyle and McParlan never slept together and McKenna's testimony to that effect is wrong."[29] Not surprisingly, the prosecution did not call her as a witness.

All the while Linden was doing this groundwork, McParlan was in New Jersey, where he had been sent with "two of our most trusty men, in order to get necessary rest and exercise, as well as to keep him out of all possible harm should any effort be made by his enemies to trace him"—efforts that had already been made, alluded Franklin mysteriously.[30] McParlan was not the only one living dangerously, however. When Linden visited the courthouse in early June, Patrick Collins, the AOH bodymaster at Port Carbon, commented, "Are you alive yet?" Linden queried why he asked, to which Collins replied, "Oh it's a wonder you aren't shot before this."[31]

On June 20, only days before the nation was seized by another startling event—the destruction of the main body of Lieutenant Colonel George Armstrong Custer's Seventh Cavalry at the Little Bighorn by Lakota Sioux and Northern Cheyenne warriors[32]—the original prosecution team again appeared at the Mauch Chunk courthouse, this time with Alexander Campbell in its sights. This was no ordinary member of the AOH, as Doyle and Kelly had been, but the secretary of the Storm Hill lodge and, more than that, a man portrayed as "a leader among leaders and a chief among chieftains."[33] The trial was also hugely significant, in that Campbell admittedly had not been at the shooting of John P. Jones, but was being tried as an accessory before the fact for planning the killing.

Campbell was represented by Kalbfus, Mulhearn, and an impressive orator from Easton, Edward J. Fox, all of whom he had retained himself, as the convictions had rapidly halted contributions to the AOH defense funds.[34] Impaneling a jury with no previous knowledge of the case proved impossible, and numerous prospective jurors admitted they had already formed opinions. One, Fisher Hazard, not only had financial interests in the Lehigh Coal and Navigation Company, but, when asked if he had any conscientious scruples about capital punishment, responded: "Not the least, sir. There ought to be more hangings than there is."[35]

The first key witness called was Kerrigan, and with damning detail the little Irishman tied Campbell to planning the murder and sending out the killers. He was followed by McParlan, who in the next two days repeated much of the background testimony he had given previously. He also recalled a remarkable series of confessions linking Campbell to the murder of Jones. According to McParlan, he met with Campbell on:

July 15, 1875, when Campbell first told him that the murder of Yost was a "clean job," but that "they would not have bothered with it but it was done on a trade."[36]

July 18, in Campbell's saloon, where Campbell introduced him to McGehan.[37]

August 4, when Campbell said that "McGehan was the man that shot officer Yost," that "he calculated for to start McGehan in a saloon for the clean job that he had done at Tamaqua; what he wanted now was a few good men from Schuylkill to go to Lansford and murder John P. Jones," and that he had prevented Kerrigan from doing the killing on July 27.[38]

August 9, in Mauch Chunk, where Campbell was trying to get McGehan a liquor license.[39]

August 13, when McParlan stayed at Campbell's house prior to McGehan's opening, and during the evening Campbell described Jones's house and mentioned the site "to have the men placed to shoot him just as he comes out in the morning and goes to his work."[40]

August 14 and 15, when McGehan and Roarity confessed their roles in the Jones murder.

August 24, when Campbell "asked me to help to get men to shoot John P. Jones."[41]

September 4, in Tamaqua, when Campbell "stated if Kerrigan had been any kind of engineer, he could have had them men at their homes in Mount Laffee before they were arrested. He stated it was the cleanest job that ever was done but the men were twisted by Kerrigan, and that he was going on the following day to Luzerne County to try to raise money from the organization there for the purpose of the defense of those prisoners. . . . He stated that on the night previous to the murder of Jones, that these men stopped in his house."[42]

Campbell also allegedly told McParlan three different times (September 30, October 4, and October 18) about securing witnesses to provide alibis for Doyle, Kelly, and Kerrigan.[43]

This was an amazing parade of confessions, particularly to a man whom neither Campbell nor the others knew particularly well. McParlan stated that "I seemed to have his confidence from the first introduction in June, 1874 ... [because] I was a member of the organization that he belonged to."[44] Nevertheless, so many confessions in such a short time—when added to those of Carroll, Kerrigan, the killers of Sanger and Uren, and others that McParlan claimed in subsequent trials—does raise questions about the likelihood of whether so many people would have chosen this one individual to confide in, or whether some confessions were fabricated.

Campbell's attorneys, however, failed to address this point, if they considered it. Instead they presented a series of witnesses who testified that Doyle and Kelly had not been at Campbell's saloon prior to the murder. They then attempted to show that McParlan was an accessory before the fact—and thus ineligible to testify—and to lessen his credibility by demonstrating that he had made no effort to warn the victims. This last strategy was taken to its extreme by Kalbfus, who said: "[I]f he saved a thousand lives it would not atone for the one he took,"[45] but Franklin and Linden refuted this by pointing out the early warnings that McParlan had given about the threatened assassination.

The defense concentrated its closing arguments on McParlan's credibility. He was a hireling of the Reading, Kalbfus said, whose task was to help in the destruction of the AOH. He had refused to save Jones when he was only a few miles away, because he had planned the crime himself. Fox then launched into an impassioned speech against informers in general and McParlan specifically, while repeating that the detective "encouraged and promulgated the murder of Jones. McParland is the man who made Mrs Jones a widow."[46]

The jury, however, did not accept the defense's premises, and on July 1, after a short debate, it returned a verdict of guilty of murder in the first degree. The defense immediately appealed the case to the Supreme Court of Pennsylvania. Although the appeal claimed four separate errors, the key complaint concerned McParlan's alleged role as an agent provocateur. If this appeal was upheld, his testimony could be eliminated not just in the Campbell case but all upcoming ones as well. "He counsels and encourages them to commit an act of murder, intending, in his own mind, to frustrate their designs," the appeal stated. "Without his encouragement, it is safe to assume that they would not have attempted the murder. His plans to secure their victim's safety fail, and he is murdered. Why is not the detective an accessory before the fact? His mental intentions may have been good enough, but his acts and declarations to the conspirators were the immediate cause which produced the death."[47]

It was for naught. The Supreme Court judges confirmed the verdict, holding that: "A detective who joins a criminal organization for the purpose of exposing it, and who, without any felonious intent and solely for the purpose of discovering, arresting, and punishing the criminals, counsels and encourages members who are about to commit crime is not an accessory before the fact, and his testimony is not to be treated as that of an infamous witness."[48] McParlan's role had been officially validated, but that would not prevent him from being vilified ever since.

Long before the Supreme Court ruling, McParlan had moved on to other cases. In fact, before he even concluded testifying in Campbell's trial, Franklin wrote to Kaercher: "As soon as he is finished I propose to send him to Pottsville in order to have him appear."[49] Therefore, four days before Campbell was found guilty, McParlan was ready when Thomas Munley went on trial for the murder of Thomas Sanger and William Uren.

From the start the Munley case appeared to be the most difficult. Although many men had been in the vicinity when the murders took place, none but mine owner Robert Heaton had seen their faces, which had been obscured by hats and coats. No one had the least idea of a motive, including McParlan— even though he had heard the confessions of the five shooters, he did not know *why* they had done it, and neither he nor the prosecution would have any help from Kerrigan, who knew nothing about it whatsoever. It appeared that the case might come down to whether the jury would convict on McParlan's word alone, without any corroboration.

Fortunately for the Commonwealth, although several of the regular prosecutors were still in Mauch Chunk, the case was led by Kaercher, Gowen, and Hughes. Nevertheless, the early testimony gave the defense hope, as only one of the first fifteen witnesses could identify the culprits: Heaton stated that "I had a full view of them; every time I fired my pistol they turned full around upon me, faced me full in the face."[50] However, under cross-examination, his claim was damaged by the admission that he had been about 550 feet away. He was still certain, he said, that one of them was Munley because, before the shooting, he had seen one of the men sitting "in a peculiar and apparently constrained position, with his hands down in his lap and his body bent in a straight line from the hips upward and forward to the head and neck, with no curvature of the back."[51] He had seen Munley sitting in the same position at the habeas corpus hearing.

With the prosecution in a rocky position, a lucky and bizarre twist suddenly strengthened its case, when Jeannette Williams of Raven Run accompanied her husband to court after he was subpoenaed to testify. On the day of the shooting, her son made motions to go outdoors after hearing the shots, but she grabbed him to prevent him from doing so. As she did, a stranger with a pistol passed her door, and she saw his face. When she entered the courtroom with her husband, she immediately recognized Munley as that man. She asked to testify, and Gowen made sure the jury appreciated her ability to make the identification. "The art of the photographer has discovered a method whereby, in an instant of time or less than an instant, in a pulsation of the heart, in the winking of an eye, you can take the picture of a man while he is moving at full speed before you," he explained. "Why should not the eye of this woman be able to do the same thing?"[52]

Despite the helpful reports from other witnesses, the heart of the case once again was McParlan's testimony. Repeating much of his usual information, he also added an account of the pre- and postmurder interactions with the killers. He described how Doyle told him that the murder would be committed, and acknowledged that he had loaned him his coat despite knowing that the purpose was "to prevent detection afterward." He also told of the confession at Lawler's saloon after the murder, during which: "I learned . . . that the name of the boss that was shot was Sanger and that the colliery he was boss at was operated by Heatons."[53]

Once again the defense hammered at McParlan for not warning Sanger. Again and again Ryon asked if he could not escape from Hurley: Could he not leave at dinner? Could he not tell him that he was going to the telegraph office? Could he not devise another means of escape? "I seen no means," McParlan replied. "[T]here might have been other men that could, but I did not see any, and I do not see any now." Could not, Ryon demanded, McParlan get the man drunk, so that he could leave him? "Well, the truth was I do not think there was enough [alcohol] in Shenandoah to make him drunk."[54]

Throughout the trial the defense proved far more vigorous than it had in previous trials. Munley's father, brother, and sister testified that he had been at home, and friends supplied other alibis. Then Ned Monaghan, the former constable for Shenandoah and a member of the AOH, attempted to discredit McParlan by testifying that he had been arrested for stealing a watch, had suggested killing *Daily Herald* reporter Tom Fielders, and had been the primary mover in planning the murder of Bully Bill Thomas. It briefly seemed that the tables might be turning, but under Gowen's searing cross-examination the damage was undone, and Monaghan's credibility was shattered when he was arrested as an accessory before the fact in the murder of Gomer James.

L'Velle and Bartholomew gave powerful summations for the defense, declaring the case an example of religious and nationalist discrimination, and demonizing McParlan as a mercenary hired to crush the AOH, a man guilty of "collaborating to allow Doyle and Hurley to escape,"[55] and a murderer who made no attempt to save Sanger.

But these were gentle waves compared to the tsunami that Gowen unleashed. In the most compelling address of the trials, for three hours he mesmerized the crowd in the courthouse, sweeping away any chance that Munley would walk free. Beginning with a point-by-point review of the prosecution's evidence, he dismissed each of the defense witnesses. Munley's brother took the brunt of Gowen's biting tongue about false alibis. "Mr Bartholomew says when an occurrence which fixes a date in the memory of a man is brought to his attention, he can probably recall from that little clue many other circumstances that occurred at that same time," Gowen stated. So, "I asked young Munley what he ate for breakfast on that morning, and he remembered . . . that he ate ham. Now, where is there an Irish Catholic in Schuylkill county that ate ham for breakfast on that Friday morning?" Michael Munley, still in the courtroom, shouted that he had said he ate eggs, but Gowen confirmed his point from the original court record. "Now he says it was eggs," he concluded, "and if we would prove that there was not a chicken in all the world that laid an egg that day this witness would take the stand and swear that he meant turtle eggs."[56]

Gowen then turned to McParlan, who, he noted, worked under an agreement of no extra compensation for achieving results, guaranteeing an honest and honorable transaction.[57] He disputed L'Velle's claim that crime had increased since McParlan's arrival, challenged the notion that McParlan was an accomplice, and denied that Hurley, Doyle, and others had truly escaped. "There is no place on the habitable globe where these men can find refuge, and in which they will not be tracked down," he roared. "Let them go to the Rocky Mountains, or to the shores of the Pacific; let them traverse the bleak deserts of Siberia; penetrate into the jungles of India, or wander over the wild steppes of Central Asia, and they will be dogged and tracked and brought to justice."[58]

Gowen also pointed out that, Irish Catholic by birth, McParlan had natural sympathy for the accused, yet could work against them because of their overarching evil. As a result, the safety of the whole of society has been greatly increased. "And to whom are we indebted for this security?" he asked. "To whom do we owe all this? . . . [W]e owe this safety to James McParlan, and if there ever was a man to whom the people of this county should erect a monument, it is James McParlan, the detective."[59]

Gowen concluded by asking the jury to link their names forever "with that of McParlan and of others who have aided in this *glorious crusade.*" [emphasis in original][60] Within days this speech had been published by a local print house in a pamphlet that sold thousands of copies throughout the anthracite region, the state of Pennsylvania, and even New York City and Boston. More important to Gowen, however, within an hour of the case going to the jury Munley had been pronounced guilty of first-degree murder. Like Campbell, he was sentenced to be hanged.

CHAPTER 10

<svg>——</svg>

ONE AFTER ANOTHER

Neither the prosecution nor the defense had time to rest after Gowen's remarkable speech, because the next day testimony began in the retrial of four of the men accused of murdering Yost—Duffy having elected to appear separately. After nine witnesses established the circumstances of the policeman's death, Kerrigan again gave his version of events, this time without contradiction from his wife, who did not testify.[1]

Yet again, however, the star witness was McParlan, whose battles with Bartholomew and Ryon reached new levels of bellicosity. For example, when Ryon interrupted McParlan, the detective quickly broke in: "Hold on. I was just going to state. You wanted his statement to me."

"I asked you a question," Ryon barked, "and, when you have answered it, that is enough."

"You asked the question," McParlan retorted, "and you answered it yourself; and the answer is not correct."[2]

Although Kaercher led McParlan through his now familiar background information and his interactions with Carroll, Roarity, and McGehan, as well as their confessions—which implicated the three of them as well as Boyle—the defense did its best to change the trial into an indictment of the detective. But as before, he wriggled off any hook they set for him, giving witty responses that always made him seem to be the victor. Thus, hoping to show McParlan was a liar, Ryon asked, "Did you tell these people to whom you applied to become a member of that organization that you wanted to go into it for the purpose of betraying its secrets?"

"I did not," said McParlan scornfully, "there would not have been much strategy in that."[3]

One issue the defense addressed regularly—unlike in Campbell's trial—was that McParlan's testimony showed him to be the recipient of an extraordinary number of confessions. Since he was always on his own or with

Kerrigan when he received them, there was no one to dispute what was said.[4] The first such incident came when, despite having met Carroll only ten days before, "We got into conversation respecting the murder of Yost, Carroll and I, he then stated that the parties that came to shoot Yost came to his house upon the night previous, the same night that Yost was shot; he stated that they had but one pistol, and that he gave them a little one-shooter."[5]

Even in the defense's initial address, Ryon pointed out that McParlan claimed only he heard the confessions, and anybody else was excluded from the conversations, even the men's friends of many years. "Four men were in that saloon. Who heard that conversation?" Ryon told the jury he had asked, to which McParlan had replied, "Nobody heard it; we were way off at the end of the counter, and they were way off at the other end, and I know they could not hear." So, Ryon continued, "[y]ou say you were talking to him, a stranger to you, in an undertone, to prevent his neighbors and friends, members of the same society with you, from hearing anything?" "O, yes," responded McParlan.[6]

How could anyone believe this, Ryon asked, as not only had McParlan just happened to go to the right saloon for that initial confession, but the owner had admitted his guilt the second time they had ever met? "That is a little too thin," Ryon said. "That is thinner than water."[7]

The defense also disputed Gowen's claim that the AOH was a criminal organization and thus membership in it made one guilty as an accessory to every one of its crimes.[8] However, as often as not, their contentions were negated by McParlan's quick, clever responses. "Was there anything immoral or illegal in the [AOH] by-laws or constitution?" Ryon asked. "O! no," responded McParlan, "there was nothing immoral or illegal; it was the violation of them where the immorality came in."[9]

After nine volatile days, the jury heard final summations. The defense concentrated on the accusation that the trial was bolstered by ethnic and religious bigotry and on McParlan's lack of credibility. With Gowen unavailable, Albright and Hughes each powerfully offset these charges. McParlan had "exposed violence and tracked the murderers into their very dens. He has taken off the thin gauze that covered their faces, and you have discovered what hideous monsters they are," Albright proclaimed. "But because James McParlan has done this are you to be told that you are not to believe him? Are you to shut your eyes to these facts and seal your consciences to the truth. . . . This is no crusade against any nationality. This is not war against any Church. This is a war against crime, and crime should not be exempt from punishment."[10]

Hughes then defended the accuracy of McParlan's testimony, as proven by his reports. "McParlan has told us upon this witness stand that he made daily reports of everything he did and said," he stated. "Is it not a shame, is it not a commentary upon this attack upon McParlan, that when he comes into this Court with the records of his life in his hands, holding them out to the gentlemen upon the other side, that they might see if he varied in his statements to the breadth of a hair, and if he had deviated in the slightest degree, they could have said, look at your reports and show your reports, and yet they never did so? . . . They did not dare to present these reports in evidence before you." Hughes waited for that to sink in, before continuing: "We could not do it. The law would not permit us to do that because the law is that a party cannot give in evidence the previous declarations of its own witness to corroborate him, but if these gentlemen wanted to contradict McParlan why did they not call for the reports? . . . The best and most infallible means of disproving the truth of the statements of McParlan, if they were untrue, were right there in their possession, tendered to them by us, and they refused to take them."[11]

The jury was convinced, and within three hours all four defendants were declared guilty.

Each of the trials so far had been for murder. That changed two weeks after the second Yost trial, when nine men were brought before Judge Walker in Pottsville, charged with aggravated assault and battery with intent to kill Bully Bill Thomas. This was no minor event, however, because among the defendants were the region's most powerful AOH leaders: John Kehoe, the "King of the Mollies"; Dennis Canning, the Northumberland County delegate; Christopher Donnelly, Schuylkill County treasurer; "Yellow Jack" Donahue, the Tuscarora bodymaster; James Roarity, the already convicted Coaldale bodymaster; Michael O'Brien, the Mahanoy City bodymaster; Frank McHugh, the secretary for Mahanoy City; and the two Shenandoah men who actually pulled the trigger: John Morris and John Gibbons. The other two in the party that attacked Thomas—Doyle and Hurley—were still on the run.

It was not just the defendants that gave the trial such import, however. Only two of the nine had actually shot Thomas; the others were charged with conspiracy for having been at the June 1, 1875, meeting in Mahanoy City where the decision to kill him had been made. And this conspiracy, according to Gowen, would prove that it was more than just a small, ruthless set of individuals that was the criminal element of the AOH, but rather it was the entire organization, which sought through terror and fear to control the southern anthracite region.

Testimony began on a sweltering morning made worse by the temperature having soared a full twenty degrees over the previous five days. McParlan—the only man other than those under indictment (and William Gavin, who had fled) to have attended the June 1 meeting—immediately took the witness stand. By now his story was well-known to anybody who could read a newspaper, but he told it again, slowly, succinctly, and in detail, not leaving the stand until the fourth day of a five-day trial. Despite efforts by the defense to prevent testimony about the secrets of the AOH, the criminal acts discovered by McParlan, and the methods of assigning and trading "jobs," all of it was introduced, as was his usual background information and a comprehensive account of his discovery and eventual flight.[12]

A powerful new element of McParlan's testimony put Kehoe in a less-than-favorable light. McParlan testified that after traveling to Girardville two days before the convention was held he found a pair of doctors at Kehoe's house, because his wife had recently given birth and the baby had a harelip. Refusing to be distracted by family problems, Kehoe asked McParlan and John Reagan, the St. Clair bodymaster, "if we had any good men in our division, good men that were good on the shoot."[13]

Although the defense counsel suggested that it was actually McParlan who initiated the murderous plan and that the story about the visit was fabrication, McParlan denied it, and although neither doctor remembered seeing him, they could not testify with certainty because they had been preoccupied.[14] Ultimately, the image McParlan created of Kehoe—a monster who thought only of murder even when medical help was needed for his baby—must have weighed heavily on the jury as its members formed an opinion about what kind of man Kehoe really was.

The key prosecution question—whether McParlan's testimony alone would have been enough to convict the conspirators—became a moot point late in the trial, when the twenty-year-old McHugh suddenly turned state's evidence in the hope of receiving a lighter sentence.[15] McHugh had been called into the convention to obtain some paper. When he returned with it, he handed it to Gavin. "He was county secretary, and I do not remember whether it was him or McParlan that said I should do the writing, but it was either one of them. All the writing that I done was that the meeting was called to order by Kehoe and to put down the date."[16] McHugh left his document behind, so there was no official record. Several times during his testimony he stated that he could not remember details, but, although his tale differed from McParlan's in a few specifics, it generally corroborated the detective's account.

The defense suffered a second surprise when the prosecution called George Beyerle, the warden of the county jail, who recounted a conversation he had with Kehoe during the Yost murder trial. "I said it would go pretty rough with them," Beyerle recalled. "He said, 'I think it will go rough with us too. I do not think we will get justice.' He said, 'If we don't get justice, I don't think the old man at Harrisburg will go back on us.'"[17]

Gasps could be heard throughout the courtroom, because a rumor already existed that Republican governor John F. Hartranft was indebted to the AOH for helping elect him, and he might issue pardons in return.[18] The defense moved that the testimony be stricken, but Gowen called it "equivalent to an admission of guilt. . . . [I]t is evidence he believes himself guilty, and that he cannot be acquitted."[19] Judge Walker determined that the testimony would remain in the record, a major triumph for Gowen, because it became politically impossible to issue pardons to those convicted.

The defense, as Pottsville attorney Samuel A. Garrett commented in his opening remarks, now faced a peculiar position, "almost without any defense whatever. That the majority of these defendants attended a meeting of the Ancient Order of Hibernians on the 1st of June we cannot deny. What took place there it is impossible for us to prove to you . . . [because] the mouths of all the parties who were present at that meeting are entirely closed, and the defendants are left without being able to prove anything."[20]

The problem for the defense was that defendants had long been disqualified from testifying on their own behalf under American common law, because they were considered to have an interest in the outcome, so their testimony was deemed untrustworthy. This was particularly true in criminal law, in which the "old common law shuddered at the idea of any person testifying who had the least interest."[21] However, in 1864, Maine had passed the first statute in the English-speaking world making criminal defendants competent witnesses. Most U.S. states followed suit within two decades, and a federal statute was adopted in 1878. Pennsylvania, however, did not enact such statutes until 1885, so during the Molly Maguire trials, defendants still could not normally testify on their own behalf.[22]

With such constraints, the defense's only hope was to break McParlan's story. Garrett started immediately, laying out the defense's basic proposition:

[W]hether this man McParlan did or did not assist in the perpetration of this crime, he, nevertheless, went to that meeting when it was conceived; he helped to perfect the plan, and he went with the men on this mission of crime; and even if he did not take any part in the actual perpetration of the offence, there is not a scintilla of evidence to show that he adopted any means to prevent its commission. On the other hand, the evidence is clear that he was always first to advise and counsel outrages, see to their execution, and never in the slightest manner adopted any means for the prevention of the same. In this way he became the main instrument in the commission of all these crimes. During all this time he was careful that no crime which he proposed should be carried out; but his conduct and acts taken together show very clearly his character, and that these crimes in their boldness, arose from his example.[23]

The defense thereafter cited the differences between McParlan's current tale and that given at the habeas corpus hearing, tried to disqualify McHugh's support by noting *his* inconsistencies, argued that McParlan had made no efforts to warn Thomas, and admonished him for permitting Hurley, Doyle, and even McCann—the confessed killer of George Major—to escape. L'Velle and Ryon continued this throughout their closing statements, with the latter insisting that "of all the men that deserve punishment this man McParlan deserves twice what anybody charged with crime in this county deserves; if it is true that anybody deserves hanging, this man McParlan ought to be hanged twice; because, if there is an author to this mischief and this deviltry anywhere, McParlan is the man."[24]

It must have been a bit of a surprise when that genius of oratory, Franklin Gowen, addressed the jury in the first closing statement rather than waiting until the end. Although he did not equal his previous masterpiece, he defended McParlan, accused the AOH of resorting to terror, and, in a masterful statement of twisted logic, insisted that any discrepancies between the testimony of McParlan and McHugh actually proved both were true.[25] Gowen then singled out Kehoe as "the chief conspirator, murderer and villain," adding that, "There is a crime which in its magnitude far transcends and exceeds any [other] crime known . . . and this is the crime not of the killing of the body, but the crime of the killing of the soul. How many young men, brought up by good parents, in good churches, and by pious priests, have been led from the path of rectitude and honesty by the influences of this society and of its leader, Jack Kehoe?"[26]

The final summation, by Kaercher, was precise, based on evidence, and unemotional. In this way it was almost the antithesis of the defense arguments, which demonized McParlan. And yet, what else could the defense attorneys do? They did not have a great deal of evidence on their side, and they could not call their clients to the stand. So they followed a time-tested tactic: attempting to get the jury members—who, like many on juries in trials for heinous crimes, felt the need to punish *someone*—to concentrate their anger on anyone other than the defendants. By expounding the thesis that McParlan was an agent provocateur, the real leader in these crimes, and a fiend of unequaled immorality and evil, the defense hoped to shift the need to blame and punish someone onto him. That the general strategy was a good one is shown by its appearance time and again throughout legal history, and that the specific argument was powerful is proven by its adoption by apologists for the Molly Maguires.[27] Sadly for the men in the dock, the jury did not buy it. After only twenty minutes of deliberation they returned with a guilty verdict against each prisoner, with a recommendation of mercy for McHugh.[28]

The floodgates had now opened, and a series of quick but successful trials followed in Pottsville. Only two days after Kehoe and company were found guilty, all of them other than McHugh, Morris, and Gibbons were back in the courtroom, facing charges for conspiracy to kill William and Jesse Major. The defense protested that this was the same conspiracy for which the men had already been convicted, but the trial went ahead, and on the third day, the defendants were again found guilty.[29]

On the very next day, Roarity, Donnelly, Donahue, and O'Brien were dragged back into court, along with three others—Patrick Dolan, Frank O'Neil, and Patrick Butler—for aiding and assisting in the rewarding of Hurley for the murder of Gomer James. These men had all been at the August 25, 1875, convention at which Hurley had pressed his claim. Three others who had been there were fugitives from justice, and the prosecution decided to postpone the trial of Kehoe.

The star of the show was again McParlan, but the major change in the process came when, for the first time—with prosecution permission—the defendants were called to the stand. Unlike McParlan, these were not men practiced or naturally gifted in the intricate arts of trial testimony, and Kaercher soon made them regret the decision. "Donnelly left the stand after receiving an awful raking," reported the *Daily Herald*.[30] Shortly thereafter it turned from bad to disastrous for the defense.

Without the knowledge of Ryon or L'Velle, Patrick Butler, the Lost Creek bodymaster, had already agreed to confess, which explains why the prosecution allowed the defendants to testify.[31] During cross-examination by Kaercher, Butler suddenly admitted that leaders of the AOH had proposed many crimes, including when Dennis "Bucky" Donnelly had ordered him and a man named Pat Shaw to murder Sanger. He also told of Hurley's plans to murder Gomer James, Hurley's subsequent claims, and Kehoe's decision for him and McParlan to investigate.[32]

The unexpected and complete nature of the confession was stunning. "Frank O'Neil actually rubbed his eyes to make sure he wasn't dreaming... Mike O'Brien suddenly became actually ghostly through terror and astonishment.... Roarity actually gave his front teeth a rest and forgot to chew.... 'Yellow Jack' gave up the attempt to take matters coolly, for it was too much, more than a man could be expected to bear calmly."[33] Any hope of an acquittal was gone, and the next day, after fifteen minutes of deliberation, all the defendants were found guilty.[34]

A couple of weeks later, Gowen's reappearance with the prosecution showed the significance of Thomas Duffy's separate trial for the murder of Yost. This time Kerrigan was the star witness, testifying for three days and covering how he and Duffy had been beaten up by Yost and McCarron, and how Duffy had sworn revenge and offered Roarity ten dollars to kill Yost.[35] So much for the motive, although it came from a notorious liar who contradicted his earlier testimony. Even so, no participation by Duffy in the murder itself could be proven, and the most damaging evidence was that he spent the night at Carroll's to provide an alibi.

Although McParlan testified for two days, his evidence was by far the weakest he had yet presented, as he did not know Duffy and had never seen McGehan and Duffy together.[36] The prosecution included McParlan's usual testimony, but even this lacked its previous effectiveness, as shown by the defense's lackadaisical attitude. When Gowen proposed reading the "goods" into the record from McParlan's reports—long objected to by the defense—Ryon simply said, "It makes no difference to us."[37]

When the case went to the jury it seemed far from proven, and Judge Walker's instructions "leaned toward the side of mercy.... [H]ardly a soul in the courtroom but was satisfied Duffy's chances of acquittal were more than even."[38] Nevertheless, early the next morning Duffy was pronounced guilty of first-degree murder.

Duffy's conviction was announced on a Wednesday morning. Before the end of the following Wednesday, another thirteen people had appeared in Pottsville court. Four—James Duffy, Bridget Hyland, Kate Boyle, and Barney Boyle—were found guilty of perjury for giving false alibis.[39]

Meanwhile, McParlan's claims were also shown to be fallible on occasion, as he admitted that Charles McAllister, in jail since February for the murder of Sanger and Uren, was the wrong suspect, and that it should have been his brother James, who looked similar. Charles was released but immediately re-arrested and charged for the attempted murder of James Riles in August 1875.[40]

That same day, Muff Lawler was tried as an accessory after the fact in the Sanger murder. McParlan testified that his old chum took several guns to hide for the killers when they came to his saloon after the murder, and added that, "I know that he knew of crimes before they were committed, because before these men came back he said he wondered how the boys got along, and he said he knew Friday O'Donnell would make a clean job of it."[41] Lawler quickly admitted his role and turned state's evidence by corroborating information about other crimes, but the jury was unable to arrive at a unanimous verdict, after voting 10–2 for acquittal.

While that jury was still debating, four men were brought before another hastily assembled one in the same courtroom. Charged with conspiracy to kill the Majors, all had been implicated by Kerrigan in the first Major trial. Two, John Slattery and Charles Mulhearn, joined the ever-lengthening list of those who turned state's evidence, but despite their testimony and that of McParlan, Kerrigan, and McHugh, John Stanton became the first man in the trials to be found not guilty.[42]

As the trials raced on, McParlan testified against former constable Ned Monaghan, who had earlier tried to undermine him, and then Thomas Donohue, both for involvement in the attack on Thomas. Monaghan had no chance, as he had claimed in the Munley trial to have attended the meeting at which men had been selected to kill Bully Bill, whereas Donohue's entire trial lasted only a couple of hours.[43]

Almost immediately after Donohue's trial, "McParlan and his guards left town. . . . They have ended their labors here for a little while, but they will not be gone for long."[44] Where McParlan went during this period is unknown, but it is probable that his younger brothers Charles and Edward—about twenty-six and twenty-four years old, respectively—accompanied him, after having been initially brought over from Ireland by Pinkerton or Gowen at his request in order that he have people he could trust around him during the later stages of his testimony.[45]

After a month spent recovering from the stresses of almost constant testimony, McParlan was back in Mauch Chunk in late October. Charles Mulhearn, while giving state's evidence, had indicated that he had been with "Yellow Jack" Donahue and Matt Donahue when they had murdered Morgan Powell in 1871. Mulhearn also stated that "Yellow Jack" had been promised one hundred dollars by Thomas Fisher, then the Carbon County delegate, to kill Powell. Fisher had become involved at the request of Summit Hill bodymaster Patrick McKenna, who had been asked by Alexander Campbell to have Powell killed because the foreman had denied him a mining job.

A series of trials for the murder of Powell now followed, in which Mulhearn, Slattery, Kerrigan, and McParlan were key witnesses. As the murder took place before McParlan came to the anthracite region, he did not have a great deal to add in a couple of the trials, but he did testify that in July the previous year, Jack Donahue—again with no one else present—admitted that he had made a clean job of it—going to Summit Hill with two men, shooting Powell, and then laying down in the bush until things were quiet.[46] McParlan also told how, while visiting Campbell one evening, his host had "stated that there was no doubt but that they would try to convict them [the murderers of Jones] very hard on account that Powell the previous superintendent had been murdered there. Campbell laughed and said that John Donahue was the man that done that job."[47]

Donahue, Fisher, and Campbell were sentenced to hang, while McKenna was given nine years in prison. Lead attorney Francis Hughes acknowledged McParlan's role—which was perhaps most significant, because the other primary witnesses were confessed criminals turned informer and he gave the cases more credibility—by stating: "Like pure gold, the harder he's rubbed the brighter he shines. If a spot of tarnish could be placed on the escutcheon of his character, the gentlemen representing the defendant . . . would have placed it there."[48]

McParlan returned briefly to Pottsville in the midst of these trials for the second prosecution of Muff Lawler. Having not succeeded with the earlier case, the prosecution used the same information but changed the charge from accessory for the murder of Sanger to that of Uren. After Kaercher led McParlan through "the story once so painfully new, now so painfully old, of how the Mollies did their work,"[49] the detective recalled the morning in Lawler's saloon where the five killers confessed, and Lawler had offered to keep their guns for them. The next day the defense pointed out that McParlan had previously stated that he was afraid to do anything in advance about the murder, and that had seemed acceptable, but Lawler was simply too afraid to do anything *after* the murder, yet was being treated differently. It was a clever—and fair—argument, but it failed nonetheless, and Lawler was found guilty.[50]

Throughout the period of the Powell trials Linden continued his detailed investigations into other old murder cases attributed to the Molly Maguires. The most important of these was the killing of Frank Langdon in 1862. Although McParlan did not play a significant role in these trials, they resulted in two second-degree murder convictions, with long sentences being passed down to Neil Dougherty and John Campbell. More important to the prosecution was the January 1877 trial of Kehoe for the same charge. The man considered the leader of the Molly Maguires already faced two seven-year sentences, but Kaercher, Albright, Hughes, and Farquhar hoped to eliminate the possibility of him ever leaving prison by putting a rope around his neck. They were successful, as he was found guilty of first-degree murder and sentenced to be hanged.[51]

Another earlier murder was that of Alexander Rea in 1868. McParlan had previously heard that Manus Cull, alias Daniel Kelly or Kelly the Bum, had been involved. Cull was then serving a sentence in Pottsville jail, so in August 1876, Linden visited him four times within a week, each time bringing him whiskey, cigars, or other treats.[52] Eventually, this generosity—or bribery—was rewarded, because in November Cull turned state's evidence. In February 1877, almost a year after McParlan had fled Schuylkill County, Patrick Hester, Peter McHugh, and Patrick Tully went on trial in Bloomsburg, Columbia County, for Rea's murder. Cull and Lawler were the primary witnesses, but McParlan took the stand to give evidence "of the character of the Order" and replay the basics from his earlier testimony.[53] All three men were found guilty and were sentenced to hang.

The same week that the trial for Rea's murder began, Bishop William O'Hara of Scranton finally followed the recommendations of Archbishop Wood and formally excommunicated the AOH in his parish, which included the Northern Field.[54] This helped lead to swift decisions at the national convention of the AOH, held in New York City that spring. In a public address, the

AOH leadership stated that "the Order does not recognize any connection . . . with that terrible band of misguided men that have committed such crimes in Pennsylvania," and that it had decided "to cut off from all connections with our organization the Schuylkill, Carbon, Northumberland and Columbia County lodges," despite the fact that "a good number of good men would suffer for the misdeeds of a few."[55] What few Molly Maguires remained out of jail were now on their own.

Eight months later, in November 1877, McParlan returned to the anthracite region for a final appearance in the trial of Bucky Donnelly, the former Lost Creek bodymaster accused of plotting the murders of Sanger and Uren. The detective again went over his well-worn facts about the AOH and the case, and implicated Donnelly based on a conversation in Danny Hughes's saloon on the day of the habeas corpus hearing for Munley and McAllister. "Donnelly took me aside in the saloon and stated it did not make any difference about this habeas corpus hearing," McParlan testified. "Said he, 'In the arrest of McAllister they have got the wrong man anyhow, and so far as Munley is concerned I am going to swear that I was well acquainted with him, and that he was not there; of course, I know different, as I know all about it.'"[56]

Despite McParlan's testimony, it was Butler and Dennis Canning—who turned state's evidence in exchange for a pardon on his conviction for conspiracy in the attack on Thomas—who provided the most damaging evidence. The latter told of Donnelly's boasts of arranging the killing and the former that the defendant had attempted it previously. The combination was too much for the defense, even with an alibi for the night before the murder and testimony that contradicted Butler.[57] Donnelly was convicted of first-degree murder and sentenced to hang, completing the prosecution for the Sanger and Uren murders.[58] It also ended McParlan's time in the anthracite region. By the end of his testimony in a remarkable nineteenth trial appearance it had been more than four years since he had first stepped off the train in Port Clinton. Schuylkill County would never be the same—nor would James McParlan.

CHAPTER 11

AN ENDING AND A BEGINNING

Before McParlan took the stand for the final time in Pottsville, the Commonwealth of Pennsylvania made its most forceful statement regarding the Molly Maguires. On June 21, 1877, in what became known as the Day of the Rope, ten of the convicted men were hanged. Six died at the Schuylkill County jail—Boyle, McGehan, Carroll, Roarity, and Duffy for the murder of Yost, and Munley for the killing of Sanger and Uren. Four others were hanged at the Carbon County jail in Mauch Chunk: Doyle and Kelly for the assassination of Jones, Donahue for Powell, and Campbell for his involvement in both murders. At the last moment, Kelly asked to see Mrs. Jones, to whom he said, "I have made your children fatherless, but I want you to forgive me." Her response was simply, "I hope God will forgive you."[1]

Eventually ten more supposed Molly Maguires were hanged. Hester, McHugh, and Tully met their ends in Bloomsburg on March 25, 1878, for murdering Rea, six days after Tully confessed to his lawyer that most of what Cull had said was true, and that all three were guilty.[2] Four days later, Fisher was hanged in Mauch Chunk for his role in the Powell murder. And the next month, Donnelly died for ordering Sanger murdered. On December 18, after exhausting his appeals, Kehoe was hanged for killing Langdon.[3] Four men were also hanged in 1879, having been convicted after McParlan left the region.[4]

Although some were appalled by the trials and subsequent hangings,[5] the Commonwealth's actions were generally supported in the press, and within a short period several books had appeared praising McParlan, Gowen, and others for their roles in suppressing a terrorist organization.[6] Over the years, however, popular opinion has changed about the fairness of the trials, as has how people view the Molly Maguires.

Some have gone so far as to claim that the Molly Maguires never actually existed but were fabricated by Gowen, Bannan, Pinkerton, and others to destroy organized labor.[7] However, the historical evidence simply does not support such arguments. It was not just the rail and mining companies and the newspapers that acknowledged the Molly Maguires existed—a whole realm of individuals and organizations did so, including: the Commonwealth's officials; many average citizens, as shown by their testimonies; the juries; the families of the men killed; the Catholic Church; witnesses called for the defense; prosecution and defense lawyers; and men who had been a part of the organization, such as McParlan, Kerrigan, Butler, and Mulhearn.[8] Even historian Kevin Kenny, one of the strongest advocates on behalf of the convicted men, has agreed that "the Molly Maguires did indeed exist as an organized conspiracy" and that "the Molly Maguires existed as a group of Irish immigrants who assassinated their enemies."[9]

Another view is that the Molly Maguires were activists who formed the beginning of the labor movement, representing oppressed miners against big capital.[10] This is intriguing, because the Molly Maguires did, in one sense, represent mine workers, but it was very much at the individual level and not as part of the larger class struggle that tends to be the modern focus on the growth of the labor movement. Many of the Molly Maguires' actions—including the murders of Powell, Yost, Sanger, and Jones—were responses to personal grievances. This was a fundamentally different approach than that of the trade unionism of the WBA, the first true labor movement to unite workers in different mining trades and from different ethnic backgrounds.

In reality, closely linking the Molly Maguires and the WBA is difficult because of their distinct modes of organization, ideology, and strategy. The WBA was representative of a large, broad group in a manner that was indirect, peaceful, systematic, and gradual; the small, sectarian Molly Maguires believed in direct, violent, and immediate action. Rather than engaging in harmonious bargaining with owners and management, as the WBA did, the Molly Maguires chose to employ threats, property damage, and personal violence. This is why the WBA, and particularly John Siney, were fundamentally opposed to the Molly Maguires, and criticized their outrages time and again. Thus, although there were arguably common characteristics in their goals, and undoubtedly a small overlap in personnel, the contrast between the trade union and the Molly Maguires could not have been greater. And ironically, it is this same dubious linking of two distinct organizations, which some try to make today, that allowed Gowen to identify them as the same body and helped enable him to destroy both.[11]

Closely related to the notion that the Molly Maguires were labor leaders is the concept that the trials and executions were the results of a conspiracy to purge innocent religious, political, or labor leaders fighting oppression and injustice.[12] Gowen has been a particular target of this theory, with claims that he was trying to eradicate Irish Catholic leadership due to its political opposition to the Reading. Although Gowen certainly wanted to control the southern anthracite region economically, and to establish a stable social order there,[13] it is doubtful that he pursued the Molly Maguires for religious or political reasons. There is a lack of any serious evidence—from his correspondence, speeches, or accounts of those who knew him—that Gowen ever showed any anti-Catholic prejudice. On the contrary, he was closely associated with Archbishop Wood and found a powerful ally in the Catholic Church. Gowen also never expressed any desire to enter politics, as he believed he could control any relevant political forces in Harrisburg from his position with the Reading.

A more frequent argument is that the trials came about because Gowen, Parrish, and Packer wished to destroy the entire labor movement. While it is true that Gowen had previously attempted to damage the WBA by linking it to the Molly Maguires, the union had been crushed the year before the trials, during the Long Strike. So it makes no sense that he would launch a conspiracy to destroy an organization that had already collapsed. Moreover, if that had been the case, Gowen would not have brought criminal charges against the saloon owners and AOH members who were the key figures in the Molly Maguire trials, but would have concentrated on Siney and other prominent union men. Further, he would not have fallen back on McParlan's evidence—he would have looked rather to those operatives who had infiltrated the union, such as P. M. Cummings and William McCowan.[14]

In recent years there has been much discussion of the Molly Maguire trials, and their legality and morality have been much debated. However, an objective assessment should not confuse these important but separate issues. A weakness of many recent appraisals of the trials is their historical inaccuracy. They do not take into account important facts, or ignore that while various practices might since have changed, they were common and acceptable at the time. The trials were not mockeries of the American and Pennsylvania legal systems of the time, as some claim, but representative of them. A case in point is the frequently criticized practice of using private prosecutors, which was long established not only in Pennsylvania but throughout the English-speaking world. Furthermore, the claim that juries were *illegally* stacked by eliminating Irish and Catholics is not only factually inaccurate—there *were* Catholics on them—but anachronistic, in that it does not take into account what was accepted legal practice at the time.[15] Such arguments also ignore that due to the way potential jurors had long been chosen from the jury wheel, the Molly Maguire trials did not violate due process any more than any other trial in the region during that period.

Further, arguments suggesting that the trials were a vast conspiracy disregard the long trail of bodies *before* the hangings. There *were* crimes committed, including cold-blooded murders. This is particularly overlooked in arguments that Gowen was involved for political reasons. More than once during the trials Gowen held forth about his time as district attorney, and how he had encountered "a secret organization, banded together for the commission of crime, and for the purpose of securing the escape or acquittal of any of its members charged with the commission of an offense."[16] There can be little doubt that his inability as a young prosecutor to successfully punish murder, violence, and arson was a key reason for Gowen's participation in the trials.

These brutal murders are also often ignored or conveniently forgotten by those who have espoused theories that the trial evidence was fabricated, perjured, or obtained by coercion. Such theories overlook the fact that at least two of the men who were executed confessed their guilt, one of them implicating those hanged with him. Certainly Kelly's confession leaves little question that he and Doyle murdered Jones. What *is* disputed is whether they did so on Campbell's orders because they were members of an organization that had decided upon the mine boss's death. Yet what other possible reason could they have had to travel twenty-five miles to murder someone they had never met? There has been no good answer generated other than that they were carrying out orders, nor a reasonable alternative to Campbell as the man behind the decision. Even if there *were* another man behind the killing, that would not change the story of AOH members killing on demand, whether the murders be of Powell, Yost, Jones, or Sanger.

Much of the criticism of the overall format of the trials has been spearheaded by an oft-quoted assessment made four decades ago by Professor Harold Aurand: "The Molly Maguire investigation and trials was one of the most astounding surrenders of sovereignty in American history. A private corporation initiated the investigation through a private detective agency; a private police force arrested the alleged offenders; the coal company attorneys prosecuted them. The state provided only the Courtroom and the hangman."[17]

The facts say otherwise, however. Although many of the arrests were made by Coal and Iron Police, that force had been brought into being by state legislation, and each member of it had officially been approved by the governor of the state, thereby making it quasi-official and responsible to higher authorities. The prisoners were held in county facilities under the care of publicly elected officials. The charges were brought by the elected county district attorney on behalf of the Commonwealth. Although attorneys affiliated with the rail and mining corporations were significant figures in the prosecution, the district attorney in each case participated in and fulfilled his legal obligations while—as had been common for a century—accepting the help of private lawyers. The district attorney carried out his role in each case for the habeas corpus hearing, the primary trial, and the appeal. The jury commissioners were public officers and the jurors were tax-paying citizens. The judges were publicly elected, and the appeals were sent to the Commonwealth's highest judicial body, the Supreme Court. When those convicted sent further requests to the Pardon Board, they were decided upon by public officials, prior to the elected governor of Pennsylvania signing the death warrants. Thus, the counties and Commonwealth were fully involved in the chargings, prosecutions, and executions of the Molly Maguires.

That being said, there is no doubt that the trials were held at a time of high emotion and intolerance, when the frenzy stirred up by the press, combined with the remarkable oratorical powers of Gowen, Albright, and Hughes, allowed the prosecution to repeatedly insist that mere membership in the AOH was evidence of guilt by association. Despite precedents established by the trial of the Lincoln assassination conspirators, this was a highly unusual argument for the time, and it raises questions about McParlan's testimony.

As early as April 1874, McParlan first reported that the bodymasters and a few other members of the AOH formed an inner circle that acted without the knowledge of the full membership in carrying out violent acts.[18] He believed at the time that it was this inner circle, rather than the entirety of the AOH, that formed the Molly Maguires. Yet two years later, throughout the trials, McParlan testified that the AOH and the Molly Maguires were the very same organization.

It has been argued recently that only the most tenuous of links can be shown to connect the two groups.[19] Yet in each case in court, the Commonwealth and its witnesses presented evidence not merely directly linking the two, but indicating that they were actually the same organization. This evidence was credible according to the juries, judges, courtroom reporters, and most other individuals who attended the trials. But what did McParlan actually think? For if there *was* an inner circle in the AOH, why did he testify that the two bodies were the same?

No definitive insight into McParlan's private thoughts exists today. Perhaps he had become convinced that the organizations were identical and that there was no inner circle. This seems doubtful, however, because the concept of the inner circle became so implanted in his mind that he used a similar model in other cases later in his career, and if the hypothesis had been disproven in this case, he would have been unlikely to cling to it so tenaciously. Perhaps he just changed his testimony to fit Gowen's plan. If so, this is not as damning as it initially sounds, because, as those familiar with modern prosecution techniques and police procedure know, it is what police and witnesses do throughout the Western world. The task of the police as it relates to court appearances is to secure convictions, just as McParlan's was as an investigating detective. This is not to say that police or other witnesses fabricate testimony, but it should not be surprising that they present the facts that best make their case, while suppressing those that do not.

So did McParlan modify his story about the inner circle simply in order to help the prosecution's case? Under the circumstances, it seems unlikely that he changed basic facts but probable that he shifted his emphasis at points. He did this in an extremely impressive fashion, because there is no doubt that he was considered to be very credible and persuasive. He showed a remarkable memory for what he considered important, and through day after day of fierce cross-examination he avoided falling into traps set by the defense, and was never proven to have lied. That he could come through that many questions in nineteen different trials during a period of a year and a half without significant contradictions certainly suggests that most of what he said was the truth, because under intelligent, searching cross-examination it is very difficult to maintain an extended web of lies. Moreover, McParlan's testimony was extensively supported by those of Kerrigan, McHugh, Butler, Mulhearn, Slattery, and Canning, the last of whom, for example, confirmed during the Donnelly trial the holding of the June 1 meeting in Mahanoy City at which it was decided to kill Bully Bill and the Major brothers.[20]

It was, in fact, only the defense attorneys who, with no other effective avenues through which to help their clients, decided to declare publicly, in ever more vehement terms, that McParlan was a liar and an agent provocateur. But this is what defense attorneys do—follow the course best calculated to gain their clients' liberty. The juries, judges, and press did not agree, although the defense attacks nevertheless set the pattern for later efforts to support the innocence of those on trial by discrediting McParlan. These attacks have never satisfactorily explained what his motive for lying would have been. Despite Patrick Campbell's intensive search to prove McParlan received a bonus of blood money, there is no evidence to support this contention.[21] It is clearly not reasonable to suggest McParlan was anti-Irish or anti-Catholic. And there is no serious indication to back up the charge that he was an inherently evil man, one "simply outside the human pale . . . a case of almost pure *evil*." [emphasis in original][22]

So McParlan appears to have been mostly honest, but not totally untainted. And if he was less than entirely truthful about his story of the inner circle, it might say something about his willingness to corrupt his other testimony. In fact, a close accounting of his witness statements makes it clear that he held back the truth in various parts of his testimony, and ultimately did, in fact, commit perjury. Moreover, he did it more than once.

Molly Maguire expert Howard Crown has argued that McParlan committed perjury in the trial for assault and battery with intent to kill Bully Bill Thomas.[23] On August 10, 1876, the following exchange occurred between McParlan and defense attorney Martin L'Velle:

Q: Prior to your joining the Ancient Order of Hibernians did you have any knowledge of their organization?
A: I did not; I had no knowledge, only what I gathered up through the county.
Q: Did you know of such an organization in Chicago?
A: I did not. There was a Hibernian Benevolent Society in Chicago that I was acquainted with.
Q: I am talking of the Ancient Order of Hibernians. Did you know it elsewhere in the West?
A: No; I did not know of it.[24]

Crown also noted a second section of testimony that he indicated furthers the case against McParlan. In the Donnelly trial, the detective was again cross-examined by L'Velle:

Q: Did you ever try to gain admission to any branch or body of the Ancient Order outside of Schuylkill County?

A: Yes, sir; at Hazleton ...

Q: You know the Ancient Order of Hibernians to flourish elsewhere?

A: Yes, sir.

Q: In Chicago?

A: Yes, sir.

Q: Of your own knowledge?

A: I have heard of them. ...

Q: It is a matter of public notoriety that such an order does exist there?

A: Yes, sir.[25]

Crown argues that in the first exchange McParlan committed perjury (of which Gowen, Hughes, and Kaercher were aware) because—as proven by the report on Irish secret societies that he submitted to Pinkerton in October 1873—he already knew of the Molly Maguires and had indicated that they had simply adopted a new name: the Ancient Order of Hibernians. Crown added that the second passage directly contradicted McParlan's previous testimony that he knew nothing of the AOH prior to coming to Schuylkill County.[26]

However, attorneys have pointed out that witnesses should always have been cautioned—both at McParlan's time and more recently—to limit their testimony to information based on their personal knowledge, as opposed to secondhand accounts, which are considered hearsay. Therefore, if McParlan's information for his report to Pinkerton was based on oral history, newspaper accounts, and other secondhand sources—as opposed to his own direct knowledge—then, assuming that he believed the question to be asking him about his actual personal knowledge, his answer (it has been argued) could be considered essentially truthful and not grounds for a perjury charge.

Further, the second passage quoted does not actually contradict McParlan's previous testimony. The AOH meeting to which McParlan gained admission in Hazleton was in June 1874, by which time he already held his membership card from the Tamaqua division of the AOH, so it was after he learned about the organization in Schuylkill County.[27] And whereas he did seem to contradict himself about knowing about the AOH in Chicago, the questions were actually not mutually exclusive. During the Kehoe case he was asked if he knew of the organization in Chicago prior to his joining in April 1874. In the second question he was asked if he was familiar with the AOH flourishing anywhere else—in November 1877, at the time of the Donnelly trial. There is nothing to prove that it was not during the intervening three and a half years that McParlan had learned of the Chicago branch of the order.

Whether one believes from these different points of view that McParlan perjured himself or not, he certainly seems to have been walking near the edge, and his earlier testimony regarding the existence of the Molly Maguires was not dissimilar. In cross-examination during the first trial for Yost's murder, Bartholomew asked him, "When did you first get acquainted with the fact there existed a secret society known as the 'Mollie Maguires' in the County of Schuylkill? When did you have the fact brought to your attention so that you knew it as a fact?" McParlan replied, "The fact was brought to my attention . . . by a man named Fitzgibbons, who was a watchman at the [Tremont] crossing." A few moments later Bartholomew asked: "That was the first knowledge that you had that there was such an organization?" McParlan responded: "Yes, sir; it was the first *in this county*." [emphasis added][28]

Although the answers might have led one to believe that McParlan had no knowledge of the Molly Maguires prior to meeting Fitzgibbons, due to the manner in which the first question was phrased and the second answered, McParlan was able to state the truth while leaving the meaning ambivalent.

Similarly, during the Munley trial, McParlan stated: "The object of my coming to the coal regions was to make an investigation concerning an organization which was supposed to exist, called the Mollie Maguires. I first learned in the county from parties living in the county that there was such an organization existing."[29] Again, the statement is strictly accurate: He learned "in the county" from those parties, even though he had previously learned of them outside the county. Once again, McParlan was able to create the impression he desired by being a careful wordsmith and implying more than he actually stated.

McParlan's ability to play games with words, and thereby dance out of the defense's traps, led Ryon to call him "the most skillful, cunning man, the most unfair witness that I ever saw on the stand in my life."[30] Even so, there are times that his written reports contradicted what the detective stated on the stand, indicating beyond question that he committed perjury.

The most significant example was McParlan's portrayal in court of his lack of knowledge about the intended victim prior to Sanger's murder. In his original report he stated that Doyle "told me he got it [the pistol] from Ed Monaghan and that he and James O'Donnell . . . and Chas O'Donnell and

Chas McAllister . . . were going down to Ravens Run to shoot Sanger, the mining boss just as he went out to get dinner."[31]

Yet, no fewer than three times in court, McParlan attempted to legitimize his inaction by claiming he did not know who was to be murdered. "Did not know the boss' name, as there were several collieries there. I did not know what boss," he testified in his first court appearance. "And in the communication which you received of the fact of the commission of this murder, that it was to be committed, you did not learn who it was that was to be killed?" Bartholomew asked. "I did not," responded McParlan.[32]

He stated similar "facts" almost two months later, adding that it was not until the morning at Lawler's bar that he discovered the victim's identity. "I then learned the name of one of the parties that was shot; that was the boss, and his name was Sanger. . . . I learned it from those parties . . . and in Lawler's saloon, that the name of the boss that was shot was Sanger and that the colliery he was boss at was operated by Heatons."[33]

The following year, in the Donnelly trial, McParlan revisited those tense hours: "I did not know what colliery the boss worked at, or what was the name of the boss," he claimed, adding that, as Hurley remained with him until ten o'clock, "I could not go to Raven Run. I did not know what boss was to be killed or what colliery he was at, but if I could have found Linden, and he had got his men stationed there, the probabilities are that the boss' life might have been saved, but those things were impossible."[34]

That McParlan lied on the stand in these trials seems as mysterious as it is inescapable. Why did he choose to do so? He was called out time and again for not trying to warn Jones, but he steadfastly maintained his position that he would not risk his life for someone he did not know, and that there was a very real danger that he would be killed himself.[35] He also stuck to his story that he could not warn Thomas of a second set of attackers due to his ill health and having Michael Carey with him until nearly midnight.[36] And yet, although he had a similar reason for his failure to warn Sanger—he could not get away from Hurley—he added a needless falsehood.

The doubts raised by the way McParlan dealt with these issues during testimony lead to still more questions. Foremost among them is: What is the likelihood that so many men involved in heinous crimes would have so lightly confessed to someone they had not known long and did not know intimately? It is also hard to believe that these confessions would have so frequently been offered in such a way that no one else could hear the conversation.

Although it is reasonable to ask questions about McParlan's testimony, his reports do seem to be relatively trustworthy. For one thing, they correlate closely to events that were reported by different people. In addition, although spies or undercover agents have often engaged in exaggeration, they have traditionally been hesitant to fabricate reports "because he would never be the only spy available . . . and his information could often be checked."[37] By the end of McParlan's undercover role there were numerous Pinkerton's operatives in the region, including Linden, so he would not have been certain if lies in his reports would be spotted.[38]

There are, unfortunately, numerous reports missing, and that they do not cover some significant periods of McParlan's investigation has encouraged the conspiratorial notions that he and Linden let murders proceed in order to obtain evidence of capital crimes, allowing them to eliminate the Molly Maguires. More than Linden, however, McParlan stands square in the midst of these theories, for which he has been cast as a treacherous informer who, without the slightest remorse, accepted payment to betray his "kind," making him worse than the murderers themselves.[39]

This portrayal is difficult to accept for a number of reasons. First, despite the underlying implication, the Molly Maguires were not more worthy of compassion and pity than the men who were killed in cold blood because of agreements between bodymasters. Those instigating and carrying out the murders and other outrages were not heroes—that role could more safely be ascribed to Siney and those who stood with him in the WBA, working for the betterment of the miners via a peaceful solution. In addition, as previously noted, there *is* no proof that McParlan received any special payment for his testimony.

Moreover, although McParlan testified against those in whose houses he had stayed and at whose tables he had eaten, he was bearing witness against men who had committed capital crimes. Just because he carried out his civic and professional duty does not mean that it was a decision he took lightly or that he did so without a sense of remorse or personal unfaithfulness. Further, to demonize him for his actions is not only to condemn the thousands of law officers who have contributed to a safer society by performing dangerous and valuable roles as undercover agents but to make the argument that McParlan would have been a better individual had he simply engaged in the supposedly lesser of the two offenses: murdering those engaged in such crimes rather than testifying against them in court. This is self-evidently ludicrous.

Pinkerton had never wanted McParlan to testify in the first place, in order to preserve his usefulness as an operative. As it turned out, McParlan's lengthy trial appearances made him one of America's most recognizable heroes, but they did not end his career of undercover and detective work. They did, however, force him to disappear from the public eye for some time afterward.

It seems unlikely that there was anyone who held McParlan in higher esteem than Allan Pinkerton. When the detective entered the anthracite region, Pinkerton's agency was struggling financially. By the time McParlan completed his assignment, not only had his exploits helped stabilize its economic fortunes, they had given the agency a glowing worldwide reputation. Despite the ongoing economic depression, which lasted until 1879,[40] Pinkerton's Chicago and New York offices had turned the corner, and it was in no small part due to McParlan's reputation.

When the thirty-three-year-old McParlan left Pottsville for the final time, the strain of so many months of testifying had triggered some of the stress-related physical complaints from which he had been suffering on and off for the previous few years. He needed a period for rest and recovery—a considerable amount of it. Almost immediately, he was taken to Allan Pinkerton's Larch Farm,[41] where, still fearful of assassination, his mind must have been eased by the manned guardhouse at each of the property's three entrances.[42]

After a few months of rest, the detective traveled to Ireland to visit his family, remaining "abroad until such a time as his health was restored."[43] One can only speculate how the wandering son was received, knowing the Irish attitude toward informers. A man who claimed to "know 'Jimmy,' as his friends call him, well," wrote in a widely published newspaper article: "From the vast body of Irish people he is virtually ostracized. 'He is an informer.' That settles it with his race."[44]

About a century later, Patrick Campbell was told by McParlan's elderly niece, then living in the "old McParland homestead" that had been passed to her from her father, McParlan's eldest brother: "He was a very brave man. . . . We were always proud of him here."[45] However, according to Irish local historians, it is unlikely that such pride would have extended outside of his immediate family—even if it existed within it—nor could they have been outwardly supportive without running the risk of alienating the surrounding community.[46]

One of the mysteries about McParlan's relations with his family is raised by his father's will, in which James was one of only two children not mentioned.[47] His father, Eneas, left his lands to his eldest and youngest sons,

Patrick and Henry, who had continued to farm them. Eneas's son Michael, a bootmaker in nearby Markethill, and three of his daughters, Rose Anne, Kate, and Eliza Jane, also received varying sums. Four of his children—John, Charles, Edward, and Teresa—each received "the sum of 2 shillings and six pence." All four had left Ireland—the two younger lads in 1876 to join their brother, and John and Teresa later, after having married—and the small sum can easily be perceived as a loving acknowledgment of his children who had gone on to better lives.[48]

But what of the two who were not mentioned in their father's will? These were the first to leave Ireland: Frank, who had settled in New Zealand, where he was married in 1868, and James. Were they left out because they were the first to leave? One would not think so, because youngsters were encouraged to go abroad for a better life. Were they excluded because they did not send funds back to those remaining in the old country, as had been expected? Or did their father simply feel that they were better off than the others and needed no token gesture? There is also the possibility that James was excluded due to his undercover role. It is impossible to know, but what it demonstrates is the risk McParlan took in fighting the Molly Maguires: exclusion from his people, and perhaps from his very own family.

Before the detective returned to Ireland, Charles and Edward—using versions of their mother's maiden name—left Pinkerton's for positions with the Philadelphia and Reading Coal and Iron Company. Charles worked in a company store in Pottsville, where he would meet both his first and second wives. Edward was at the East Norwegian Colliery, where McParlan had earlier investigated a fire. The detective wrote to Gowen that he was unhappy with the amount that Edward was being paid, but that when he mentioned it to General Pleasants, he had been told that if it weren't for him the pair would not even be employed, as "there was no necessity for them whatsoever."[49]

McParlan's brothers were not the only people receiving special treatment from the Reading. In March 1877, Butler, who had turned state's evidence, was given a job at a colliery under a new name. Within a week and a half, the hire proved a mistake. "I had arranged for Patrick Butler to have steady work at our best colliery," Pleasants wrote to Franklin. "[T]he difficulty is that Patrick Butler wants good pay and light work. . . . [H]e evidently expected a 'soft thing' from the company."[50] Such an attitude did not disturb Franklin, who subsequently employed Butler. In court, Butler later denied that he was a detective but admitted that "I did just anything going around. I told him what was going on."[51]

The Reading also provided employ to Muff Lawler at the Indian Ridge shaft—where McParlan had done his first stint—and to Frank McAndrew, about whom Gowen noted, "You will remember that this man is the one who saved McParlan's life, and I think it no more than justice that he should have some work in our service."[52] Conversely, despite his attempts to get a job via Gowen, Pleasants, and even Kaercher, Kerrigan found himself "in a reduced condition at present myself & family, and no prospect of any supper."[53] He and his family were eventually resettled in Virginia, where he held a position as a fireman with a railroad.

Other Molly Maguires did not find such forgiveness. "Mr Linden is at the present time in Nevada hunting up some of the fugitive Mollies, as we have strong reasons to believe they are there," Franklin wrote to Kaercher.[54] But despite a flood of claimed sightings, the most wanted men continued to elude capture. Friday O'Donnell and James McAllister were reported near Montreal in September 1876, but two months later the same source indicated that they had reached Ireland.[55]

The next year O'Donnell was reported in Salt Lake City. Two Coal and Iron Police who claimed they knew him were sent to pick him up, and they brought a man back to Chicago. He turned out to be James Dugan, who had known McParlan so well that the detective had served as his second in a prizefight. Dugan was released, and it was not for three decades that McParlan learned that O'Donnell, under the name James McDonald, had worked for years at the Daly West Mine in Park City, Utah. Having grown a full beard, he proved impossible to identify but "was always regarded there as a very harmless man, earned good wages and spent all he earned, and did not have a dollar when he died," around 1905.[56]

Hurley, too, remained at large, but one of the strangest stories came from a man who was actually in prison. About three weeks before he was hanged, James Roarity gave an interview to Tom Fielders of the *Daily Herald*. "I don't believe that McParlan was ever a detective until Kerrigan squealed and I am not the only one," Roarity stated mysteriously. He went on to say that: "McParlan wrote a letter, telling me to clear out. . . . [W]hen I got it I wouldn't do anything of the kind, because I knew that there was nothing that I had done for which I could be punished. . . . Some days before I was arrested a man came to me and told me . . . there was danger for me in staying, but I laughed and said I wouldn't go because no man could prove anything against me. . . . I little thought fifteen months ago that today I would have the halter around my neck."[57]

The entire interview is perplexing. Was Roarity being honest, and, if so, what did he mean about McParlan not being a detective until Kerrigan turned state's evidence? Why would McParlan send a note to him? Did he know that Roarity was not guilty and wanted him to escape? If so, why did he not give different testimony at the trial? There are no certain answers. This kind of doubt would continue throughout McParlan's life and work, as in the ensuing years he once again found himself in an undercover role, and later still he was able once more to bask in the fame of being America's greatest detective.

CHAPTER 12

✦

A NEW LIFE

The 1880s was a decade of upheaval and confrontation throughout the United States, and nowhere saw more change, more unrest, and more violence than the territories west of the Mississippi River, which were in a state of constant expansion. Railroad entrepreneurs, mining magnates, industrialists, and livestock ranchers accumulated almost unimaginable wealth and holdings, while others less fortunate—including displaced Native Americans, Chinese immigrants, and followers of the Mormon Church—faced punitive social legislation, economic sanctions, and widespread public prejudice.[1] Whole new regions were opened up, settled, and brought into the Union. Cattle being driven to market replaced the disappearing buffalo as the most numerous creatures on the plains. Workers joined together in record numbers to gain or protect their rights. Bloodshed was rampant, from racist riots in Wyoming and Washington to violent labor strikes and demonstrations in Kansas and Chicago to gunslinging killers on both sides of the law. In a nine-month period, beginning midway through 1881, Billy the Kid was shot dead in New Mexico; the Earp brothers and Doc Holliday gunned down three members of the Clanton gang near the O.K. Corral in Tombstone, Arizona; and Jesse James was killed by Bob Ford in St. Joseph, Missouri.[2]

Pinkerton's National Detective Agency was connected in one way or another with virtually all of these events. Building on its success in the anthracite region, during this decade Pinkerton's began providing services to more diverse and greater numbers of big businesses—particularly railroad and mining companies, heavy industry, and the large ranching community—as well as to local governments. Certainly hunting down criminals continued to play a major role in Pinkerton's income and image, but antiunion activities, as well as protection against and suppression of strike actions, became increasingly important. So well-known did the agency become for these activities that detectives and private police in general—and there was a large number of such organizations, as by 1892 Chicago and New York each had more than twenty "detective agencies"³—began to be generically labeled "Pinkertons."

No Pinkerton's operative, or member of any other investigative outfit, was more deeply involved in tracking down villains and fighting to subvert the new and growing unions than the country's most famous detective, James McParlan. In fact, his investigations mirrored in their way the entire development of the criminal-justice system of the Old West.

McParlan did not immediately just jump back onto the national scene after he left Schuylkill County, however. Despite the time he spent at Larch Farm and with his family, he did not make a quick physical recovery. In the autumn of 1879, a friend wrote that he still was "broken up badly. The excitement, great labor, poisonous mine gases, and more poisonous miners' whisky or 'mountain dew' he was compelled to freely use and distribute . . . nearly wrecked him. At one time his eyesight was despaired of." He also suffered in other ways. The writer continued: "Not all the wealth on earth would induce McParlan to again go through what he has. . . . I believe he regrets it. . . . Never a more honest, upright and sincere man lived. But this is a load that he carries. No man can contemplate a score of scaffolds and a score of souls plunged into eternity through his instrumentality free from a regret which must be eternal."⁴

McParlan's experiences had, in some ways, made a new man of him, one appropriate for the tasks his career would require in the future. "He was formerly simply 'a broth of a boy,' kind-hearted, impulsive, not ignorant, but what is termed quick-witted, and that's all," the friend wrote, noting that if he had not worked for Pinkerton's, "he would have remained to this day what he was before, and what I believe he often wishes he still was—a sort of a porter or man of all work about stores and wholesale houses. But now he is a man of brains and intellect. . . . Intellectually, in experience, in thought, motive and purpose, he has virtually been recreated."⁵

Changes were occurring in the detective's personal life as well. At some point in the mid-1870s his relatives in Ireland added a "d" to the end of the family name—"McParland." In fact, his brother Frank had been using the new spelling since at least 1868, when he married Margaret Kennedy in New Zealand.⁶ By 1879, the Pinkerton's operative had added a final "d" to his name as well.

An even bigger change took place on August 26, 1879, at St. Joseph Church in Chicago—which had reopened the previous year, having been rebuilt following the great fire—when the thirty-five-year-old McParland married Mary Ann Fitzgerald, age nineteen, following which they went to Larch Farm for their honeymoon.⁷ The marriage was a political coup, because Mary Ann was the daughter of James Fitzgerald, the captain of Pinkerton's Preventive Police in Chicago.[8]

McParland had courted Mary Ann while still assigned to the Philadelphia office, where major changes were occurring. In the spring of 1878, Franklin—citing his role with the Molly Maguires—had pressed for a 50 percent pay increase. Unlike those in Chicago and New York, however, the Philadelphia office had not been a financial success, and Pinkerton was not pleased by the request, writing to Bangs that "I beg him [Franklin] to remember that first the praise, honor and glory of breaking up the MM's belongs to MacParlan."[9] Franklin's continued demands—reportedly at the insistence of his wife, who annoyed Pinkerton—were the final straw for the principal, who had long been concerned about Franklin's drinking, which had led to his earlier dismissal from the Philadelphia police.[10] In late 1878, Franklin was replaced by Linden.[11]

With his good friend in charge, leaving Philadelphia was not something McParland would have done without serious thought. This was particularly true as his brothers left the Reading and moved to the Philadelphia area, both working as shoemakers, the same profession as their older brother Michael in Ireland. Charles, going under the surname Laughlin, a variation of their mother's maiden name, began operating a shoe store in Conshohocken, while Edward did the same in Philadelphia proper, where he used another variation of her maiden name: Loughren.[12]

Nevertheless, soon after his marriage, McParland transferred to Chicago.[13] Then, in March 1880, his father-in-law died suddenly of typhoid fever,[14] and McParland—appointed administrator of the estate and guardian of Mary Ann's sixteen-year-old sister Margaret—took over Fitzgerald's family and financial responsibilities. This was not easy, because Fitzgerald left behind not only the two daughters and his son Edward—a member of Pinkerton's Preventive Police—but his widow, Bridget, the stepmother to the three children, with whom she was not popular. Fitzgerald's financial holdings included four valuable lots of property stretching along Menominee (later changed to Menomonee) Street between Larrabee and Hurlbut (now Cleveland) in the well-to-do area of Lincoln Park in northern Chicago.

By summer Bridget had left the family home and relinquished her widow's inheritance and rights to the property in exchange for eleven hundred dollars paid by Edward and Mary Ann out of their share of their father's insurance policy.[15] Meanwhile, McParland, his wife, and her two siblings were joined at 146 Menominee by two girls, Jenny and Lilly Robertson—aged twelve and five—whose father, David Robertson, was a Scottish immigrant employed as chief clerk by Pinkerton's. Robertson was not listed as living in Chicago in the Tenth U.S. Census that summer, although he was in that year's city directory.[16] This was likely because he was away on an assignment; although a clerk, he was in the process of shifting to more of an operational position.[17] Always politically aware, McParland undoubtedly took in the children because he was currying favor with another rising star. Four years later Robertson became an assistant superintendent, and he was later promoted to superintendent, and then assistant general superintendent for the division of Pinkerton's covering the center of America.[18]

For a while it looked like the household would expand even further. In April 1881, Mary Ann gave birth to the couple's first daughter, Mary, only for the baby to die five hours later due to a congenital defect exacerbated by atelectasis (collapse of a lung).[19]

In the midst of these changes and traumas, McParland was required to submit an agency form entitled History of Detectives, in which he detailed his background. The supplement to the form, completed by Chicago superintendent Frank Warner, gives an intriguing look at how the famous operative was seen by his superiors, including his strengths and weaknesses:

General deportment and appearance	Genteel Irishman
Classes of society can become readily adapted to; whether higher or laboring class, sporting men or thieves	Both
Class of "Roper"; whether makes acquaintance easily, and ability to obtain friendship and confidence	Good
Class of "Shadow"	Not good
Ability for making investigations	Good
Knowledge of criminals	Not good
Whether Moderate in expenditures or inclined to be extravagant	Medium
Impulsive or cautious	Impulsive
Determined or timid	Determined
Secretive or talkative	Talkative
Self-reliance and ability to originate a plan of operations beyond instructions	Good
Failings to be guarded against	Operating too fast[20]

The report is as interesting for what it says about the attitudes at Pinkerton's as what it records about McParland. To the hierarchy of the agency, "Genteel"— refined or well-mannered—differentiated McParland from the stereotype it long had held of the common Irishman: the low-class, hard-drinking, undesirable thug personified by some of the men in the Molly Maguires. The report also shows that McParland was not particularly good at one of the basic skills of being a spy—"shadowing," or tailing a suspect—and that he clearly was not guarded enough, as he was listed as both "impulsive" and "talkative."

In his remarks, Warner noted that "whilst in Philadelphia Agency [while undercover] he acquired the habit of excessive drinking. He reformed however and married previous to joining Chicago Agency. He is suspected of having fallen from grace since employed here, but no harm resulted."[21] The abstemious Pinkerton abhorred drinking, and in 1875 almost fired even Bangs for being intoxicated on the street.[22] It is almost certain that McParland's "fall from grace"—a term used by those in the temperance movement—referred to his heavy drinking, which, although curtailed again, is rumored to have reappeared on and off for the rest of his life.

Drinking was probably not the only thing about which McParland was at odds with his supervisors. He showed throughout his career that he regularly thought he knew best about anything in which he was involved, and it must have been difficult for Warner and the assistant superintendents to have as a subordinate the country's most famous detective, who was also a favorite of Pinkerton. In 1882 the conflict apparently escalated to a point where McParland was ready to leave the agency, as he and his brother Charles—who had joined James and Mary Ann in the cottage on Menomonee and gone back to using the name McParland—established a furniture business. However, the new enterprise quickly proved unsuccessful, so McParland remained while Charles returned to shoemaking.[23]

Shortly thereafter, McParland and Mary Ann welcomed a second daughter, named Kate on her birth certificate, but generally called Kittie.[24] But all was not well on the family front. In February 1882, two months before Kittie's birth, Mary Ann's sister Margaret turned eighteen and, six days later, for a small sum of money, she conveyed to her sister her one-third interest in the real estate their father had left them.[25] This gave sole ownership to McParland and Mary Ann, who had previously paid Edward $980 for his part of the property. Although Margaret had reached her majority, McParland did not make his final report as guardian until May 25, thereby, in effect, continuing in that role in the interim. In June, Margaret married Peter Larkin, a fireman who moved in with the McParlands.[26]

Likely encouraged by her husband, Margaret soon filed suit in Cook County Circuit Court against McParland, Mary Ann, Charles, and Michael J. Dunne and Conrad L. Niehoff (the last two holding liens on the property) to return her former share of the property, which had proved to be worth considerably more than what had been paid for it. After bitter proceedings, the court found on Margaret's behalf, but rather than declaring the transfer deed void, referred the matter to a "special master" to "ascertain the value of the land and improvements, and the amount of the encumbrances, and to take an account of rents and taxes" prior to making a final decree.[27] There the matter lay fallow, as, for several years, no report from the master was received. When McParland and the others appealed the decision, the Illinois Supreme Court ruled that the appeal itself must be dismissed, as no final decree had been entered due to the absence of the master's report, and without such a decree, there was no decision that could be appealed.[28]

The special master, forced by the criticism implicit in this ruling, then submitted his findings, and the Circuit Court entered a final decree on behalf of Margaret. Once again, McParland and the others appealed, but in 1895, in what is considered a classic judgment, the Illinois Supreme Court affirmed the lower court's decision. Although the final decree would not have hugely impacted McParland financially or personally—by that time he had remarried and moved to Denver—its findings are important in assessing his ethics.

The Supreme Court—having indicated that unless the influence of the guardian upon a ward has ceased, "such transactions are always to be regarded with suspicion"[29]—concluded that: "the ward was a female, barely past the age of 18 years, practically without knowledge or experience in business affairs. The peculiar interests of the guardian were opposed to her own. . . . The ward was induced to execute a deed, prepared by the guardian for her signature, for an inadequate consideration, greatly less than the real value of her interest."[30] Under such circumstances, the court noted, it was not necessary to prove intentional fraud but only that the guardian "gained some advantage by the transaction with his ward" in order to "throw the burden of proving good faith and absence of influence . . . upon the guardian. This we are not prepared, after the most careful consideration of the evidence, to say has been done, and the decree . . . setting aside the deed must be affirmed."[31]

In essence, the courts at both levels believed that the McParlands, while standing "in loco parentis to the minor" and supposedly caring "for her as though she was their child,"[32] had taken advantage of Margaret's naïveté to better their personal economic situation at her expense. This is a significant assessment of McParland's ethics. During the Molly Maguire trials he had been attacked as corrupt and unscrupulous, but his honor was equally vehemently defended. However, in these much less public legal proceedings, his principles and morality once again were questioned, and this time they seem to have been shown wanting.

Throughout his career McParland had always been blessed with the strong support of both Pinkerton and Bangs, the agency's general superintendent. That changed in September 1883, when Bangs died suddenly in Roselle, New Jersey.[33] The following July, Pinkerton himself passed away.[34] These losses might have inspired McParland to consider an alternative career, as in the 1885 Chicago directory he was not listed as a detective, as usual, but as a "commercial traveler."[35] Of course, that might simply mean that he had actually gone undercover again, or that he was taking on additional jobs. But what *can* be stated with certainty is that even if he had any serious thoughts about leaving the agency, they were soon set aside due to the persuasion of Pinkerton's sons, both of whom were as positive about McParland as their father had been.

The year after Pinkerton died, McParland received an even tougher personal blow. On August 10, 1885, having suffered from consumption for an extended period, Mary Ann died at the age of twenty-four, leaving him a widower with a three-year-old daughter.[36] In a state of extreme emotional distress, McParland was saved by an event that occurred only three days later and forced him to think about work rather than just his sorrow.

Around 2:00 A.M. on August 13, the residents of Columbus, Kansas, were woken "by a terrific explosion which shook every building in the town . . . The court house vault, a brick structure attached to the main building, and by its peculiar construction has long been dubbed the court house 'bake oven,' was found to be blown to atoms. . . . It is a wreck that would put to shame the best cyclone invented, as records and papers are torn to shreds, the great vault door blown out and the accumulation of years of the county's valuable books totally destroyed."[37]

Pinkerton's was brought in to discover the perpetrators. Leaving Kittie with Charles and his brother's new wife (also named Mary Ann), McParland proceeded to Columbus, located in the volatile southeast corner of Kansas, only thirteen miles from both its formerly hostile neighbor Missouri and the Indian Territory that would become Oklahoma. McParland's suspicions quickly fell on two men, Richard Lawton and C. L. Woodruff, whose firm—normally engaged in real estate, insurance, and moneylending—had been making abstracts of the records that had been destroyed, suggesting to the detective that the crime could have been not just for gain but to cover up a misdeed.[38]

While McParland was investigating, the records that had survived the explosion were targeted once again. They had been moved into the Register of Deed's office in a building near the courthouse, and on an extremely cold night in January 1886, a saddle and harness maker who slept above his shop, near the rear of the office, was awoken by smoke. He broke down the door to the office to find flames consuming the records, which had been doused with coal oil. Although he contained the fire, many more volumes were damaged.[39]

About three weeks later McParland arrested nine men, who were charged with "making forged mortgages, forged deeds, and the execution of forged papers" in order to cover up fraudulent land transactions.[40] Two of them—Lawton and Luther Archer—were also charged with arson. McParland worked a confession from Archer,[41] and then convinced one of the others to turn state's evidence. Most of the accused were convicted, but Lawton was pronounced physically unable to go to trial. Immediately after he was released from jail on bond, he bolted. His bondsman again sought out Pinkerton's, and McParland, finding that Lawton had traveled to Cincinnati, assigned an operative named Greenfield to shadow him. On the morning of June 24, Lawton was found dead in his bed, having, according to the coroner's report, died from "paralysis of the heart resulting from fatty degeneration and accelerated by mental depression consequent on business complications."[42]

A month later McParland was brought back into the case when rumors surfaced that Lawton had faked his death. The detective accompanied several Columbus representatives to Lawton's burial site in Greenville, Ohio, so that they might disinter and identify the body.[43]

The visits to Columbus were not the Great Detective's only reasons for being in southeast Kansas. In March 1886, while he was still involved in Columbus, the Knights of Labor—the country's largest union, which included railroad machinists, trackmen, switchmen, car repairers, engine wipers, coach cleaners, and baggage and freight handlers—went on strike against the Southwest Railroad System controlled by Jay Gould. Perhaps the most reviled and ruthless commercial entrepreneur of the Gilded Age, Gould was also a financial and business genius[44] who at times controlled not only the Western Union Telegraph Company, *The World* newspaper of New York (which he later sold to Joseph Pulitzer), and the elevated railways of New York City, but the largest railroad network in the country, including the Texas & Pacific; the Missouri

Pacific; the International & Great Northern; the Wabash, St. Louis & Pacific; the St. Louis & Iron Mountain; and the Missouri, Kansas & Texas railroads. At its height, the system contained more than fifteen thousand miles of track, making it the biggest transportation structure in Texas, Arkansas, Missouri, the Indian Territory, and Kansas, while also extending into Louisiana, Nebraska, Colorado, and Illinois.[45]

The strike—set off when C.A. Hall, a carpenter in Marshall, Texas, was dismissed after attending a meeting of his local union, despite having received permission—quickly spread throughout Gould's system,[46] with the early days marked by strikers taking over shops and workhouses and doctoring the engines, "making them unfit for service until the missing parts are returned or new ones made."[47] The rail companies quickly employed detectives from both the Furlong Secret Service Company and Pinkerton's. One of these was McParland, because one of the flashpoints in the strike was Parsons, Kansas, an important railroad junction with a major car repair shop only thirty-five miles northwest of Columbus.

McParland quickly discovered that Parsons, the largest city of Labette County, was no place for the weak and timid. In the heart of southeast Kansas, it was located in a region that had a remarkable history of mayhem.[48] The settlers had experienced conflict with the Cherokee and Osage Indians, been a part of the violence between the "free-soil" and proslavery advocates that created "Bleeding Kansas," and had seen the murder and pillage of guerrilla warfare during the Civil War. Many of those ruffians found uncontrolled violence suited their temperament in the postwar years, so they continued that life in what was as unbridled a region as any farther west. In the early 1870s western Labette County was the home to the Benders, four serial killers whose well-placed homestead allowed them to rob and murder travelers lured in to what seemed to be a store and inn. The railroads brought their own brand of thieves and outlaws to Labette County, as did the Shawnee Trail, one of the great cattle trails from Texas to Kansas.[49]

The rampant violence of the area is demonstrated by a few headlines from a Parsons newspaper in the first half of 1886:

"Epps in Eternity—The Murderer of Farmer Dobson Taken from Jail and Hanged"

"A Destroyer of Domestic Happiness Shot Down on the Public Streets"

"Graham, the Wife-Murderer, Pays the Penalty for His Crime—
He Is Taken From Jail by a Mounted Mob and Hanged to the
Limb of a Tree"

"A Brute's Fate—Arrested for an Outrage and Shot by an
Injured Neighbor"

"Eli Owens Forcibly Taken from Jail, Severely Pummelled and
Left to Ornament a Lonely Tree"[50]

Yet all this bloodshed was nothing compared to what was allegedly happening in the center of Parsons.[51] At that time, a bloodthirsty killer named Jacob McLaughlin owned the sixty-room Grand Central Hotel in Parsons. Men moving along the rails or returning from the cattle sales in Kansas City were entertained there with liquor (which had been constitutionally prohibited in Kansas in 1881), women, gambling, or anything else they wanted. Hopefully they enjoyed it, because afterward, unable to defend themselves in their drunken stupors, they were "chloroformed and robbed" and their bodies "dropped into the basement for burial," filling up the vast vault beneath the structure to such an extent that McLaughlin had to import more than three feet of earth to cover the corpses. In another basement room "McLaughlin, and a man who was said to be a big eastern detective used to sell boot-leg whiskey and manufacture counterfeit money." And that mysterious detective, it was written, was none other than James McParland, "wielding the dagger of assassination in the subterranean tunnels . . . the infamous, heartless detective [who] grinned with delight and gloried in his crime."

One might ask how this astounding transformation from detective to butcher and purveyor of pure evil had occurred. And the answer, of course, is that it hadn't. The author of the defamatory claims was George Shoaf, a sensational journalist who wrote for *Appeal to Reason*, a weekly socialist newspaper published in Girard, Kansas.[52] Shoaf had a passionate hatred for McParland, whom he saw as the epitome of the capitalist abuse of labor, and he and two colleagues at *Appeal to Reason*—Walter Hurt and P. M. Eastwood—launched an all-out smear-campaign against him.[53] This included such pettiness as always referring to him as "McPartland," an effort to link the detective in the reader's mind to a much publicized criminal case in which an ex-convict named James McPartland—known by the police as Sharkey the Brute—brutally murdered a woman in front of her bedridden husband.[54]

In a series of outrageous yarns, Shoaf created a story of McParland's involvement at McLaughlin's Grand Central Hotel, including cleverly expanding their supposed relationship to include more illegal and immoral activities by McParland. Unfortunately, even though there is no indication of any truth in Shoaf's stories, they have occasionally been accepted as accurate.[55]

On the other hand, there is little dispute that McLaughlin was a bad, bad character.[56] In the summer of 1885, he and his associate Wash Bercaw were fined for violation of the Kansas liquor prohibition. When they refused to pay they were put in the county jail in Oswego, where another inmate, Frank P. Myers, was awaiting trial for stealing a span of mules. McLaughlin and Bercaw were eventually released on bail, but Myers yo-yoed in and out. In July, the three men broke out, supposedly forcing Myers to accompany them; the next morning, he gave himself up. Myers escaped again later that month but was quickly caught. Then, in early August, he yet again went missing—"this time singularly not a lock, door, or bar was broken, and his cell was locked as securely as it was the night before and it would have required the unlocking of five locks to open it."[57] The following week boys swimming in the Neosho River found his body, and an autopsy confirmed he had been killed before being thrown into the water.

The next spring, McLaughlin and Bercaw were charged "with taking Myers from the Oswego jail ... and bringing him to Parsons and strangling him to death."[58] At a preliminary hearing, Frank and George Davis, brothers who had been in the jail at the time, stated that McLaughlin and Bercaw took Myers out of his cell, at which point McLaughlin said: "If you boys say anything about this or tell [jailor] Charlie Wooden your necks will be stretched before morning. We are only taking Myers out to set him free."[59] Further testimony from Mrs. Myers indicated that she saw the clothes Myers had on when he was in jail being worn by bus driver Frank Goultrie, who, in turn, reported that he had obtained them from McLaughlin.

When McLaughlin went on trial in June 1886, however, the stories had changed. Not only did Goultrie's brother declare that he had bought the clothes and given them to Frank, but the Davis boys suddenly remembered things differently, claiming that their earlier statements were not true. Questioned intensely, George Davis broke down on the stand and stated "that E.C. Ward, the defendant's attorney, had agreed to pay him two hundred dollars if he would go on the witness stand and swear that his former statement was a lie. . . . The most singular part of the affair is that Davis claims that his first statement was actually false, but that he was to get the two hundred dollars for admitting that it was untrue instead of standing up and insisting that it was true."[60] The next day, McLaughlin was found not guilty, and the charges against Bercaw were dismissed.

That was not the end of the matter, however. The judge—commenting, "I never saw such unblushing and shameful perjury as has been flaunted in my face during the past few days"[61]—appointed a committee to investigate the shenanigans since the preliminary hearing. The Davis brothers were later found guilty of perjury and sent to state prison, and Ward was disbarred.[62]

And this is where the accounts of Shoaf and Eastwood incorporated claims that were unconfirmed by any court or newspaper records. First, Shoaf wrote, "Myers was in possession of information about McLaughlin which the latter was afraid would be sprung during some pivotal case.... McLaughlin determined to send the fellow to ... whence no traveler ever returns and so be rid of the nuisance."[63]

Further: "McPartland's principal business was to shield ... McLaughlin from punishment for innumerable crimes and misdemeanors ranging in import from gambling, counterfeiting and violation of the state liquor laws to wholesale robbery and cold-blooded murder. In manufacturing evidence to clear McLaughlin from one charge of murder, McPartland was the direct cause of ruining E.C. Ward ... and, as a result of McPartland's bribery, two brothers, Frank and George Davis, were sent to the penitentiary ... But McPartland's manufactured evidence cleared McLaughlin."[64]

What a story! But it went strictly against the evidence of W. B. Glass and Albert A. Osgood—two of the three members of the committee appointed to investigate. They interviewed Ward, George Davis, Kate McLaughlin, and others, and found that "said testimony, which said Davis said he would and agreed to give was then written down by Ward in the form of an affidavit, which was subscribed by said Davis, and was sworn to by him before R.D. Talbot, a justice of the peace of this county, which affidavit said E.C. Ward retained in his possession." They concluded that Ward was primarily at fault for the situation and that "information [should] be filed against him for practices unbecoming a gentleman and unworthy of an attorney, with a view of disbarring him from the practice of the profession."[65] Nowhere did their report mention—or hint at—McParland.

Nor did Shoaf truly address the most obvious questions his story raised: Why would McParland be involved with McLaughlin in the first place? And wasn't he actually in Parsons to investigate aspects of the railroad strike? But

Shoaf would have just laughed, and answered that all one needed to know about McParland was in his other articles. "It is known that he has been instrumental in doing away with heirs-apparent to large fortunes," he had written, for example. "He has put women beneath the ground at the instigation of their paramours. It is whispered that he has officiated at the birth of several still-born babes in the city of Denver, and that today he levies tribute upon the sons of wealthy men as the price of keeping their secrets ... amidst all this holocaust of crime and murder, in which he has been an active participant, enough evidence ... has leaked through his guarded bounds of secrecy to stamp him the greatest and most horrible Gorgon of this monster-bearing age."[66]

Those who believed such things of McParland would have been doubly horrified to know that he was soon to be joined at Pinkerton's by—according to Shoaf's term—"Satan's spawn," the man who, for the next two decades, would be the Great Detective's chief troubleshooter.

CHAPTER 13

◆━◆━◆

A NEW DETECTIVE IN TOWN

When McParland returned to Chicago from Kansas, his move was mirrored by that of a small, wiry, extremely confident young Texan. His name was Charles Angelo Siringo, and it would not be long before he crossed paths with McParland. Siringo—whom William Pinkerton once claimed "is as tough as a pine knot and I never knew a man of his size who can endure as much hardship as he does"[1]—would become McParland's closest associate, as their careers were intertwined for more than twenty years.

Charlie Siringo was born on the Matagorda Peninsula on the east coast of Texas on February 7, 1855.[2] His father, an Italian immigrant, died when young Siringo was only a year old, leaving him and his two-year-old sister Catherine to be raised by their Irish mother, Bridgit. He grew up in the region of the Texas coastal plain, with many of his early memories coming from the hard times of the Civil War, including an occupation by the Union army. In 1867, age twelve, Siringo took a job on a ranch as an apprentice cowboy. It was a fateful move, because he was becoming part of a new epoch in American history—that of the cowboy of the Old West.

At the end of the Civil War, much of Texas was impoverished, with few economic assets other than a seemingly endless supply of longhorn cattle. Despite the growing demand for beef, it was extremely expensive to transport cattle by rail from Texas, and Missouri and Kansas had issued quarantine closures to prevent Texas cattle from bringing in ticks that carried the disease known as Texas fever, which was fatal for Midwestern cattle.[3]

It took the vision of Joseph G. McCoy of Illinois to resolve the problem and create a marketing revolution. In the spring of 1867 he convinced officials of the Kansas Pacific Railroad to build a spur to the tiny town of Abilene, Kansas—west of the quarantine area—where he built stockyards, loading stations, and other facilities, thus creating a "cattle hub": a station to receive

Texas cattle and send them east far more cheaply than had hitherto been possible. McCoy advertised widely in Texas, and soon cattle were driven north to Abilene, up what would become known as the Chisholm Trail. By the end of the year McCoy had shipped thirty-five thousand head to eastern markets, and that number doubled each year until 1871, when it reached six hundred thousand.[4]

The new procedure was a financial bonanza for ranchers, trailing contractors, cowboys, and shippers, particularly because when longhorns were able to graze and drink their fill while traveling ten to twelve miles a day, they actually gained weight on the trail. Equally as important, it "spawned a new, distinct type of American character—a strong, resourceful man on horseback who took trouble in his stride and changed the face of the prairie."[5]

No one was more representative of this new breed than Siringo, although his early experience was interrupted midway through 1867, when he nearly died from typhoid fever. Shortly thereafter, his mother fell prey to an age-old con, when she married a man who promptly squandered her savings and the proceeds from the sale of her land on alcohol before abandoning her and Catherine in Illinois. A short while later, Bridgit moved to St. Louis, but somehow Charlie did not receive her new address, and he spent much of the next two years traveling on the Mississippi, working in hotels, on farms, on riverboats, and in packing houses, all the while searching for his family.

Returning to Matagorda at the age of fifteen, Siringo took a job on Rancho Grande, a mammoth cattle and pony ranch owned by Abel "Shanghai" Pierce and his brother Jonathan.[6] The Pierces were among the few ranchers who delivered their own stock rather than hiring trailing contractors, but it was not until 1876 that Siringo finally helped drive twenty-five hundred head to Wichita, Kansas.

The next year, he took thirty-five hundred steers to Dodge City for the famous Texas cattleman George W. Littlefield. While there, Siringo and another cowboy were involved in a bust up with a group of buffalo hunters in the Lone Star Dancehall, which was managed by lawman Bat Masterson. In the midst of the fight Masterson, who was tending the bar, threw several beer glasses at Siringo, one of which "clipped [me] behind the right ear and didn't feel like a mother's kiss either."[7]

Soon thereafter, Siringo left behind those he derisively called "Kansas short horns" and helped drive twenty-five hundred steers south to the LX Ranch in the Texas Panhandle. After taking a job there, Siringo became friendly with another youngster, born Henry McCarty but known as William

Bonney, or Billy the Kid. Two years later Siringo led a group of men from the LX into the New Mexico Territory to recover several hundred cattle stolen by the Kid. While there they met Pat Garrett, the sheriff of Lincoln County, who was looking for volunteers to go after the Kid. A couple of Siringo's men obliged, but Siringo followed his employers' orders and collected the missing cattle. He returned to Texas in June 1881, within weeks of Garrett killing Billy the Kid at Fort Sumner, New Mexico.[8]

In 1883, David Beals, one of the owners of the LX, bought a farm near Caldwell, Kansas, so he could winter cow ponies there. Siringo was put in charge, and bought nearby property himself. Located three miles north of the Indian Territory, Caldwell was one of the last Kansas towns to serve as the destination for Texas cattle drives as the quarantine area moved west. But Siringo's mind eventually wandered to other things. In March 1884, soon after being ordered to bring some of the ponies back to the LX, he met a fifteen-year-old, black-eyed beauty named Mamie Lloyd. Six days later they were married, and Siringo then headed south with one hundred ponies.

By September Siringo was back in Caldwell, but when Beals asked him to bring more ponies south, he resigned to stay with his pregnant wife. He opened a tobacco store, which was so successful that he expanded it into an ice cream and oyster parlor. When a daughter, Viola, was born in 1885, he looked for other ways to make money and stumbled upon what would earn him his lasting reputation—writing autobiography. "No other cowboy ever talked about himself so much in print [but] few had more to talk about," the Texas historian J. Frank Dobie wrote.[9]

Siringo's first effort was his greatest. *A Texas Cow Boy, or Fifteen Years on the Hurricane Deck of a Spanish Pony*, appeared in the autumn of 1885, quickly sold out, and became arguably the most influential book ever written about the Old West. The first cowboy autobiography, it was written in an engaging, humorous, and at times sentimental style, while presenting a self-serving picture of a daring, clever, and outgoing young man. More importantly, it popularized the romantic image of the American cowboy, his work, character, aspirations, relationships, and love of whiskey, women, weapons, and his horse. It told of months-long cattle drives, hunting for missing steers, riding through the Indian Territory, and suffering from sweltering heat, dust storms, and freezing rain. It generated the popular image of the wild west based on Abilene, Dodge City, Wichita, and other Kansas towns where cowboys rubbed shoulders—and exchanged gunfire—with frontier lawmen like Bat Masterson, Wyatt Earp, and Wild Bill Hickok. And it placed forever in the

American psyche the great cattle trails from Texas to Kansas, especially the Chisholm Trail, which, before falling into disuse after 1884 due to new quarantine laws and miles of barbed wire, saw more than five million cattle and one million mustangs make the long journey north.

The immediate success of *A Texas Cow Boy* convinced Siringo to give up his shops and move to Chicago, where he could oversee the publication of a second edition. He had not been there long when a series of memorable events changed his life.

On Saturday, May 1, 1886, large numbers of workers rallied in support of demands for a national eight-hour workday, with more than forty thousand in Chicago participating in a general strike.[10] The next Monday, a confrontation between strikers and replacement workers at the McCormick Reaper Works in Chicago exploded into violence, and the police—assigned to protect the strikebreakers—shot into the crowd, killing between two and six people.

In response, local socialist and anarchist leaders organized a protest rally for the next evening at Haymarket Square (about two and a half miles from McParland's house). At 10:20, after several speakers had addressed a crowd that had dwindled from about fifteen hundred to six hundred as the night grew colder and rain threatened, approximately 180 police marched up from the Desplaines Street Police Station. When Police Captain William Ward ordered the remaining crowd to disperse, a bomb was thrown into the police ranks, killing officer Mathias Degan and fatally wounding several others. The police opened fire, with some of the crowd shooting back, most fleeing, and an undetermined number wounded. A final tally showed seven policemen killed and at least sixty injured.

Following a police investigation, eight men said to be anarchists were tried and found guilty of murder. Four were executed, three received lengthy prison sentences, and one committed suicide before his scheduled execution. Like the Molly Maguire trials, that of the Haymarket defendants has long been a focal point of arguments about injustices of the legal system and the oppression of the working classes.[11]

Siringo attended much of the trial, which lasted from June 21 to August 19. Living on Harrison, not far from Haymarket Square, he and Mamie had heard the explosion, and when he found out the next day what had occurred, he was horrified and "wanted to help stamp out this great Anarchist curse."[12]

The idea of being a detective had first been raised after a lecture given by a blind phrenologist in Caldwell in 1884.[13] After feeling the bumps on the heads of several others, the blind man "laid his hand on the top of my head and then said: 'Ladies and gentlemen, here is a mule's head.' When the laughter had subsided he explained that I had a large stubborn bump, hence was as stubborn as a mule. He then said I had a fine head for a newspaper editor, a fine stock raiser, or detective; that in any of these callings I would make a success."[14]

After some thought, Siringo applied to William Pinkerton, giving as references David Beals of the LX; James East, the Tascosa, Texas, sheriff; and Pat Garrett, who had killed Billy the Kid. Pinkerton told him that if the references came back positive they would hire him, and "give me a position in a new office which they were opening in Denver, Colo. He said they would need a cowboy detective there, as they figured on getting a lot of cattle work" and would want someone familiar with cattle, horses, and living and travelling on the open range.[15]

Siringo's first assignment—given by David Robertson, by then the Chicago superintendent—was "to watch the [Haymarket trial] jury, to see that lawyers for the defense did no 'monkey work' in the way of bribery."[16] Although he maintained a dislike of anarchists for the rest of his life, Siringo questioned the verdict's fairness: "I couldn't see the justice of sending Neebe to the pen. . . . The evidence was in Neebe's favor, except that he was running with a bad crowd." He also had mixed emotions about certain aspects of the trial's background: "A million dollars had been subscribed by the Citizens League to stamp out anarchy in Chicago, and no doubt much of it was used to corrupt justice. Still, the hanging of these anarchists had a good effect and was worth a million dollars to society."[17]

While Siringo was at the Haymarket trials, McParland was in Duluth, Minnesota, working under the name of James S. Mack. The previous year what was thought to be the richest vein of iron ore in the United States had been discovered in the square mile known as Section 30 in Township 63, Range 11 of the Vermilion Range, three miles east of Ely, Minnesota. By the end of 1886 thirty-one claims had been filed for it. One of the longest court battles in state history then began, due to the many claims, arguments for right of possession, and judgments overturned based upon conflicting state and federal laws.[18] Pinkerton's was hired by one set of claimants to obtain information. However, it would be half a dozen years before McParland actually testified.[19]

Meanwhile, one of the detective's old companions—Thomas Hurley—finally met his maker. As the killer of Gomer James and one of the shooters of

Bully Bill Thomas, Hurley had remained high on the Pinkerton's most wanted list for a decade. It had been rumored that he was in Ontario, Canada, where, under the name John Skivington, he worked as a laborer on the construction of the Third Welland Canal, between Port Dalhousie and Allanburg.[20] He left there for South America, but ended up instead in Texas, where Linden learned that he was going under the name of Thomas McGee.[21] Yet again, however, Hurley evaded capture, fleeing to Gunnison, Colorado, where he adopted the name Hugh McCabe.

Hurley thereafter worked in a mine at Baldwin, in Gunnison County, where he was considered a "tough customer" and "usually carried a long clasp dirk knife which he used to cut his plug tobacco."[22] One evening in August 1886, after watching a professional prize fight, several men got into a tussle, and a miner named Luke Curran had his stomach slit open by a sharp knife—he died within minutes. Three suspects were arrested, but knowing Hurley "was as dexterous with a knife as he was with his fists,"[23] the suspicions of the county sheriff fell on him—and they were confirmed when his knife was found covered with dried blood.

The sheriff of Gunnison County was Cyrus Wells "Doc" Shores, one of the most respected lawmen in the history of the West, who, in a law-enforcement career spanning more than thirty years, often worked as a special Pinkerton's operative, at times paired with Siringo. The story eventually went around that although the murderer was arrested as McCabe, on information from the East, the sheriff was able to identify him as Hurley. Taking him aside, the sheriff said, "Your time has come, Tom Hurley! McParland is on his way here to take you back to Pennsylvania."

"Who is McParland?" demanded Hurley.

"You used to know him as James McKenna."

No sooner had he heard the name than he slipped his hand under a mattress, and pulling out a razor, cut his throat from ear to ear. As he dropped dying to the floor, he said, "Mac will never get me alive."[24]

In fact, according to Shores, the reality was quite different, although still dramatic. At the time of Hurley's arrest the county jail was also occupied by the notorious cannibal and murderer Alfred Packer, who was awaiting a second trial for killing five men, after the verdict in the first trial had been overturned on appeal.[25] Hurley's preliminary hearing was held the same day that the jury was deliberating its verdict for Packer. When an indictment was returned for Hurley at the city hall, a crowd gathered, thinking to lynch him. Shores took Hurley by the arm, pulled out his revolver, and ran the gauntlet back to the jail, having to threaten to shoot those people trying to stop him. Once at the jail he locked Hurley in Packer's cell, while he took Packer to the courthouse to await the verdict. Fetched by the jailer shortly thereafter, Shores returned to the jail. "I found McCabe lying on his stomach in the front part of his cell. Blood was streaming across the iron floor in all directions," he later wrote. "I grabbed the fallen man by the shoulder and turned him on his side. Although accustomed to sights of violence, I shuddered as I looked down at his grotesquely dangling head, which was nearly severed from his body. Blood was spurting from a deep gash which extended nearly from ear to ear. His jugular vein had been cut, and he had bled to death within only a few minutes. He certainly knew how to handle a knife even when it was directed against himself."[26]

Looking around the cell, Shores found a bloody, straight-edged razor that belonged to Packer. Shores had no idea if the deceased had any family, but shortly thereafter Hughie Frill, the dead man's closest friend, claimed the body. And then the telegraph operator showed Shores a telegram that had been received in response to one Frill had sent to the man's family. "Bury Tommy in Gunnison," it read. When Shores looked at the name and address on the telegram, they read "Hurley" and "Pottsville, Pennsylvania." It was then that he realized that the most notorious of the fugitive Molly Maguires had refused to let anyone else end his life, and had chosen to finish it by his own hand.[27]

Within two months of the end of the Haymarket trial, Siringo—having already told William Pinkerton "that the east was too tame for me, hence I wanted a position in the west"[28]—was sent to the new Denver office. Allan Pinkerton had long avoided expansion, believing that a limited number of offices allowed the agency to be run by people he implicitly trusted in a manner that followed his long-established ethical codes. His sons, however, added four offices—in Denver, Boston, Kansas City, and St. Paul—within five years of their father's death.

The Pinkerton's Denver office came about due to expansion into that city by the Thiel Detective Service Company. One of Pinkerton's most trusted operatives during the Civil War, Gus Thiel had set up a rival company in St. Louis in 1873, an action that Pinkerton considered a betrayal.[29] In 1885, Thiel sent his star agent, John F. Farley, to open an operation in Denver, which was considered the most significant city between Chicago and the Pacific.[30] In response, the Pinkertons made it their fourth branch location in 1886, opening the office under Charles O. Eames, a former assistant superintendent in Chicago.[31]

Siringo became suspicious of the goings-on within the agency almost immediately upon his arrival in Denver, in October 1886. Eames, a trusted officer, had been allowed to select his own operatives—other than Siringo—and it seemed to the cowboy that they were all occupied in shady practices. Although Siringo did engage in what he called "city work"—such as catching a gang of dishonest streetcar conductors—he welcomed the opportunity to get into the field for investigations, because the ethos and actions in town disturbed him.

Siringo's first major case came early in 1887, when he was sent to Archuleta County, in southwest Colorado, to investigate an ugly political dispute.[32] The county included only about seventy-five voters, most of whom were English-speaking. But in the recent election, three members of the Archuleta family—wealthy Hispanic sheep ranchers from Amargo in northern New Mexico—and two of their cronies had won the five positions as county commissioners by sending their employees into Colorado on election day to cast votes. Their English-speaking opponents rebelled and marched the five members of the Archuleta group over the state line, warning them never to return. Bendito Martinez, one of the five, hired Pinkerton's to put down the insurgents and restore the deposed commissioners.

Siringo thought neither party was totally in the right, but, posing as a Texas outlaw, he bought a horse in Durango and pretended to join the insurgents, who numbered about seventy-five. The Archuletas had sixty heavily armed New Mexicans, and the two sides faced each other across a bridge over the San Juan River, threatening serious violence. Twice the insurgents laid plans to murder the commissioners, and twice Siringo managed to warn them. "This came very near costing me my life," he wrote, "as a rope had been prepared to hang me as a spy. But I lied out of it."[33] A truce was finally brokered between the two sides, but meanwhile, Siringo found proof of a number of crimes by the insurgents, including illegal vote buying. He testified to a grand jury in Durango and then disappeared when sixteen of the insurgents were indicted.

Soon thereafter, Siringo was ordered to hunt down a brakeman for the Atchison, Topeka and Santa Fe Railway who had stolen ten thousand dollars from Wells Fargo following a train wreck. Siringo traced him to Mexico City but found there were no extradition laws with Mexico, so he played tourist for two months while waiting for the man to return north. When he finally did,

Siringo had him arrested in Leavenworth, Kansas.[34] The cowboy detective followed that with cases in Colorado, where he figured out who was robbing a wealthy widow, and Wyoming, where his search for a killer who had broken out of jail included going undercover.[35]

When he returned to Denver, Siringo continued to be bothered by his colleagues' corruption. Eames, in league with the bookkeeper Morton, had started his own watch patrol—claiming it was Pinkerton's—to furnish protection to businesses.[36] He also had operatives take on multiple assignments and charge several clients concurrently for the same full day's work. The operatives also padded their expenses, accepted bribes, became involved in cases that Pinkerton's would not normally accept, and committed crimes themselves, which they then pretended to investigate.[37]

The worst were two thugs known as "Doc" Williams and Pat Barry; the former had served time in an eastern prison for safe blowing. The pair kept a large part of their ill-gotten gains—such as stolen clothes and jewelry, some of it purloined from merchants for whom they were conducting investigations—in trunks in the room shared by all the operatives. One day Siringo was there when he heard cries from the superintendent's adjoining office. Looking through a peephole, he saw Barry trying to beat a confession out of a man for a robbery that Siringo knew Barry and Williams had committed. Grabbing his Colt .45, Siringo rushed in, pointed it at Barry's face, and demanded he stop immediately. He then told the whole story to Eames who, rather than support Siringo, unsuccessfully tried to convince Pinkerton to sack him.[38]

But that was not the worst of the situation. "For the next few months, I had to keep my hand on 'old Colts 45,' my best friend in those days, while in the operatives' room when Doc Williams or Pat Barry were present, as they had sworn to get even with me," Siringo wrote. "At one time pistols were drawn, but I had the drop and made the future chief of police of Portland, Ore., Pat Barry, lay down his gun."[39]

In the midst of this, in November 1887, McParland was appointed assistant superintendent. For several months, while outwardly concentrating on criminal investigations, he took note of everything that happened inside the office as well as outside of it. He was impressed with the abilities and honesty of Siringo but reported negatively about the others to the Pinkerton brothers, who promptly sacked virtually everyone in the Denver office. "A new set of employees were sent from the East," Siringo reported, "I being the only one of the old 'bunch' left. This swelled my head, of course."[40]

McParland, too, remained, as on February 23, 1888, Robert A. Pinkerton informed his other superintendents that "Mr Jas McParland has been appointed Supt of the Denver office."[41]

His sudden rise to the head of the agency's westernmost office dramatically changed McParland's life. The man who had earned his spurs as an undercover detective was now foremost an administrator. He still served as primary investigator at times, but more often he was an overseer and facilitator of other men's work. To help run the Denver office—initially located at 1 and 2 Opera House Block—he was joined by assistant superintendent Charles K. Hibben, who was replaced by John C. Fraser in 1891. As the watch service had already been introduced, Captain John Howard was brought in from Chicago to run the now official Pinkerton's Protective Patrol.[42] When Farley became police chief in 1889, McParland had an understanding individual in charge of the city force, and therefore was able to maintain an alliance with the official local law-enforcement agency.

McParland's personal life also changed. For some time the widower of three years had been courting Mary H. Regan, a woman about ten years his junior and of Irish descent, who had been raised in Princeton, Wisconsin. In May 1888, McParland returned briefly to Chicago, where he and Mary were married.[43] They settled into a house in Denver at 814 Broadway, along with his daughter Kittie and his precious bull terriers, which he had raised ever since his days in Schuylkill County.[44] The move to Denver did require him to leave his brothers, however. Charles, with whom he was always closest, continued to live on Menomonee, and that same year their older brother John, also a shoemaker, moved into the same property. Edward, also now using the name McParland, had finally left Philadelphia and moved to Glencoe, in the Chicago area, the previous year.[45]

Of his new associates in Denver, McParland became closest to Siringo. They clearly developed a mutual respect, and each identified with the work ethic and professional approach of the other, although they did not work in the field together, as Siringo did with Shores or another rugged outdoorsman, W. B. Sayers.[46] McParland's position—and even more, his temperament—meant that he remained, to a great extent, a lone wolf within the agency. It is clear, however, that he trusted Siringo more than his other operatives, and liked him more as well, as he extended him the unique power of—at least on occasion—choosing to turn down investigations that did not appeal to him.

McParland and Siringo also formed a significant personal relationship. The Great Detective never had many intimate friends—those people most important to him tended to be older and to have helped advance his career—but Siringo appears to have been closer to him than most anybody other than his brother Charles. It is easy to imagine that—as they both enjoyed having a drink and telling stories, true and otherwise—the man who could be the embodiment of Irish blarney and the tough-as-an-old-boot range rider spent more than one evening together, bragging, fabricating, and scheming. Within a few years, they were also united in tragedy.

Around the time that McParland took charge of the Denver office, Siringo was working with Doc Shores to hunt down three men who had robbed the Denver & Rio Grande Railroad in western Colorado.[47] Knowing that two of them, the Smith brothers, were from near Cawker City, Kansas, the detectives went there, and Siringo took a job on their father's farm. Their sixteen-year-old, dark-eyed sister was not much younger than Siringo's wife, and he probably didn't have trouble paying her special attention, with the result that she showed him a letter from her brothers that had been mailed in Price, Utah. With this information, Siringo and Shores headed to Utah, and Shores sent a telegram to his brother-in-law, undersheriff Roe Allison, to search the area. By the time they arrived in Utah, Allison had arrested all three.

The lawmen still did not have any proof of their captives' crimes, however, so when Shores took the three men back for trial, he kept Siringo, posing as a desperate felon, shackled and chained like the others. When they reached Gunnison they were thrown into the same cell in which Hurley had committed suicide. "My three bedfellows were a dirty lot and were alive with vermin," Siringo wrote. "And one of the Smiths had a bullet wound through the head, which gave out an odor that put on the finishing touch to the already foul air in the cell."[48] Yet Siringo's talent for acting was so great that several outsiders thought he was by far the worst of the bunch. Not long after, all three confided in Siringo, which Shores used to prompt an official confession from them. They were each sentenced to seven years in the Colorado penitentiary.

In the ensuing period, McParland assigned Siringo to a case with huge political ramifications.[49] The lord mayor of London had purchased the Mudsill silver mine near Fairplay, Colorado, for one hundred ninety thousand dollars, and had then paid forty thousand dollars to Fraser & Chalmers—the world's largest manufacturer of mining equipment—to build a mill on the property. The foundations of the mill had already been laid when a sample of silver proved to be different than those that had been tested prior to purchase. Pinkerton's was asked to investigate, and McParland explained to Siringo that the case was particularly tricky because the findings might result in a cancellation of the mill order, and Chalmers of Fraser & Chalmers was married to the Pinkerton's sister.

Going undercover as Charles T. Leon, Siringo targeted Jack Allen, the right-hand man of the swindler who had sold the mine to the lord mayor. After a night on which Siringo and Allen became gloriously drunk together and danced with the "free-and-easy girls" until morning, Allen confided that he had spent several years in the state penitentiary in Lincoln, Nebraska, and also spilled enough about the mine to confirm Siringo's assessment that it had been "salted" to make it appear productive. It took Siringo eight months to gather all the required information, during which he sent for Mamie and Viola, who moved into a hotel in nearby Alma. Four nights a week, Siringo went out drinking and dancing with Allen, and the other three he sneaked out to see his family. At one point his visits were noticed by the hotel's landlady, who warned Mamie not to associate with Siringo because he was a "bad-un." Eventually, Siringo learned the full story "from Jacky as to how he and his partner Andy, had spent three years salting the Mudsill mine," allowing them to fool the two experts who had been sent by the lord mayor.[50]

It was important to not let it be known that Charles T. Leon was actually a Pinkerton's operative, so the case now passed to McParland. He obtained the prison record and photograph of Allen, and then decoyed him to Denver. Once there, McParland had him brought to his office, where, by all accounts, the Great Detective could play "good cop, bad cop" all by himself, smiling sweetly and crooning gently or being dangerously intimidating. Realizing that Allen did not want his background and true identity known in Fairplay, McParland used it to force a full confession. The courts were thereafter able to attach the property of the rogue who had developed the scam, as well as his primary financial backer, in order to allow the lord mayor to recover the vast majority of his funds.

The year after he took over the Denver office McParland lost two more men who had made a substantial impact on his life. On July 12, 1889, his father, Eneas, died without so much as acknowledging his fifth son's existence; it is uncertain how McParland took the news. Five months later, he was followed by a man who had helped propel McParland to the heights of fame—Franklin B. Gowen.

Gowen's apparent success in his early years as the president of the Reading had been, in many senses, a mirage. He had forced the Reading to borrow so heavily to purchase coal lands that it was never able to recover economic stability. When other business decisions led to the Reading formally declaring bankruptcy in May 1880, it led to Gowen's ouster as president. Undaunted, he formed an alliance with William Vanderbilt of the New York Central Railroad, whose power politics helped Gowen regain the presidency of the Reading. But Gowen's new policies could not overcome the huge debt the company faced, and in January 1884 he resigned. He returned for a third reign before being forced out once and for all in 1886 by a syndicate led by J. P. Morgan.[51]

Gowen returned to his private legal practice, but despite seeming to be in good health and spirits, on December 13, 1889, he killed himself in his room at the Wormsley Hotel in Washington, D.C. Linden was called in from Philadelphia to investigate whether he had been murdered by the Molly Maguires, and reluctantly made the assessment that Gowen had committed suicide.[52] When asked about the case, McParland showed the same perplexed attitude as most of those who knew Gowen: "I don't see how he could have put an end to himself unless it was because he had over-taxed himself since leaving the Reading. . . . [H]e has been engaged in a desperate fight against Standard Oil."[53]

Linden was not the only superintendent actively conducting investigations. In the spring of 1890—with Siringo on a lengthy case concerning the dynamiting of two mine owners' houses in Tuscarora, Nevada[54]—McParland, at the request of the Denver & Rio Grande Railroad, headed an investigation of complaints from mine owners that the weights of the ore they were shipping on the railroad kept coming up short, meaning that the ore was being stolen.[55] In mid-July, Sheriff John White of Aspen, Colorado, arrested one man and McParland two, all of whom were switchmen in the railway yard. The next day, two more were picked up.

When McParland confronted one of them, Charles Sligh, with details of the crimes, the man "saw he was caught and made a clean breast of everything. He said McParland knew too much and more than he wanted him to know and he thought he had better tell him straight."[56] From Sligh's confession it was evident that it "was an easy matter to throw the ore from the cars onto the platform and then sweep it up as if it had fallen from the wagons in loading onto the cars."[57] This simplistic scheme had allowed the thieves to steal four or five tons of ore at a time.

Once he began talking, Sligh revealed even more. He and three other men had several times broken into a warehouse owned by a wholesale liquor dealer and had stolen kegs of beer and boxes of cigars. The other three "beer burglars" were promptly arrested, and when they attended the preliminary hearing,

Sligh's testimony revealed that he was not the cleverest man. Having pled "not guilty," he promptly confessed, and when asked why, he "said that the reason he plead [*sic*] not guilty was because he was not under oath. He said he was under oath at the present time and was telling the truth. He was guilty and expected to go to the penitentiary."[58]

In November, McParland returned to Aspen to testify in the ore-stealing case. By that time his personal losses had continued to mount. On September 19, 1890, his friend George Kaercher, the former Schuylkill County district attorney—who in 1883 had been appointed the general solicitor for the Reading—was killed in a train wreck.[59] A much greater tragedy—from McParland's perspective—occurred a week later when his beloved daughter Kittie died of diphtheria at the age of eight.[60]

The personal losses continued that winter, as the wives of the two men to whom McParland was closest both died. On January 28, 1891, Charles's wife, Mary Ann, gave birth to their fourth child, Agnes. But Mary Ann thereafter fell ill with what was diagnosed as puerperal fever, and on February 1 she died at the age of thirty-one. Later that month the three-week-old Agnes went into convulsions and died at home.[61]

Meanwhile, Mamie Siringo's health also deteriorated. She had been operated on earlier in the year for what doctors diagnosed as pleurisy, but her lungs had already been too damaged for a recovery. Once Siringo was back from Nevada, McParland made sure that the detective could stay home with his ailing wife. During that same winter, at the age of twenty-two, she died in his arms as he held her at an open window so she could get some fresh air. Soon thereafter, unable to look after Viola himself, Siringo let Mamie's childless aunt and uncle take her, knowing they would raise her better than he could.[62]

Around the time of Mamie's death, Siringo, distraught from the tragedy, got into a fight outside a pawnshop with a policeman named Rease.[63] Both reached for their guns, but Siringo was quicker and, pointing his at Rease's heart, pulled the trigger. Fortunately another policeman grabbed the pistol, and the hammer came down on his thumb. Dragged by six members of Denver's finest to a police wagon, Siringo was hauled off to jail. That night McParland visited Farley, the police chief, to negotiate the release of his operative. Having so recently experienced the loss of Kittie, McParland would fully have understood Siringo's grief, and it is likely that these two men—at times so hard, cold, and determined—would have found comfort in each other's presence, friends brought even closer by tragedy.

CHAPTER 14

CALLING THE SHOTS

Many years after the death of Kittie McParland in 1890, it was suggested that her passing had taken the last true happiness and joy from her father's life, particularly as he and Mary remained childless.[1] Although this may have been overstated, the reports of him being a free-spirited, devil-may-care Irish lad certainly disappeared, and he began to be seen as a distant, dour, and businesslike supervisor. The novelist and former Pinkerton's agent Dashiell Hammett caught the essence of this view when he created a character based on McParland—"the Old Man"—who had "no more warmth in him than a hangman's rope."[2]

Then again, McParland's role was not to be popular but to efficiently run a major office in a growing and ever-evolving business, in which the requirements of the clients and the level of participation demanded of the agency were constantly changing. His promotion had made him one of seven superintendents responsible directly to Robert and William Pinkerton, who, on the death of their father, had assumed the titles of general superintendent, Eastern Division and general superintendent, Western Division, respectively.

The seven offices emphasized different investigative priorities, due to the primary concerns of their local clients, but they were organized similarly, into four main sections: clerical, criminal, operating, and executive.[3] The clerical department consisted of a chief clerk, who reported directly to the superintendent, and under whom were a bookkeeper, cashier, several stenographers, an office boy, and a janitor. The department was responsible for keeping the financial accounts, typing the detectives' edited reports, and assisting the other departments with their correspondence.

The criminal department was headed by the assistant superintendent, who drew personnel from the operating division as required. He was in charge of criminal investigations and correspondence and for the maintenance of the card index file and the Rogues' Gallery—photographs of and information about all known criminals.

The operating division was composed entirely of operatives, of which there were three kinds. The special operative was, in fact, the least special. Hired essentially as a freelance detective on a case-by-case basis, he was required to shadow a target or undertake an investigation when there was no general operative available.

The general operative was the public image of an operative. Like Siringo or W. B. Sayers, he was "an all-round able man, bright, intelligent, and capable of assuming any role, or impersonating any kind of character . . . and who will at all times act in a cool, discreet and level-headed manner."[4] General operatives were so important that every office was required to keep a few on staff at all times, and every effort was made to retain them once they had established themselves.

The third kind of agent was the secret operative—whom unions called a "labor spy"—whose job was to infiltrate an organization, discover as much information as possible about its plans, and take any actions within or against it, as instructed. Although such tasks were relatively unusual when McParland took charge of the Denver office, as time passed they became the most frequent and significant, making the agents carrying them out also the most important, both to Pinkerton's and other detective agencies.[5]

The final section, which expanded as the offices' workload increased, was the executive department, consisting of the superintendent and, as time went on, a variable number of assistant superintendents, depending on the volume of business. Among their functions were studying and analyzing incoming reports from operatives, editing or revising them for sending to the client,[6] and suggesting policies or recommending actions for the employer. In addition, "letters of criticism and instruction are sent almost daily to the operative."[7] The executives were also expected to canvas for new business.[8]

Although the seven offices were thus similar on the surface, the relative isolation of McParland's Denver headquarters, as well as the fact that it covered the entire vast region to the west, north, and south, made it distinctive, and it gave McParland a day-to-day control that was greater than that of his counterparts at the other offices. It also made his leadership ability and managerial style somewhat more observable than those of the men who were more closely overseen by the Pinkertons.

McParland tended to give his operatives more freedom—particularly those

he trusted the most, like Siringo and Sayers—than some of the other superintendents did. He was also not averse, like other superintendents, to jumping
into an investigation himself or taking it over totally if it interested him. He
also was happy to delegate a certain amount of responsibility and didn't feel
the need to micromanage, such as chasing his men for daily reports. This is
probably something he learned from his own experiences with the Molly Maguires, when safely sending reports was not always possible. An examination
of several intensive operations gives a fuller view not only of McParland's leadership but of the tasks that, as superintendent, he carried out.

The events leading to one of his major cases as a superintendent began on a
frigid evening in February 1891, in Santa Fe, the capital of the New Mexico
Territory. Two men, armed with a rifle and a shotgun, fired through a window
of the law offices of Thomas B. Catron, a member of the Territorial Council,
or upper legislative house. Joseph Ancheta, another councilor and a powerful
figure in the local Republican Party, was severely wounded by the shotgun
blast, while Catron was saved only by the stack of legal books and papers that
happened to be between him and the window. Meanwhile, a rifle bullet just
missed Elias Stover, another high-ranking political figure.

After the Territorial Council offered a reward for bringing in the assassins,[9] Governor L. Bradford Prince contacted William Pinkerton, who referred him to McParland. Shortly thereafter McParland assigned Siringo to
the case.[10] Again using the name Charles T. Leon, the cowboy detective soon
found the case featured a remarkably complex set of political, social, religious,
and ethnic issues.[11] He also learned that no one knew if the target was Ancheta, Catron, or Stover, each of whom had numerous enemies.

The investigation was further complicated by the presence of a secret Hispanic society known as Las Gorras Blancas, or White Caps, for the hoods worn
over their faces and their horses' heads during night raids. Organized by Juan
José Herrera, the group was struggling against the expansion of Texas ranchers
and other English-speaking settlers, who were claiming pasture lands and water rights long considered common property. The White Caps cut stock fences,
burned barns and haystacks, and damaged railway tracks.[12] Some also believed
that the White Caps were a subset of the Knights of Labor, who had opposed
land speculation and fencing in New Mexico.[13]

Despite not being fluent in Spanish, Siringo was assigned to infiltrate the
White Caps. Seeking a way into their group, he built a relationship with Herrera's brother Pablo and entertained the White Cap leaders with frequent

meals, drinks, and cigars.[14] His plan worked, and in early April Pablo success-fully pushed for his "Gringo friend" to be inducted into the secret order.

Meanwhile, McParland's role was to maintain a regular correspondence with Prince, in which he kept him informed of Siringo's movements and find-ings, explained away any difficulties the operative was facing, badgered the governor for payments, and soothed any worries Prince might have about the operation (so that the lucrative payments would continue).[15]

Siringo's admittance to the White Caps did not help him identify a guilty party, however, and when he reported that the group had had nothing to do with the assassination attempt, Prince became unsettled by the lack of return for the high costs.[16] This fear was exacerbated when John Gray, the marshal in Santa Fe, found evidence suggesting that the shooters were Victoriano and Felipe Garcia from the mountain village of Cow Springs.[17]

Siringo headed to Cow Springs and cultivated the friendship of the Garcia brothers, but his investigation slowed to a crawl when he contracted smallpox. "I was swelled up like a barrel, and every inch of my body even to the soles of my feet and the inside of my throat was covered with soars," he wrote. "In ly-ing so long on my back, these sores had become calloused, but on undertaking to turn over on to the fresh sores so as to try to get up, I would scream with pain and fall over on my back again."[18] He lay at death's door for two weeks before recovering and then, after confirming the Garcias' participation, he was suddenly called back to Santa Fe.

Prince had complained about excessive charges by Pinkerton's ever since Siringo spent forty dollars on a horse and saddle, although McParland assured him that "when the horse is disposed of you will be credited with the amount received."[19] Then, in July, Prince objected to being billed eight dollars per day for the time Siringo was incapacitated with smallpox. McParland responded

> I am sorry that I cannot take the same view of this matter that you do. It is true that the Opt has been sick and it is equally true that in the discharge of his duty, in order to obtain the necessary infor-mation, it became necessary for him to go into a hot bed of small pox—something that few men would do except Mexicans—: it is also a fact that the very circumstances of his sickness has in my opinion . . . been the cause of his obtaining a great deal of information. . . . There is a doctor's and druggist's bill amounting to $51, which has not been charged and as the case is one in which the Opt, through no choice of his own nor choice of the Agency but

in discharge of his duty, was forced into a neighborhood where he contracted this loathsome disease, I think that it certainly is right that the Agency is paid for his services during that time and also his expenses. Besides, it is not a case where the Opt, although sick, was lying there idle but . . . was attending to his business even at that time when, from the nature of his disease, almost anyone else would have been thinking of taking a trip to another world.[20]

Nevertheless, a week later Prince discontinued the investigation. Siringo recommended that the Garcia brothers be arrested, but nothing was done, and the case was closed. To this day it is uncertain whether Prince abandoned the investigation because he believed the Territory was being overcharged or because he was concerned that the Garcia brothers had indeed carried out the attempted assassination, and, as self-proclaimed Republicans, their prosecution would cause problems for the party. Either way, the crime officially remained unsolved, and the identity of the target was never determined with certainty.

An intriguing point about the investigation is what it showed about how McParland's mind worked. In response to Prince closing the investigation, he replied:

I am sorry, as I do not think it would take much to bring this to a satisfactory conclusion. . . . The circumstances point plainly to who committed the deed and also to the parties who actually instigated it: however, under the condition of affairs, with Knights of Labor and White Caps, it would be difficult to convict anyone of this crowd but I want to say that the time is not far distant when the Territory of New Mexico will be confronted with even graver questions than the attempt to assassinate Senator Ancheta and when this illegal organization of White Caps and of Knights of Labor who claim to be legal, will have to be exposed to the public. . . . The country is certainly in a bad state, although it may not appear so upon the surface, but we have the inside facts. It is true that in all such cases there are a lot of blow hards, who never do anything but talk, but at the same time, they excite other people to commit crime. This was just the case in the Mollie Maguire regime in Pennsylvania: the men who did the most talking and blowing never did anything themselves but they incited others to show the utmost disregard for human life and property and the authorities were almost powerless until it came to the time they had to be annihilated. I consider that the secret society of White Caps is traveling in the same direction.[21]

One can understand on a basic level why and how McParland would link the White Caps to the Molly Maguires—the use of hoods to mask the identities of violent men conducting "outrages" against agrarian expansion would naturally have smacked of the Irish organization. But beyond that, his past experiences clearly helped dictate how he viewed the present, mainly in making this connection between the White Caps and the Knights of Labor to the Molly Maguires and the AOH. There were also other examples that linked the anthracite region to New Mexico: the perceived inability to convict people brought to trial, the attempted assassinations of men due to political or financial differences, and probably even the way that Siringo's investigation forced him to drink vast amounts of alcohol.

Perhaps most important, McParland's response showed that there remained indelibly sketched in his mind the notion that there were those who "incited others" to do their dirty work, so that they would not be caught themselves. Once again, here was an inner circle. It would not be the last time he would see organizations and individuals in such a light, and at various points during the rest of his career he would direct his operatives in such a way as to find the small group of villains whom he believed were really pulling the strings.

Coincidentally, a man notorious for doing others' dirty work had come under McParland's own direction in 1890. Born near Memphis, Missouri, in 1860, Tom Horn left home at the age of thirteen. By 1875, he was driving a stagecoach in the New Mexico and Arizona territories, and the next year he became a civilian scout for the Fifth Cavalry.[22] In 1885, he was named chief scout for the U.S. Army operation to capture the Apache chief Geronimo, and around 1887 he served as a hired gun in the Pleasant Valley War, an Arizona range conflict. He thereafter bought into a mine and became a star rodeo performer.

In 1890, Doc Shores entered Arizona on the trail of cattle rustlers, and the owner of a ranch where Horn was foreman recommended him as a deputy. Shores described Horn as "a tall, dark-complected man with a mustache . . . an imposing figure of a man—deep chested, lean loined, and arrow straight," with "black, shifty eyes."[23]

The two initially got along very well, and after they caught the cattle thieves, Shores said, "Tom, you ought to go into the law enforcement business. You sure have done a good job for me, and with your background as an Indian scout and understanding of the Mexican lingo, I believe I could get you a job with the Pinkerton National Detective Agency. I'm pretty well acquainted with Jim McParland, the superintendent of the Denver office."[24] Horn was enthusiastic about the possibility, so Shores wrote to McParland, who offered Horn a job. However, it did not take Horn long to realize that the Pinkerton's way was not his own. "My work for them was not the kind that exactly suited my disposition; too tame for me," he wrote. "There were a good many instructions and a good deal of talk given to the operative regarding the thing to do."[25] Horn took a simpler approach—and even though it was outside the normal protocols, McParland must have appreciated his no-nonsense style, and his unquestioned results.

Before long he had the opportunity to show both, as he and Shores again paired up after the Denver & Rio Grande Railway was robbed. They chased two men from Colorado into New Mexico, Texas, and the Indian Territory, where they caught one in a house in which they had been hiding out. Shores took him back to Denver, while Horn waited for the other to return.[26] A few days later, "as he came riding up to the house I stepped out. . . . He was 'Peg Leg' Watson, and considered by every one in Colorado as a very desperate character." Even men as tough as Watson knew Horn's reputation, however, and "I had no trouble with him."[27]

For a couple of years, Horn was engaged in "running down robbers and roping in gangs of toughs . . . to rope in some train wreckers . . . eating, sleeping, drinking, and gambling with 'tinhorn gamblers' for the purpose of catching crooked men."[28] He was obviously valued by the agency, because when he was arrested in Nevada for robbing a faro dealer, William Pinkerton himself came to Reno to testify on his behalf, as did McParland's assistant superintendent, John C. Fraser.[29] Horn was found not guilty.

Although Horn claimed he left Pinkerton's in 1894, it's more likely that he did so in 1892, when he moved to Wyoming. There he found work as a "stock detective" for the Wyoming Stock Growers Association, which was trying to end widespread cattle theft. Horn developed his own style of dealing with rustlers—he killed them. "Killing is my specialty," he remarked. "I look at it as a business proposition, and I think I have a corner on the market."[30]

Siringo worked with Horn more than once and later mentioned that "he had a contract with wealthy cattlemen of Wyoming to murder suspected cattle rustlers. . . . It was understood that whenever a corpse was found with a stone under its head for a pillow, Horn was to be paid six hundred dollars and no questions asked. Horn claimed the stone under the corpse's head as his 'private' brand."[31]

Horn continued to work occasionally for Pinkerton's, which suggests that McParland was willing to look the other way if the right results came in.[32] This, of course, followed Allan Pinkerton's old notion of the ends justifying the means—although Horn apparently took this concept to an extreme.

Even when he was not working *for* Pinkerton's, Horn received recommendations *from* them. In April 1895, for example, Frank Canton, an undersheriff in Pawnee County, Indian Territory, sought help from the agency in finding an escapee from the Wyoming State Penitentiary. William Pinkerton told Canton that he was forwarding his letter to McParland, but noted that, "Tom Horn who used to be with our Denver office would be a good man." McParland did not mention Horn by name, but wrote: "I know of a man although not working for me but I could recommend him as he formerly did work for me. . . . I can guarantee the man. If he undertakes this matter no better man could be found for the work."[33] Particularly if that work was killing, because, as Siringo noted: "It is said that Horn killed seventeen men since first going to work for the Pinkerton agency."[34]

However, that reputation eventually caught up with him, and Horn was arrested and tried for the July 1901 murder of fourteen-year-old Willie Nickell. It has been cogently argued that he was actually innocent of that particular murder but was condemned to death because of a dubious "confession," unfair trial procedures, and his bragging on the stand, which not only connected him with other crimes but left many of his former employers wondering whom he might implicate next.[35] About three years later, McParland said that if Horn had kept his mouth shut, he would have been able to save him.[36] Instead, Horn was hanged in Cheyenne, Wyoming, on November 20, 1903.

Despite his power and reputation—and a strong ego—McParland could also be effective as part of a team rather than having to be the leader. At no time was this better demonstrated than his involvement in one of the most unusual murders of the era.[37] On Monday, April 13, 1891, Josephine Barnaby, the widow of a wealthy Providence, Rhode Island, clothier, was visiting Denver with her friend Florence Worrell. That evening, while staying at the home of Mrs. Worrell's son Ed, they broke open a bottle that had arrived for Mrs. Barnaby through the post several days earlier. The bottle had come in a wooden box with a sliding top on which was stamped LIEBIG'S EXTRACT OF MEAT, and attached to the bottle was a label that read: "Wish you a Happy New Year. Please accept this fine old Whiskey from your friend in the woods." Thinking it must be from Edward Bennett, a guide they had met in the Adirondacks, the women had a drink. Within ten minutes they were both feeling extremely sick, and it soon became apparent they had been poisoned. Although Mrs. Worrell recovered, Mrs. Barnaby died on April 19 after days of intense pain.

Mrs. Barnaby's son-in-law was the wealthy Montana mining magnate John Howard Conrad, and he swore that he would spare no expense in hunting down the killer. Virtually immediately he determined that man was Thomas Thatcher Graves, Mrs. Barnaby's physician and business adviser. Conrad had no love for Graves, who a few years before had convinced Mrs. Barnaby to contest her husband's will, which had left her very little but large amounts to her two estranged daughters. She gained a huge settlement in the resulting litigation, in part at the expense of the Conrads. Although Conrad's own wealth made the loss insignificant, he had not forgiven either her or Graves.

Conrad approached Pinkerton's about investigating the murder, which it did "commencing at Denver and extending East throughout the New England States."[38] Eventually, both the Denver and Boston offices were involved, although the eastern press tended to lay the success of the investigation at the door of John Cornish, the superintendent in Boston, and his assistant superintendent, Orinton M. Hanscom.[39] Much of this credit was due to Cornish's unabashed self-promotion, the extent of which is shown by Robert Pinkerton's response to one publication: "[Y]ou will note from this article that J.C. is throwing a few bouquets at himself."[40]

It is unclear whether Conrad asked Pinkerton's to investigate the murder or to investigate Graves, but he was the prime suspect from the beginning, particularly as he received twenty-five thousand dollars in Mrs Barnaby's will. He was tall, distinguished, and charming, and had risen to the rank of major during the Civil War, when he had been a staff officer under Major General Godfrey Weitzel, whose XXV Corps first occupied Richmond. Graves was selected to be in the party accompanying Abraham Lincoln when he entered the fallen capital in April 1865, and he became known for his elegant written description of the president's visit.[41] After the war, Graves graduated from Harvard's medical school, and later settled in Providence, where he met Mrs. Barnaby and eventually progressed from physician to confidant and adviser.

An autopsy showed that Mrs. Barnaby had died from poisoning by arsenite of potassium. According to J. A. Sewall, who led the postmortem, a chemical study of the bottle's contents indicated "it contained arsenic, alcohol and other ingredients. Twenty-one per cent about was alcohol. Nearly 2 ½ per cent was arsenic. . . . The entire bottle contained 132 grains of this poison, about 11 grains to the ounce." Two grains would have been a fatal dose. "I may also add that the person who mixed the solution was no novice," Sewall stated. "He, or she, knew how to prepare it so that the largest amount of arsenic could be kept in solution."[42]

This assessment made Graves the likely culprit, rather than Bennett, whose potential involvement was dismissed by McParland at an early stage. "[T]he reference to 'your friend in the woods' on the New Year's greeting can only refer to the Adirondacks," he stated. "It was therefore practically certain that suspicion would at once fall on Bennett as 'the friend', but that he would be so foolish as to leave a clue pointing directly to him is unthinkable. The inevitable conclusion therefore must be that the murderer intended that Bennett should be suspected and that the message on the bottle was written solely with that end in view."[43]

McParland next turned to finding out whence the bottle had come. It had originally been unwrapped at the investment firm of Schermerhorn & Worrell—of which Ed Worrell was a partner—and the wrapping paper was thrown away. However, John Schermerhorn had kept the stamps for his son's collection, and they enabled a new phase in the investigation. "[T]he package was mailed in Boston," McParland concluded. "I have learned that the postage was overpaid thirty cents, indicating that the sender didn't care to take the chance of having it weighed for fear that later he might be identified. I have sent the cancelled stamps to Superintendent John Cornish of our Boston office and have asked him to ascertain if they were purchased in Boston."[44]

The point man in the eastern investigation was Hanscom, who discovered that a new series of 15¢ stamps had been issued on February 22 to commemorate George Washington's birthday, and that no older format stamps, as were on the package sent to Mrs. Barnaby, had been sold there since. Pushed by Conrad to investigate every one of the more than nine thousand postal branches in New England if necessary, Cornish's operatives found that it had only been possible to obtain the older stamps at the Providence post office.

Meanwhile, Hanscom joined Conrad in an amateurish effort to gain an admission of Graves's guilt. Inviting the doctor to the Barnaby household in Providence several times, the two—with Hanscom introduced as Conrad's brother Charles—again and again tried to weasel a confession that he had sent the bottle, even if it had not contained any poison. Later they testified that he had admitted just that, although Graves vehemently denied it.[45]

The investigation convinced Denver district attorney Isaac Stevens that he could gain a conviction. But to put Graves on trial, he needed him in Denver, where there was no reason he would go if he were the chief suspect. In early May, McParland wrote and sent a telegram—signed as if it were from the chief of police—indicating that there was clear evidence that the poison had been put in the whiskey after its arrival in Denver. Claiming an indictment of Ed Worrell was in preparation, it stressed the significance of Graves returning to Denver to give a deposition about Mrs. Barnaby's physical condition prior to her death.[46]

The deception was successful, and shortly thereafter, Graves headed for Denver. He was questioned upon his arrival, and a week later was indicted for murder and arrested. "I have been fully expecting this," he told reporters. "I am glad it has come to an issue, very glad indeed, for now I shall have the opportunity to vindicate my character."[47]

The result was not, however, what Graves had expected. The trial took place in December and January, and although McParland testified briefly, the key witnesses were Conrad and Hanscom, who claimed Graves had admitted sending Mrs. Barnaby the bottle. Graves disputed their statements, but the jury found him guilty, and in January he was sentenced to hang. He appealed, and when his conviction was overturned, remained in prison waiting for a retrial.[48] On September 3, 1893, he was found dead in his cell, having, according to the official determination, committed suicide, a verdict since disputed.[49]

Through his early years as a superintendent McParland showed that he could obtain results, crack difficult cases, and put away criminals (one way or another), whether as a primary investigator, as a member of a team effort, or by enabling the efforts of others. He demonstrated that he could keep a handle on the vast area of the United States that fell under his purview, including acting as the key planner behind Western operations, serving as a salesman by seeking out new customers, and showing diplomatic skills by elegantly easing any concerns or doubts that existing clients might have about ongoing investigations. These abilities, combined with his formidable reputation with the press, public, and other law-enforcement agencies—based primarily on his Molly Maguire successes—would be of great significance in future years when he was considered for further promotion.

At the same time, McParland's personal characteristics earned him esteem (and perhaps fear) from those who served under him. There could be no question that he understood the operative's problems and tasks, and there could never be the excuse that he didn't know what a younger man was going through. His no-nonsense manner, that he had risen through the ranks (unlike the Pinkertons), and the fact that a subordinate always felt he knew where he stood with him would all also have garnered respect from his men.

But most important of all, both with the Pinkertons and his operatives, was the knowledge that McParland had almost always been successful, and that in order to achieve that success time and again, he would do anything necessary—whatever it took.

CHAPTER 15

+⟨≻=≺⟩+

A NEW DIRECTION

When McParland was in Schuylkill County Pinkerton's was comprised of three regional offices: Chicago, New York, and Philadelphia. By 1890, there were seven; by 1903, a dozen; and three years after, there were twenty. The key reason for this exponential growth was not a concentration on criminal activities against banks, jewelers, and railroads, but rather the concurrent expansion of what became the agency's greatest targets and critics: the labor movement and its large unions.

Although there were national labor organizations for various trades, the first national labor federation in the United States—attempting to bring together all the country's unions—was the short-lived National Labor Union, founded in 1866 and dissolved seven years later.[1]

In the midst of that period, the Knights of Labor was founded in Philadelphia by members of a local tailors' union. The new organization grew slowly, and in 1879, when Terence Powderly became its head, membership still numbered only about ten thousand. However, the success of the Knights in the Union Pacific Railroad strike of 1884, and in Powderly's early negotiations with Jay Gould during the strike against his Southwest Railroad System, led to a surge in membership, increasing it to more than three quarters of a million. After incidents of violence, arson, and sabotage helped turn public opinion against the strikers, several governors ordered out state militias, contributing to the strike's eventual disintegration in the summer of 1886.[2] That failure, combined with negative publicity linking the Knights to the Haymarket affair, severely tarnished the organization's reputation, and its numbers fell dramatically in the next few years, to below one hundred thousand.

Into the vacuum created by this collapse stepped the American Federation of Labor (AFL), led by Samuel Gompers. The new body was essentially a reincarnation of the Federation of Organized Trades and Labor Unions, which had been founded in Pittsburgh in 1881 and was, like the National Labor Union, a federation not a union. Formed in great part due to widespread union dissatisfaction with the Knights of Labor, the new organization emphasized the autonomy of each affiliated union; the federation tended to be composed primarily of skilled labor while somewhat ignoring unskilled workers and women.

These organizations proved fervent opponents of Pinkerton's, but they also benefited the agency by bringing in new employment from big businesses willing to pay to have operatives infiltrate them. An especially valuable boon to the agency's coffers came from one industry that had not yet been effectively unionized nationally—mining. In 1883, in the aftermath of the failure of John Siney's WBA and Miners' National Association, the coalfields saw the formation of the Amalgamated Association of Miners, which, decimated after a strike, was succeeded by what would become the National Progressive Union of Miners and Mine Laborers. In 1890 that body merged with Trade Assembly 135 of the Knights of Labor to found the United Mine Workers of America.[3]

But hard-rock mining—for quartz, gold, silver, iron, copper, zinc, and other valuable metals and minerals—had not been organized successfully on any national scale, despite local efforts starting in the 1860s in Nevada's Comstock Lode.[4] Certainly local unions dotted the western mining regions, but the very absence of a large-scale union encouraged the wealthy companies that owned the mines to prevent the formation of one and, as a step in that direction, to crush any fledgling locals. For this task, many such businesses looked to Pinkerton's.

Ever since Allan Pinkerton's early investigations of embezzlement and fraud by postal and railway workers, his agency had been viewed by some as a tool of big business.[5] McParland's involvement with the Molly Maguires only enhanced that reputation. In 1874, the miners at the bituminous coalfields near Braidwood, Illinois, were locked out when they rejected lower terms offered by the Chicago, Wilmington and Vermillion Coal Company. When the company brought in strikebreakers it also hired fifty armed members of Pinkerton's Protective Patrol for security.[6] Three years later, when the company announced another wage cut, miners in both Braidwood and Streator walked out, and Pinkerton's agents again served as guards for the strikebreakers.[7]

Pinkerton's quickly became a fixture in major strikes throughout America, with some holding that the agency caused more violence than it prevented. In 1886—the same year its operatives entered Kansas during the railroad strike—a member of Pinkerton's Protective Patrol killed a bystander during a series of strikes at the Chicago stockyards, inciting a riot. The next year, a boy was killed by a Pinkerton's guard during strikes at the Jersey City coal wharves. And in the 1888 strike against the Chicago, Burlington and Quincy Railroad, Pinkerton's not only provided guards and detectives but helped recruit the strikebreakers.[8]

It was against this background that McParland began his major antistrike, antiunion actions in the gold, silver, lead, and zinc mines of Colorado, Montana, and Idaho.

One of the most mineral-rich regions on Earth was a district in the northern panhandle of Idaho known as the Coeur d'Alenes. To the east of the lake bearing that name, and near the border of Montana, was a mountainous area covered with heavy pine forests and gouged by deep canyons, through which rivers fed by winter snows raced down steep grades. There, along the South Fork of the Coeur d'Alene River, surrounding the nascent towns of Kellogg and Wallace and dotted up ancient streambeds bearing names such as Nine Mile, Deadwood Gulch, and Silver Creek, were developed mines that eventually earned the region the nickname Silver Valley. In the century and a quarter since the first of these opened, more than 1.2 billion troy ounces of silver, 8.5 million tons of lead, 3.2 million tons of zinc, and sizable deposits of gold, copper, cadmium, and antimony have been extracted.[9]

It was in 1883 that the first gold was found on the North Fork of the Coeur d'Alene River, sparking a rush that brought thousands of prospectors.[10] The initial frenzy had subsided within a few years, but those still seeking their fortunes spread out. The lucky ones found that the South Fork was rich in other precious metals.[11] The Bunker Hill Mine—near what is now the town of Wardner—became the most productive in the region, and the smelting complex built in Kellogg was at one time the largest in the world. Another mining center grew up down the river along Canyon Creek, where the tiny towns of Gem and Burke were founded in response to the discoveries of ore deposits that led to the start of the Frisco, Black Bear, and Gem mines. Just down the canyon a few miles, nestled along the Coeur d'Alene, was Wallace, the area's most important mercantile center.

Not long after the beginning of mining operations, the inevitable differences between the goals of the owners and the workers began to appear, and in 1887 the Bunker Hill men formed the Wardner Miners Union. Others soon followed.[12] Conflict became inevitable within several years, and the unions joined together to establish an executive committee. Thirteen owners followed suit, founding the Mine Owners Protective Association of the Coeur d'Alenes (MOA). Relations between capital and labor were further soured by a fall in the price of silver. The turndown meant some mines closed and others decreased wages.[13] As the two sides jousted for control, gauging the intentions and strengths of the other, the MOA employed Pinkerton's to provide them with inside details about the unions.

In August 1891, McParland told Siringo that he was sending him to the Coeur d'Alenes, because the "Miners' Union of that district was raising Hades with the mine-owners," and the MOA "wanted a good operative to join the Miners' Union, so as to be on the inside of the order when the fast approaching eruption occurred."[14] Siringo told his boss that his sympathies lay with "labor organizations as against capital," so McParland agreed to send another man and detailed Siringo to a railroad operation in Utah and California.

A month later, Siringo was recalled to Denver. "Now Charlie, you have got to go to the Coeur d'Alenes. You're the only man I've got who can go there and get into the Miner's Union," McParland told him. "They are on their guard against detectives and they became suspicious of the operative I sent up there, and ran him out of the country. We know the leaders to be a desperate lot of criminals of the Molly Maguire type and you will find it so. I will let your own conscience be the judge, after you get into their Union. If you decide they are in the right and the Mine-owners are in the wrong, you can throw up the operation without further permission from me."[15]

McParland's flexibility won Siringo over, and he headed to Idaho, where, under the name of C. Leon Allison and with the knowledge of the mine superintendent, he took a job as a mucker in the Gem Mine. For an unknown reason, his reports were sent to John McGinn, the superintendent in St. Paul, where they were typed and sent on to the secretary of the MOA.[16] As the postmaster in Gem was a member of the union, Siringo had to walk to Wallace, four miles down the valley, at irregular intervals to send them.

Two weeks after arriving, Siringo joined the Gem Mine union; in so doing he took "an iron-clad 'Molly Maguire' oath that I would never turn traitor to the union cause; that if I did, death would be my reward."[17] A few months later he was elected the union's recording secretary, placing him in frequent contact with its financial secretary, George A. Pettibone, "a rabid anarchist."[18] From this position, Siringo could access the union records and monitor the key dissidents. Not long after, he contrived to be fired from his job in such a way that it would be impossible to find another in the local mining industry. Having informed his coworkers that his wealthy father would help him financially, he was able to spend all his time "working for the benefit of the union."

In the winter, Siringo was horrified by the union practice of "gathering up scabs . . . taken from their homes, sometimes with weeping wives and children begging for mercy. They were marched through the streets of Gem and spat upon amidst the beating of pans and ringing of cowbells, this being a warning to others who might . . . criticize this noble union, or refuse to pay dues." Then, high up the canyon above Burke, they "were told to hit the trail for Montana and never return, at the peril of their lives, and to give them a good running start shots would be fired over their heads. In this Bitter Root range of mountains the snow in winter is from four to twenty feet deep, so you can imagine what those scabs had to endure on their tramp without food or shelter to Thompson's Falls, the first habitation, a distance of about thirty miles."[19]

Siringo "found the leaders of the Coeur d'Alenes unions to be, as a rule, a vicious heartless gang of anarchists . . . while others were escaped outlaws and toughs."[20] He therefore decided he had no qualms in revealing their schemes, one of which was to flood several mines that used nonunion workers. Siringo recorded the details while keeping the minutes of a meeting, but Oliver Hughes, the president of the Gem union, ordered him to cut out the page where he had done so, so it could not be used in evidence. Siringo did so, but then sent the page directly to the secretary of the MOA.[21]

The long bubbling cauldron of mistrust finally boiled over during an exceptionally hard winter. When the railroads increased their rates for hauling ore, the MOA, arguing profits would disappear, shut down the mines in January 1892.[22] When the MOA finally offered employment again it was at substantially reduced rates, and in April, as the owners hoped, the miners went on strike.

The MOA now decided to break the unions once and for all.[23] The unions were no less determined to prevail, and Pettibone told Siringo that "they had selected a secret crowd of the worst men in the unions to put the fear of Christ into the hearts of 'scabs'; that if these secret men committed murder the union would stick by them."[24] Arms, which had been stealthily obtained, were openly distributed when it became known that immigrant miners were being taken to Wallace as strikebreakers. The local sheriff, a union sympathizer, was "on his fine horse with a gang of union deputies to preserve order, but in reality to help shoot down 'scabs.'" However, Siringo got a message out, and the train stormed through Wallace and straight to the protection of the Union, Gem, and Frisco mines.[25]

James McParlan was considered one of the most dangerous Molly Maguires in Schuylkill County during his undercover operation.

Allan Pinkerton, founder of Pinkerton's National Detective Agency and the man who chose McParlan for the Molly Maguire investigation.

Franklin Gowen, president of the Philadelphia and Reading Railroad and its subsidiary, the Philadelphia and Reading Coal and Iron Company.

Benjamin Franklin, the head of Pinkerton's Philadelphia office and McParlan's direct supervisor, annoyed Pinkerton by claiming too much credit for the Molly Maguire operation.

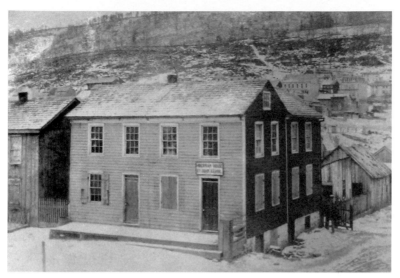

Hibernian House, John Kehoe's tavern in Girardville. Kehoe's great grandson, Joseph Wayne, continues to operate it today.

John "Black Jack" Kehoe, Schuylkill County delegate for the Ancient Order of Hibernians and, according to McParlan, head of the Molly Maguires.

George Kaercher was the young district attorney for Schuylkill County and one of the key prosecutors during the trials of the Molly Maguires.

A threatening coffin notice typical of those sent to mine bosses and owners.

A woodcut showing Tom Hurley murdering Gomer James at an evening picnic.

Robert J. Linden, McParlan's primary Pinkerton's contact in the anthracite region, who later headed the agency's Philadelphia office.

The small pistol that was used in the murders of both Policeman Yost and John P. Jones.

McParlan testifying during the trial of Kehoe and eight others for the attempted murder of "Bully Bill" Thomas.

The famous "cowboy detective" Charlie Siringo, armed with his Colt .45 and a walking stick with a hidden 20-inch blade.

"Doc" Shores, the sheriff of Gunnison County, Colorado, and sometimes a special Pinkerton's operative, was one of the most respected lawmen in the history of the Old West.

Charlie Siringo and his good friend and fellow "cowboy detective" W. B. Sayers on the trail of outlaws.

Tom Horn, the famed Old West scout, lawman, hired gun, detective, and killer.

Josephine Barnaby, the wealthy widow whose murder by poison initiated one of McParland's most high-profile cases.

The tiny mining town of Gem, Idaho, showing how Siringo escaped from the mob hoping to kill him. A: Siringo's house, where he sawed a hole in the floor. B: Hotel through which Siringo crawled through a window to escape on one of his surreptitious visits to the mine. C: Saloon building, to the back of which Siringo crawled from under the sidewalk. D: Miners' Union hall. E: Where Siringo entered the culvert. F: House next to which Siringo emerged from the culvert. G: Daxon's saloon. H: Company store.

The notorious train and bank robber Robert LeRoy Parker, better known by his adopted name of Butch Cassidy.

Harry Alonzo Longabaugh, alias the Sundance Kid, with his partner Etta Place, before they sailed for South America in 1901.

The portrait of the Wild Bunch taken in Fort Worth in 1900. From left: Harry Longabaugh, alias the Sundance Kid; Will "News" Carver; Ben "the Tall Texan" Kilpatrick; Harvey Logan, alias Kid Curry; and Butch Cassidy.

Frank Steunenberg, the former governor of Idaho who was assassinated on December 30, 1905.

The Steunenberg house. The fence, path, and total lack of a gate show the effects of Harry Orchard's bomb.

Albert Horsley, alias Thomas Hogan and Harry Orchard, at the time of his arrest for the assassination of Frank Steunenberg.

The Great Detective at the time of the trial of William "Big Bill" Haywood.

James H. Hawley, one of Idaho's greatest lawyers and politicians, and the lead prosecutor in the trial of William Haywood.

Steve Adams was tried for murder three times but was never convicted.

McParland's "Inner Circle" of the Western Federation of Miners awaiting trial. From left: George Pettibone, William Haywood, and Charles Moyer.

The defense team in the murder trial of William Haywood. From left: Edgar Wilson, Leon Whitsell, John Nugent, Fred Miller, Clarence Darrow, and Edmund Richardson.

Idaho senator William Borah, the associate counsel for the prosecution in the trial of William Haywood.

Judge Fremont Wood, whose directions to the jury in the murder trial of William Haywood helped ensure a not-guilty verdict.

Harry Orchard after having been spruced up in preparation for the trial of William Haywood.

Orchard giving testimony during Haywood's trial. In front of him are the court reporters, and Haywood and his defense team sit around a table, with Darrow chin in hand.

The Great Detective and his cowboy sidekick: McParland and Siringo chatting together in Boise during the Haywood trial.

The grave marker of McParland and his wife Mary at Mount Olivet Cemetery, with the mysterious date given for his birth. The smaller marker to its immediate right is that of McParland's beloved nephew Eneas.

Siringo's valuable reports almost proved his undoing. In June, the *Coeur d'Alene Barbarian*, a weekly newspaper representing the mine owners, included information that had obviously been leaked from an insider. Gabe Dallas, the secretary of the Butte, Montana, union, arrived to investigate. Described by Siringo as "a one-eyed, two-legged, Irish hyena,"[26] Dallas soon began to suspect Siringo, and called a meeting at which it was thought he would unmask the spy. Warned in advance that he was suspected because he had so often been seen mailing letters, Siringo nevertheless attended the meeting. In a packed union hall, Dallas launched into a fiery speech in which he vowed the traitor would never leave the hall alive and glanced ominously at Siringo. The detective, outwardly calm, was in fact thinking about the Colt .45 in his shoulder holster and the pearl-handled Bowie knife strapped to his waist. Siringo later recalled: "My mind was made up to start business at the first approach of real danger. Of course I didn't expect to last long among those hundreds of strong men, many of whom were armed, but I figured that they couldn't get but one of me, while I stood a chance to kill several of them. I would have been like a cat thrown into a fiery furnace—spit fire so long as life held out."[27]

After a speech that impressed even Siringo, Dallas announced a recess, at which he expected the detective to flee. But Siringo did not fall into such a simple trap, and calmly presented his minute book for examination. After several minutes Dallas found the page that had been cut out. "Here's a leaf cut out of this book. We want an explanation," he said triumphantly. When Siringo mentioned that the union president had told him to cut the page out, Hughes jumped up and called him a liar. But Siringo reminded him of the exact instance wherein they had planned to flood the mines, and the president had to acknowledge it was true.[28] For the moment, Siringo had dodged a bullet, but he knew that his time was running out.

In the following days, Siringo's success in staying alive owed a great deal to Kate Shipley, his landlady when he first arrived in Gem. In the spring, Siringo had paid three thousand dollars—most of his savings—for a two-story building in the center of the town. Upstairs were furnished rooms, and downstairs he opened a small store. He moved Mrs. Shipley and her five-year-old son in behind the store and paid her half the income to run the place. His room— removed from prying eyes—was upstairs, and to prevent anyone from prowling around the house, he built a sixteen-foot-high fence. "As a precaution," he noted, "I left the bottom of one wide board loose so that I could crawl out instead of going over the fence."[29]

Not long after the union meeting, Mrs. Shipley told Siringo that she had seen a man following him. Watching out, Siringo recognized "Black Jack" Griffin, who had been involved in the dynamiting of two mine owners' houses in Nevada a few years before, a case that Siringo had investigated. Siringo had no doubt Griffin would tell Dallas that the man going by "Allison" was the detective "Charles T. Leon." But Siringo did not feel that he could leave yet—Pettibone had told him that a major uprising was planned for early July, to take possession of the mines and run the owners and scabs out of the country.[30] Wanting to provide as much advance information as possible, Siringo waited.

All Canyon Creek, from Burke to Wallace, seemed on edge. Guards at the Gem Mine prevented anyone from entering, while union men outside prevented anyone from leaving. A friend warned Siringo not to attend a union meeting on July 9, or "I was doomed to die the death of a traitor."[31] Instead, he gave the guard at the door his minute book and a letter that denied he was a spy but included his resignation from the union due to the unwarranted suspicions. A short while later he was told by a late arrival that the "Homestead, Pa., riots of a few days previous would be child's play as compared to our approaching storm."[32] Before he reached his house, Siringo was accosted by a group of about twenty men in an ugly mood. "I sprang out into the street and with my hand on my cocked pistol, threatened to kill the first man who undertook to pull a gun. In this manner I backed across the street to the hallway leading up to my room."[33]

By the next day, more than one thousand union men had arrived. Despite the danger, that night Siringo slipped out the back, dislodged the piece of fence, wriggled out through the hole, and crept to the river, wading through it in a dark place that the guards on the bridge could not see. He then crawled on his stomach until he neared the Gem Mine, where he warned the superintendent that rioting would start the next morning.[34] When daylight came, Siringo boldly walked back into town, his rifle under his coat, and returned home. At precisely 6:00 A.M., shooting started from near the Frisco Mill, the targets of which were the replacement workers and their guards.[35]

Siringo realized this was his chance to leave, but when he peeked outside he saw strikers blocking all the possible exits. He then saw a man from the Thiel Detective Service Company, which had been hired to guard the Gem Mine, walking into town. The operative was shot dead in his tracks. Shots were then fired in earnest, at the mine and all around it. After considering barricading himself upstairs and defending the place until he died, Siringo decided to try to escape. His store was built on an uneven piece of land, and although the building rested on the ground at the rear, it was built on piles at the front. So he sawed a hole in the floor and, still holding his rifle, squeezed beneath the house.

Siringo found he could see through the cracks of the board sidewalk on the main street, and standing nearby with a shotgun was Dallas. "I up with my rifle and took aim at his heart," Siringo wrote, "but before pulling the trigger, the thought of the danger from the smoke going up through the cracks and giving my hiding place away, flashed through my mind."[36] Moreover, just then there was a huge explosion from the direction of the Frisco.

Shortly thereafter, Mrs. Shipley agitatedly told Siringo through the hole in the floor that the Frisco mill had been blown up, many men killed, and "now they're coming after you to burn you at the stake."[37] He calmly told her to recover the hole with the rug and put the trunk on top of it. Just in time, as soon there were hundreds of men in the street baying for Siringo's blood. They kicked in the door to the store and demanded to know where the "dirty Pinkerton detective" was, but Mrs. Shipley insisted she hadn't seen him.

Knowing it was only a matter of time until the hole was found, Siringo wormed his way under the sidewalk, pulling his rifle behind him. When he paused to rest he could hear men directly above talking about killing him. With no room to crawl on hands and knees, he wriggled on his belly, inch by inch, the length of three buildings before reaching the saloon; there he could see light coming from an open space toward the rear. Emerging, he saw three armed men only thirty feet away, but their attention was on the main street, so he sneaked past them and rushed toward the creek, reaching a culvert that led under the railway embankment toward the Gem Mine just as a bullet whizzed past his head. Making his way through, he raced across hundreds of yards of open ground to where the guards allowed him in. He was safe—for the moment.

Siringo had not been at the mine long when a union messenger demanded they surrender or else the mill would be dynamited. The superintendent, having been ordered by the owners to avoid loss of life and destruction of the mill, surrendered. Meanwhile, Siringo, certain he would be murdered, escaped with a nonunion miner by crawling on his stomach through the surrounding brush, and then slipped into the local mountains. As he paused at the crown of a nearby hill he could see the union men looking into the face of each remaining man, hunting him.

Siringo and the miner stayed hidden in the hills for several days, while the strikers marched on Wardner and forced the closure of the Bunker Hill facility. Governor Norman B. Willey thereupon declared martial law and, at his request, federal troops were sent to quell the strike. After several days, non-union workers returned to the mines with military protection, while hundreds of miners were arrested and, as local jails were inadequate, placed in hastily built stockades, or "bullpens."[38] Siringo was appointed deputy sheriff to help round up those who had escaped. Among them was Pettibone, who had lit the fuse to blow up the Frisco mill, killing one.[39]

Siringo later testified in the trials, helping to convict eighteen union members, including Pettibone.[40] So intense was the feeling of some of the union miners against him that the building he owned in Gem—into which Mamie's uncle and aunt had moved with Viola—was burned to the ground. On appeal, the conviction of the union leaders was reversed by the U.S. Supreme Court, and the men spent less than a year in prison.[41]

Not long after their release, five of the former prisoners met other labor leaders representing miners in Montana, Colorado, Utah, and South Dakota. Together they founded exactly what the mine owners had long feared: "a grand federation of underground workers throughout the western states," consolidating a number of individual unions into the Western Federation of Miners (WFM).[42]

Even before the disastrous intervention by Pinkerton's at Homestead in July 1892 there had been growing concern about equipping what were essentially private armies for use in the increasingly aggressive struggle between big business and the unions. Pressure was brought to bear by numerous groups, including the Brotherhood of Locomotive Engineers, which, following the Burlington Railroad strike in 1888, began lobbying Congress to abolish the use of Pinkerton's detectives.[43]

Although such legislation received some support, serious congressional action did not begin until after Homestead. After this, both the Senate and the House of Representatives held hearings about the use of "large bodies of armed men to discourage strikers from interfering with the orderly operation of business."[44] In response, an amendment to the civil appropriations bill for that year included what became known as the Anti-Pinkerton Act. This act prevented the federal government and that of the District of Columbia from employing Pinkerton's or similar organizations.[45] More broadly, however, the hearings determined that it was not up to Congress but to the states to pass such legislation, if desired. By the end of the century twenty-four states had forbidden armed guards to enter their jurisdictions.[46]

Most of these laws focused on the prevention of employing organizations that "offered for hire mercenary, quasi-military forces as strikebreakers and armed guards."[47] Therefore, this did not greatly affect McParland's operation in the West, which concentrated not on protecting strikebreakers but on using detectives for criminal investigations and as undercover operatives.

McParland's agents were not significant, however, in the first major test of the Western Federation of Miners. In January 1894, a dispute arose in the gold mines around Cripple Creek, Colorado, an area that had expanded rapidly during the gold rush of the first years of the 1890s. When mine owners increased the workday from eight to ten hours for the same pay, the gold miners, who had only recently affiliated with the WFM, went on strike.[48] Minor violence and a brief appearance by the state militia followed, but by late April, all but seven of the thirty-seven local mines were working an eight-hour day.

The more militant owners and union men would not give in, however, and the situation turned ugly when the owners hired Sheriff M. F. Bowers to assemble a large force to protect the strikebreakers.[49] As Bowers deputized some twelve hundred men—called by the local union president "the scum from nearly all the cities in Colorado"[50]—the union armed and began training. The actual conflict began on May 24, when the miners captured the nonunion Strong Mine from armed deputies and ordered everyone to leave. Shortly thereafter, the shaft house was blown up, trapping the superintendent, foreman, and engineer in it. Each side blamed the other for the explosion, with McParland writing: "This gang of union men ordered every man to leave the Strong Mine. Mr McDonald, the Supt and a few others did not come out of the mine quick enough, so they dynamited the tunnel and left those men in there to die. A large number of deputy sheriffs . . . eventually cleared away the debris and released Mr McDonald and his men more dead than alive."[51]

The next day the strikers approached the deputies' camp not far from several mines and gunfire broke out, killing two and wounding several others. Fearing anarchy, Populist governor Davis H. Waite asked the strikers to lay down their arms and declared the deputies an illegal force that must disperse. When that did not happen, he called in the state militia, which quickly took control of the situation and successfully quelled the violence. Waite also later served as the arbitrator for an agreement between the owners and the union to end the strike.[52]

The strike was widely considered a union victory, and the WFM had huge success in organizing workers in its immediate aftermath.[53] At the same time, it taught the leaders of the federation some of the wrong lessons. The famed muckraking journalist Ray Stannard Baker wrote: "The strike at Cripple Creek in 1894, and that of Telluride in 1901, were called great victories for unionism. They were not. They were defeats. Victories obtained by such violence and bloodshed are always defeats. They laid the foundation for other violence. They encouraged the unions, once successful with rifles and fists, to use rifles and fists again."[54] The seeming success therefore masked not only that the government still maintained the power, but that the image of the WFM was damaged with both the owners and the public by gaining a reputation for violence and lawlessness. Further, it increased the call of the owners for antiunion measures by Pinkerton's, the Thiel Detective Service Company, and other such organizations.

For McParland, the conflict with the WFM had one personally negative aspect. In the early 1890s, his brother Edward had moved to Cripple Creek, where he hoped to strike it rich in the gold rush. Not doing so, he returned to his shoe business, but in the interim he became friendly with members of the WFM.[55] Many years later, Kittie Schick—the youngest daughter of Charles McParland, who had lived with her uncle James in Denver—was reported to have said that Edward was "a bit of an anarchist" who was "really a little off."[56] Exactly why she said so is unknown, but it is obvious that any alliance between Edward and the WFM would have been particularly distressing to McParland.

McParland's success throughout this period—as the leader of the Denver office, in the early struggle against the WFM and other labor organizations, and in a number of personally led criminal investigations[57]—gained him a major promotion. In 1892, William and Robert Pinkerton jointly took on their father's old title of principal. George D. Bangs, the son of Allan Pinkerton's former number two, thereupon became the general superintendent, making him the number three man in the agency and directly in charge of operations in the eastern United States. Simultaneously, two new positions were created. McParland, while remaining superintendent of the Denver office, was named assistant general superintendent, Western Division, and his old colleague David Robertson became assistant general superintendent, Middle Division.[58]

McParland was now more than ever one of the key players in the agency, but that only meant he would be expected to work even harder. Fifteen years before, Allan Pinkerton had decided that employment in his agency meant working seven days a week, a requirement that would continue under his sons into the twentieth century.[59] However, in his initial year in charge of the Western Division, McParland found himself taking Sundays off for the first time since his recuperation at Larch Farm. Unfortunately, it was due to a serious bout of typhoid fever,[60] which left him weak and listless. But this time there would be little chance to relax and enjoy life while regaining his health: He had half a country to oversee.

CHAPTER 16

BUTCH CASSIDY AND THE WILD BUNCH

A s the 1890s passed, Pinkerton's Western Division continued to grow in both reputation and the number of clients it serviced. Some were railroad companies, for which the old task of testing conductors was still carried out, in addition to chasing train robbers. Others were mining companies, disturbed by the growth of unions, wanting help when they purchased a salted mine, or worried by the theft of ore or bullion. Yet others were banks, jewelry sellers, cattle ranchers, money brokers, or public officials who simply could not cope with the numbers of murderers, robbers, kidnappers, con men, and general thugs who made the Old West so wild.[1] McParland's vast domain stretched from Mexico to Canada—and at times into them—and from the shores of the Pacific to the Mississippi. And in that realm were more than enough "desperate men"[2] to keep his expanding forces constantly busy.

McParland himself continued to be more administrator, salesman to potential clients, and diplomat than anything else, but he did manage to keep his hand in the investigation business. He particularly liked to swoop in at the last moment, round up the criminals, and frighten, bribe, or cajole confessions out of them. It was not unusual at the time to read newspaper notes such as: "The real object of his [McParland's] visit was the possible capture of a lot of confidence men who have been operating on the Union Pacific to the great annoyance of the company . . . and the discomfort of the passengers."[3]

As always, McParland employed numerous operatives, but the man as often as not assigned to the toughest investigations was his friend Siringo. In the period following his stint in the Coeur d'Alenes, Siringo spent three weeks in a Pueblo, Colorado, jail with two killers, eventually wrangling a confession out of them that allowed him to give testimony that led to a seventeen-year prison sentence. On one job he posed as a wealthy mining man in Denver, and on another as a hobo hitching rides on railways in Colorado, New Mexico, Arizona, and California. After having been thrown off the train in the Mojave

Desert, he had to walk fifteen miles without water, and when he finally came to a house, the rancher told him to "git" before he let his dog loose on him. Fortunately for Siringo, just a short while before he had noticed a couple of milk cows in a deep arroyo. "Only one cow would let me go up and rub her head, and she was a Jersey with a bag full," he wrote. "While she chewed the cud of contentment, I got down on my knees and milked the fluid into my mouth."[4]

On one of Siringo's assignments, McParland sent him to Alaska to find ten thousand dollars in gold that had been stolen from the Treadwell Mine on Douglas Island, one of the largest gold mines in the world.[5] Before Siringo left, McParland emphasized the political importance of the job—both within the company and without—because three detectives from the new Portland office had failed to find anything, and so it had been reassigned to Denver by an embarrassed William Pinkerton. Although both offices were under McParland as assistant general superintendent, Western Division, he was also the direct superintendent at Denver, so he wanted to show that his own office was still the best.

Using the name Lee R. Davis, Siringo worked at Treadwell for three weeks before determining that the robbers were Charlie Hubbard and Hiram Schell, two mill hands who had quit work, bought a schooner, and disappeared in the waterways near Juneau. Siringo was then joined by W. B. Sayers, one of McParland's most talented and dedicated horseback trackers, whose investigations included many exploits in the badlands and barren, rocky regions of the West. While Siringo was feigning an accident so that he could leave the mill without engendering suspicion, Sayers happened to see a trim schooner come into Juneau. Before she left the next morning he had a conversation with the two men sailing her, who turned out to be Hubbard and Schell. While chatting, he discovered that they had just come from the west coast of Admiralty Island, and although he did not find out exactly where they were heading, he suspected it was the same area.

The two cowboys bought a forty-foot canoe "painted all the colors of the rainbow," added a sail, and loaded up with Canadian rye whiskey. "The main object in taking the whisky along was to pass ourselves off as whisky peddlers among the Indians, and as bait for Schell and Hubbard in case we found them."[6] One day, while following the route that local Native Americans indicated the thieves had taken, the two detectives decided to take a rest, and they paddled toward a small, black island. Suddenly, they realized the island was actually a whale, and Siringo, ignoring Sayers's warning, ill-advisedly engaged in big-game hunting. He fired a shot, but it proved ineffective—and worse—as he later acknowledged: "The bullet hadn't more than struck him when I wished I had taken my partner's advice. He went around and around with the rapidity of a cyclone, churning the water into a foam, the waves reaching our canoe. Then straight down he went, leaving a hole in the water. This hole filling up again, sucked us toward it, and I imagined I could see Hades at the bottom of the hole."[7]

Fortunately they were able to escape and continue with their manhunt. After sailing and paddling about six hundred miles, they found the men. The glib Siringo soon convinced them that he and Sayers were experts on assaying gold and that they had gone there to make their fortune. The liquor enticed Hubbard to visit their camp regularly, and the four soon became, on the surface, the best of friends. After several weeks, desperate to know how to deal with their stolen gold, Hubbard confessed to the crime and offered to pay Siringo and Sayers to melt it down. Not knowing where the gold was hidden, the detectives had to go through a charade of Siringo returning to Juneau to buy clay to build a furnace as well as chemicals and other materials to melt the gold. At the same time, he arranged for a U.S. marshal to station himself not far from the camp.

Before long, the four started melting the gold into ingots, and when the others went to bed one night, Siringo sneaked out of camp to fetch the marshal. They returned the next morning and arrested the thieves. Hubbard, outraged, walked up to Siringo, and, "looking me square in the face said: 'Davis, how in h—l can you ever face the public again, after the way you have treated me?' I laughed and told him that . . . my conscience wouldn't bother me on that score."[8]

Siringo also worked again with Doc Shores and relieved Tom Horn on one assignment, but he partnered up with Sayers more than anyone else. At one stage he missed going with Sayers on what he thought would be the trip of a lifetime. Siringo had been working on an ore-stealing case in Salt Lake City, and for three weeks had been receiving letters from McParland telling him to finish quickly, as he was needed in Denver. Fearing he would be assigned to another "tramp operation," Siringo responded that certain work couldn't be hurried. He could have finished the job two weeks before he actually did, but "I didn't believe in dropping a good thing so long as it could be held onto without injuring the Agency."[9] When Siringo finally returned to Denver, "Mr McParland informed me that my friend, W.B. Sayers, had started two days before for New York City, there to ship for London, England, to meet our clients, and from there go to South Africa to work up a big ore-stealing case. . . . Robt A Pinkerton had selected me for the operation and had been waiting on me for nearly a month, but that the clients got tired of waiting, and then Sayers was detailed to go. He was allowed to take along another operative, Harry Akin, to help him. My bones ached for a week on account of losing this trip."[10]

Throughout this period, McParland and his wife, Mary, led quiet lives, focusing on work, church, and family. Once lean and muscular, McParland could now better be described as "stocky," and he sported a heavy mustache, but was otherwise clean-shaven, with a complete lack of sideburns. His health was not particularly good. His assistant superintendent, J. C. Fraser, wrote years later: "Mr McParland is anything but a strong man. Ever since he had the typhoid fever [in 1892], he is easily alarmed over any spell of illness he may have."[11] One thing that certainly was problematic was his eyesight, which had been poor even during his time in Schuylkill County. In 1895, he suffered from what was diagnosed at the time as choroiditis, and he had an operation that seemed to improve the condition.[12] It has also been claimed that he was a very heavy drinker, but—although certainly a distinct possibility since he had been during his Molly Maguire days and the supplement to his History of Detectives form suggests his drinking issues had continued—there is no firm proof that it was the dominant feature that it has been portrayed to be.[13]

Although lacking children of his own, McParland remained close to his brothers and their families, most notably Charles, who went into the real estate business and long remained in the house on Menomonee Street. Not long after Charles's wife, Mary Ann, died, the widower rediscovered Emma Schoepple, an old flame from his time in Schuylkill County. In September 1893, they were married, the same year that Edward married his wife, Frances, in Colorado, shortly after she had immigrated from Ireland. Within the next few years Charles and Emma had two children—Charles's fifth and sixth—John and Kittie, the latter of whom would become an important part of McParland's life in Denver. Sadly, Emma died of cardiac collapse in May 1898, at the age of only thirty-eight.[14]

In 1897, James and Mary acquired, in a sense, another family member, when Eneas McParland, the second son of James's older brother Frank, moved in with them. Born in 1872 in Charleston on the South Island of New Zealand, Eneas worked at an early age as a storeman at his father's store and bakery in the nearby town of Cobden. He moved with the family to Wellington in 1895, where he worked as a baker.[15] But he was a bit of a wild lad, and, hoping to calm him and instill a sense of responsibility, Frank sent him to live with his uncle James. The two hit it off famously, giving McParland the closest he would ever have to a son. Eneas soon found a good job as a mail agent for the Globe Express Company, and he lived with his uncle and aunt until 1899, the year that, after living at seven different addresses since he had moved to Denver, McParland bought a house at 1256 Columbine, where he and Mary would remain the rest of his life.[16]

McParland seemed to have had an instinctive understanding of how to use the popular press, and in the days before such things as regular press conferences were held, he would still call together the reporters from the newspapers that he thought would be most helpful (and positive) and give "a little something to the press" in order to make sure they distributed the information that he wanted made known.[17] He was also known to leak developments to friendly reporters on a more personal level, sometimes doing so on the condition that he could go over the story before it was submitted.[18] This meant that he essentially was able to vet numerous newspaper articles that mentioned ongoing developments in his investigations, and also that he was presented positively in regard to assessments of cases, views on crime, financial donations to charities, and contributions to other good causes.

Among those good causes or associations, McParland was "a strong advocate of the Benevolent and Protective Order of Elks"—the highly respected American fraternal organization—and was extremely active in "any undertaking to further the interests of the Church."[19] Mary also participated in many charitable causes, particularly Church-related ones.

At times McParland even was able to link charity and crime. In January 1898, he was the guest speaker at a "conference of charities and corrections" in Colorado Springs. "After a number of discussions along the line of caring for discharged convicts," a newspaper account summarized, "Governor Adams arose and stated that he would give $100 toward the starting of a Prisoners' Aid Society. . . . Among those who spoke in favor of the Prisoners' Aid Society were . . . W. H. Conley, warden of Arapahoe county jail, and Superintendent McParland of the Pinkerton detective agency. The latter gentleman . . . said that convict labor should be employed and that they must also be given instruction. He was opposed to the system of contract labor."[20]

It was somewhat ironic that proposing such a society thereafter led Colorado governor Alva Adams to be portrayed as "soft on crime," because less than two months later, on March 14, 1898, he, Wyoming governor William A. Richards, and Utah governor Heber Wells decided to pull out all stops to exterminate outlaws in the region. The three agreed on "a concerted action by the three states . . . to break up the infamous 'Robber's Roost' gang which has been terrorizing portions of the three states for the past two years. In all probabilities the work will be done by special officers."[21] The original thinking was that those "special officers" would be men sworn in for this particular purpose, or would be bounty hunters paid to curtail the criminal activity. Ultimately, however, the efforts focused on the members of one gang, and many of those seeking them would be McParland's operatives, including Siringo, Sayers, and Shores. Their quarry: the violent gang of bank and train robbers most often known as the Wild Bunch and led by Butch Cassidy.

It was in 1866, the year before McParland moved to the United States, that Robert LeRoy Parker was born to a hardworking Mormon family in the remote Circle Valley of Utah's southwest quadrant.[22] As the oldest of fourteen children, Parker went to work early, being hired at the age of thirteen at a nearby ranch, where he began his lifelong relationship with horses: "stealing them, raising them, racing them, and selling them—and eventually escaping on them with other people's money."[23] He also fell under the spell of a hand named Mike Cassidy, who taught the youngster how to shoot and rebrand stray cattle, and whose last name Parker would eventually take on.

It wasn't long before Parker had his first brush with the law, although it appears to have been more of a misunderstanding than anything else. Having ridden into town to buy a pair of overalls, he found the general store closed, and not wanting to have come so far for nothing, he searched out a way into the building. He went through the shelves and found the clothing he wanted, then wrote a note to the store owner, leaving his name, telling him what he had done, and promising to be back soon to pay him. The owner did not take this arrangement in the best of spirits, however, and reported Parker to the town marshal, although the matter was eventually settled without Parker receiving any jail time.

At the age of eighteen Parker moved to the mining town of Telluride in southwest Colorado, taking along twenty horses that likely had been stolen by a friend and he had been paid to drive over the border, where they would fetch a good price. He had started down the path he would follow the rest of his life.

Parker seems to have drifted through Wyoming and Montana during the next three years. At some point in 1887 he returned to Telluride, where he met Matt Warner, another Mormon cowboy who had proven adept at both stealing horses and racing them. There was an instant rapport between the two, and that summer, after a horse race in Cortez, Colorado, Warner introduced Parker to Tom McCarty, an experienced horse thief. The three were looking for easy ways to make money, and although Parker and Warner both worked occasionally as cowboys and horsebreakers, they knew they were never going to get rich that way, so they turned their eyes toward other folks' property. There are stories that the three were involved in the robbery of the eastbound Denver & Rio Grande passenger train near Grand Junction, Colorado, in November 1887, but nothing was ever proved. What does seem certain, however, is that in March 1889, either Warner and McCarty or Warner and Parker robbed the First National Bank of Denver, taking twenty-one thousand dollars after having threatened to blow the building up with nitroglycerin.

That was just the start. Three months later the trio and a fourth man held up the San Miguel Valley Bank in Telluride. They rode out of town shooting their revolvers to intimidate anyone who might be about. That did not stop the local sheriff from forming a posse and following them, but the bandits managed to evade capture due to having organized in advance a relay of horses along their route. Eventually they reached Brown's Park, the thirty-five-mile-long valley on the Utah-Colorado border through which the Green River runs. That it was exceptionally isolated made the park "a popular hiding place for stolen stock" and it "became a general hangout for rustlers and eventually outlaws of all kinds."[24]

Thinking they were safe, the outlaws settled down to rest at a mountain cabin belonging to a friend of Warner's. But within days they discovered that they had been followed as far as the friend's nearby ranch, so, according to Warner, they raced down to a new hideout in record time, riding by night and hiding by day.[25] The new place was Robbers Roost—a location even more remote than Brown's Park. Located in the high desert of southeast Utah, Robbers Roost was a desolate, barren region of deep canyons, sheer cliff walls, and countless mesas. The extreme summer heat, general dearth of water, and twisting gorges that ended in unassailable rock faces made it nearly impossible for lawmen to hunt down their prey. And here Parker and his friends waited out their pursuers.

Now a wanted man, some time the next year Parker started using the alias George Cassidy. He also spent some of his ill-gotten gains on a ranch in the dry, sagebrush region near Dubois, Wyoming. An honest living did not hold his attention for long, however, and eventually he moved north to Johnson County, a center for both cattle ranching and cattle and horse rustling. As the large ranchers had difficulty getting court judgments against stock thieves, it was just the place for Cassidy, and he purchased about six hundred acres on Blue Creek, some ten miles from another favorite hiding place for criminals, called Hole-in-the-Wall.

For a while, Cassidy ran a round-trip transportation business in which he took horses stolen in South Dakota to Utah. After selling them he used part of the proceeds to buy horses stolen in Utah, which he drove back to the Dakotas. In 1891, he met up again with Warner and McCarty, and that summer the three only just escaped after being seen by a party of range riders armed with Winchester repeating rifles and hired to put an end to rustling. Leaving behind the fifty or so head they had gathered, they split up and somehow managed to outrun the larger party and avoid the potshots taken at them. Things could have been worse, as it was only the next year that the Wyoming Stock Growers Association brought in a party of forty-six ranch owners, stock detectives, and hired gunmen to kill rustlers and other "undesirables," in what became known as the Johnson County War.[26]

In 1892, Cassidy, by this time going by the nickname "Butch,"[27] was arrested for possession of a stolen horse, one of three that he claimed he had purchased from a cowboy named Billy Nutcher. The trial was postponed, and a year later he was acquitted. But that same week a second complaint was registered, alleging the theft of another of those three horses. Again the trial was delayed, and Cassidy left the state. But in 1894 he returned for the trial; he was convicted and sentenced to two years in the Wyoming State Penitentiary in Laramie. He served about eighteen months before being released in the middle of winter, January 1896. The first thing he did was head straight to Brown's Park to find Warner. There Cassidy fell in with two other minor criminals: Elzy Lay, an Ohio-born counterfeiter,[28] and Henry "Bub" Meeks, a Wyoming Mormon looking for excitement. They were going to get more than any of them bargained for.

The event that started a new phase in Cassidy's career of crime was the arrest of Matt Warner and two other men for the murder of a pair of prospectors who they had tried to frighten off a claim. Warner had no money for a lawyer and asked Cassidy for help. In response, on a hot afternoon in August 1896, Butch, Lay, and Meeks robbed the bank in Montpelier, Idaho, of an amount estimated between $5,000 and $16,500.

It was a classic job. Shortly before closing time, the three robbers rode up to the bank, and while Meeks watched over the horses, Cassidy and Lay pulled their bandannas over their faces, drew their pistols, and entered the bank.

Ordering everyone against the wall, Butch stood near the door and covered them while Lay told A. N. McIntosh, the assistant cashier, to give him all the money. When McIntosh said there were no bills, Lay smacked him on the forehead with his pistol, which angered Cassidy, who ordered him not to hit the clerk again. McIntosh then forked the cash over, little realizing that Cassidy's comments were the first noted instance of an attitude that would—years later—contribute to his portrayal as a Robin Hood–type figure. He was, it would be said, a happy-go-lucky rogue who stole from banks and railroads, but not from common people, and one who chose not to engage in violence—including not killing anyone until late in his career.[29]

Whether that assessment is accurate or not, for the time being, Cassidy waited inside the bank, allowing Lay to walk calmly outside and tie the sacks with the money onto the horses. Butch then warned everyone not to leave the bank for 10 minutes, and the three men rode off. Quickly pursued, they again made an effective escape due to having stashed fresh horses partway to the Wyoming state line. They then headed to Robbers Roost, where they spent the autumn and winter. Warner, meanwhile, was convicted of manslaughter and sentenced to five years in the Utah Penitentiary.

By the spring of 1897, Cassidy had started recruiting men to form a gang. He was already well-known in the criminal world, and his description would have been familiar to law officers in Utah, Wyoming, and the surrounding states. He was, according to a Pinkerton's description, five feet nine inches tall, 165 pounds, with "light complexion, blue eyes, medium build, flaxen hair . . . small red scar under left eye . . . eyes deep set."[30]

What that description did not emphasize was that he was intelligent, quick-witted, and a very careful planner. That said, he needed a good deal of luck for the next big heist, because his target—the payroll office of the Pleasant Valley Coal Company at Castle Gate, Utah—was one of the most difficult places to rob in the entire West. Castle Gate was a small company town located in a deep valley reached by a railroad spur of the Denver & Rio Grande Railroad, which owned the coal company. Horses, which would be needed for a getaway, were uncommon there, as the miners had no need for them, and anyone who brought them into the valley was immediately the subject of suspicion. Moreover, even knowing when to try to carry off the robbery was next to impossible because the cash and gold delivered for the company payroll were sent every two weeks on a train running on differing days and at undisclosed times. The only way the miners knew when they were going to be paid was by a special blast of the mine's whistle: At that sound they would descend on the office for their pay, giving any robbers an extremely limited time to carry out any plan.

In order to have horses available, Cassidy started sending a couple of men into the town at a time, under the pretense that they were training for bareback horse races in Salt Lake City. On one of these excursions, he and Lay just happened to be there when the train arrived with the payroll. While the paymaster and his clerk collected the money, Cassidy quickly moved into position. As the two men returned to their office, he confronted them on a set of stairs and ordered them to drop the bags. They did so, but the clerk then scampered off for help, and as a miner approached, having heard the disturbance, Lay, who was already mounted, pointed his pistol at him and growled, "Get back in there, you son-of-a-bitch, or I'll fill your belly full of hot lead!"[31]

Meanwhile, Cassidy grabbed the bags and tossed them to Lay, who caught them but dropped the reins to Butch's horse. Frightened, the horse bolted down the road, only just to be headed off by Lay, allowing Cassidy to leap in the saddle and the two men to gallop off. The paymaster ran to the telegraph office and tried to contact the sheriff but found the lines had been cut. He immediately commandeered the train and headed to Price, the county seat, to form a posse. Yet again, however, the stashing of fresh horses allowed the outlaws to make excellent time to Robbers Roost, after which they split their time hiding out between there and Brown's Park.

Even before the Castle Gate robbery, Cassidy's criminal circle had been increasing, and he hoped to form a gang that he wanted to call the "Train Robbers Syndicate."[32] The name didn't stick, but the gang did, and one man who joined early on was a fellow who, like Cassidy, had a special talent with and affection for horses—Harry Alonzo Longabaugh.[33] Born of devout Baptist parents in 1867 in Phoenixville, Pennsylvania, he had received only intermittent schooling but could still read and write, and at a surprisingly early age he had joined a local literary society. Longabaugh left home at the age of fifteen and moved with the family of his cousin to a ranch near Durango, Colorado. A couple years later, they headed to Cortez, and Longabaugh began working as a wrangler and horsebreaker. It is possible that at this stage he met Bob Parker.

By 1887, having fallen on hard times, Longabaugh stole a horse, a saddle, and a pistol from cowhands in Crook County, Wyoming. He was caught, escaped, and was recaptured. Found guilty at trial, he was sentenced to eighteen months in prison, but spent the time instead in the Crook County jail in Sundance, from which he most likely adopted his nickname of the Sundance

Kid. After his release, he drifted, working at ranches near Calgary, Alberta, and in Montana. Then, in 1892, Longabaugh, Bill Madden, and Harry Bass held up a passenger train of the Great Northern Railroad. Madden and Bass were caught soon thereafter and sent to prison, but Longabaugh disappeared into Wyoming's Big Horn Mountains.

Within a few years, the Sundance Kid, also using the alias Harry Alonzo, had joined Cassidy's gang. By all accounts he had a certain style and class unusual for a desperado. Standing about five feet nine inches tall and weighing around 170 pounds, Pinkerton's described him as: "Complexion medium dark, black hair, blue or gray eyes, combs his hair pompadour, bow legged, walks with feet far apart, mustache or beard, if any, black, nose rather long, slim build, features Grecian type, marks his clothes 'H.L.' with worsted thread."[34]

At about this time, the band began to be known popularly as the Wild Bunch, a name "probably derived from the gang's antics in riding into towns for a little fun and excitement" and short for "that wild bunch from Brown's Park."[35] There was little formality in its membership, as the men were caught, left to carry out their own robberies, and drifted back when they felt like it. But there were usually about eight or nine at a time, including a number of villains who had been engaged in lives of crime long before meeting Cassidy. One was Harvey Logan, a rough cowboy and cattle thief originally from Iowa, but who had lived in Missouri, Texas, Colorado, and numerous other parts of the West. In 1895 Logan fled to Wyoming from Landusky, Montana, after killing the man for whom the town had been named. One story was that Pike Landusky had started a brawl over Logan's attentions to his daughter—only for her to acknowledge after her father's death that she was pregnant by Logan's brother Lonnie. Also known by the alias Kid Curry, Logan was the smallest of the bunch—at five feet seven and a half inches and about 145 to 150 pounds[36]—but he was also the most violent, and before he joined up with the Wild Bunch he and Lonnie had ridden with the feared train robber and murderer Tom "Black Jack" Ketchum.

Other well-known members of Cassidy's crew included: Lonnie Logan; George "Flat Nose" Currie, who had probably met Cassidy in the Blue Creek area years before; the slow-talking, round-faced Texan David Atkins; Will "News" Carver, another Texan who had also ridden in Ketchum's gang; Ben "the Tall Texan" Kilpatrick; Bob Lee, the Logans' cousin; and Tom O'Day, listed on a Pinkerton's wanted poster as "smelling like a polecat."[37]

Only a few months after the robbery at Castle Gate, the Wild Bunch tried to rob the Butte County Bank at Belle Fourche, South Dakota. Although Cassidy might have planned the robbery, he was not there on the day, as he was allegedly trying to find his friend Bub Meeks. What he didn't realize was that Meeks had been arrested in Fort Bridger, Wyoming, a couple of weeks before for robbing a general store and post office of $123. While Meeks was in custody, a cashier who had been serving at the bank in Montpelier when it was robbed, identified him as the man who had held the horses. Eventually, Meeks was tried and found guilty of bank robbery and sentenced to thirty-five years in the Idaho State Penitentiary in Boise.

Meanwhile, on June 28, 1897, five or six members of the Wild Bunch rode into Belle Fourche, expecting that the bank would be holding more cash than usual, as the town had just hosted a reunion of Civil War veterans.[38] Four dismounted outside the bank, and three or four—thought to be "Flat Nose" Currie, Harvey and Lonnie Logan, and perhaps Walt Punteney[39]—stormed inside and ordered everyone to raise their hands. The head cashier pulled out a pistol, pointed it at Harvey Logan, and pulled the trigger. But when it misfired, he meekly laid it down and followed the gunmen's instructions.

Currie ordered the bank's patrons to put their money in a sack, but before more than one man could do so, the owner of a hardware store across the street, having seen everyone inside the bank raising their hands, yelled that a bank robbery was in progress. Realizing that the town would mobilize within moments, the robbers raced out to their horses, and all but one mounted and rode away. The horse of the last man, Tom O'Day, bolted, leaving the bandit on his own. He ran off, trying to lose himself in the crowd, but was quickly caught and put in jail. The others rode hard into Wyoming, where they split up, having gained only ninety-seven dollars, the amount dropped in Currie's bag.

Later that summer, Longabaugh, Harvey Logan, and Punteney ventured into Montana, planning on robbing the bank in Red Lodge. But after unsuccessfully soliciting the aid of a local marshal they thought to be corrupt, they decided they'd better make themselves scarce and headed north toward Lavina. Near there they were caught by a posse, and Logan was wounded. When Longabaugh and Logan were identified as two of the men involved in the bank robbery at Belle Fourche, the three were taken to jail in Deadwood, where O'Day was still awaiting trial. On October 31, the four were broken out of jail, and Longabaugh and Logan—whose identities had not been established with certainty because they both claimed to be named Jones—made good their escape. The other two were recaptured, but O'Day was eventually acquitted, and the charges against Punteney were dropped.[40]

By the end of 1897 a great deal of the crime in the region—whether bank robbery, highway robbery, or cattle or horse theft—was being blamed on mysterious gangs that emerged from the great emptiness of places such as Robbers Roost or Brown's Park and then simply melted away, disappearing back into those areas. The Robbers Roost Gang, they were called, or the Hole-in-the-Wall Gang, or, most often, the Wild Bunch.

Just when cattlemen, banks, and other large business owners began demanding that something be done, an event occurred that changed everything.[41] In February 1898, a ruffian called Patrick Johnson killed teenager Willie Strang in Brown's Park. When Johnson and two escaped desperados he had fallen in with—Harry Tracy and David Lant—were cornered, Tracy killed Valentine Hoy, a rancher who had joined a posse. The case became a cause célèbre and quickly pushed the governors of Colorado, Utah, and Wyoming to issue a joint edict about breaking up the region's bands of outlaws. In the face of the growing pressure, some of the Wild Bunch left the area. Cassidy and Lay made their way to New Mexico. Enough of the gang stayed together, however, to pull off their most notorious robbery and killing yet, in the aftermath of which they would find themselves pursued by the most relentless hunters they had yet encountered: the operatives of the Western Division of Pinkerton's National Detective Agency.

CHAPTER 17

ON THE TRAIL OF THE WILD BUNCH

Early in the morning on June 2, 1899, the Union Pacific Railroad's Overland Limited No. 1—which had left Omaha the day before carrying unsigned bank notes, gold, and silver—made an unscheduled stop a few miles west of Wilcox, Wyoming.[1] Reports gave conflicting information about why the train halted. One indicated that up to four men had boarded at Wilcox, one of whom crawled over the locomotive's coaling car and forced the engineer to stop at gunpoint. Another claimed men had flagged it down with emergency lamps. Whatever the cause, just beyond an old bridge about six outlaws took control of the train and then forced the engineer and fireman to accompany them back to the two mail cars. When the clerks inside refused to open up, the robbers first put a couple of bullets through the wall and then set off explosives that jolted the entire car. Convinced that the next blast would destroy them along with the car, the clerks opened the doors.

Shortly after the mail car had been opened, a light was seen approaching from the east. It was section No. 2 of the Overland, officially part of the same train but actually a second one pulled by its own locomotive, although always traveling in close conjunction with No 1. Having been told that there might be soldiers aboard, the robbers ordered the engineer to move the train forward, but not before the fireman made a clumsy effort to pull down one of the gunmen's masks. He was quickly told that another such effort would result in him being shot.

Once clear of the vicinity of the bridge, dynamite was lit beneath the structure. Although the explosion did not bring it down, it was enough to prevent No. 2 from crossing. The back cars were then unfastened, and the train moved ahead two miles, pulling only the baggage, express, and mail cars. Perhaps concerned about a lack of time for a thorough search, the robbers ignored the other cars and ordered the express agent, C. E. Woodcock, to open his door. When he refused, they blew it open and promptly blasted open the safes, using so much explosive that damaged bank notes and other financial documents were strewn far and wide. Grabbing the unsigned bank notes, cash, gold, and other valuables, they escaped on their waiting horses with an estimated fifty thousand dollars.

The next day the robbers were joined by another man—usually assumed to be Cassidy, receiving a share for the planning—and the money was split up. The parties then headed in different directions, one going north and another evidently riding west. There is little certainty exactly who was in which group, but three of them hid out in a quiet cabin on Casper Creek in Natrona County. They might not have been so relaxed if they knew what was behind them.

Immediately after the robbers rode away the engineer had carefully driven the damaged cars into Medicine Bow, where he telegraphed news of the event to the Union Pacific Railroad office in Omaha. Union Pacific officials immediately dispatched a specially outfitted train from Laramie to Wilcox. Aboard were company detectives and operatives from Pinkerton's, which had a contract with the railroad. They were joined by local posses and members of the state militia, and within twenty-four hours more than one hundred men were in the field searching for the criminals.[2]

The discovery of the three men at Casper Creek was essentially accidental. When a neighbor came by to see who was using the cabin, two armed men emerged from it and told him to "hit the road and hit it quick."[3] He left, but reported the incident to law officers in Casper, and a posse was quickly formed. When the posse reached the cabin, the three bandits were gone. Following their tracks in the mud, the posse soon caught up with them. But without warning, the outlaws opened fire. Josiah Hazen, the Converse County Sheriff, was badly wounded and the posse had to withdraw to take him back to Casper—it was in vain, as he died the next day.

Sheriff Hazen was among the most respected lawmen in the state, and his death launched one of the largest manhunts ever undertaken in Wyoming.[4] Nevertheless, the three outlaws managed to escape despite losing their horses in the shootout. Reaching the area near the Powder River on foot, they were given horses by a sympathetic rancher, and were able to elude any number of posses seeking them.[5]

It has long been debated which members of the Wild Bunch were involved in the Wilcox train robbery. Were George Currie and Harvey and Lonnie Logan the three participants in the firefight that killed Hazen? Or were they Currie, Harvey Logan, and Longabaugh? And who were the other three—if that is even the correct number? Different reports suggested Ben Kilpatrick, Will Carver, Elzy Lay, or Bob Lee. Regardless, they were now all in the sights of law-enforcement agencies throughout the West, including that headed by James McParland.

For more than eleven years, McParland had served as superintendent of Pinkerton's Denver office—the last four officially as "resident superintendent"—as well as, most of that time, being the assistant general superintendent of the Western Division. Not long before the Wilcox train robbery, his longtime assistant, John C. Fraser, was promoted to resident superintendent, and Frank Murray—who had been superintendent at the Chicago office but was suffering from consumption, and so needed to move to a "healthier" location—was brought in as an assistant superintendent. This allowed McParland to focus on the broader goal of controlling Western operations instead of the day-to-day dealings of the Denver office. As he responded to Bangs after being congratulated on the job he was doing: "I have always wished to have made more comments and suggestions to the Supts of the Western Division, but I was handicapped on account of the pressure of business as Supt of this office. It was impossible for me to do justice to the Asst Genl Superintendency so long as I had to assume the Superintendency of this office. I am very highly pleased that my work is satisfactory."[6]

Not only did the letter show McParland's gratitude to the Pinkertons and his desire to serve them as best he could, it also illustrated what the brothers thought was one of his weak points—his verbosity. McParland's gift—or curse—of the gab seemed to increase as time passed. He was quoted at longer and longer length in the press, and his statements in newspapers and in courtroom testimony seemed to reflect both self-satisfaction and a desire to prove himself an expert in all aspects of crime investigation and enforcement. It is apparent that at some stage he was carrying on too long in his reports, because handwritten on McParland's letter was a brief note from Robert Pinkerton, instructing Bangs: "In replying to this, ask him not to be too voluminous in his replies, but to get right to the point and make his letters as brief as possible."[7]

There was certainly no beating around the bush in the aftermath of the Wilcox train robbery. In almost no time McParland and Fraser had men in the field, including Siringo and Sayers, the latter recently returned from South Africa. They were told to start at Salt Lake City and track down two men—presumably the robbers—who had been seen driving thirteen horses toward Brown's Park. Before they left, however, Siringo made contact with Shores, who was then working for the Denver & Rio Grande Railroad. Shores shared with them a letter he had received from an agent in Hanksville, Utah, that said two men with thirteen horses had passed there heading south. Realizing that this was undoubtedly the same pair, Siringo convinced Shores to give them the use of a stockcar to take their supplies and horses south so that they could reach the Colorado River around the same time as the robbers. But Fraser told them to stick to their original instructions. After five days hard riding toward Brown's Park, they found a telegram waiting for them at Fort Duchesne stating that the two men in Utah likely *were* the robbers, and to turn south after them. "We were not mad," wrote Siringo, "but the cuss-words hurled over towards Denver left a sulphuric taste in our mouths for a week."[8]

Fraser's mistake also left them ten days behind their suspects, as they found when they reached Hanksville. But the owner of a local hotel also gave a report about another man, who fit the description of Harvey Logan and had herded five horses across the Colorado River only days before. At this stage Siringo suspected that Logan was the mastermind of the robbery as well as the leader of the Wild Bunch, so he followed the tracks, ascending an impossibly steep bluff and picking his way through rocky arroyos before finally losing them and turning back within half a mile of Logan's campsite.[9]

The next day, Siringo and Sayers continued after their original prey, encouraged that they were on the right track by the appearance of some of the stolen bank notes.[10] But when they reached Bluff, in southern Utah, they were angered to find that Fraser had sent two additional operatives south by train, and they were now ahead of the cowboy detectives. According to Siringo: "Sayers and I figured that we were born leaders of men, hence we didn't like the idea of bringing up the rear." They put their horses to pasture and, taking a train, caught up with the other two operatives. They then "led the chase by riding on trains, in buggies, and on hired saddle horses. We left the other two boys far in the rear, and they finally lost the trail entirely and returned to Denver."[11]

Meanwhile, having heard from the old Pinkerton's client J. M. Archuleta— whom Siringo had once saved from assassination—that the men had been seen in Lumberton, New Mexico, the two cowboy detectives followed them there. Once again, their quarry was gone, and shortly thereafter the two followed different leads, after disagreeing over where to go next. Siringo returned to Colorado and followed the robbers' trail along the Arkansas River. He eventually passed through Dodge City, Wichita, and his old home in Caldwell, before crossing the Indian Territory to Arkansas, and thence proceeding into

Tennessee, and eventually Mississippi. Finally, still several weeks behind the outlaws, he was recalled to Denver.[12]

Sayers, meanwhile, traced some of the unsigned bank notes to Harlem, Montana, where Lonnie Logan and Bob Lee—going under the name Curry—owned a saloon and were laundering their stolen money. Sayers found out their true identities, but before he could arrest them they had sold the saloon and skipped town. In the process, Sayers's own identity was exposed, so he was unable to proceed with the investigation. He was named assistant superintendent of the new San Francisco office—a position that Siringo had turned down—and Siringo was sent up to Helena so that he could replace him in hunting down the Logans and Lee.[13]

Using the name Charles L. Carter, and claiming he was a fugitive outlaw from "old Mexico," Siringo went to Landusky, where he became friendly with a ruffian who shared ownership of a ranch with Harvey Logan. Siringo also met Pike Landusky's widow and daughter Elfie, with whom Lonnie Logan had a three-year-old son. He quickly turned Elfie's head, gained access to her personal items, and read the letters she had received from Lonnie. In this way, and from Harvey's partner, he learned a great deal about them and the other men with whom they rode. But as to the whereabouts of Harvey Logan, Siringo was still at a loss: "[H]e would never give a hint as to where 'Kid' Curry was, though I found out enough to convince me that they kept up a correspondence."[14]

Meanwhile, other Pinkerton's operatives were enjoying greater success. When Lonnie Logan and Bob Lee disappeared from Montana, they went to Cripple Creek, Colorado, where Lee returned to a job as a faro dealer that he had worked at on and off since 1894. Logan traveled on to Dodson, Missouri, to visit his aunt. In February 1900, Pinkerton's agents traced him there. When Lonnie saw lawmen outside the farmhouse, he attempted to run out the back to escape, but he was shot down, falling dead in a snowbank.[15] The same day, Lee was arrested at the Antlers Saloon in Cripple Creek.[16] Three months later he went on trial in Cheyenne, Wyoming, where his mother hired a Kansas City lawyer to dredge up an alibi. Instead, while the attorney was working with the Logan family, Siringo "was introduced to him, and learned all of his secrets."[17] With knowledge of the defense plans, it was easy for the prosecution to put together a case to prove Lee guilty of involvement in the Wilcox robbery; he was sentenced to ten years in prison.[18]

Not long after the Wilcox robbery, another former Pinkerton's agent, Tom Horn, was called in—possibly by the Union Pacific but equally as likely by

McParland[19]—to help find the three robbers who had headed north after the holdup.

By late December 1899, Horn was still conducting his search in Johnson County. Convinced that a man named Bill Speck knew more than he would admit, Horn visited him in early January. "In the morning it was snowing and I stayed all day," he later wrote. "Occasionally I would bring up the train robbery, and he never wanted to talk about it, so on the morning of the fourth when I was going to leave I told him that he had some information that I wanted and he must give it to me, or I would kill him and be done with him." Speck broke down and pleaded that the robbers would kill him if he told Horn anything. "I told him I was worse than they, because I would surely kill him then and there if he did not tell me, as no man was within eight miles of us."[20]

Not surprisingly, Speck told him a great deal, including that George Currie had picked up four horses from Billy Hill's ranch after the gun battle in which Sheriff Hazen was killed. Currie had told Speck and Hill all about the robbery, and had said that the two other men at the shootout were Harve Ray and a stranger "from the British possessions . . . [who] could blow Christ off the Cross with dynamite."[21] Frank Murray, the assistant superintendent in Denver, later enclosed a copy of the letter to U.S. Marshal Frank A. Hadsell, who was also leading a search for the Wild Bunch. In it, he speculated that Harve Ray might actually be Harvey Logan, meaning that he might not only have led the robbery but have been guilty of killing Hazen.[22]

Horn's discovery meant that investigations intensified regarding both Flat Nose Currie and Kid Curry. This was significant, because as late as the end of November, McParland was still writing that "it is a 'dead cinch' that the Roberts brothers, Geo. Curry and very possibly 'Butch' Cassidy are the main movers, if not the entire outfit, that held up the train."[23] In other words, it had not yet become clear that the mysterious Roberts brothers were actually the Logan brothers.

It was not only the Pinkerton's and the railroad detectives who were chasing the Wild Bunch. With large rewards on the criminals' heads, apprehending them "dead or alive" became an alluring prospect for other citizens. One man interested in doing so was former U.S. Deputy Marshal Frank Canton, who, after having left government employ in Alaska, decided a route back into official law enforcement might be as a successful bounty hunter.[24] In November 1899, Canton asked if Pinkerton's would pay his expenses if he went after the robbers. McParland responded that he was not able to "offer any other inducements to you other than what is offered in the circular." But, McParland told him, "if you want anything run down that you are not able to get after yourself, let me know."[25]

When Canton developed a strategy to waylay Flat Nose Currie, McParland told him that although he was dubious of the plan, he did "hope your scheme will be successful, not only on account of rounding up these people, but for your own self. . . . [Y]ou will have a nice piece of money." McParland then added some confidential agency information, noting, "This information is strictly for yourself and for your guidance and will help you in case you have got to act. You needn't say where you got [it] . . . just give whatever story you see fit."[26]

As it turned out, Canton's efforts came to nothing, and he, like other lawmen, must have felt he was chasing wisps of smoke, because although there were many rumors, hard evidence about the gang was slim. Then, on April 17, 1900, a man was seen changing the brand on a cow near Green River, Utah. A pair of sheriffs—Jesse Tyler of Moab and William Preece of Vernal—rushed to the scene, thinking it was a small-time rustler named Tom Dilley. Shots were exchanged until Tyler, coming up behind the man, shot him through the head. It was then that they discovered the dead man was actually Flat Nose Currie.[27]

While a wide range of law-enforcement officers searched high and low for the Wild Bunch, several of the outlaws were spending most of their time hiding out. For example, it is likely that the two men that Siringo and Sayers had followed south were Cassidy and Elzy Lay, who were en route to the WS Ranch in New Mexico, where they worked under the assumed names Jim Lowe and Willie McGinnes. However, although the pair generally stayed out of mischief while there, they appear to have taken a couple of weeks off to participate in the Wilcox robbery.[28] Lay then made a major mistake in an effort to make a similar "score." On July 11, 1899, he was one of three men— along with Sam Ketchum and Will Carver—who held up train No. 1 of the Colorado and Southern Railway about five miles outside Folsom, New Mexico, making off with between fifty thousand and seventy thousand dollars.[29]

Five days later a posse stumbled upon the three hiding out about eighty miles away in a place called Turkey Creek Canyon, not far from Cimarron. Alerted to their presence by a smoking campfire, the posse sneaked up on them. They might or might not have demanded that the robbers surrender, but, even if they did, they opened fire immediately thereafter. Lay was hit in the shoulder and back, and Ketchum had a bone just below his shoulder broken by a bullet, but Carver and the injured Lay took a heavy toll on the posse, killing Sheriff Edward Farr and wounding two others, one of whom died shortly thereafter. When the posse pulled back, the three men escaped, although Ketchum and Lay were captured a few days later. On July 24, Ketchum died in jail from blood poisoning. Lay, still insisting he was Willie McGinnes, was tried in October, found guilty of murdering Farr, and sentenced to life in prison.

About a month after Lay's trial, Murray showed up at the WS Ranch, still following the trail of money from the Wilcox robbery. Some had been spent by a ranch hand named Johnny Ward at a store in Alma, New Mexico, not far from the WS. Murray spoke to ranch owner William French, who called in Ward; the cowboy admitted to passing the money, which he had received for selling a horse to another ranch hand named Clay McGonagill, who had since moved on.[30] Surprisingly, Murray allowed Ward to keep the remainder of the stolen money.

Murray then showed French pictures of three men, and when the owner recognized one of them as his trail boss, Jim Lowe, Murray told him that it was actually Butch Cassidy. Only that very morning, Murray said, he had seen Cassidy in Alma. But when French asked if he intended to arrest the man, the assistant superintendent said that to do such a thing he "would need a regiment of cavalry," and that he would instead turn his attention to finding McGonagill.[31]

When French next saw Cassidy, he mentioned the meeting, but the outlaw "only grinned when I told him the name he had given him, and said that he and Tom [Capehart] had already spotted him. In fact, they had stood him a drink when he returned to Alma. As he put it, they suspicioned who he was, and they invited him to drink to make sure."[32] It did not take long to confirm his true identity, and it appears that at least several men intended to kill Murray before he could leave Alma and send in his reports. It is thought that there were other men at the WS who had ridden with the Wild Bunch, such as Capehart—a popular cowboy who has been rumored at times to have been the Sundance Kid under another alias—or possibly Will Carver, Ben Kilpatrick, or Harvey Logan.[33]

But Cassidy evidently liked Murray, because Siringo later wrote that the agent would have been killed had it not been for Jim Lowe, but instead was just driven out of town.[34] One suspects that Murray was grateful to Cassidy for saving his life, because he did not ever mention that Lowe was Cassidy, and he later told Siringo that he was wrong when the cowboy detective said the two were the same man.³⁵ On the other hand, although Cassidy gave all appearances of not being too worried about another Pinkerton's agent showing up, before long he sold off his holdings in the area and once more disappeared.

Unlike Cassidy, it is safe to say that not many wanted outlaws would have let Murray leave Alma alive. Included in those who would have finished off the Pinkerton's operative were most of the members of the Wild Bunch, men who were neither gentle nor very nice. But of all of them, Harvey Logan was the nastiest.

On May 27, 1900, Sheriff Tyler of Moab was still searching for Tom Dilley, this time near Hill Creek, some seventy-five miles northeast of Green River, Utah. Seeing three men wrapped in blankets around a campfire, he left one of his deputies behind and rode toward the men with Deputy Sam Jenkins to ask if they had seen Dilley. Suddenly the three opened fire, killing both lawmen. The other deputy raced off for help, but the killers escaped despite an intensive search. It was later shown that the murders were planned by Logan as revenge for the killing of his mentor, Flat Nose Currie.³⁶

Three months later, on August 29, Logan was back in action. Shortly after the second section of Union Pacific No. 3 left Tipton, Wyoming, and headed over the Continental Divide, a masked man slid down from the coal tender, pointed a gun at the engineer, and ordered him to stop the train when he saw a fire next to the track.³⁷ Three more men then forced the engineer to uncouple the passenger cars and move the rest of the train a mile up the track. Leaving the mail car untouched, they blew open the Oregon Short Line Express car, which suffered comparatively little, and the Pacific Express car, which was considerably more damaged.³⁸ Inside the latter was their old acquaintance from the Wilcox robbery, C. E. Woodcock. Although the Union Pacific claimed the robbers left with almost nothing, according to Woodcock they netted fifty-five thousand dollars.³⁹

After the robbers rode off, the engineer drove the train toward Green River, Wyoming, where a report was sent to the Union Pacific headquarters. Posses were immediately organized, and they headed to the scene of the crime, where, led by U.S. Marshal Frank Hadsell, U.S. Deputy Marshal Joe LeFors, and Sheriff Pete Swanson, they joined into one unit and set off in pursuit. Within a short time they saw the tracks of the four riders had been joined by those of a fifth. Riding hard, with LeFors leading the way, the posse covered 120 miles toward Colorado that day, but dwindled from about fifty men to a dozen as their horses gave out. At dusk they could see three men in the distance, but they had to stop due to fears of losing the trail in the dark. The next day they gave up after finding the outlaws' horses, which had been switched for fresh ones.

From the beginning authorities believed that both Cassidy and Logan participated in the robbery. There have since been strong arguments against Cassidy's involvement, however, and although Logan undoubtedly was at Tipton, the other men's identities have not been established with certainty.[40]

What does appear to be a possibility is that if the weather had turned out slightly differently a short while before, Cassidy might not have been robbing anyone. At some point during the previous year, he seriously considered turning away from a life of crime.[41] His initial idea had been followed by a visit to the influential Salt Lake City attorney Orlando Powers, and then a request to Parley Christensen, another prominent lawyer and rising Utah politician, to arrange a meeting with Utah governor Heber Wells to discuss a deal. Remarkably, Wells granted the request and met with Cassidy not once but twice while considering an amnesty should Butch turn himself in and reform. The potential plan was ultimately rejected when Wells was told that Cassidy was wanted for murder in Wyoming. Of course, even had Wells moved ahead, he did not have the power to speak for the governors of Wyoming, Idaho, Colorado, Montana, or South Dakota.

Undeterred, Powers and Cassidy's longtime Wyoming attorney, Douglas Preston, proposed a meeting with Union Pacific officials to consider the same offer—presumably hoping that if the railroad decided to stop its pursuit of Cassidy, the states would follow suit. A meeting was arranged for a remote location, but on the day that Preston was scheduled to bring the railroad officials, a terrible storm delayed them. When they finally reached the meeting place, Cassidy had departed, leaving behind a note: "Damn you Preston, you have double-crossed me. I waited all day but you didn't show up. Tell the U.P. to go to hell. And you can go with them."[42]

As a last-ditch effort, Powers approached Wells again, and in August 1900 the two men sent Matt Warner, recently released from prison, to find Cassidy, explain what had happened, and try to get him to reconsider. Warner was on the train heading for the area where he expected his friend to be when he was handed a telegram from Wells: "All agreements off. Cassidy just held up a train at Tipton."[43]

Cassidy had not, in all likelihood, been involved in the Tipton robbery, but that was most likely because he was already on his way to another heist. On September 19, three men without masks robbed the First National Bank of

Winnemucca, Nevada, of $32,640. With fresh relays of horses, they easily left behind the hastily organized posses. The target was so far out of the Wild Bunch's normal stomping grounds that the authorities initially gave little consideration to his potential involvement, but it later became accepted that the three robbers were Cassidy, Longabaugh, and Will Carver.[44]

Siringo was now assigned to the Tipton case, and he began his search by going after two men reported to have been seen near Grand Junction, Colorado, one of whom, being very tall, was thought to be Ben Kilpatrick. At one point he found that his quarry—evidently Kilpatrick and Logan—had left only the previous morning.[45] He could not close the gap on them, however, so he rode to Circle Valley to see what information he could obtain from Cassidy's family instead. He spent a week in Circleville, where "I had hard work to keep from falling in love with Miss Parker, the pretty young sister of Butch." He also "found out all about 'Butch's' early life and much about his late doings. His true name was Parker, his nickname being 'Sallie' Parker when a boy. This nickname of itself was enough to drive a sensitive boy to the 'bad.' "[46]

Ordered to go to Alma, since it was the "southern Rendezvous for the Wild Bunch," Siringo drifted south into Arizona, then on to New Mexico, finally arriving at Cassidy's old hangout to finish his "horseback ride of over a thousand miles through the most God-forsaken desert country in the United States."[47] In Alma he heard tales of how Murray had talked to the barkeep Jim Lowe without realizing this was the very man he was looking for—stories that did not exactly match the reports that Murray had submitted. Siringo wrote to Murray, telling him that a friend of Lowe's had mentioned that he and his friends were nearby preparing for a raid, and that he was planning to try to get in with the gang. But the assistant superintendent replied quickly, telling Siringo that he "was mistaken about Jim Lowe being 'Butch' Cassidy, as he had met Lowe and found him to be a nice gentleman."[48] Instead, Murray ordered Siringo back to Denver to follow up on other members of the Wild Bunch.

In the following months, "after much planning and scheming," Siringo, going by the name Lee Roy Davis, "got in solid" with Jim Ferguson, who had furnished horses and food to Logan, Kilpatrick, and the Texan Bill Cruzan—usually considered the best horse thief among the members of the Wild Bunch—before the Tipton robbery.[49] Ferguson had remained in close contact with several members of the gang, and Siringo was able to wheedle information from him about the Wilcox robbery and other unsolved cases. Then, obtaining a letter of introduction from Ferguson—"This is to introduce you to my friend," it stated. "He is righter than hell."[50]—Siringo went to Rawlins,

Wyoming, where he fell in with more men who were friendly to Cassidy, Logan, or other members of Wild Bunch, from whom he learned a few key trade secrets of the gang. One was that "they kept a system of blind post offices all the way from the Hole-in-the-Wall in northern Wyoming to Alma in southern New Mexico, these post offices being in rocky crevices or on top of round mounds on the desert. In passing these post offices, members of the Wild Bunch would look for mail or deposit notes of importance."[51]

Siringo then headed to Santa Fe to interview Elzy Lay in the New Mexico Penitentiary. In the following months he returned to his "friends" in Wyoming, and then made another slow pass through Arizona and New Mexico, all the time gathering information about relatives, hideaways, and secrets of the Wild Bunch, while once missing Logan by just two days.[52]

More than a quarter of a century later, Siringo wrote that he had actually gone undercover and been a "member of the Wild Bunch for four years under many assumed names,"[53] a story that various writers have repeated ever since. However, although he certainly dealt with men who were on the fringes of the gang during the several years of his investigation, and he indeed used many different names with them, he never rode with the Wild Bunch himself, as shown both by his own earlier accounts and by the timing of his other investigations, which would have made his active participation impossible. His claim to be more involved than he truly was was simply an old man with a very active imagination remembering things as he wanted them to be rather than how they were. In enlarging on stories like this, he once again showed himself similar in this respect to that other master storyteller—his friend and boss, McParland.

The end of Siringo's assignment did not conclude the agency's role in the hunt for the Wild Bunch. Nor did it end the history of the gang. Following the Winnemucca robbery, the key remaining players—Cassidy, Longabaugh, Logan, Carver, and Kilpatrick—met up in Fort Worth, Texas, although it has been debated whether it was for a celebration of their success, the wedding of Will Carver, or just a good time.[54] On November 21, 1900, they donned Sunday suits and bowler hats for a now famous photograph, taken by John Swartz at his studio. Apparently Swartz was so pleased with the photo, he displayed an extra copy in his gallery. When Wells Fargo agent Fred Dodge happened to spot it and recognized Carver, he sent copies to a variety of law-enforcement agencies. Pinkerton's then used the pictures on new wanted posters that were distributed throughout the West.[55]

The almost mocking portrait of the Wild Bunch made it seem that once again they had had the last laugh, and before long a picture of Longabaugh and his partner Etta Place taken in February 1901 in New York City, created another stir at Pinkerton's. "What a great pity we did not get the information regarding the photograph while this party was in New York," William Pinkerton wrote to his brother. "It shows how daring these men are, and while you are looking for them in the wilderness and mountains, they are in the midst of society."[56] A few weeks later—on February 20, 1901—Longabaugh, Place, and, most likely, Cassidy boarded the steamer *Herminius*, bound for Buenos Aires, Argentina.[57]

The disappearance of the leader of the Wild Bunch and his closest crony did not interfere with the Pinkerton's investigation. Two weeks later, McParland was scheduled to go to Laramie to interview Bob Lee, although he had to postpone the trip when he came down with "a case of Grippe" and "discovered that my temperature was 101."[58] Nor did the departure of Cassidy and Longabaugh change the manner in which the remaining members still figured to make money—stealing it. In March, Logan, Carver, and Ben and George Kilpatrick began planning the robbery of the First National Bank of Sonora, Texas.[59] But late that month, the Kilpatrick family ranch was visited by a neighbor, Oliver C. Thornton, who had been complaining about the pigs of the Kilpatricks' brother, Boone. Whether that issue escalated or Thornton heard plans for the robbery, he didn't leave alive: Logan killed him on the spot. On April 2, Carver and George Kilpatrick rode into Sonora, where the local sheriff and several deputies tried to arrest Carver for Thornton's murder. When the outlaws resisted, Carver was shot dead.

Two and a half months later—on July 3, 1901, as much of the country prepared for celebrations of the 125th anniversary of the signing of the Declaration of Independence—the Wild Bunch pulled off its last great robbery—the Great Northern Railroad's Express No. 3, outside of Wagner in remote northern Montana.[60] The robbery was likely led by Logan, who, along with Kilpatrick, O. C. Hanks, and from one to three other men, escaped with up to forty thousand dollars in unsigned bank notes, gold, and silver coins. That was the beginning of the end, however. In November 1901, Kilpatrick—having been mistaken for Longabaugh—was arrested in St. Louis. Once officials discovered who he actually was, he was indicted for seventeen federal currency offenses. Rather than risk extradition to Montana—which had instituted the death penalty for train robbery—he pled guilty and was sentenced to fifteen years in prison.[61]

That same month, Logan began spreading his stolen bank notes around Knoxville, Tennessee, and one evening there he became involved in a brawl in a poolroom.[62] Two policemen—William Dinwiddie and Robert Saylor—came in to break up the fight, and Logan shot each repeatedly, disabling both of them. Logan made a getaway, but was injured, and was caught a couple days later. When tried in federal court, he was convicted of stealing, forging, and passing forged federal bank notes. He was sentenced to between 20 and 130 years in prison. His lawyers appealed, but were unsuccessful. In June 1903, when he was about to be transferred to federal prison in Columbus, Ohio, he somehow escaped on the sheriff's horse.

On June 7, 1904, Logan, George Kilpatrick, and a man thought to be Dan Sheffield—the brother of Boone Kilpatrick's wife—held up the Denver & Rio Grande Western's No. 5 train near Parachute, Colorado. After a posse hunted down the three, Logan was wounded in a shootout. Choosing to avoid capture, he fatally shot himself in the head.

Meanwhile, Cassidy, Longabaugh, and Etta Place settled on a large piece of public land—where they could raise sheep and cattle—in the southern Argentine valley of Cholila, overlooked by the Andes and close to the Chilean border. They had not been there long before, in March 1903, the highly successful Pinkerton's operative Frank Dimaio, who was on assignment in São Paulo, Brazil, was sent to Buenos Aires to confirm their whereabouts.[63] By studying Argentine public records and ship company documents, checking bank and hotel records, and conducting numerous interviews, he was able to learn exactly where the desperadoes were living. However, the U.S. vice consul in Buenos Aires advised him not to try to reach their retreat during the rainy season, as the roads would be impassable. With months to wait, Dimaio returned to New York, but not before he had arranged for wanted posters of the two men to be printed in Spanish and distributed throughout the country.

The Pinkerton brothers had every intention of sending their operative back to capture Cassidy and Longabaugh, but, to their surprise, the railway companies and the American Bankers Association refused to pay for the operation. The railway reasoning was simple: Rather than extradite the criminals and risk their escape upon return to the United States, better to leave them in South America, where those authorities would be forced to deal with them.[64] The Pinkertons, not wanting to invest their own money, put any intervention on hold.

In the following years, Pinkerton's operatives continued to monitor the movements and resumed criminal activities of Cassidy and Longabaugh.

These continued until early November 1908, when, following the robbery of a mining company payroll in a remote area of the Bolivian Andes, the two were discovered in the village of San Vicente, where they were killed during or after a gun battle with Bolivian army and police forces.[65]

Meanwhile, shortly after Dimaio had first located Cassidy and Longabaugh in South America, an article in *The Sun* of New York—headlined "Last of the Train Robbers"—allowed McParland to take credit for the end of the Wild Bunch. "As a result of the work of the Pinkertons, assisted by local officers and posses, the train and bank robbers who have infested various States and Territories of the United States for more than forty-five years are at the present time a thing of the past," he said smugly. "The two greatest gangs of train and bank robbers this or any other country in the world has ever known were the Logan or Curry gang of Wyoming and Montana, and the Black Jack [Ketchum] gang of Texas." Despite this surprising lack of knowledge about the leadership of the Wild Bunch, McParland maintained that the end of the gang could be credited to the efforts of the men under his own leadership, with a result that "the train robber of the future will have to find a new country in which to operate and a new place in which to hide."[66]

CHAPTER 18

THE MAN IN CHARGE

I t is not surprising that at times James McParland seemed the epitome of self-satisfaction. He was powerful, successful, and respected, and he enjoyed a celebrity in which he relished. He was also a cornerstone of a famed nationwide organization and the master of every aspect of the agency in the Western states.

In 1902, the Pinkerton brothers made a slight reorganization, reestablishing exactly who the agency's power brokers were. George D. Bangs—previously in direct control of the Eastern Division—gave up that charge to serve strictly as the number-three man, the day-to-day national administrator, with his title changing from general superintendent to general manager. Simultaneously, Robert Pinkerton's son, Allan, who was being groomed in the family business, was promoted to assistant general manager, in anticipation of his eventually becoming a principal. The three regional divisions remained, with the chiefs having "assistant" dropped from their designations. McParland's title thereby became general superintendent, Western Division, while his old friend David Robertson was replaced by Edward S. Gaylor in that role in the Middle Division. John Cornish, formerly of the Boston office, was promoted to the head of the Eastern Division and stationed in New York. Two years later McParland's title was changed to manager, Western Division.[1]

Soon there were twenty offices, eight under McParland, with nearly two hundred operatives in the West alone. The increase in business was so pronounced that Denver had more than thirty agents under Fraser, with four assistant superintendents: Murray, H. Frank Cary, Arthur E. Carver, and E. E. Prettyman.[2]

Located adjacent to the Denver office in the Opera House Block was McParland's private headquarters. He was thus neighbor to many operatives who hoped to emulate his success, although it is unlikely that they were on social terms with him, or even felt comfortable in his presence. Although the novelist Dashiell Hammett never personally knew McParland—joining Pinkerton's Baltimore office in 1915 and working out of Spokane only after McParland's death[3]—he definitely knew his reputation, which led him to write about the character based on him: "The Old Man . . . was also known as Pontius Pilate, because he smiled pleasantly when he sent us out to be crucified on suicidal jobs. . . . The Agency wits said he could spit icicles in July."[4]

It is obvious from numerous accounts that McParland at times got what he wanted by way of intimidation, bluster, and coercion, both within the company and with other agencies, including public law enforcement. "To-day I had a long confidential chat with John Leyden, who has been on the City Detective Force here in Denver for a number of years and owes his position to me," he once wrote to William Pinkerton. "While Leyden is the best officer in the city, he used to go on a periodical drunk and get discharged, but each time I was in a position to get him reinstated."[5]

McParland also had considerable charm and charisma, and to some he was the picture of all that was desirable. "He is regarded as one of the most skillful directors of detective work in the country," reported *The Seattle Daily Times*, "and in personal intercourse is most agreeable. His forte is story-telling, a form of entertainment in which he excels."[6] Similarly, the famous Ringling Brothers Circus proudly linked itself to him in a yearly account of its successes: "Detective Ryan . . . entertained McParland as the circus played in Denver."[7]

The Benevolent and Protective Order of Elks, perhaps the most respected fraternal organization in the United States—and the one that most emphatically espoused American values—found McParland to exemplify its ideals of "a loyal, reverent, and dutiful American."[8] At a meeting in Salt Lake City of Elks lodges from around the West, the person who first drew attention from the press was "a medium sized man . . . whose keen blue eyes looked out from behind a pair of steel-rimmed spectacles, and who apparently missed nothing that was going on. He was James McParland and . . . is the man who broke up the famous Molly Maguire gang."[9]

Even decades later the hierarchy of the Catholic Church was still honoring him for his work on that case, as well as for his devotion to the parish and his many contributions to the building of Denver's Cathedral of the Immaculate Conception.[10] He was on excellent personal terms with Denver's Bishop, Nicholas C. Matz, who, like McParland, was an outspoken opponent of the Western Federation of Miners.[11] But some of Denver's large Catholic community undoubtedly still considered McParland a traitor, and perhaps his actions in Schuylkill County were held against him when he tried to gain entrance to the Knights of Columbus, America's preeminent Catholic social and charitable organization.[12]

Or so claimed Edmund Richardson—a defense lawyer who was prepared to use such a story to smear McParland's reputation with a jury.[13] According to Richardson, when the Knights wished to expand into Denver in 1900, one of the national organizers visited McParland, on account of his connections with the Church hierarchy. McParland gladly met with Bishop Matz on their behalf, after which an application for a charter was submitted that contained the names of twenty-five of the most significant Catholic men in Denver— including McParland. The application was quickly granted, but when Denver Council 539 was instituted and its new members initiated, McParland was out of town on business. He therefore had to apply for membership and be voted in, like any other new member. As Richardson later recorded: "When his name was proposed, a number of the members decided that he would not make a desirable member. . . . When the ballot had been taken a number of the members, who had not voted, stated as a reason that the black balls [for a vote against] were exhausted and they did not care to vote. The vote was 29 black balls, 12 white balls and 24 members not voting for the reason as stated. According to the bylaws of the organization, this would debar him from membership." Months later, Richardson continued, McParland sought admission as a charter member of Council 615 in San Francisco, and it was there, in a place he supposedly was little known, that on January 19, 1902, he was finally able to gain admittance.

Although Richardson's story was later accepted as fact,[14] it remains uncorroborated. The national archives for the Knights of Columbus shows no record of McParland on the charter list for Denver but does show him as a charter member in San Francisco. According to the archivist, the only source that might provide such information would be the minutes book for the council of that period, but there is no record in Denver of the original meeting minutes.[15] The accuracy of the story is therefore open to debate. What *is* certain is that McParland eventually became a fourth-degree member of the Knights, the highest ranking in the order.[16]

It is also certain that McParland was not "little known" in San Francisco when he became a member in the Knights of Columbus, because immediately before that he had received a great deal of acclaim there for solving one of the most widely publicized robberies of the period.

On the morning of August 6, 1901, it was discovered that thirty-seven bars of gold bullion—some as heavy as eighty-five pounds—had been stolen from the Selby Smelting & Lead Company's plant south of the Mare Island Naval Shipyard, near Vallejo. The thief had burrowed under the building and cut out a section of the iron floor into the walk-in safe. He had then taken the gold out the way he had come, through a railroad tunnel to the shore, and had apparently sailed off with it, inexplicably leaving behind two bars worth nearly $50,000. The heist was proclaimed "the largest theft of gold bullion known in this country"—with a loss estimated at $283,000.[17]

Within hours of the discovery, Harry Morse, a local detective, was on the scene, and his biographer claims that he quickly determined the identity of the thief.[18] However, no arrest was made until the following day, when W. B. Sayers, by then superintendent of Pinkerton's San Francisco office; former San Francisco police chief Isaiah Lees; and John Seymour, the captain of San Francisco detectives, tracked a man called Buck Taylor—a former employee at the plant who had been acting suspiciously—to his girlfriend's house in San Rafael.

Later that day McParland joined the three officials and interrogated Taylor in the police "sweatbox" in San Francisco. Initially, despite the discovery of Taylor's cap in the tunnel and several items at his home being covered with tunnel mud, he denied any involvement. But McParland persisted until the prisoner "understood perfectly from me that we had all the evidence to convict him and give him a long term in prison. I warned him that he would never have a chance to get near the bullion he had stolen. I told him that if he was in prison for thirty years, when he came out we would have a man with him day and night until he died."[19]

Hoping that returning the gold would mean a lighter sentence, Taylor confessed, admitted that he was Jack Winters, a longtime criminal from the East Coast, and turned over the bullion. He had dropped it into thick mud that at low tide was covered by only about a foot of water, at a place down the coastline from the smelting plant, hidden behind coal bunkers at the end of a railroad wharf.

"I am convinced that Winters stole the bullion solely with the idea of securing a big reward," McParland announced. "His work was crude and he left a clear trail behind him. His idea was to join in the hunt for the gold and when a large reward was offered to fish it up in the presence of witnesses and claim the reward. I consider Winters a far more dangerous criminal under these circumstances than one who intended to get away with his plunder. . . . Our organization secured the evidence against him and the prosecutors will not be delayed."[20] McParland was not wrong about the timing: A little more than a week later, Winters was sentenced to fifteen years in prison.

At the dawn of the twentieth century Pinkerton's was synonymous to many union men not with solving crimes but with undercover operatives subverting labor. At McParland's direction, the previous few years had seen secret operatives infiltrating more and more unions. This pattern had actually been restarted in 1896, when the Cloud City Miners Union, a local branch of the WFM, went on strike in Leadville, Colorado, one of the world's major sources of lead ore.

In September of that year the union demanded a pay raise of fifty cents per day for all workers not making at least three dollars daily, returning them to the pre-1893 level.[21] The mine owners, who had agreed to be bound by the decision of their majority, making it impossible for the union to play one against the other,[22] offered a sliding wage scale tied to the price of silver and lead. This was rejected, leading to nearly a thousand miners striking and the owners locking out more.

The owners began hiring undercover agents from both Pinkerton's and the Thiel Detective Service Company to keep them apprised of union decisions and activities.[23] They also brought in nonunion workers—primarily from Missouri, where there was stronger opposition to unions[24] The strikers attempted to persuade them not to go into the mines, but when that proved unsuccessful the union ordered one hundred rifles, ten to fifteen pistols, and ammunition.[25]

On September 21, union members attacked the Coronado and Emmet mines—both of which had been using nonunion miners—causing an estimated fifty thousand dollars in damage by dynamiting an oil tank and a wooden structure. Three union members and a fireman were killed, leading Colorado governor Albert McIntire to send in troops. With armed forces protecting the mines, the violence soon ended.[26] By February 1897, most of the miners had gone back to work or moved to other areas.[27] However, the actions had driven the two opposing forces further apart than ever.

The WFM leaders, particularly new president Ed Boyce, quickly adopted more militant policies. At the 1897 WFM convention, Boyce stated: "I strongly advise you to provide every member with the latest improved rifle . . . so that in two years we can hear the inspiring music of the martial tread of 25,000 armed men in the ranks of labor."[28] Boyce also campaigned for the WFM to adopt socialism and fight for "the over-throw of the profit-making system." His vision and vigor made him the role model for new union fire-brand Bill Haywood.[29]

Following the Leadville strike, mine owners' associations turned to undercover agents. They were not all McParland's men: The key supplier in the 1899 Coeur d'Alene labor confrontation—when union men blew up the Bunker Hill concentrator in Wardner—was the Thiel Detective Service Company. Wilson S. Swain—Thiel's manager in Spokane and a man McParland loathed[30]—inserted operative Edward L. Zimmerman into a local union in the Coeur d'Alenes. Zimmerman was soon elected financial secretary, allowing him to destabilize the union from within,[31] and giving both Zimmerman and Swain star status with some of the Idaho mine owners, thereby providing Thiel the upper hand with them. Conversely, Pinkerton's was the agency of choice for the mine owners in Colorado, particularly in Telluride and Cripple Creek. It was there that McParland's secret operatives would wage a deadly war with the WFM.

Although not all detectives did undercover work, being visible did not necessarily make them more popular. In 1900, in an effort to stop "high-grading"—the theft of high-quality ore as miners exited the mines—eight companies in the Cripple Creek region required everyone working underground to undress and pass naked before a detective prior to getting dressed in the next room. Two such checks were carried out at the Independence Mine at Victor before the miners refused to comply. Eventually mine owners agreed to stop using Pinkerton's agents for the process, men would strip down only to their underclothes to pass between changing rooms, and anyone suspected of high-grading would be searched by a union representative with a guard present.[32] The decision was seen as a WFM victory, because it also included an agreement that the mines would hire only union men.

Two years later, more serious trouble arose. In 1902, Boyce was replaced as president by Charles Moyer, and the union's new secretary-treasurer became the volatile socialist Haywood. That autumn, in response to fears about Haywood's revolutionary ideas, Republican James Peabody—a reactionary candidate of the propertied classes[33]—was elected Colorado governor. Meanwhile, in a referendum, Colorado voters approved by a 3-to-1 margin an amendment to the state constitution limiting the working day to eight hours. However, neither the legislature nor the new governor acted upon the amendment, thereby letting it die and drawing from muckraking journalist Ray Stannard Baker the comment: "Rarely has there been in this country a more brazen, conscienceless defeat of the will of the people."[34] The eight-hour working day would be a primary cause of the labor strife soon to follow.

Among the key groups still working a twelve-hour day were the smelters in Colorado City, a bleak little place near the base of Pikes Peak. Not long after Moyer and Haywood took charge, the WFM organized them into a union.[35] Charles MacNeill, the general manager of the United States Reduction and Refining Company (USRRC) was one of the most vehement antiunion operators in the state. He promptly turned to Pinkerton's, which inserted operative A. H. Crane into the union.[36] When Crane was elected secretary of the union he was able to supply MacNeill with the names of members, who MacNeill began discharging, firing twenty-three on the same day in February.

The union immediately demanded the men be reinstated and pay raised for all workers. When MacNeill refused, the union called a strike. Within a short time, Crane's role was exposed. Informants later confessed to McParland that "Heywood [sic] had offered fifteen hundred dollars for the assassination of [Crane].... Heywood said it was a nice state of affairs to think that when they organized a union of smelter and mill men they elected for their secretary a detective, and he had to be taught a lesson, and the best way to teach him was to kill him, and show that detective agencies could not place men within their ranks." Several attempts on Crane's life were unsuccessful, before he was given a "good licking" and "put aboard a train and told to never return."[37]

Despite the presence of other Pinkerton's operatives in Colorado City, Victor, and Florence,[38] MacNeill requested help from the governor, who, over the objections of local authorities, sent in the National Guard. In a short time the troops broke up the picket lines, began protecting replacement workers, and searched the homes of union supporters. But heavy political pressure forced Peabody to negotiate an accord, and a tentative agreement was reached. The National Guard withdrew, the picket lines disappeared, two of the three mills were unionized, and the USRRC agreed to reemploy those men who had been fired.

In July 1903, after the legislature adjourned without passing laws pertaining to the eight-hour day, men working for the American Smelting and Refining Company (ASARCO) of Denver requested that Franklin Guiterman, the general manager, reduce their workday by four hours, to the agreed limit.[39] When he refused, the local union went on strike against the two main mills in Denver, and the Colorado City union followed suit when it became obvious

MacNeill would not fulfill his promises at USRRC. After a tense month, about thirty-five hundred miners in Cripple Creek joined them, thereby drying up the supply of ore to the mills, effectively shutting them down.

Within days, Guiterman requested an operative from Pinkerton's. McParland supplied A. W. Gratias, and personally oversaw the operation. The union members soon recognized Gratias's abilities, and he was elected secretary of the local.[40] McParland then ordered him to agitate among the men for strike benefits, so that the WFM would be forced to pay them. When this was accomplished, the grateful strikers elected Gratias chairman of the relief committee, allowing him to control payments. At McParland's instruction, he paid the strikers extremely liberally, helping to drain the federation's treasury while becoming so popular he was elected president. The next year, with the strike still dragging on, Haywood objected to the payments. McParland thereupon ordered them cut, so that the strikers could barely make ends meet. This, he hoped, would throw blame on Haywood, resulting in his dismissal and the appointment of a less able opponent. The plan did not work, but it did make life difficult for Haywood.

"At first we had been giving out relief at such a rate that I had to tell the chairman that he was providing the smelter men with more than they had had while at work," Haywood wrote. "Then he cut down the rations until the wives of the smelter men began to complain that they were not getting enough to eat. Years later . . . I discovered that the chairman of the relief committe [sic] was a Pinkerton detective, who was carrying out the instructions of the agency in . . . deliberately trying to stir up bad feeling between the strikers and the relief committee."[41]

Meanwhile, soon after the strike started, members of the Citizens' Alliance—a large, well-funded group organized to support the mine and mill owners[42]—began pressuring shopkeepers and merchants to stop extending credit, further increasing hardship for the strikers. When the mines reopened with nonunion workers from Missouri and Minnesota, tensions mounted and sporadic violence followed, including, on August 29, the burning of the shaft house at the Sunset-Eclipse Mine.[43] That was all the mine owners needed to appeal to Peabody for a return of the National Guard. When the governor dithered due to expense, the owners agreed to pay.

By the end of September more than one thousand troops had been sent to Cripple Creek under the command of Sherman Bell, the state's adjutant general. Bell made no bones about his goals. "I came to do up this damned anarchistic federation," he said, adding that he intended to "[k]ill 'em—when one of 'em pokes his head up, slug it—shoot 'em down—exterminate 'em."[44] When labor leaders protested that the National Guard exceeded its authority by holding union men without charge, suspending the right of habeas corpus, shutting down newspapers, and denying the right to free assembly, Thomas McClelland, judge advocate of the National Guard and one of Bell's cronies, spat out: "To hell with the Constitution; we are not following the Constitution!"[45]

By this time the strike had spread throughout the state. Efforts had also been made to organize the bituminous coal miners in central and southern Colorado, but the Colorado Fuel and Iron Company had hired Pinkerton's undercover agents to thwart such attempts. McParland's operatives were so successful that one was named the national organizer for the United Mine Workers at the same time that he was helping prevent the formation of a local.[46]

As dissatisfaction mounted on both sides, violence increased. In November, an attempt was made to derail a train carrying replacement miners by pulling spikes from the tracks. No one died, but killing had already been a part of the scene at Telluride, where Arthur Collins, the Cornish manager of the Smuggler-Union Mine, was murdered in his parlor by an assailant who blasted him through the window with a shotgun while he and three friends played bridge whist.[47] The killing led to Collins's replacement by Bulkeley Wells, who became one of the most vehemently antiunion managers in Colorado, and in April 1905 succeeded Bell as adjutant general of the National Guard.

Almost a year to the day later—on November 21, 1903—an explosion at the six-hundred-foot level of the nonunion Vindicator Mine outside of Gold-field killed the superintendent and the shift boss, who were descending in a cage. This occurred despite the presence of the National Guard, leading to the claim that it had been perpetrated by the mine owners to make it look like a union atrocity. Two months later, a cable hauling sixteen nonunion miners to the surface at the nearby Independence Mine was cut, and all but one were killed when the cage dropped down the shaft. Arrests were made, but nothing was proven.

For months the strike ground on.[48] Then, early in the morning of June 6, 1904, a large gang of workers from the Findley Mine were at the Independence depot waiting for their train when a colossal explosion rocked the area, destroying much of the station, killing thirteen, seriously injuring six, and flinging arms, legs, and torsos hundreds of yards in every direction. The cause of the explosion: 150 to 200 pounds of dynamite placed beneath the station.

Events moved quickly thereafter—owners and the Citizens' Alliance lay the blame on the WFM, as all of the casualties had been nonunion workers. Within hours the local sheriff, a member of the WFM, was forced to resign, as a coiled rope was dangled in front of him with the threat of being handed over to a mob. The new sheriff, Edward Bell, was a member of the Mine Owners' Association, and he rapidly appointed a hundred new deputies.

Bell then accompanied Clarence C. Hamlin, the secretary of the Mine Owners' Association, to a large lot in Victor—about six miles from Independence—where several thousand people had gathered. Perched above the crowd on top of a wagon, Hamlin proclaimed: "The badge of the Western Federation of Miners is a badge of murder, and everyone who is responsible for the outrage at Independence should be driven from the district."[49] As things turned ugly, about fifty union men fled to the union hall for protection. Sheriff Bell demanded they leave, and when they refused, a group opened fire, wounding four before the others surrendered. Hamlin's call went far and wide, and Citizens' Alliance members smashed union halls and wrecked four WFM cooperative stores. They also occupied several union mines. By that night, hundreds of union men had been detained and placed in hurriedly built bullpens in Victor, Goldfield, and other communities.

Individuals who were not part of the union but were sympathetic to it were also taken into custody. That night, McParland's brother Edward, a shoemaker in Victor, was forcibly taken from his shop. "They marched me up the street and about every five steps I got a blow from a gun across the kidneys until I reached the bullpen," he testified.[50] He was left there for four days with two hundred other men, after which seventy-three of them were marched to a train between lines of deputy sheriffs and militia with fixed bayonets. They were forced aboard and "at five o'clock on Sunday morning we were dumped off in a swamp at the Kansas line and three volleys were fired over our heads with the instructions, 'don't come back under the penalty of death.'"[51]

Edward's case was not uncommon. Within days, a seven-man commission was appointed to determine who had the "right to remain" in Cripple Creek. People wishing to stay were required to renounce any allegiance to the WFM and needed a card issued by the Mine Owners' Association to gain employment. Within a few months the commission "tried" 1,569 men, of whom more than 230—including elected officials—were deported to Kansas or New Mexico. Sherman Bell did not mind that they had not been legally convicted.

"They are men against whom crime can not be specified," he stated, "but their presence is regarded as dangerous to law and order."[52] Numerous other union workers and sympathizers were beaten and driven from the region in a violent process known as "whitecapping" for the masks worn by the perpetrators.[53]

These events—known as the Colorado Labor Wars—had more losers than those run out of the state. The strike in Denver resulted in the closing of ASARCO's giant Grant Smelter, leaving its plant unoccupied and its 375 employees out of work. Its massive 350-foot chimney was a sad reminder of the strife until it was demolished in 1950 to make way for the Denver Coliseum.[54] The political process was also a loser. Governor Peabody's handling of the strikes gave powerful ammunition to his opposition when he ran for a second term in 1904. Former Democratic governor Alva Adams apparently won the election, but the Republican-controlled legislature voted to unseat him due to voter fraud. Siringo later confirmed this, writing that he "voted eight times, as per McParland's orders—three times before the same election judges." But Peabody's side was equally at fault, and he was declared winner only upon condition that he resign immediately after taking the oath of office. He was succeeded by Republican lieutenant governor Jesse F. McDonald, giving Colorado three different governors in one day.[55]

Although the WFM never officially terminated the strike, its program had been crushed by the violence following the dynamiting of the Independence depot. By the end of 1904 the WFM was no longer a force in Cripple Creek, Telluride, or Idaho Springs. Its leaders had to seek strength by realigning with other organizations, such as the short-lived American Labor Union or the Industrial Workers of the World.[56] But to McParland that only meant the WFM was like a chameleon, changing its name or outward appearance while remaining the same within, and at the top. Therefore, the Great Detective still had the organization and its leaders in his sights.

Actually, having anything literally in his sights was a serious worry for McParland. The year 1903 had started well, when his much loved nephew Eneas married his sweetheart, Emily Pfeiffer, in Ocala, Florida, on January 14. "Mr McParland is a young man, prominent in both business and social circles in Denver," a Florida newspaper stated, "where he holds a responsible railroad position."[57] Eneas then returned to Denver with his new wife, who, like her husband, was doted upon by the McParlands.

June, however, brought unpleasant events, as McParland's weak eyesight took a serious turn for the worse. "On getting up on the morning of the 3d I

discovered that everything in front of me looked hazy or smoky while side-
ways I could see about as usual," he wrote to Robert Pinkerton. "But on arriving at the office and opening my mail I discovered that I was unable to read."[58]
Soon thereafter McParland consulted his oculist, Dr. Walker, who informed
him that he was again suffering from choroiditis. "The Doctor stated that a
speck of this choroiditis had gotten right on the center of vision. That caused
everything in front of me to be clouded, just the same as though you would
put a little black patch in the center of a bulls eye lantern; there would be light
around the sides of the lantern but the center would be dark."

Walker's treatment consisted of applying "leeches just behind my left
ear . . . and he kept up the bleeding process brought on by the leeches after they
had done their work for a couple of hours."[59] He also prescribed heavy dosages
of "iodides"—used at the time for anti-inflammatory purposes—but several
days later decided that the treatment "was depressing to the system, and the
iodides, when taken in such doses as I was now taking them were very debilitating in this altitude, and if continued for any length of time, would result in
my having to discontinue the treatment entirely for some time, and therefore
no progress would be made in eradicating the disease."[60] The solution, Walker
said, was that McParland "get to sea level just as quickly as possible, and suggested that I go to some hot spring at sea level, or at least I must be somewhere
where I could take Turkish baths occasionally, but a hot spring where I had an
attendant to rub me down would be more preferable." Typical of McParland's
work ethic was his request that Pinkerton allow him to go to the San Francisco office, as it was at sea level and would allow him to "take Turkish baths
and attend to the business of the Western Division."[61]

From a modern medical standpoint, Walker's treatment plan was ques-
tionable,[62] although it was supported by another doctor, who told the detective that "while my heart was in good condition, having no organic trouble,
nevertheless my pulse was slow, and that was caused by the iodide that I was
taking, and in his opinion it would only be a question of time when I would
have to discontinue taking iodides and rest up."[63]

Yet four days later—before he finalized any travel plans—McParland reported such sudden improvements "that neither Dr. Walker or myself can
hardly realize it. . . . I have simply been improving every day, not only the sight
but physically. I really think I have not felt better in 20 years."[64] Several days
later he noted that "My eyesight has continued to improve, so that on yester-
day on testing it, and comparing the test with the record . . . he made after the
operation on my right eye eight years ago, my vision is more acute, and I can

partially read one line more than I could read at that time. All that is left of the Coroditis is simply a little haze in the distance which is improving from day to day."[65] One surprising result was that despite being expected to lose weight, McParland actually gained substantially. This was never taken off for any extended period, and McParland's once svelte figure became progressively paunchier.

Concern about losing his eyesight encouraged McParland to think a little about his life away from the office. In September, mentioning the agency's new policy of allowing each clerk a Sunday off in rotation, he asked Bangs if, "owing to my long service in the agency . . . the Principals and yourself might permit me in the future while in Denver to remain at home on Sundays. . . . [I]f anything transpired . . . I would immediately get down to the office. . . . I do not want the Principals or yourself to strain a point to grant me this favor. If it is not granted matters will remain just as they are now."[66] It is uncertain whether he thereafter received regular time off, but McParland did note in the same letter that he had never taken a holiday. A year later that changed, as he wrote to Doc Shores that he would shortly be leaving for Chicago on vacation.[67]

McParland's eyesight was far from his only physical complaint. In March 1904, he sprained his right foot while in Los Angeles, and on the way back to Denver, it "burst" in an unidentified way. The skin between his toes was thereafter prone to suffering serious cracks. The following winter the foot was further damaged when it was frostbitten during a storm, and the skin between his big toe and the next one broke open. Blood poisoning set in, and there "was a red streak from the big toe about as big as a pencil near the vein, to within two inches of the groin." McParland was put on medication and, despite having no solid food for nine days, regained his health. About six months later, he again suffered blood poisoning, suddenly becoming very ill at work. His temperature rose to 104 degrees, and he spent two weeks in the hospital under the care of two physicians and a specially trained nurse. Again he recovered and returned to his daily routine.[68]

These health problems inevitably left McParland with concerns about the future, particularly as at the same time he lost one of his oldest and closest colleagues. On April 15, 1904, Robert J. Linden, after being ill for about a month, died in Philadelphia of pneumonia at the age of sixty-nine.[69]

Age also seems to have brought with it a tetchiness and pedantry that annoyed McParland's employers. "Mr McParland raises too many technical arguments on matters brought to his attention," Robert Pinkerton wrote to his brother in 1905, continuing:

> The General Management have too much to do to have to keep up a continual correspondence, writing letter after letter to get Mr McParland to carry out what has been outlined in our Orders. There is no [other] Manager that raises the arguments that Mr McParland does. . . . [W]e have more trouble with that Division in having our ideas understood and carried out than with the other two Divisions together. . . . [F]or the future Mr McParland, instead of finding matter for argument, must accept the ruling of the Principals and Management and carry out their directions. . . . Let Mr McParland study how to avoid or at least curtail his correspondence; put it in as few words as possible instead of continually jumping into an argument. This must stop. . . . Mr McParland personally knows the very high regard that our father, you and I have always had for him. There is nothing within reason that either of us would not do for him, but he is getting old, as we are . . . and these constant and unnecessary arguments that he unfortunately brings up are exceedingly annoying, and worse than all, very wearing on everyone.[70]

McParland was actually only about sixty years old,[71] but it is clear that he was becoming less physically able. He had grown portly and taken to carrying a gold-headed cane to help him walk. He was also becoming increasingly curmudgeonly. More important, he seemed to think that he always knew best and realized he could get what he wanted either by charm or a bullish dominance, which he had in equal measure. Butting heads with him would have generally been futile—apparently even for the Pinkertons. But if the brothers thought they saw a difficult side of McParland, it was nothing compared to what the leadership of the WFM would endure—him at his most determined, inflexible, and merciless.

In 1905, John Ingram—a former chief constable in Rossland, British Columbia, a center of gold mining—was killed in a mine explosion similar to those attributed to the WFM in Colorado and Idaho.[72] As that union had a local in Rossland, and Ingram had played a prominent role in putting down strikes, suspicion quickly fell on the local WFM leaders. Ingram's brother, a

Member of Parliament, asked Pinkerton's to find out what had actually happened. After investigating personally, McParland reported that dynamite had been stored at the site and that Ingram's death was accidental, nothing to do with the WFM.[73] It was the last time that he would find on behalf of the WFM or present it as anything less than a criminal organization led by an inner circle of anarchists, dynamiters, and killers. They needed to be stopped at all costs, and McParland knew he was the man to do it.

CHAPTER 19

A MURDER AND A CONFESSION

I
t was on a snowy evening in a bleak Idaho winter that the opening act in the final showdown between McParland and the Western Federation of Miners was played out. It was a scene that would precede both what was arguably the most remarkable confession in U.S. legal history and a series of courtroom dramas peopled with more famous investigators, witnesses, defendants, prosecutors, and defense attorneys—as well as more stunningly murderous testimony—than perhaps any other American trial on record.

About twenty-five miles west of Boise is Caldwell, the seat of Canyon County. There, on December 30, 1905, former Idaho governor Frank Steunenberg ran several errands—including renewing his life insurance policy[1]—and then followed his usual late Saturday afternoon routine. Braving temperatures that hovered only slightly above 0 degrees Fahrenheit (–18 degrees Celsius)—as well as the eight inches of fresh snow that carpeted the town he had helped build from its rough foundations—the forty-four-year-old Steunenberg headed for home shortly after 6:00 P.M.

Steunenberg's bulk—235 pounds packed on a frame of six feet two inches—made the man still called "governor" by many of Caldwell's twenty-two hundred inhabitants a figure easy to spot, even when dressed against the weather. Less recognizable was the much smaller man who passed him, hurrying back the other way toward the center of town from near Steunenberg's house.[2]

Steunenberg reached the gate to his home, pulled back the slide to open it, stepped through, and, before he could close it, was hurled ten feet through the air by an explosion so powerful it was heard sixteen miles away.[3] As his wife and daughter raced out to help him, one glance told the whole story—the gate was gone, replaced by a giant divot, and the nearby fence and boardwalk had been shattered, their debris blown throughout the neighborhood. Steunenberg himself was a broken and mangled remnant, the clothes on the lower half of his body totally destroyed, the right side of his body shredded and crushed, both his legs broken, and his right hand "having the inside blown completely out." Both his eardrums were also apparently broken, leaving him deaf. Within about twenty minutes, despite the desperate ministrations of his family and three of the town's doctors, he breathed his last.

The news quickly spread through Caldwell that the governor had been murdered. Canyon County sheriff Jasper Nichols and his deputies formed a posse to surround the town and prevent the perpetrator from escaping. Assistance was sought from the surrounding communities, and a phone call placed to the current governor, Frank Gooding, who hurried from Boise on a specially chartered train and quickly helped organize a twenty-five-thousand-dollar reward for the capture of the killer.

Early the next morning, investigators at the scene uncovered some waxed fish line and what appeared to be a trigger mechanism, suggesting there had been a bomb attached to the gate. Meanwhile, several strangers in the town were hauled in for questioning. One man not immediately obvious to the authorities was a round-faced, ruddy-complexioned fellow called Thomas Hogan, who was staying at the Saratoga Hotel. He was not a total stranger, as he had been in and out of town for months and seemed to be an affable, engaging man looking to buy, depending on the conversation, sheep or real estate. Within moments of the explosion, he calmly helped the hotel bartender tie a bow on a parcel, pressing a steady finger on the knot.[4]

Yet, for a man who in the preceding weeks had shown a peculiar curiosity about Steunenberg, Hogan demonstrated an inexplicable lack of interest about the assassination, even interrupting one conversation by asking if someone knew where to purchase wethers—castrated rams.[5] His odd behavior made several locals suspicious, as was Sheriff Harvey K. Brown of Baker County, Oregon, who, happening to be in Boise, had hopped on Gooding's train to Caldwell. Baker thought he recognized Hogan as a miner from Cracker Creek in eastern Oregon, although Hogan denied he had been there. However, when Sheriff Nichols made a surreptitious visit to Hogan's hotel room, he found traces of explosive powder and plaster of Paris—ingredients used in making bombs. This was enough for Hogan to be questioned, following which, on the afternoon of New Year's Day 1906, he was arrested and charged with first-degree murder.

The day after the murder, Charles O. Stockslager, the chief justice of the Idaho Supreme Court, arrived in Caldwell, joining a rush of public figures who saw political advantage in being there. Keen to be the next governor of Idaho, and wanting to be seen as "tough on crime," Stockslager jumped into the investigation by phoning an old colleague—James McParland. The Indiana-born Stockslager had known McParland since the case of fraud and arson in Columbus, Kansas, back in 1886. At that time, as Cherokee County attorney, he had successfully prosecuted the case, and the men's mutual respect meant they had stayed in touch.[6]

Stockslager asked McParland if he would take over the Steunenberg investigation,[7] but the manager of the Western Division referred him to James Nevins, general superintendent in Portland, because the agency was inflexible about the manner and routing of initiating operations. Furthermore, McParland told his friend, the official request must come from Governor Gooding. The next day the uneasy bedfellows Stockslager and Gooding agreed to contact Nevins, but before they could, Gooding heard from Wilson Swain, the Spokane manager of the Thiel Detective Service Company. Swain announced that *he* would arrive that day, having been hired by the Coeur d'Alene mine owners. Pinkerton's was thereupon put on hold, as the county and state governments liked any deal that meant they did not have to pay. The decision infuriated McParland not only professionally but personally, as he disliked Swain intensely.[8]

Swain was self-important, bombastic, and overbearing. He immediately flooded the area with operatives and personally took charge of dealing with Hogan. On January 2, he and several sheriffs searched the suspect and found keys to his trunk, suitcase, and traveling bag. In the trunk they discovered not only clothes, toiletries, business cards, and fishing gear, but also: a loaded Colt automatic pistol with a shoulder holster; a Winchester sawn-off pump shotgun with a shoulder strap (for carrying it concealed under a coat); a pair of brass knuckles; a cloth mask; wire cutters; a fuse; plaster of Paris; four packages of chemicals; and shoes that matched tracks made through the vacant lot adjacent to Steunenberg's house.[9]

Not only was Swain certain that Hogan was the killer, he was equally sure he had accomplices. "There is now no doubt," he told a throng of reporters while stroking his walrus mustache, "that Governor Steunenberg's death was the result of a conspiracy that was most carefully planned, and which the conspirators were months in bringing to a conclusion."[10] What he did not say was that the detectives felt certain that the chief conspirator was a man who had spent considerable time with Hogan in the prior months, registering at hotels as J. Simmons. Swain had his men produce a photograph of Jack Simpkins—a WFM executive board member active in the Coeur d'Alenes[11]—and was gratified that hotel employees confirmed his suspicions that Simmons and Simpkins were one and the same. However, he had not been seen in Caldwell for weeks.

On January 3, Swain conducted a lengthy interview at the jail, and his first question produced gold. "What is your right name, Thomas Hogan?" he asked. The prisoner responded in the negative. "What is it?" Swain asked. Without pausing, the man replied, "Harry Orchard."[12] That day, other sources confirmed the claim. Sheriff Edward Bell of Teller County, Colorado, arrived and not only identified Orchard, but said that he was wanted for the Independence depot bombing. At the same time, Sheriff Brown also confirmed him as Orchard.[13]

By the end of the interview, Swain and his colleagues had learned that Orchard had joined the WFM in the Coeur d'Alenes before the 1899 troubles, and had later worked in Cripple Creek during the Colorado Labor Wars, although he did not admit any participation in the Independence bombing. He acknowledged knowing WFM leaders Charles Moyer and Bill Haywood, had recently been in contact with Simpkins, and conceded that the materials found in his hotel room were his, although he insisted that they were for making loaded dice.[14]

Orchard's significance to the WFM became doubly mysterious when a telegram arrived from the Spokane law firm of Robertson, Miller and Rosenhaupt—which represented the WFM—stating that attorney Fred Miller was leaving the next day for Caldwell. As Orchard had not sent any messages, it was obvious that someone else had arranged for him to receive legal assistance, even before he had confessed his real name. And as Simpkins was thought to be in Spokane, it appeared that a member of the union's executive board was keen to protect Orchard.[15]

These details led the investigators to the same conclusion held by Governor Gooding, Steunenberg's brother Will, and many of the newspapers around the nation that were giving extended coverage to the murder: Steunenberg had been assassinated, probably with the backing of the WFM, because of his actions in the Coeur d'Alenes in 1899.[16]

That a former typesetter for a small Iowa newspaper had been in a position to influence events in the Idaho mining wars was rather surprising. Steunenberg was born in Iowa in 1861 and left school at sixteen to apprentice as a printer at the *Knoxville Journal*, where he stayed for four years before going to Des Moines. He returned to his hometown as the publisher of *The Knoxville*

Express before moving to Caldwell in 1887 to help his brother A. K., who had purchased a declining paper named *The Caldwell Tribune*. The Steunenbergs turned it into a success, and writing about aspects of Idaho life, culture, and affairs of state led Frank to politics. In 1889 he was one of sixty-eight delegates to the Territory's constitutional convention, and the next year he was elected to the Idaho Legislature.[17] Only six years later, running on a "fusion" ticket that joined the Democrats and the Populists, he was elected Idaho's fourth governor. He lost much Populist support during the next two years, but with the backing of the "Silver Republicans"—who had split from the Republicans over the issue of "free silver"[18]—he was reelected.

Steunenberg's opportunity to show that he was truly the friend of the masses and unions who helped elect him came in 1899. Problems had been bubbling in the Coeur d'Alenes ever since 1892, and a U.S. House of Representatives investigation determined: "A secret organization controlled the civil authorities in Shoshone County. The mandate of the 'dark lantern' order was more powerful than the law of the State. Whatever was the desire of the secret clan became the law of the community."[19]

The organization referred to was the WFM, which had overseen an improvement in the pay rate of most mine workers, a notable exception being those at the vast Bunker Hill and Sullivan operation in Wardner and Kellogg. In late April 1899, Wardner union representatives demanded wages matching those of other local mines and recognition of the union. The acting manager of the Bunker Hill and Sullivan immediately granted the pay, but acceptance of the union was flatly refused. Three days later a large group of armed union men seized the Bunker Hill tramway, shutting down most mining and milling operations. At the same time, others forcibly turned away nonunion workers.

On April 29, after a tense week, about 250 miners from Burke—some armed and masked—commandeered the train that ran down Canyon Creek to Wallace.[20] Stops at Black Bear and Frisco mines and at Gem added hundreds of miners to the train, as well as eighty boxes of dynamite. Although the train normally terminated at Wallace, the engineer was forced to drive on another company's tracks to Kellogg, by which time almost a thousand miners were involved. A phalanx of armed union men marched on the Bunker Hill concentrator, where shots were exchanged. One man was killed and another mortally wounded before the guards fled. The raiding party placed sixty boxes—three thousand pounds—of dynamite in three different locations and lit the fuses. Within moments one of the world's largest concentrators had been reduced to rubble.

Despite being in the hospital, Steunenberg flew into action. With the Idaho National Guard in the Philippines in the aftermath of the Spanish-American War, he asked President William McKinley to "call forth the military forces of the United States to suppress insurrection in Shoshone County."[21] McKinley did not delay, and troops of the Twenty-fourth Infantry Regiment were ordered to the region. Under the command of Brigadier General Henry Clay Merriam—working with Steunenberg's representative, Bartlett Sinclair—they swept into the county. A massive program of arrests, starting with 128 men in Kellogg and Wardner, began shortly thereafter.[22]

Troops from the Fourth Cavalry next made a sweep through Burke, searching every house and breaking down doors if no one answered. They arrested "the entire male population of that town, consisting of about 300 persons; among them were clergymen, school teachers, druggists, merchants."[23] Men were taken at work, at home, at dinner. Although some were released within hours, 243 were herded into boxcars and held in a barn in Wardner, which became known as the "old bullpen" in reference to the structure built in 1892. When about 350 more men were arrested two days later at Gem and Mullan, the lack of space meant that they were kept in the boxcars until a new bullpen was built.[24]

The bullpens were cramped, uncomfortable, and unhealthy, but it was more than that which engendered the inmates' undying hatred for Steunenberg. Most were held for months without being charged. Those who *were* released found it difficult to obtain jobs, because Sinclair instituted a permit system that required each man to sign a declaration before he could return to work that he had had nothing to do with the events of April 29, and that he did not belong to any organization that had incited or approved of the crimes.[25] The system proved so effective that it was later instituted in the aftermath of the Colorado Labor Wars.[26]

Even more significant for many miners was the use of the Twenty-fourth Infantry—one of the nation's "colored" regiments. Few occupations were more xenophobic than mining, and in the Coeur d'Alenes the white miners, whose ethnic bigotry never lay far beneath the surface, were united in their hatred of Chinese and blacks. "Not only did the miners share the turn-of-the-century American view of 'niggers' as second-class citizens," wrote J. Anthony Lukas, "they regarded them as pawns of the mine owners."[27] That loathing was intensified by the knowledge that the Twenty-fifth Infantry, another colored regiment, had been used to suppress the 1892 uprising.

Now bitter complaints were made about the Twenty-fourth. Its soldiers were accused of brutality in making arrests and transporting prisoners, harassing and abusing incarcerated men, and making sexual advances toward the miners' wives.[28] Such charges came even from the highest union levels—Haywood claimed that while his brothers-in-arms were held illegally, "black soldiers were at home insulting, outraging, ravishing their wives, mothers, sisters and sweethearts."[29]

Steunenberg also generated union hatred because it was believed he had betrayed his supporters. An honorary member of the International Typographical Union, he had nonetheless determined to break the WFM, while concurrently throttling anything he saw as insurrection. As his attorney general, Sam Hays, said: "We have taken the monster by the throat and we are going to choke the life out of it. No halfway measures have or will be adopted. It is a plain case of the state or the union winning, and we do not propose that the state shall be defeated."[30]

Steunenberg's decisions severely damaged the WFM, but it was obvious that the personal consequences for him might be equally disastrous. Socialists, the labor press, and union sympathizers vilified him, and he met with strong labor opposition throughout the remainder of his term as governor. There were also those who wanted more than the end of his political career. In 1899, he told his wife that he thought his actions would eventually cost him his life.[31] Through the following years, his concerns about assassination apparently decreased,[32] but someone had not forgiven him. The question now became: was that simply Harry Orchard or was there something darker and more dangerous looming behind the scenes?

Despite Swain's progress with Orchard, the Thiel operatives soon annoyed many people in Caldwell, including Sheriff Nichols and Frank J. Smith, the judge of the Seventh Judicial District. None liked the way Swain had pushed in to take over the operation with what Smith called "a gang of the dirtiest low lived sons of bitches . . . he ever saw congregated in one place."[33] With nine agents in town and more in the surrounding region, the Thiel men were also running up high bills—without much to show for it.

On January 4, in a colossal error of judgment, one of Swain's assistants phoned Edwin Taber, the superintendent of Pinkerton's office in Spokane, to request that he "take this matter up in conjunction with the Thiel Agency."[34] Assuming that such a request had already been passed through Pinkerton's hierarchy, Taber sent assistant superintendent Gus J. Hasson to Caldwell to discover how the investigation stood. What Hasson learned was that not only were the Thiel agents inept, but that Swain expected him to share information without returning the favor—something Hasson was unwilling to consider.

Seeing how poorly the Thiel investigation was progressing, Hasson called on Governor Gooding to discuss hiring Pinkerton's, with the understanding that they would report directly to him and would not share information with other investigators. Gooding agreed, and the result was an accord between the State and the agency that Taber tailored so that the payment rate would be the regular eight dollars per day for the first thirty days, and six dollars thereafter. Most likely "done so for the purpose of meeting any rate Thiel would give," this nevertheless led to McParland censuring Taber for agreeing to it without consulting him.[35]

On the afternoon of January 7, Taber telegraphed McParland: "Gooding desires see you Boise immediately." McParland was "highly pleased" not only to be taking charge of a high-profile case but because of its potential impact on company business in the region: "[I]t means a great deal to the Spokane office so far as the mine operators of Idaho are concerned and in fact all mine operators in the whole district."[36]

Met by Stockslager and Hasson at the Boise train station on the evening of Wednesday, January 10, McParland was taken to the Idanha, the city's finest hotel, where he settled in to suite 35 and, after dinner, was joined by Stockslager and Gooding. "The Governor wanted us to work in conjunction with Swain," McParland noted. "This I refused to do."[37] At this point, Stockslager interjected: "Governor, I told you that you might as well try to remove Plymouth Rock as to change the established rules of the Pinkerton's, their plans are right, look at the information you have got from the fine reports of Mr Hasson who has only got on the ground as it were." After some consideration, Gooding acquiesced, noting that Swain—whom he had not personally employed— was waiting in the hotel, as he had expected to bring him to the meeting. Now he could be dismissed for the night, which was presumably done when the chief justice departed shortly thereafter, undoubtedly leaving McParland extremely gratified.

McParland and Gooding continued their discussions until midnight, after which the detective met with Hasson. In a report produced only a few hours after arriving in Boise, McParland wrote: "I am satisfied that there were other people in this plot besides Orchard and feel almost sure that Orchard was the tool of the others." He noted particularly that Orchard and Simpkins had not only visited Caldwell and nearby Nampa multiple times, but had shared a hotel room. "I think we will be able to convict the man [Orchard], but this conspiracy is so wide spread and so well and secretly conducted that it would not surprise me to find out that the W.F. of M. has one or more men posing in Caldwell as bona fide residents, for the purpose of proving an alibi."[38]

Swain had said much the same, but confirming his rival's analysis did not mean McParland's attitude toward him had mellowed. Instead, in the following days he began elbowing him out. His cause was given a boost when it turned out Swain expected the county to pay the daily charge per detective—already around two thousand dollars—when he had been brought aboard in great part because the commissioners had understood they would not have to pay. Gooding supported McParland: "I can see now why you could not work with a crowd of bunco men," he exclaimed, bursting into the detective's room. "I have sent for Swain and will order him to discontinue all his men. . . . I will be damned if I like to be buncoed in this way . . . and will tell him that he must not in future incur a dollar for time or expense without getting my participation."[39]

Swain was not ousted at once because McParland "wanted this man Simpkins badly," and Swain claimed "he could lay his hands on Simpkins at any moment."[40] However, McParland had clearly achieved a victory for both Pinkerton's and himself. "I have done what I could to overthrow Swain never letting an opportunity pass," he crowed smugly to Fraser, who now was head of the San Francisco office as well as assistant manager of the Western Division. Further, he noted, he had "done it in such a way that I am not suspected."[41]

Meanwhile, McParland focused on Orchard and quickly decided that he should be moved from the Canyon County jail to an isolated cell on death row in the state penitentiary in Boise—partly to wage psychological warfare, but also for greater security, as "his friends would not hesitate to remove him by poison or even dynamiting the jail."[42] The problem with the plan was that Nichols, supported by Judge Smith—whose position on the bench made him the man who would preside over any trial of Orchard—insisted there was no legal authority to remove him.

Facing a stalemate, Gooding set up a meeting with Smith and McParland, for which he arranged to be "unexpectedly" called out, to avoid being seen taking sides.[43] On the night of January 12, they met in McParland's suite, where the governor raised the issue of a transfer, thereby allowing the detective to give his reasons for it. The judge "agreed with us that our reasons for desiring such a step taken were good ones . . . but at the same time he was not sure whether or not the action would be legal, and he did not wish to jeopardize the state by making an illegal move, which might result in getting the prisoner free on a writ of habeas corpus."

At that point, Gooding was called from the room, and the judge, studying McParland's carefully placed lapel pin, said, "I see that you are an Elk?" Smiling, McParland replied, "So is the Governor but I never allow myself to so far forget my obligation to the Order to use it in any way to forward my plans in any case." But that is just what he did, for, having identified their bond, the two men forged an agreement. By the end of the meeting four hours later Smith had agreed to "use his influence with the Sheriff to have him transfer the prisoner to Boise further he would not issue a writ of habeas corpus except so directed by the [Idaho] Supreme Court."

The latter possibility was put to rest the next morning, when McParland visited Stockslager and Associate Justice Isaac N. Sullivan, who "both agreed that it was perfectly legal to remove the prisoner to the Pen. and would sustain Judge Smith in denying a writ of habeas corpus."[44]

Nichols, however, was inflexible and stuck by his position that Orchard could not be taken. But Gooding personally brought him to see McParland several nights later. Faced by the governor and the country's most famous detective, the small-town law officer backed down. After two days Orchard was transferred to the state facility, where he was put in a cell on death row, the only people near him being two convicted murderers awaiting execution and a set of guards who watched him day and night, without uttering a word.[45]

Now, McParland had Orchard right where he wanted him.

Having patiently waited for the isolation to do its work on Orchard, at 2:15 on Monday, January 22, McParland took a streetcar to the eastern end of the line, where he met state penitentiary warden Eugene L. Whitney, who accompanied him to the facility. After setting up in Whitney's private office, McParland—without identifying himself—became the first person to speak to the inmate in more than three days, during which Orchard had not been allowed to bathe, shave, or exercise.

"Orchard has about as determined a countenance as I have ever seen on a human being," McParland recorded, "with the most cold, cruel eyes I remember having seen."[46] Undeterred, the detective explained to Orchard how, if he admitted his part in the murder, gave up any conspirators, and testified for the prosecution, he could reasonably expect the State to consider his cooperation as mitigation for his sentence.

After twenty-five minutes, Orchard interrupted, saying: "You speak your piece very well, but I don't know what you are getting at. I have committed no crime. I have heard and read over forty times just such talk as you have made, and there are instances where such talk has only made innocent men confess to crimes that they never committed and to implicate others who were also innocent. Talk about acting square with the state! I never heard tell of a man that did but what he afterwards paid the penalty."

But McParland had not been obtaining confessions for thirty years for nothing. He waited calmly while Orchard added that his lawyer—Fred Miller, at that moment in Denver collecting a fifteen-hundred-dollar retainer from the WFM—had told him not to say anything. Then, although "during my conversation with Orchard I did not for a moment intimate that by turning states evidence he would be granted immunity," he cited "cases in which the state witnesses went entirely free ... [including] the Mollie McGuire state witnesses who saved their own necks by telling the truth, and more especially Kelly, who, although he swore on the witness stand that he fired the first shot into Alexander McKee, exclaiming 'Dead dogs tell no tales,' went free."[47]

Still skeptical, Orchard responded that "McParland had that all fixed, and he saw to it that whatever promises he made were kept."

"I then asked the man if he had ever seen McParland," the detective wrote, "to which he replied that he had not, but added 'McParland would go to any extreme to convict a man, but as a rule he kept his word.'" McParland looked the prisoner in the eye, and "I then told Orchard who I was and stated that my main reason for interceding for the men who turned states evidence was not because they were innocent but because they had allowed themselves to become the tools of the men of the inner circle of the Mollie Maguires, who were more guilty than they who actually committed the crimes, ... that they did the biddings of the inner circle of the Mollie Maguires just as he had done the biddings of the inner circle of the W.F. of M."

Here was McParland again drawing on the model he had long before developed about the AOH—that criminal organizations had an elite inner circle comprising the worst of the lot, with the rest consisting of drones unquestioningly obeying orders. Certainly he was providing reasons for Orchard to confess and to implicate the WFM leaders, but at the same time McParland believed implicitly in this overworked scenario.[48] Nor was the theory of an inner circle unique to him, as it was expressed in newspapers around the country, which were giving the case extensive coverage, referring to it as "the crime of the century."[49]

McParland was not finished, however. He continued to attempt to unsettle

Orchard and undermine his allegiance. "I told him that in the case of the Mollie Maguires the attorneys for the tools had advised them . . . not to speak, knowing that if they did it would endanger the lives of the inner circle, who in reality were the clients, . . . just as the inner circle of the W.F. of M. is now the client of the lawyers and not himself, as he thinks he is. I told him that it is the duty of the lawyers to buoy up the spirits of the tools . . . until they have been executed."

He then explained how "taking him to the penitentiary was for the purpose of protecting him from his friends, as he was a menace to those whose orders he had obeyed until such time that they killed him or that the state convicted and hanged him." And so it went for three hours, until McParland left with the promise to "use my influence to see that he got some exercise."

For three days McParland allowed Orchard "time to reflect." Then, on January 25, he returned to find the prisoner—who had been allowed to bathe, shave, and exercise—pleased to see him. "[H]is manner was entirely changed from what it was on my [first] visit."[50] For three and a half hours, McParland reasoned, warned, encouraged, assured, and comforted Orchard, also giving him legal, moral, and spiritual guidance. Stating that he knew by his forehead Orchard was "a man of intelligence and reasoning," McParland explained how that showed he had "the ability of doing a large amount of good, as well as evil . . . if he had formed associations with law-abiding citizens when he first started out in the world instead of a crowd of socialists, anarchists and murderers, he would have become a shining light in any community."

McParland also reminded "him that he was not the client in this case, but that the clients were the Inner Circle of the Western Federation of Miners who paid the lawyers, not for the purpose of clearing him but for the purpose of keeping his mouth shut. His lawyers in advising him this course knew full well that he would be convicted and eventually executed."

But, Orchard asked, "[I]f I become a States witness in giving my evidence I would probably have to admit some crimes that I committed in the State of Colorado. . . . Then what?" No problem, McParland smoothly assured him, since "if he acted properly in this case we would get the leaders and that was all that the State of Colorado and the State of Idaho wishes, and that I thought I could assure him that he would not be prosecuted for any crime that he committed in Colorado."

But wouldn't the public demand his execution, Orchard asked, to which the detective responded: "if he acted in good faith . . . that the sentiment that now existed would be reversed, that instead of looking upon him as a notorious murderer they would look upon him as a saver . . . of all States where the blight of the Inner Circle of the Western Federation had struck."

After a while, McParland "asked him if he believed in an Allseeing and Divine Providence," and Orchard said, "Yes." McParland quickly pounced, pointing out "what an awful thing it was to live and die a sinful life, and that every man ought to repent his sins, and that there was no sin that God would not forgive." Then McParland "spoke of King David being a murderer, and also the Apostle Paul." Orchard asked about this, and McParland "told me about King David falling in love with Uriah's wife, and ordering Joab . . . to put Uriah in the thick of the battle, and then ordering the rest to retreat, so he would be killed; and of St Paul, who was then called Saul, consenting to the death of Stephen, and holding the young men's coats while they stoned him to death."[51]

Through all this, Orchard's belief and trust in McParland was clearly growing. "My God, if I could only place confidence in you," he said, walking over to the detective. "I want to talk. . . . I know every word you have said is true. . . . You certainly have not got to build a reputation as a detective and I am satisfied that all you have said is for my good." Wanting to build a more intimate relationship, he asked McParland about his home in Denver and whether he still kept bulldogs. These details took McParland aback, while reinforcing his conspiratorial notions: "By this conversation the indications are that the Inner Circle was keeping tab on me."

Eventually Orchard stood, to conclude the interview, but then suddenly asked why "you never arrested Thomas Hurley. . . . You certainly knew where he was and it has been a mystery to me and several others why you did not take him back to Pennsylvania." Actually, all evidence points to McParland *not* knowing Hurley's whereabouts, but that did not stop him using the question for his own ends. "Hurley was simply the tool of Jack Kehoe, the head of the Inner Circle of the Molly Maguires, just as you are the tool of Moyer, Haywood, Simpkins and others," he said. "While I might have known where Hurley was located, as we had convicted all of the Inner Circle, including the leader of the gang, what did I want with convicting and hanging a poor tool like Hurley?" The explanation was hardly honest, but, McParland would have thought in true Pinkertonian form, the ends justify the means.

When McParland returned to the penitentiary the next morning, Orchard's confession was his for the taking. Orchard later claimed that this was because he had tried to pray on the previous night, but, plagued by overwhelming guilt, "the only real hope I could see for me was to make a clean breast of all, and ask God to forgive me."[52] However, an examination of Orchard's continually expanding confessions—from the one he gave to McParland to another serialized in *McClure's Magazine* to what later appeared in a full-length book[53]—indicates that Orchard's religious conversion came *after* he met Edwin Hinks, the dean of the Episcopal St. Michael's Cathedral in Boise, several months later.[54] Thus his confession was likely based not so much on easing his spiritual suffering as on trying to make sure he did not hang.

The confession poured out after McParland arrived on a gloriously bright Saturday morning, accompanied by the penitentiary's chief clerk, George C. Huebener. For three days, McParland asked, Orchard answered, and Huebener recorded—hour after hour. By the time he was finished, Orchard had given seventy-six typed pages of confession.[55] On January 31, McParland returned with Wellington B. Hopkins, his own secretary just arrived from Denver. By the end of the day there were another forty typed pages further attesting to Orchard's guilt.[56]

In this detailed, compelling, and historic statement,[57] Orchard admitted to killing eighteen men, making attempts on the lives of numerous others, and causing massive property damage. He claimed he had set off one of the three charges that destroyed the Bunker Hill concentrator in 1899, carried out the bombing that killed two men at the Vindicator Mine in 1903, and executed the Independence depot bomb massacre that killed thirteen in 1904. He acknowledged murdering detective Lyte Gregory in Denver not long before the Independence depot bombing and attempting to assassinate Fred Bradley—one-time president of Bunker Hill and Sullivan—first by poison and then by explosive, in San Francisco later that same year. He also set bombs to kill Colorado governor Peabody and Associate Justice Luther J. Goddard and Chief Justice William H. Gabbert of the Colorado Supreme Court, the last of which was foiled when an insurance salesman was killed instead. Orchard had then "taken care" of Steunenberg.

Orchard claimed that several of these crimes—including the Independence Mine and the Gregory murder—had been carried out with an accomplice named Steve Adams, who had also murdered Arthur Collins of the Smuggler-Union Mine in Telluride in 1902 and two claim jumpers in northern Idaho in 1904. Most important, he said all the acts had been committed at the order of—and with payments from—the WFM inner circle, including Haywood, Moyer, Simpkins, George Pettibone, and Vincent St. John, the former president of the Telluride union.

McParland now had everything he needed and more—dates, accomplices, details. In four days Orchard had either claimed responsibility himself or had implicated others in virtually every major outrage and mysterious incident in the Colorado and Idaho mining disputes of the previous decade. And virtually all led back to the inner circle of the WFM. In fact, they led there so conveniently that ever since there have been those who have questioned the accuracy and honesty of the confession, and have even suggested that McParland himself was its author.[58]

Clearly McParland expected such refutation, and he prepared for it by including two questions on both January 29 and 31: whether he or the stenographer made any promises of immunity, and whether he or anyone else used "force or coercion to get you to make these statements, and if not, then why did you make this statement, being that it not only incriminates a number of your associates but also yourself?"[59] Answering "no" in both cases, Orchard elaborated:

> On meeting Mr McParland and talking with him on three different occasions I awoke, as it were, from a dream and realized that I had been made a tool of, aided and assisted by the members of the Executive Board of the Western Federation of Miners, and once they had led me to commit the first crime I had to continue to do their bidding or otherwise be assassinated myself, and therefore, not caring what would become of me, knowing that I did not deserve any consideration, and on account of the crimes that I assisted in, I resolved as far as in my power to break up this murderous organization and to protect the community from further assassinations and outrages from this gang.[60]

Although McParland saw this statement as bolstering the validity of the confession, in some ways it actually detracts from it. The language sounds so much more like his than Orchard's that it empowers the arguments stating he had a hand in shaping the final document.

Conversely, there are significant reasons to believe that the statement *was* Orchard's. For one thing, McParland obviously took great pride in having extracted it. For another, Orchard unreservedly claimed it as his own—he eventually testified to and published facts that were slightly different, but he never disputed anything in the original confession. Most important, for months thereafter McParland went to great lengths to validate the information, clarify the details, check its accuracy, and find corroborating testimony, something he would not have done so assiduously had he been the real author of the confession.[61] Meanwhile, even as McParland's operatives did this legwork, the Great Detective turned his own attention to the men named as the instigators of the atrocities—men he intended to see hanged.

CHAPTER 20

BATTLE LINES ARE DRAWN

From the moment news of Steunenberg's killing was made public, it was of huge national interest to a press and readership not yet fully recovered from the startling assassination of President William McKinley four years before in Buffalo, New York.[1] Much of the press quickly attributed Steunenberg's murder to a plot of the WFM, and the fact that Haywood, the union's best-known leader, was a rabid exponent of socialism—a movement closely connected to anarchism in the public mind—made a yet stronger link to the presidential assassination, which had been carried out by anarchist Leon Czolgosz.

By the beginning of February, a month after Steunenberg's assassination, it was known that Orchard had been arrested, but the content of his confession—even that he *had* confessed—was limited to the prosecution team and the highest levels of Pinkerton's. In fact, McParland had given Orchard detailed instructions about what he could even say to Miller, his lawyer.[2]

Although the confession was an enormous first step toward prosecuting the alleged conspirators, there was still a vast amount of work to be done: finding corroborating evidence; establishing a motive; locating witnesses; and taking into custody the men who would be tried. Normally, by this stage, the lead prosecutor would have taken charge of these operations. For that position, the State of Idaho had selected its most renowned legal figure, James H. Hawley.

Born in Iowa in 1847 Hawley moved to Idaho at the age of fifteen; within three years he had achieved such success in mining that he sold his holdings to pay for a college education in San Francisco.[3] After returning to Idaho he was elected to the territorial House of Representatives when he was only twenty-three, and shortly thereafter was admitted to the bar. Four years later he was chosen for the Territory's Senate. He twice served as a district attorney for the State's Second Judicial District, before being named a federal district attorney. In 1892–93, Hawley represented the miners on trial in the Coeur d'Alenes, and was credited with being the man who suggested that they join with the Butte union, leading to the formation of the WFM.

In general, Hawley cared little about the way he dressed or looked. When he was mayor of Boise he would hold meetings slouched in a chair, legs crossed at the ankles, boots on a table, and a faraway look in his eye. But once in court he became a tiger, and he was said to connect with a jury better than any other lawyer in Idaho. He had already become a legend in criminal law and was reputed to have been involved in more murder cases than any lawyer in American history.[4] His appointment as the prosecutor was therefore a major coup for the State.

Yet, despite the involvement of Idaho's governor, chief justice, and most prominent attorney, there is no doubt that the true leader of the prosecution was McParland. Not only did his recent experience with the WFM in Colorado make him the most familiar of the prosecution team with the union, but his army of agents could not be equaled by the State. The others therefore were guided by his decisions on how to proceed.

In the days following the confession McParland concentrated on six members of the WFM whom Orchard had closely linked with major crimes. Moyer, Haywood, and Pettibone were in Denver. St. John was in Burke—where he had fled after being arrested but not charged for the murder of Arthur Collins and under the name John W. Vincent had become the leader of the local miners union.[5] Adams and Simpkins had disappeared. There could be no doubt about the importance of the last two, and not just because of their own alleged roles. The Idaho statutes held that the testimony of an accomplice was not enough to convict unless it was corroborated by other evidence,[6] and Adams or Simpkins were needed to support Orchard's confession. However, the search for Simpkins was not going well (in fact, he was never found, and his disappearance remains one of the case's greatest mysteries[7]). Thus, locating Adams was vital, and McParland repeatedly emphasized its importance.

With his operatives searching for Adams and Simpkins, and maintaining a watch on St. John, McParland's primary task became the "procedure relative to extraditing Haywood, Moyer and Pettibone from Colorado to Idaho. Owing to the fact that neither of these three parties has been in Idaho during this conspiracy we cannot say that they are fugitives from justice, and we may have considerable trouble in extraditing them." Therefore, McParland was "perfecting plans by which we hope to get them into Idaho in a legal manner, where there is little doubt but that we can convict them."[8] This plan—and the way it was carried out—would prove to be the most legally and socially contentious aspect of the murder investigation and trials.

Before any action was taken, McParland needed to make sure that Haywood, Moyer, and Pettibone did not disappear. As the three appeared uneasy about Orchard acknowledging their or the WFM's involvement, he decided to "relieve their suspicion to a certain extent." This was done by Hawley "leaking" the story to the editor of *The Idaho Daily Statesman* that detectives had "discovered that there were two men at Caldwell on the night of the murder who assisted Orchard"—one being Simpkins—and that they were "hot on the trail." The editor then slipped the "confidential" story to the Associated Press to make sure it went nationwide, meaning that the trio in Denver, who would have known there was no other assassin in Caldwell at the time—were "thrown off the track and will rest secure for the time being."[9]

Once that was accomplished, McParland, Hawley, and Gooding developed the two main prongs of their attack.[10] The first was for Idaho and Colorado to agree formally but secretly to the extradition of the three WFM leaders. The second was for them to be arrested and rushed to Idaho with such secrecy and swiftness that there was no chance the operation could be stopped by any legal process. They also aimed to arrest Adams and St. John before they found out what had happened to their cronies.

To prevent anyone from discovering the particulars of the plan, on February 6 McParland put together an extensive "cipher list of names of parties interested in this matter" for use in telegraph and written communications.[11] For locations, he substituted names of southern towns, and for the individuals, he took code names from the animal world. The inner circle received names of vicious, dangerous creatures—thus, Haywood was Viper, Moyer was Copperhead, Pettibone was Rattler, Simpkins was Scorpion, and St. John was Coyote. The men whom McParland hoped would help the prosecution were given ambivalent names: Possum for Orchard and Fox for Adams. The prosecution team was rather grander, with Gooding being the curiously spelled Lyon, Colorado governor Jesse F. McDonald the most noble (to McParland) Elk, Hawley, Tiger, and Colorado associate justice Goddard, Bear. Finally, he assigned bird names to Pinkerton's men, including Eagle to William Pinkerton, Hawk to Robert Pinkerton, Blackbird to Fraser, Lark to Hasson, who had just replaced Taber as the Spokane superintendent, and for himself the wisest of all: Owl.

The plan was initiated six days later, when Canyon County attorney Owen

Van Duyn, as directed, filed complaints against Haywood, Moyer, and Pettibone, charging them with the murder of Steunenberg. It was clear that the
three had been in Colorado at the time, and therefore the filing of these documents has long been controversial.[12] However, Hawley argued that a technical-
ity of Idaho law allowed the men to be prosecuted as principals to the murder,
and therefore for Van Duyn's affidavits to be considered suitable for sending
to the judge, and thence to Gooding.[13] According to this interpretation,
Gooding was thus legally justified in ordering extradition papers, which were
presented to Governor McDonald on February 16.

The period leading up to that day had seen McParland at his conspiratorial
finest. On February 8, he prepared a detailed document for Gooding and
Hawley outlining the step-by-step procedure by which the three WFM leaders would be detained and brought to Idaho. He also noted that if Adams were
located, he should be arrested: "If able to break Steve Adams down or get a
confession from him, and at the present it looks to me as though I will be able
to do so, we will at the same time have the Colorado authorities arrest Vincent
St. John at Burke, Idaho, for the murder of Arthur Collins, manager of the
Smuggler Union mine at Telluride."[14]

The next day, McParland visited Orchard, and requested that he sign an
affidavit confirming his confession, in case it needed to be presented to Governor McDonald. "I look upon you as my father at the present time," Orchard
responded, "as these statements are correct and true I should not have hesitated a minute to sign them and swear to them, which I will do."[15]

That same afternoon, McParland sent a letter to Colorado Supreme Court
associate justice Luther Goddard, whom he hoped would support the plan to
grab the WFM leaders and would convince other important individuals in
Colorado to do so as well. Praising his own work in extravagant terms, McParland wrote:

> In making my investigation I have unearthed the bloodiest
> crowd of anarchists that ever existed, I think, in the civilized
> world, not even excepting Russia. . . . the outrages committed by
> the Molly Maguires in Pennsylvania were simply child's play when
> compared with the acts of these bloodthirsty assassins; and I think
> it was through an act of Devine [sic] Providence that I have been
> enabled to get at the bottom of this conspiracy.[16] This matter is of
> more importance to the State of Colorado, and all the western
> states where the blight of the Western Federation of Miners has

taken root, than all the cases that you might try on the Supreme Court bench of Colorado in a year, or in fact, during your lifetime."[17]

The day after writing to Goddard, McParland took the train to Denver, not knowing that at the same time Gooding was sending a highly complimentary letter to William Pinkerton: "Words fail to express my appreciation of the splendid work done for the State of Idaho by [McParland]. . . . In my judgment he is the only man in America that could have accomplished the results attained by him here."[18]

Those results continued in the following days, starting with confirmation of Judge Goddard's support. McParland had expected Goddard to be agreeable—after all, Orchard had tried to kill him. In fact, the unexploded bomb was still on his property, and as Goddard met with McParland, Colorado adjutant general Bulkeley Wells—trained as a mining engineer and an expert on explosives—removed it. Goddard "assured me that he will arrange with a few prominent citizens to have the Sheriff act just as I want him to," McParland noted. "The judge is of the opinion that as soon as the extradition papers arrive here that we should at once have these men arrested and taken out on a special train as we do not know what District Judge they would be tried before providing a writ of habeas corpus is obtained and he doesn't want any writs or legal points tried here."[19]

On February 16, McParland, Hawley, Goddard, Chief Justice Gabbert, and several others finally met with McDonald.[20] McParland summarized Orchard's confession and explained the plans for taking the WFM officers to Idaho. The governor was initially hesitant to sign the extradition papers, as "[t]he custom in Colorado . . . is for the Governor to refer the application to the Attorney General." However, it "was shown to the Governor that . . . it would be death to the case to refer the papers." Therefore, McDonald—who must have thought it was an easy way to get rid of some of the state's leading troublemakers—said, "I will sign them, and the record will not go into the Secretary of State's office until some time next week."[21] The road had been cleared for the transfer of the men to Idaho. The only question was: Could McParland pull it off?

Everything was now ready for the arrests, which were planned for early morning on February 18—a Sunday, chosen so that courts would not be open and lawyers and judges would be more difficult to find.[22] A special three-car train was provided by the Oregon Short Line Railroad of the Union Pacific system, with priority over all traffic except one express passenger train. The crews and engines would be changed regularly—at least eight times during the trip—in order to have men familiar with the track as well as engines specifically designed for plains, mountains, or other terrain through which the train would speed. Changing engines would also cut down on the loss of steam caused by the fireboxes filling with ash and on the chances of the friction bearings overheating, forcing a stop. Each engine would be fully fueled and watered when taken on, but other stops would need to be made for coal or water, and rather than these occurring in towns or rail yards (where union men might try to stop the train from restarting), they would take place at isolated sidings, such as Separation, Point of Rocks, and Church Buttes. McParland was particularly concerned about going through Cheyenne, where U.S. Marshal Frank A. Hadsell was based, because he could serve a writ of habeas corpus and release the prisoners. Therefore, it was agreed that the train would maintain a speed of thirty miles per hour through Cheyenne, too fast for anyone to board.

Concerned lest any unexpected troubles arise, a Union Pacific chief dispatcher was placed in one of the cars to make sure the tracks were kept clear. It was also decided that no Pinkerton's agents were to be aboard, so that the agency's participation in the later trials could not be compromised. McParland therefore "wanted not only a man of intelligence but a man of nerve to take charge." The one he selected was Bulkeley Wells, who, he knew "will not obey the order of any sheriff en route, that you can depend on."

McParland even oversaw the train's provisioning. "It will consist of plenty of good chicken and ham sandwiches," he wrote. "We will not be able to get any coffee and knowing the men that I am detailing on this matter I will place a case of beer in charge of Gen. Wells . . . as I know he will see to it that nobody will get any more of the beer than they are entitled to."[23] The actual purchase of the supplies also allowed him to throw off potential attempts by supporters of the three men to ascertain where they were being taken. They were obtained at a café where the cook was a friend of Haywood's. The Pinkerton operative picking up the food would say to him that he had to hurry to take the provisions to Burnham, a station to the south. When news of the arrests broke, it was hoped that the cook would go directly to Haywood's house and tell them he was being taken south.

The arrests were carried out under the auspices of one of McParland's longtime friends, Sheriff Alexander Nisbet. Three coaches were sent out, each containing four trusted deputies and a Pinkerton's operative who could identify the target. The arrests were to be made concurrently and the prisoners brought to the Fortieth Street yard, from where the special train would leave. The prisoners would be transported in a locked train car under the watch of Wells; James Mills, the deputy warden of the Idaho state penitentiary; and four special deputies, including Wells's assistant, "Hair Trigger Bob" Meldrum, a former Telluride deputy sheriff turned gunslinger. Even the Union Pacific's dispatcher and crews of engineers, firemen, conductors, and brakemen would not be allowed in this carriage.

On the afternoon of February 17—with the anticipation building—McParland received what he called the best news yet: Adams had been found at his uncle's ranch in Haines, Oregon. McParland promptly sent operative Chris Thiele (not to be confused with the Thiel Detective Service Company) from Boise to Oregon. "We will arrest Adams at the same time that we arrest the parties here," he wrote. "I will then see what can be done with St. John, Carpenter and others, but suppose that I must come up to Idaho right away in order to break Adams down. Put Adams through the same course of sprouts that we put Orchard through."[24]

Within hours McParland's glee shifted back to anxiety, as his plan required sudden revision. At about 8:00 P.M., Moyer left his home to catch a train to Deadwood, South Dakota. McParland had operatives watching all three WFM officers, and the one shadowing Moyer instantly phoned the office. Worried that Moyer would continue to Canada, McParland ordered his immediate arrest, and the party of deputy sheriffs that took him into custody found he was carrying more than $520 in cash, a .44 caliber revolver, and a hundred rounds of ammunition.[25] However, his arrest attracted the attention of a large crowd of onlookers, which meant that Haywood and Pettibone needed to be picked up before they got wind of what was happening.

At 9:30, Haywood was arrested at the Granite rooming house, where, only feet away from "a huge revolver that he had laying on the dressing case," he was found "stark naked and in bed with a woman notwithstanding the fact that he has a wife and child living here in Denver."[26] McParland called the place a "house of assignation," and undoubtedly would have been even more critical had he known the woman was Haywood's sister-in-law and longtime lover Winnie Minor.[27] Almost three hours later, Pettibone was arrested as he returned home. After being confined in the jail until all three were in custody, they were then moved in the early hours of the morning to the Oxford Hotel, and, at 5:40 A.M., taken to the waiting train, which had been moved from the Fortieth Street yard to Union Station on the north side of Denver.[28]

At exactly 6:00 A.M., the train headed north.[29] An hour later Wells told the three prisoners—each of whom was kept handcuffed throughout the journey—that they were under arrest and were being taken to Boise. By 9:00 A.M., the train had passed into Wyoming, and begun chugging west through the southern reaches of the state. While the prisoners played cards, the guards kept a close watch, going on extra alert each time they passed through a town. In the afternoon, between lunch and dinner, Wells broke out the cigars, which, with the compartment hermetically sealed, must have made quite a fug. That night, as the prisoners dozed fitfully in the beds in the back of the carriage, the train reached the Idaho state line, and in the middle of the night it raced at thirty miles per hour through Pocatello, a strong union center. Around 3:00 A.M. they stopped to cool and repair an overheating housing on the undercarriage. Finally, at 9:15 A.M. on February 19, the train rolled into Boise, a little more than twenty-seven hours after leaving Denver. The three prisoners were taken straight to death row—and it was then that all hell broke loose.

Despite the elaborate precautions, the Denver press found out what was happening, and stories were published before the train that would soon be nicknamed "the Pirate Special" even reached Boise.[30] The one that most enraged McParland appeared in *The Denver Republican*, stating that the arrests had come about due to Orchard's confession.[31] McParland furiously blamed the leak on McDonald's private secretary, who had once worked for the newspaper.[32] By the next day the story was in newspapers across the nation; some, such as *The Rocky Mountain News*, were already calling the act "kidnapping."[33]

Hoping to control the speculation about the case, and particularly Orchard's role, McParland told Gooding that he gave "a little something to the press in order to assure the public that we will convict all parties now under arrest and others that will be arrested."[34] It was more than "a little," as he engaged in the highly unusual practice of distributing a press release in which he was acknowledged as author. He blatantly denied that any confession had been made: "There have been statements made by various persons, but I know of none made by Orchard, and as I have been the only man at work on the case I think I would have known of it had there been one."[35]

Nevertheless, he claimed, the authorities had ample evidence of the men's guilt. And responding to taunts in the socialist press that he was too old for such tasks, he haughtily retorted: "These fellows thought that it was so long ago that I had broken up the Molly Maguires that I must now be in my dotage.

They were not afraid of me. But there is a weak spot in every wall, especially such a one as that upon which the Western Federation was founded, and that weak spot I found. It will cost Moyer, Haywood and Pettibone and as many more their lives."[36]

In hopes of getting the press totally "onside," McParland then took the rare step of meeting privately with individual reporters. His message, dutifully relayed in the newspapers, stated: "We have unearthed a conspiracy that will make the blood run cold. This is not a war against organized labor, but it is a war against organized anarchy and dynamite. It is a war against the most damnable and fiendish crimes that ever degraded humanity, and it is a war against as heartless a band of criminals as the authorities of any state or any civilized country have ever had to deal with, and I need not except Russia."[37] In fact, he confided, it was the threat of violence that prompted the manner in which the three men had been brought to Idaho. "They knew that if they were captured they would never be able to clear themselves, and were about to leave the country when arrested," he blustered, ignoring Haywood's arrest in his love nest, "They had planned to blow up the train if any attempt were made to remove them to Idaho, and for this reason I insisted on having a special train to take them to Idaho."[38]

However, a problem more dangerous than the involvement of the press was emerging. Within twelve hours of the men's departure from Denver, Edmund F. Richardson, the WFM's leading lawyer, was hot on their heels. Born on a farm in Massachusetts in 1862, Richardson had studied law while working in a tailoring business, and at the age of twenty-two had moved to San Francisco, where he was admitted to the bar.[39] In 1886, he moved to Del Norte, Colorado, nine years later joining a prominent firm in Denver, through which he became affiliated with the WFM. Despite a big-city elegance and hauteur, he was tall, powerfully built, and considered a man's man. In the courtroom he was keen, aggressive, shrewd, and one who "scorned oratorical and sensational methods, and sought to win on merit."[40]

Richardson immediately approached the Idaho Supreme Court to ask for a writ of habeas corpus for his three clients. Stressing the constitutional requirement that an individual must have fled from a state to be extradited back, he pointed out that his clients had clearly not been in Idaho at the time of the murder, and that the governors of the two states had conspired to perpetrate a fraud in the claim that "these men were present and actually committed, by their own hand, the crime of murder upon the body of Governor Steunenberg." Their removal from Colorado had therefore been "under the semblance of the forms of law, preserving the shadow, but destroying the substance."[41] His argument filed, Richardson turned his attention to an event that would have an incalculable impact upon the case—the hiring of his "associate counsel." The man selected was already on his way to becoming a legend: Clarence Darrow.

Born in rural Farmdale, Ohio, in 1857,[42] Darrow attended Allegheny College for a year before returning home and spending three years studying law on an informal basis. He then went to the University of Michigan Law School for a year before working in a Youngstown, Ohio, law firm. After being admitted to the bar in 1879, he practiced in Ohio for eight years before moving to Chicago. There his campaign work for a successful mayoral candidate helped lead to his appointment as a special assessment attorney for the city. Three months later he was promoted to assistant corporation counsel, and within a year he had become the head of Chicago's legal department.

Darrow's political connections soon enabled him to join the legal department of the Chicago and North Western Railway, but even while seemingly in the pocket of big business, he joined liberal colleagues demanding a pardon for three men imprisoned for their roles in the Haymarket affair and the overturning of the death penalty for Eugene Prendergast, the convicted assassin of former Chicago mayor Carter Harrison. But the big shift in Darrow's career came in 1894, when he began acting on behalf of labor. His first major case in this new calling was defending union leader Eugene Debs, who had been charged with conspiracy to obstruct the mail and contempt of court during the American Railway Union strike against the Pullman Palace Car Company.[43]

In 1898 Darrow successfully defended Thomas Kidd and several other union members against charges of criminal and civil conspiracy for their roles in a contentious woodworkers' strike in Oshkosh, Wisconsin. His closing argument was immediately regarded as a classic, and was quickly published.[44] Then, in 1902 and 1903, he became a legal celebrity for his defense of the United Mine Workers before the government arbitration commission following the miners' strike in Pennsylvania's anthracite region. Darrow's eight-hour closing argument was an important factor in the commission eventually awarding union members back pay, significant pay raises, and a maximum nine-hour working day.

Upon being approached about the Haywood, Moyer, and Pettibone case, Darrow traveled to Denver, where, on February 26, after meeting with labor leaders and Richardson, he agreed to join the defense,[45] although in exactly what capacity would later be vehemently disputed.

While the defense was recruiting its team, the prosecution made two important moves. On the very night that the train carrying Haywood, Moyer, and Pettibone rattled toward Boise, Shoshone County Sheriff Angus Sutherland and several deputies burst into the house in Burke rented by Vincent St. John and took him to the county jail in Wallace. Four days later, Coyote was placed in the state penitentiary in Boise.[46]

Meanwhile, on the day the train reached its destination, Pinkerton's operative Chris Thiele and Baker County Sheriff Harvey Brown visited the Oregon ranch owned by James Warren Lillard, who happened to be on business in Texas. They found, as expected, Lillard's thirty-nine-year-old nephew Steve Adams—a native Missourian with "a marked face, a wide mouth, a cunning eye with curious drooping eyelids, and a complexion blotched by liquor and exposure"[47]—who had quietly moved there with his wife and two stepchildren. Held in the Baker County jail overnight, Adams was sent to Boise the next day, having, he claimed, been reassured by Brown that "you go down there and do what those fellows want you to and you will come out all right. I am on the inside and I know what I am talking about."[48]

While some of the prosecution team rejoiced over the arrests, McParland was livid when he found out that some of his key instructions had not been carried out. Having been forced by other duties to remain in Denver, he ordered that Adams be placed in solitary confinement on death row and treated as Orchard had been. But the detective was ignored, and Adams was put in the same cell as Orchard. Moreover, he was allowed to see a lawyer, who suggested that before any discussions with the authorities they get an agreement from Governor McDonald that he would never stand trial in Colorado. "Now, this is a very unfortunate state of affairs," McParland fumed when he discovered what had happened. "It is unnecessary for me to say that with the leverage I had, founded on Orchard's confession, it would have taken me about ten minutes to have Adams make a full confession with no promises."[49]

McParland was also uncertain of the status of St. John, since his operative was "not able to inform me why St. John was arrested"—that is, on what specific Idaho complaint, as the major charge against him was for the Collins murder in Colorado. "And except that Adams met St John in Burke and told him that he was going to murder ex-Governor Steunenberg we cannot convict

St. John, and if St. John is discharged I do not see how we are going to take Adams to Telluride to prosecute St. John, as Adams himself was the principal in the murder of Arthur Collins."[50] It is clear from McParland's comments that—despite hopes to link St. John to several disappearances that had been assumed to be murders[51]—in actuality he had little true evidence of criminal activity by him other than Orchard's confession. However, after so many years obtaining confessions from defendants, McParland so implicitly trusted his own skills that he tended to believe he could tell truth from lies. This was particularly the case when the information matched what he wanted to hear anyway—such as Orchard's confession.[52]

Despite McParland's disgust, Orchard transpired to be the ideal first step for the process through which the detective wanted to put the new prisoner. As Adams later recalled: "Orchard commenced to talk at once. Said he had made a confession that implicated me in . . . all the crimes in Colorado and everywhere else that I had been around. . . . That he and I would never be tried on these charges if I would corroborate what he had said. He said their object was to get evidence against the officials of the WFM. That they were the men they wanted and he named Haywood, Moyer, Pettibone, St. John and Simpkins. . . . He told me over and over again that Governor Gooding, McParland and the States lawyer had promised to stand by us and see that no harm came to us." Moreover, wrote Adams, "He kept this up continuously for four days."[53]

But Orchard's promises of freedom were only the carrot—the stick was provided by Fred Bond, a convicted murderer awaiting execution. Hoping for clemency, Bond had been to see Gooding, and he returned to repeat the governor's remark that if, as Adams said, "I did not tell what they knew I knew and what they knew I ought to know they had evidence that would hang me so damned high salt peter would not save me."[54]

Meanwhile, on the afternoon of February 25, in order to control growing speculation about how Orchard's statement related to the abduction of the WFM leaders, Gooding suggested to McParland, Whitney, and Hawley that he "give out to the public through the press that Orchard had made a confession, [and] would also state . . . that he had withdrawn the reward. . . . This is something that will help the prosecution, as one cannot go from house to house and tell people that the Pinkerton Agency never operates for rewards."[55] The next day, in a widely released story, Gooding referred to "a full confession" that "implicated all those now under arrest and others, including J.L. Simpkins." He attributed the confession "to the great brain of James McParland, who has been employed by the state to run down the murderers," adding: "McParland was aided in his work by Orchard's early training. In his boyhood the Bible was read night and morning . . . The impression of the early days came up and smote his conscience when he was brought face to face with his God. He told me that he believed in a Supreme Being and a hereafter, and that now his one thought was to make his peace with his Maker."[56]

Meanwhile, knowing his lawyer was away, McParland visited Adams, wasting no time in pointing out that the prisoner was effectively on his own. Soon he was telling Adams that: "It is your duty that you owe to your family, your fellow men and your God to corroborate Harry Orchard's confession against the officials of the Federation. There isn't a doubt but what they are guilty." Moreover, McParland continued, "if you don't you will be taken back to Cripple Creek and hung, and then where would your wife and poor little children be. You do this and you will never be prosecuted and you will come out all right and be away ahead."[57]

For two hours McParland "went over it again and again, stating it in all its different ways. All of the time repeating that if I did not corroborate Orchard I would be sent to Cripple Creek and mobbed or hung by the people there."[58]

After a night in solitary, Adams was again visited by McParland. "You better go ahead and make a statement corroborating Orchard and save yourself," the detective stated, adding that if Adams "was turned loose [he] would be killed immediately by some member of the Western Federation of Miners."[59] With similar words from Orchard still ringing in his ears, Adams gave in, although he still had several concerns. The first—his wife and family—was put to rest when McParland assured him that he would "get her a good place to stay and the state will take good care of them and see you through."[60] To reassure him about another worry—what would happen to him—McParland cited the story of Kelly the Bum. However, unlike Orchard, who took it to heart, Adams seemed totally mystified by the tale, as he did by the detective's Bible stories.[61]

For the rest of the day, Huebener, Whitney's clerk, recorded Adams's confession, and when the process continued the next day, McParland's own secretary, Hopkins, transcribed the confession. "Adams seemed in better condition today," McParland reported the second day, "although at times big beads of sweat broke out on his face and later on his hands. He was quite nervous. As I had been made aware by [Chris Thiele] that Adams smoked continuously I had provided myself with a pocket full of cigars, and I never saw cigars disappear so fast in my life."[62]

But by the end of these smoky sessions, McParland had what he wanted—a lengthy confession that tended to corroborate Orchard's.[63] Most important were the sections pertaining to the Steunenberg murder, particularly how, in 1904, Adams had met Haywood and Pettibone in Denver, where they said they wanted to "get" the governor. Haywood gave Adams two hundred dollars for expenses necessary for the murder, but Adams drank most of the money away, and, unable to replenish it, gave up on the job, after which it was passed on to Orchard.

But that was just the beginning. Adams also admitted to helping Orchard in the attempted murders of former governor Peabody and Supreme Court justices Goddard and Gabbert. He was there when Orchard shot Lyte Gregory, had killed Arthur Collins with a shotgun himself, and he and Orchard had together set off the explosion at the Independence depot that had killed thirteen nonunion miners.

Adams was not as impressive an informer as Orchard. He did not remember dates, times, or details as well, but, he later claimed, when he told the detective that they would have to get the dates, McParland said, "I will help you with the dates all right." Then, according to Adams, McParland "took some papers out of his pocket and he would read to himself and then ask me questions, and then I would answer it back as nearly as I could remember what Orchard had told me about the same transactions. He said that it did not make any difference whose names I mentioned in my statement, none of them would be prosecuted except these men connected with the Federation, Moyer, Haywood, Pettibone, St. John and Simpkins."[64]

This recollection did not align with McParland's account that the information he obtained the first day had come tumbling out in narrative form rather than in questions and answers as on the second day.[65] But for the time being, such delicacies did not matter, because on the following day McParland was scheduled to appear before the grand jury in Caldwell.

"As to what transpired in the jury room I am not at liberty to state," McParland reported haughtily the next day, March 1, "except to say that I was treated with the utmost courtesy, and the Grand Jury men just stood in amazement at the statement that I made of the crimes committed by the inner circle."[66] A day later it was Orchard in front of the grand jury, but McParland still dominated the larger newspaper headlines, as he released a statement that Adams had made a sweeping confession corroborating Orchard's in every substantial point.

"This second confession is far more important than that made by Harry

Orchard," he bragged. "Adams knows far more of the workings of the inner circle than Orchard did, and was able to give a mass of detailed information that Orchard's confession did not cover."[67]

In the following days—while McParland was slowed by a "bad attack of Lagrippe or cold"[68]—legal issues dominated the Steunenberg case. The first of these was a victory for the prosecution, when William E. Borah, a firebrand known for the power and dynamism of his oratory, agreed to serve as Hawley's associate counsel—and for only a quarter of Hawley's twenty-thousand-dollar fee.[69] Born in Illinois in 1865,[70] Borah briefly attended the University of Kansas before being admitted to the bar, and then, in 1890, moving to Boise, where he established a flourishing legal practice representing large mining, timber, and livestock interests. Concurrently, he became a major figure in Idaho's Republican Party. By the time he joined Hawley it seemed inevitable that he would be selected as the next U.S. senator from Idaho.

Hard on the heels of signing up Borah, the prosecution had another triumph when, on March 7, the Caldwell grand jury returned indictments against Orchard, Moyer, Haywood, Pettibone, and Simpkins. An indictment was not returned for St. John, causing speculation that: "he is to be used as a witness for the prosecution, and as compensation for this he will be permitted to go free."[71] But McParland knew otherwise, as he groused in a report to Gooding: "Swain, of the Thiel detective agency, who had forced himself on the Grand Jury . . . testified that he had St. John under surveillance for the past year, and that he was not out of the city of Burke during that time. I do not know how much Swain was paid for this; however, his positive testimony prevented an indictment being found against St. John. . . . As St. John was at Wallace, Idaho, twice in conference with Orchard during last summer you can see as to the truthfulness of Swain's testimony."[72]

Here was yet another example of McParland having such confidence in his own skills that he unhesitatingly believed what Orchard had said of St. John. Part of his response was that, like others,[73] he did not trust Swain as far as he could spit, and that he viewed St. John as being responsible for several murders in Colorado, so was not about to give him the benefit of the doubt. But mostly McParland simply believed that when he wheedled, threatened, and enticed a confession, he had so controlled the exchange that any admission was the truth, the whole truth, and nothing but the truth. Although this confidence generally proved well-founded through his long career, he had perhaps not previously met quite such a fabricator as Orchard, who made a number of statements that were shown to be false, including about St. John.

The lack of an indictment did not stop McParland from moving against St. John once again, however, as that very day he wrote to H. Frank Cary, the new superintendent of the Denver office, telling him to contact Sheriff Calvin Rutan of San Miguel County (in which Telluride is located), "to come forward with extradition papers at once."[74]

Coincidentally, at the same time McParland was hoping to extradite St. John *to* Colorado, Hawley and Borah made their arguments to the Idaho Supreme Court regarding Richardson's writ for habeas corpus about the extraditions *from* Colorado. After much debate about how to address Richardson's contention that the three labor leaders could not have fled Idaho when they had not even been there, Hawley chose to portray the argument as simply an irrelevancy. Even accepting "that Moyer, Haywood and Pettibone were kidnapped from the state of Colorado, forcibly and illegally brought to this jurisdiction, the fact is they are here," he declared. "It makes no difference how the prisoners were brought here. They are here. That is the point."[75]

It was an argument that raised the hackles of newspapers across the country—particularly those on the left. But the Idaho Supreme Court was concerned solely with strict legal interpretation, and on March 12, it agreed with Hawley and denied Richardson's writ, stating that "The question as to whether or not a citizen is a fugitive from justice is one that can only be available to him so long as he is beyond the jurisdiction of the state whose laws he is alleged to have transgressed. . . . The jurisdiction of the court in which the indictment is found is not impaired by the manner in which the accused is brought before it."[76] In other words, the way the labor leaders had been brought to Idaho might or might not have been legal, but that was beyond the purview of the court, and once there, they belonged to Idaho's justice system.

Richardson had undoubtedly expected this, so he immediately appealed to the U.S. Circuit Court in Boise, again filing applications for a writ of habeas corpus. In an expedited process, arguments were heard a week later, on March 19, and on the next day Judge James H. Beatty upheld the Idaho Supreme Court's ruling and denied the writ. Richardson thereupon filed a petition for writ of certiorari, that is, an appeal to the United States Supreme Court. This was granted, and arguments were scheduled for October.[77] The question of whether McParland had organized arrest or abduction had reached the highest court in the land, and little did any of the main participants realize that the Supreme Court's eventual decision would establish national and international precedents still in effect.

CHAPTER 21

THE LULL BEFORE THE STORM

When the Supreme Court of the United States agreed to hear the appeal filed by Richardson, the Steunenberg murder trial, tentatively scheduled for May, was postponed indefinitely, at least until the Supreme Court's ruling after the hearing in October. Both the prosecution and the defense therefore had more time to investigate the murder, its relation to other crimes attributed to the WFM, and the tactics being used by the opposing side. No one was more expert in this than McParland, who immediately proceeded with numerous and varied inquiries.

One of the things at the top of his agenda was continuing the search for Simpkins. On March 16, McParland received a telegram stating that a man answering Simpkins's description was being held in Oakley, Idaho.[1] Unable to determine the individual's identity with certainty via telegraph, he sent Thiele to collect him so that Orchard or Adams could identify him. However, he proved not to be Simpkins, and the search went on.

The hunt for Simpkins was particularly frustrating, because when Gooding had asked Swain to arrest him, the Thiel operative had procrastinated for so long that the labor leader was able to disappear. Swain then claimed that he had gone to the authorities to have Simpkins arrested, but Sheriff Sutherland of Shoshone County called that a bold-faced lie, leading McParland to muse: "[T]aking into consideration what Orchard learned through Miller . . . relative to the fact that he could buy Swain for a little money . . . it now looks to me as though Mr Swain let Simpkins escape purposely, and that he was paid for the same."[2]

At the same time, McParland had St. John taken back to Colorado, first making sure that, even though the Caldwell grand jury had failed to indict him, he was left incarcerated without charge.[3] On the same day that the Idaho Supreme Court ruled on the extradition, Sheriff Rutan and Bulkeley Wells's assistant, Bob Meldrum, caught the train north from Telluride armed with an extradition request charging St. John with murdering a deputized ore trammer named Ben Burnham at Wells's Smuggler-Union Mine in July 1901. Before they could reach Idaho, however, a district court judge ruled that St. John should not have been held without an indictment and ordered him released. Within moments, Canyon County Sheriff Nichols rearrested St. John for assisting in the murder of Steunenberg, and "the smile faded from his countenance and he was chewing a tooth pick nervously as he was led away." But Nichols had no intention of keeping his new prisoner; when Rutan arrived, Gooding immediately signed the papers allowing St. John to be taken to Colorado.

During this time, McParland suffered a devastating personal tragedy. Early on the morning of March 16, the operator at a little station west of Pueblo, Colorado, on the Denver & Rio Grande Railroad, fell asleep at his post.[4] At 2:30 A.M., the heavily loaded westbound No. 3 from Denver barreled headlong into the No. 16 from Salt Lake City on a curve near Adobe, twenty-five miles west of Pueblo. Derailed in a blinding blizzard, several cars burst into flames, incinerating an estimated fifty passengers, with the final figure forever unknown because, as one headline read, "Flesh Literally Cooked from the Bones and no Means of Identifying Them." Shocked survivors told of people being hurled from the cars into the snowstorm and only being able to watch the ghastly scenes as—in another headline—"Cars Became Charnel Houses for Injured."

One of those identified in the disaster was thirty-three-year-old Globe Express messenger Eneas McParland, the detective's beloved nephew. Although McParland was too professional to mention the tragedy in his report, he did speak to Orchard about it when he saw him the next day. Orchard had been considering suicide, but McParland: "Talked to me about the hereafter, and . . . said if I would truly and sincerely repent and pray for forgiveness that there was no sin that God would not forgive. He told me he had been praying nearly all day, as he had had word that his nephew, whom he thought a great deal of . . . had been virtually burned alive."[5]

As it turned out, it was not only Eneas who was taken from McParland. Not long after, his nephew's young widow, Emily—who was also a favorite of McParland and Mary—took her sons Francis, aged two and a half, and Eneas James, seven months, to New Zealand, where they settled with the children's grandfather, McParland's older brother Frank.[6]

McParland's distress at these personal losses was intensified during this time by also being under vicious attack as part of an intensive campaign on behalf of Moyer, Haywood, and Pettibone by *Appeal to Reason*, the weekly political newspaper published in Girard, Kansas, "as an advocate of International Socialism."[7] The campaign started with a lead article by labor leader Eugene Debs, in which he declared: "If they attempt to murder Moyer, Haywood and their brothers, a million revolutionists, at least, will meet them with guns."[8]

Soon thereafter, *Appeal to Reason* began aggressively attacking those people and organizations perceived as enemies to labor, including the governors, legislators, and judicial systems of Idaho and Colorado, the mine owners' associations, and the Pinkerton's and Thiel agencies. But a particular object of its venom was McParland. More than Gooding, McDonald, Hawley, or Orchard, more than other investigators, in fact more than any other individual, McParland was the target of vicious diatribes penned by George Shoaf, P. M. Eastwood, or Walter Hurt. His operations against the Molly Maguires and many years of antiunion activities meant that McParland had been bitterly criticized for years in the labor press. Yet these condemnations paled compared to the defamatory articles that were now churned out, particularly by the rabid Shoaf.

Born in Lockhart, Texas, in 1875, Shoaf had early fallen under the spell of Debs and wanted to be someone who could inspire common people to fight for economic emancipation and socialism.[9] However, after starting in journalism in San Antonio, he moved to William Randolph Hearst's *Chicago Morning American*, which gave him a powerful introduction to "yellow journalism," and encouraged him to "sidetrack idealism, and pursue the capitalist newspaper game."[10] In 1903, Shoaf found himself able to unite sensationalism and idealism when he joined *Appeal to Reason* while continuing to write for the Hearst newspapers. Sent to Colorado to cover the conflicts between the WFM and the mine owners, he met Haywood, whom he idolized. He also came across his bête noire—James McParland.

Shoaf detested McParland, and initiated *Appeal to Reason*'s practice of calling him "McPartland" in order to tie him to a highly publicized murderer of the same name. He also created the stories linking McParland to Jake McLaughlin in Parsons, Kansas, claiming without evidence that the detective had committed murders beyond count—"crouched in the shadow there with a clenched dagger.... An unexpected thrust from behind is in perfect keeping."[11]

Such sensational stories had a certain irony coming from a man who had hoped to commit murder himself. As he wrote:

Vincent St John . . . and myself were blood brothers in our hatred
of capitalism and in our desire to liquidate the damnable economy
with force and violence. . . . St John and I concocted a plan to assassinate Pinkerton Detective James McParlan. . . . [I]f we slew the
detective chief, the act would put the fear of God in the hearts of
Colorado capitalists. . . . For days and nights we camped on the
trail of the detective chief, but his ever present body guard of
several huskies prevented us from getting near enough, . . . [but]
St John and I had murder in our hearts.[12]

Little wonder that McParland hoped to find incriminating evidence about
St. John. Meanwhile, Shoaf continued to besmirch the detective's reputation.
"McPartland, the premier thug of Pinkerton's aggregation of assassins," he
raved, "seems utterly to lack all those qualities that attract and which might
attach to himself the sympathy or affection of others of his species. He is the
one person on record who can not claim a single friend. In all other known
cases, even the vilest of human vermin holds the regard of some creature of its
kind. But McPartland not only is cut off from the rest of his race, but even the
dogs of the street, informed by instinct, slink away at his approach."[13]

Shoaf's talent for plumbing journalistic depths was perhaps only matched
by his colleague Walter Hurt, who wrote: "McPartland is a degenerate whose
particular perversion is the shedding of human blood—and to gratify his id-
iosyncrasy to the greatest extent the blood should be that of an innocent person." Then, having warmed up, he concluded: "Were the world's supply of
emetic poured down the hot throat of hell, the ultimate imp of the last vile
vomit would be an archangel in good standing compared with this feculent
fiend."[14]

While *Appeal to Reason* battered him, and his personal losses weighed heavily
on him, McParland went about the business of locating evidence to support
the confessions. Among the first materials he sought were five bottles of what
Adams called Pettibone dope, or hellfire—an incendiary mixture of phospho-
rus, bisulfide of carbon, alcohol, benzine, and turpentine that could not be
extinguished by water and was similar to what in the Middle Ages had been
called Greek Fire.[15] The bottles of this primitive form of napalm had been
produced by Pettibone during the Cripple Creek strike. With nonunion miners traveling there from the Coeur d'Alenes, Moyer ordered Adams to Pocatello, where he could throw the concoction in a window when he saw a cab

full of strikebreakers heading south. Finding the scheme impractical because strikebreakers did not travel in the same car together, Adams abandoned the idea and buried the bottles.

On March 27, a party including McParland, Thiele, Gooding, Warden Whitney, Adams, and a pair of newspaper reporters traveled to Pocatello to try to find the hellfire.[16] Although uncertain the bottles could be used in the trial, McParland still wanted them for public relations reasons: "[T]he trades and labor assemblies and other unions have been passing resolutions condemning the action of . . . extraditing these men, we wished to show to the public the class of men the labor organizations were trying to represent as good citizens."[17]

Adams eventually identified what he thought was the old mill in which he had buried the bottles, and after a great deal of digging, a glass stopper and a bucket that might have contained the bottles were discovered. The next day, with the help of a few locals, a large amount of fused glass that had been moved from that location a year or two before was found, suggesting that it had once been the bottles for which they had searched, and that had melted due to the mixture they were holding. The evidence was far from definitive, but McParland nevertheless declared the mission a huge success.[18]

Through much of April, McParland continued to interview Orchard and Adams, in hopes of gleaning small details that had been left out of their earlier confessions. Although Orchard acknowledged having previously told falsehoods, McParland still believed he "is a true penitent, notwithstanding all the crimes that he committed, and notwithstanding his weakness, is not a bad man at heart, and if he had fallen into good company he would still be a good citizen."[19]

As his reports show, McParland also believed that both confessions were honest and genuine,[20] and he organized a number of missions to prove their accuracy. Orchard's stories, for example, led McParland to seek the spade the killer had used for hiding the bomb to murder former governor Peabody, as well as to obtain a statement from the secretary of the San Francisco bartenders union, who had helped Orchard collect a registered letter from Pettibone, which included several hundred dollars needed for the assassination of Fred Bradley.[21]

McParland also sought the identity of a man in Denver, who, one night while Orchard was planting a bomb, "came across the path. The man came on him so suddenly that Orchard did not observe him until he was right beside him; then Orchard feigned that he was drunk. The man spoke to him but

Orchard lay with his face to the ground pretending that he was drunk and said he would be all right in a little while, and the man passed on."²² Hoping to show Orchard had been in Seattle in September 1905, McParland wrote to P. K. Ahern, superintendent in that city, that: "There is no doubt but what he called on several real estate offices, more especially such real estate men as deal in farms and ranches. . . . [T]ake Orchard's picture and make a careful canvass of all the real estate offices."²³

At the same time, McParland tried to corroborate Adams's confession, asking Cary in Denver to find "Andy Stark, who was either superintendent or foreman of Vindicator No. 2" when Adams and two other men reputedly severely beat him. Further, he ordered Thiele to go to Ogden, Utah, to "investigate the statement made by Adams relative to the time that he was arrested in company with [Ed] Minster, . . . wherein Detective Mason of Ogden at the request of Adams wired Heywood [sic] for seventy-five dollars, which Heywood subsequently sent. . . . There is no doubt but what Adams says . . . is true, but the point is to get the corroboration."²⁴

Throughout these investigations, McParland insisted on keeping discoveries secret, so as not to help the defense. "[I]n investigating such matters as this letter contains you must impress upon the parties called upon the necessity of keeping these matters secret," he instructed Cary, "and also try to find out whether or not they would be willing to come to Caldwell, Idaho, and testify."²⁵

Even more secret was a plan to take Adams to Telluride to find the body of William Barney, a one-time stonemason at the Smuggler-Union Mine who disappeared in June 1901 and was rumored to have been killed by members of the WFM, including St. John. It was one of at least four disappearances speculated to be murder.²⁶ It was also one of the deaths that Adams had confessed to knowing about. "I helped to move the body of Barney from the place where he was first killed," he was quoted by Hawley as stating. "Assisted O.N. [sic] Carpenter to do this. Mr Carpenter seemed to know I had killed Collins and that I was a safe man. He told me that St. John had once moved this body and had buried it but wanted it moved again. I did so and can take you to the place where the body is now buried."²⁷

The idea of taking Adams to Colorado came to McParland within a couple weeks of Adams's confession. At that time Adams had mentioned reburying Barney with the help of a man named Kelly, who disappeared from later reports and was replaced by Carpenter, the secretary of the Telluride union when St. John was president. As Carpenter was one of the men McParland hoped to prove was involved in the Steunenberg murder, this convenient alteration seems more than a little suspicious.[28] It also led to one of the more bizarre footnotes to McParland's reports. Commenting on a meeting with Adams on March 14, the detective recorded:

> I took up the matter of the location of Barney's body, and he again informed me that it would be utterly impossible for him to describe where they put this body, and except by the best of luck it would take him personally a couple or three hours to locate this body. He said, however, he was satisfied he could locate it, but it was impossible for him to describe just where they put it. He said the time he was out riding with Kelly-the-bum when he got the latter to indicate where the body of Barney was located that he and Kelly met General Bulkeley Wells going into Telluride.[29]

How Kelly the Bum was transported from 1870s Pennsylvania to twentieth-century Colorado is a mystery. McParland's reports were typed by a stenographer, in theory checked by McParland, then forwarded to the Denver office and, at least officially, on to William Pinkerton, who signed off on them before they were sent to Governor Gooding. That such a faux pas could get through that many stages of the agency's rigorous process is astonishing.

Although not directly relevant to the Steunenberg case, the idea of finding Barney's remains did not fade away. Rather, it became a significant part of McParland's ongoing investigation for one primary reason: money. The Steunenberg inquiry was not only one of the largest ever mounted by Pinkerton's, it was also one of the most costly, involving fees for several of the highest-paid attorneys in Idaho and numerous other costs. Neither Idaho nor Canyon County were able to pay for all this, and Gooding was extremely worried because he had ill-advisedly signed the financial guarantee that the agency always required previous to starting an investigation. This meant that if the State did not pay, Gooding himself would be liable for the charges.[30] Although the Idaho mine owners were covering some expenses, there were political pressures—including from President Theodore Roosevelt—not to let them be seen to be behind the prosecution of a case so flagrantly in their interests, as opposed to those of the workingman. So the money trickled rather than poured in.

The problem was suddenly resolved when Hawley received a letter from

Bulkeley Wells setting up a new—and confidential—fiscal conduit. "The various parties in interest in Colorado have retained in the interest of you gentlemen in Idaho, who are prosecuting these cases, Mr Jacob Filius [*sic*] of Denver, an attorney of long and large experience and one in whom we all have the greatest confidence."[31] They were not the only ones with such confidence. Any lawyer involved in labor issues knew of the fifty-nine-year-old Fillius, who was general counsel for the Smuggler-Union Mine and Wells's other holdings, as well as principal legal counsel for the Colorado Mining Association (CMA), the organization uniting the state's mine owners. Now those engaged in the death struggle with the WFM found themselves flush with funds, as the Colorado owners saw the chance of eliminating the hated unions while ostensibly keeping their own hands clean. As Lukas observed: "Their message to their counterparts in Idaho was blunt: Here are the bodies, here is the money, please kill them for us."[32]

Fillius was also an old friend of McParland's,[33] which was not surprising, as the detective had long before helped establish Pinkerton's as an essential service provider for the Colorado mine owners, and had become particularly enmeshed with Wells. It was Wells who exerted the pressure to rid the CMA not just of the three men awaiting trial in Boise but of one of Wells's greatest annoyances—Vincent St. John. In early March, Cary wired McParland: "Wells suggests get sketch from Adams location Barney's body, mail it to Telluride. Wells goes there Sunday night, motive, exhume body before others interested dispose same."[34]

McParland was unable to act on Wells's demands immediately, but the adjutant general persisted, and on April 17, the two met with Hawley and Fillius to discuss the case. "During our conference the matter came up as to how Steve Adams could be taken from Boise to Telluride in order to locate the place where Barney's body is buried," McParland reported, continuing:

> We readily agreed on a plan whereby this could be done without any person knowing that Steve Adams was in Colorado, but the matter will have to be taken up with Gov. Gooding and Mr Borah as the former and probably both would object to letting Adams out of the state until after the trial.... We are placed in a very peculiar position; it is all important that we should recover the body of Barney before Carpenter might take a notion to have the same removed, and while there is no risk in taking Adams into

Colorado so far as anybody recognizing him is concerned, still
there is one risk, that is in case of an accident and Adams getting
killed we lost the most important witness we have got.[35]

With snow blanketing Telluride, it was not a good time to start digging for
corpses, but Wells did not let the others forget his intentions and brought the
idea up again at a meeting in Denver on May 2.[36] Finally, at the end of the
month, the plan went ahead, with Wells, deputy warden Mills, and Telluride
Marshal Willard Runnels taking Adams to Colorado. He was guarded day
and night and kept for three days at the Smuggler-Union office in Pandora.[37]
Due to the snow making the area unrecognizable to Adams, nothing was accomplished, but he did tell McParland, "[I]f General Wells is not able to discover this body after the snow has gone he could go there at night just as he
did at the time that Carpenter and he re-buried the body, and could uncover
it, as there is no doubt about it providing that it has not been removed, and he
does not believe it has."[38]

Five days later Adams had another long talk with McParland, in which he
revealed gruesome details about Barney's body, including that Carpenter, who
"took sick at his stomach as he could not stand the stench," left most of the
work to Adams. "He said he [Adams] just pulled the feet out of the sockets at
the knees and put them into the sack, then pulled the thigh bones out of the
socket at the hips and put them in the sack. He said the magots had got their
work in in the intestines and were just in black balls about the size of eggs."[39]

Yet another three weeks passed, and Wells—still searching—told McParland that he had discovered a sack containing boots and some pieces of bone,
and asked "if it might not be possible that some of the bones were placed in the
sack that contained the clothing and boots. He would also like . . . [to] have
Adams draw a description showing the location of the body to the place where
the boots and clothes were buried."[40] Adams obliged, but the map was so vague,
it was useless. And when McParland raised the idea of Adams returning to
Colorado,[41] the notion was forcefully rejected by the attorneys. Despite Wells's
financial power, this particular mystery would have to wait in the queue.

Finance was not a problem faced solely by the prosecution. The defense, too,
needed scads of money, at least in part because Darrow received a minimum
of thirty-five thousand dollars for his services.[42] There were hopes that at least
some of this would come from organized labor, but no matter how many

donations were made, it was a huge sum—and Richardson was on a retainer of ten thousand dollars a year.[43]

Funds were also needed for the corps of detectives that Darrow hired. Unlike Pinkerton's, many detective agencies were willing to work for unions, and McParland more than once accused Thiel's agency of doing so after Swain had been cut out of the State's investigation.[44] Since he was based in Chicago, Darrow was familiar with the Mooney and Boland Detective Agency, founded in 1871, from which he hired some twenty operatives. These operatives performed a wide variety of tasks, from shadowing Pinkerton's field operatives to attempting to infiltrate the Boise Elks lodge, hoping to pick up gossip dropped by Gooding, Hawley, Borah, Van Duyn, or the members of the professional and business elite who were on social terms with them.[45] For undercover agents to discover the prosecution's most precious secrets, he went to George Dickson of the Workmen's Legal Security Company.[46]

One thing that the defense had in abundance and did *not* have to pay for was publicity. Socialist and labor newspapers and magazines throughout the country were joined by many more centrist publications in condemning the way the WFM leaders were whisked into Idaho and the subsequent habeas corpus decisions in court.[47] In addition, demonstrations and public meetings were held in Chicago, New York, San Francisco, and many smaller cities.

One such event reputedly focused on McParland. According to *Appeal to Reason*, at a meeting in Parsons, Kansas—chaired by the treasurer of the city's socialist local—McParland was noted to be "of infamously bad character, being associated while here with the notorious McLaughlin, of Grand Central fame." McParland was, it claimed, "engaged in the commission of almost all crimes known to criminal law," and although he had disappeared twenty years before, upon hearing of his involvement in the Steunenberg investigation, those at the meeting voted to "warn the courts and law officers of Idaho to be watchful of every move made by James McPartland, as we unhesitatingly declare that where there is a money consideration, he will do anything no matter how low or vile, to accomplish his purpose. . . . [T]here is not today in the United States, outside prison walls, a more conscienceless and desperate criminal."[48]

That a meeting dominated by socialists condemned McParland is not surprising, as he, Pinkerton's, and the prosecution were vilified nationwide in a well-organized propaganda campaign. Yet the report is too extreme to accept, as McParland had evidently not used his own name in Parsons—it was too recognizable—so linking him with the WFM trio would not have provoked civic outrage. Moreover, there is no evidence that at the time he had been considered an undesirable character. It is more likely that the report was simply part of *Appeal to Reason*'s ongoing attempt to discredit McParland.

Even when they did not become personal, such events drew McParland's ire. When socialist meetings were proposed to be held in Caldwell, he wrote, "Now these meetings have been stopped in Chicago, Cincinnati, Denver and other places, and I see no reason why they should be given so much rope in the City of Caldwell. . . . They are a gang of cut-throats and murderers and have no right to parade the streets and air their grievances or their imaginary grievances. . . . I think something should be done to stop them. . . . It is no use to lie down and let these fellows trample on good citizens that are prosecuting these murderers."[49]

With that in mind, he must have been delighted by the actions of his old friend Doc Shores, then a special agent for both the Denver & Rio Grande Railroad and the Utah Fuel Company. McParland noted that: "[W]hen the socialists commenced to flood the Utah Coal camps with the Appeal to Reason, Toledo Socialist and other anarchistic literature he conferred with the postmasters at the different camps and got a list of the company's employees that subscribed. . . . [then], to use his own expression, he had them 'walk down the canon.' He simply had them discharged and gave them to understand . . . that neither an anarchist nor a socialist could work in any of the camps. . . . He said his action had had a wholesome effect."[50]

More worrisome than the rhetoric, however, was that it was being followed up by violence. At the end of April a fire was started in the barn of the editor of a pro-prosecution newspaper in Parma in Canyon County.[51] Shortly thereafter, an editor at *The Caldwell News* received a threatening letter. "It looks to me as though they [socialists and anarchists] are going to inaugurate a reign of terror not only in Caldwell but in Canyon County in general," McParland wrote. "I would like to be Sheriff of Canyon County for one week or for twenty-four hours and this gang . . . would either be in the County jail, run out of town or as a last resort there would be a job for the Coroner."[52]

Others hoped that last resort would apply to McParland himself. On May 9, he received an unsigned letter addressing him as "McPartland," threatening that "we are after you. . . . be on the lookout you are the man that killed the exGov and not the three innocent men which you put the blame on . . . remember if those men aint freeded mighty quick we will drop on you and the

Gov. yous people has gone far enough its got to be stoped or we will have a war with you. . . . if Haywood Moyer & Pettibone are hanged we will tear you and all to small bitts."[53]

Months of travel, late-night conferences, tense interrogations, overseeing every detail of covert operations, and constantly trying to outwit intelligent men— as well as being subject to personal attacks, and even threats on his life—must have told significantly on McParland, who was, after all, about sixty-two years old. In late July he joined William Pinkerton in Chicago for three days of meetings, after which, "I told Principal W.A. Pinkerton that I had never taken a vacation excepting ten days about two years ago and that I would like to take a vacation at this time, to which he agreed." McParland and Mary stayed in Chicago, where they were able to visit relatives on both sides of their family, but McParland still felt obliged to check his business mail each day. "Correspondence comes from yourself, referring me back to certain documents on file here and some at Denver, so, in point of fact, I am not having any vacation at all," he wrote to Bangs. "Not being familiar with what a vacation might be, I would state if this is called a vacation, then I do not want any more of it."[54]

As it turned out, McParland did not return to Denver until August 15, more than three weeks after his departure, and he was then overwhelmed by the work that had accumulated. He told Gooding and Hawley that, even after being in the office for more than a week, "owing to a pressure of business it will be impossible for me to go to Boise before the middle or latter part of next week."[55] Exactly what McParland was working on so diligently is unknown, although he did visit the Kansas City office for two days. Part of the time might have been used to help his niece settle in with Mary and him. McParland had spent a good deal of time in Chicago with his brother Charles, and at some point before Christmas 1906, Charles's youngest daughter—Kittie, age eleven—moved to Denver, and for McParland was a sort of replacement for Eneas and his family.[56] The exact timing of her move is unknown, but it is logical that she would have traveled with her uncle and aunt in August.

McParland had not, of course, forgotten about the case, and more than once he encouraged an idea Orchard had first presented in June: to write "a short history of his life up to the time he became connected with the Western Federation of Miners, and then detail every outrage that he had been connected with and that he knew of." McParland was extremely supportive, as doing so would not only keep the inmate busy, but "will refresh his memory on the events of the past and make him still a better witness than he would be otherwise."[57] Orchard finished his manuscript by late August, and McParland suggested that both Hawley and Borah go over it carefully, as "Orchard having written this biography it will simply be impossible for any counsel to shake his testimony."[58]

McParland wanted Adams to do the same, as he "has a poor memory of dates and places, in fact has a poor memory upon some facts, and while he will tell the truth on the witness stand and has told the truth in his confessions, still I am afraid he will not make a first-class witness." Therefore, he wanted Hawley and Borah to "get him to write out a history of his life covering everything from childhood just as Orchard has done.... [I]t will impress him so that it will be very hard to confuse him in the cross-examination. We know that Adams is telling the truth, but his memory is deceptive.... [I]f Adams had as good a memory as Orchard he would stand on the same ground but he is not to blame for not being as bright as Orchard."[59]

When McParland finally returned to Boise on September 9, he was accompanied by an old friend—Charlie Siringo. McParland had recently received a report stating that Guy Caldwell, a "slugger [hit man] for the Socialist members of the Western Federation [had] claimed he had been looking out to get a chance to assassinate me."[60] As a result, "Principals W.A. and R.A. Pinkerton will not allow me under any circumstances to go up in that country any more without having somebody to accompany me, and while ... I am not in any way afraid of those people that are making threats ... I have a man that I can depend upon to be constantly on the lookout in Opt Siringo."[61]

He was back, but little did McParland know how much his delay—and the concomitant lack of foresight by other members of the prosecution—was going to cost the State's case.

CHAPTER 22

THE FIGHT FOR ADAMS

While the prosecution dithered in Idaho, Darrow—who from the beginning had considered Adams's confession the key[1]—made his move. Gooding had thought the case secure, because neither Darrow nor Richardson was allowed to see Orchard or Adams, the latter of whom had been placed with his wife and two stepchildren in a small cottage on the penitentiary grounds. But in August, with McParland still in Denver, Adams's brother Joe was granted permission to visit several times. Hawley immediately expressed concern to Fillius that Joe was "working on the other side," yet nothing was done to find out what was discussed, a point that alarmed McParland.[2]

A meeting in Boise of Darrow, Richardson, Miller—who had been brought onto the defense team—and spymaster Dickson should have set off alarm bells when the prosecution's operatives reported its occurrence, but still the team in Idaho did not understand the danger. Meanwhile, Darrow began to maneuver, twice traveling to Oregon to see James W. Lillard, Adams's "Uncle Warren." Darrow soon convinced Lillard to visit his nephew and persuade him to renounce his confession. As part of the arrangement, Darrow agreed that he and the union attorneys would defend Adams if he were brought to trial.

Lillard traveled to Boise and had dinner with Adams on the night of September 3. Although it would have been difficult to prevent Lillard from seeing Adams, the prosecution team still should have been more aware of the meeting's negative possibilities. As far back as April McParland had pointed out that Lillard had "talked about giving a bond for Adams' release" and had noted that they could "take no chances of allowing him out on bond. There is too much money on the other side for us to take any chances."[3]

Lillard later maintained that Adams told him he was being detained against his will and asked for assistance in gaining his freedom. But Adams was already prepared for the specifics of such a discussion, because on the morning of September 7, his wife, Annie, managed to sneak a message out of the prison that changed the course of the trial—and she knew exactly where to take it. Like her husband, she had been confined—without charge—to the prison grounds. Claiming that her new baby had diaper rash, she received permission to go into town for ointment. Once on her own she hurried to the law office of John T. Morrison, Gooding's predecessor as governor of Idaho and an attorney engaged by Darrow to represent Lillard and Adams. Annie gave Morrison a handwritten note that stated: "This is to certify that the statement that I signed was made up by James McParland, detective, and Harry Orchard, alias Tom Hogan. I signed it because I was threatened by Governor Gooding, saying I would be hung if I did not corroborate Orchard's story against the officers of the Federation Union of Miners. Stephen Adams. Witness: Annie Adams."[4] Within hours, Morrison filed a habeas corpus petition to force Adams's release.[5] The next afternoon, Judge George Stewart ordered him discharged.

But the defense had not planned on such quick reactions from McParland, who, the night before Adams's release, was briefed about the situation over the telephone. He flew into action and had a Colorado warrant issued that evening for Adams's arrest for his involvement in the murder of detective Lyte Gregory. The Denver sheriff then telegraphed his counterpart in Ada County, in which Boise is located, as well as the district attorney, asking them to hold Adams while the warrant was brought to Idaho. Therefore, moments after Adams was released on September 8, he was rearrested and placed in the Ada County jail.

The next morning, McParland arrived in Boise to explain to Gooding and Hawley that the Colorado charges were simply a delaying tactic. At that very moment, Shoshone County Sheriff Angus Sutherland was on his way there to charge Adams with the 1904 murder of two Idaho claim jumpers, Fred Tyler and Ed Boule. Orchard had tied Adams and Simpkins to these killings, and Adams had thereafter confessed to them.[6] If McParland could lay enough of a smoke screen, he could have Adams taken to Wallace without any legal ructions. Once there, McParland would try to convince him to recant his recantation, after which the threat of being tried for a capital offense would keep him on the prosecutorial straight and narrow.

The next day, Darrow hit back with equal cunning, paying a surprise visit to Borah and tearfully confiding that "Adams had deceived him in not telling him that he had committed the two murders. . . . If he had known this he would never have made this move as it now put him in a hole if Adams were convicted . . . for he would always feel that he had caused Adams' conviction."

Darrow asked Borah "to see to it that Sheriff Sutherland . . . not leave for a day at least as he (Darrow) was going down the road for a day and wanted to be here in Boise before Adams was taken away."[7]

McParland immediately suspected that Darrow would take that day to arrange a habeas corpus petition, which would be presented when the train to Wallace entered Oregon—which it had to do before returning to northern Idaho. He must have smiled to himself, because he was still a step ahead of Darrow, but he nevertheless assigned a man to shadow him.[8] More concerning to McParland was how Darrow had learned of his plans and activities.

On September 11, the Colorado deputies were missing when Adams was arraigned. The charge was dismissed, but once again Adams was not out of the courtroom before he was arrested—this time on the Shoshone County charges—and turned over to Sutherland, who promptly put him back in the state penitentiary for safekeeping. McParland was already waiting there—having arrived "unseen by the numerous Thiel detectives who were shadowing me, three hours before"—and when Adams saw him, "I thought he would faint."[9]

McParland talked—harangued according to Adams—for two or three hours.[10] "These lawyers will do anything for money," McParland reputedly said. "You will be tried and convicted and they will still pat you on the back and tell you the case will be reversed. They will appeal and still pat you on the back and tell you that you will be all right until the case will be affirmed and you will stand on the scaffold a doomed man with the rope around your neck and all to save the lives of three of the worst cut throats, sons of bitches that ever breathed, and then where will your wife and babies be and where will you be."

Every so often McParland paused to allow Adams to speak, but he refused. Then the detective told him "of a number of cases of horrible deaths where the lawyers patted their clients on their back until they had been swung into eternity at the ropes end. Among other cases he mentioned was that of Tom Horn and he said he could have saved him if he only could got to him. He said that they sung a cow boy song for fear he would say something when he got on the scaffold."

Still Adams would not talk to McParland, so two days later, early in the morning, Sutherland, Whitney, and prosecution detective Eugene Johnson sneaked him out of the prison, past Darrow's Thiel detectives, and headed north. After five days of dodging efforts to track them down, they reached Wallace, much to the frustration of Darrow, who grudgingly acknowledged McParland as "the greatest detective in the West."[11]

McParland was less complimentary to Darrow. From the beginning he suspected that the defense had bribed Lillard, writing that Darrow had admitted "he didn't give a d—n what happened to Adams, he simply had him placed where he wanted him." Similarly, Lillard "did not seem to care whether Steve was convicted or not. He seems to think it would be much better to see Moyer, Haywood and Pettibone go free whereby he would receive the thirty pieces of silver like Judas of old, which no doubt has been promised him if he will keep Adams from testifying."[12]

Five years later, McParland still believed this, writing that Lillard had received seventy-five thousand dollars, two-thirds earmarked for "Uncle Warren" and the rest for Adams. "Lillard at that time was trying to defend himself . . . in the matter of some 14,000 acres of land that the United States Government claimed that he had got unlawfully," McParland wrote. After the trial, "Adams raised hell, demanded of his lawyers and old man Lillard the $25,000.00 that was promised him if he denied his confession, and also claimed that Lillard held that money. . . . [I]t looks as though old man Lillard got the $75,000.00 and used it and left Stevie, as he called him, to hold the bag."[13]

It was not the first time McParland accused jurors, witnesses, or detectives of accepting bribes. However, he was not the only one who doubted Darrow's ethics in this particular case. John Nugent, who accompanied Darrow to Lillard's farm, later called Darrow "Old Necessity," because, "necessity knows no law."[14] Even Darrow's closest friends were skeptical, such as the author, soldier, and lawyer Colonel Charles E. S. Wood, who noted the "crooked methods" by which "the defense was manufactured."[15]

But the most damning evidence suggesting Darrow bribed Lillard was the attorney's own behavior. In October 1910, a suitcase holding 16 sticks of dynamite was set off in the alley behind the building housing *The Los Angeles Times*, the publisher of which, Harrison Gray Otis, was one of the nation's most powerful antiunion voices. The explosion started a devastating fire that killed twenty-one workers. Then, on Christmas Day that year, the Llewellyn Iron Works in Los Angeles was bombed, causing significant damage.[16] The famed detective William J. Burns took charge of the investigation,[17] which led to the arrests of James and John "J.J." McNamara, brothers active in a campaign of violence by the International Association of Bridge and Structural Iron Workers.

Darrow agreed to defend the McNamaras—in what was his first major case after the Idaho trials—but before the trial even started, he discovered that they were guilty and realized that he had not the slightest chance of winning.[18] During jury selection two jurors were approached with bribes to vote for acquittal. When the alleged middleman was caught in a sting operation, Darrow was charged with two counts of bribery and prosecuted in separate trials. In the first he was found not guilty, but the second ended with a hung jury that had voted 8–4 for conviction. Darrow's shining reputation has long obscured the fact that most of the trial reporters as well as many colleagues and friends were convinced that he was guilty. In an authoritative and exhaustive study, Geoffrey Cowan concluded: "On the basis, then, of all of the available evidence, it is fair to conclude that Darrow bribed both Lockwood and Bain."[19]

Such an assessment makes it reasonable to assume that Darrow had bribed Lillard in 1906, and in so doing, had swung the momentum back in favor of the defense.

Early in Adams's confinement in Wallace, McParland visited him in the hope of winning him back. Afterward, McParland recorded that, "He told me he did not want to talk; he had his mind made up and there was no further use in me calling upon him as he realized what he was doing. . . . [H]e did not want to see anybody but his lawyer and his people in the future, from which it will be seen that he is wholly in the power of his lawyer, wife and uncle."[20]

That being the case, on Monday, September 24—six days after Adams arrived in Wallace—a preliminary hearing on the murder of Tyler began. Hoping to gain information about Orchard's confession, Darrow looked forward to cross-examining McParland, but to save its thunder, the prosecution chose not to call him to the stand, relying instead on Thiele—who had recently been promoted to assistant superintendent in Spokane.[21] McParland was in attendance nevertheless and noted: "Owing to the long drawn cross examination of the witnesses by Darrow, the proceedings were very slow, and it would appear as if he was trying to kill time or make a showing for his fees."[22]

Presiding judge Boomer had a different view. At the hearing's conclusion he informed McParland "that he could see through the way that Darrow cross-examined Asst Supt Thiele that his main object was to discover what evidence the State had against Moyer, Heywood [*sic*], and Pettibone, and as he, Judge Boomer, did not want this case to be a medium through which the defense would get information, . . . he over ruled all questions asked by Mr Darrow on that line."²³

On September 29, Adams was bound over for trial, but in the next fortnight, labor supporters finally had a major triumph. Back in March, St. John had been brought to Colorado on a charge of conspiracy to murder Ben Burnham. After being denied bail, a change of venue, and a request for the local magistrate to recuse himself, St. John was committed to trial in Telluride.²⁴ In the following months, Orrin N. Hilton, a former judge turned WFM attorney, obtained a change of venue to the Mesa County District Court in Grand Junction, and then managed to get six of the eight counts against St. John quashed.²⁵ When the case finally went to court, Judge Theron Stevens dismissed all charges when "District Attorney Selig announced that the State had not secured evidence to convict him."²⁶

St. John was but a sidelight, however, compared to the events across the country the following week, when Hawley, Borah, Richardson, and Darrow appeared in the same courtroom for the first time to argue the habeas corpus petitions before the U.S. Supreme Court. The arguments were necessarily similar to those made before the state and circuit courts, and on December 3 they heard that the decision they'd been waiting almost two months for would prove the same as well. Effectively combining the appeals from the two court systems into one, the Supreme Court affirmed the decisions of the Circuit Court (and therefore the Idaho Supreme Court) by a 7 to 1 vote.²⁷

The key elements of the decision were three lower-court rulings that were upheld. The first was that Governor McDonald had not infringed any rights by accepting the extradition papers at face value, without demanding further proof that Pettibone (the petitioner in the case ruled upon) was a fugitive from justice. This proof was in theory provided under the Constitution's Full Faith and Credit clause, which effectively stated that McDonald had reason to trust official documents from another state. The second issue addressed the speed with which the men had been removed from Colorado and if it denied them the right to a legal means to challenge their deportation. The Supreme Court agreed with the lower courts that the Constitution did not guarantee the petitioner the right to be arrested and extradited in such a way as to provide a convenient opportunity to test whether the extradition was legal.

The most contentious point in the ruling related to whether the men should be released on habeas corpus if the methods by which their presence in the state had been secured were themselves illegal or had violated their rights. Or, as Justice John Marshall Harlan wrote in the decision: "As the petitioner is within the jurisdiction of Idaho, and is held by its authorities for trial, are the particular methods by which he was brought within her limits at all material in the proceeding by habeas corpus?"[28] Basing their decision to a great extent on two previous Supreme Court rulings—*Ker v. Illinois* and *Mahon v. Justice*[29]—the Court ruled that such considerations were *not* material, once again supporting the lower courts' decisions. In summation, it stated:

> Even were it conceded, for the purposes of this case, that the governor of Idaho wrongfully issued his requisition, and that the governor of Colorado erred in honoring it and in issuing his warrant of arrest, the vital fact remains that Pettibone is held by Idaho in actual custody for trial under an indictment charging him with crime against its laws, and he seeks the aid of the circuit court to relieve him from custody, so that he may leave that state and thereby defeat the prosecution against him without a trial. In the present case it is not necessary to go behind the indictment and inquire as to how it happened that he came within reach of the process of the Idaho court in which the indictment is pending.[30]

The decision received widespread condemnation from socialist and labor critics, who by sheer repetition, made famous one line from the dissent by Justice Joseph McKenna: "Kidnapping is a crime, pure and simple."[31] Regardless of reaction to the ruling, it established a precedent that has been followed ever since by state and federal courts, and even, on occasion, international courts.[32] Moreover, it remanded the three prisoners to the Canyon County authorities, who were now able to proceed with the trial.

McParland's return to poor health did not receive such publicity. "I was stricken down with rheumatism in my left leg and ankle on Nov 7th," he wrote to Bangs, continuing, "and was in a very precarious condition. . . . The ankle and leg up to the knee swelled to such an extent that all the smaller blood vessels under the skin broke. . . . I could not under any circumstances allow my foot to touch the floor or in fact did it go within twelve inches of the floor for over two weeks." Equally unpleasantly, McParland suffered severe headaches, high fevers, and "During my sickness I think I must have lost at least twenty to twenty-five pounds."[33] Moreover, he worried about his wife, who was also suffering badly from rheumatism: "you can imagine the condition we were placed in at our house, my wife lying in one bed and I in another."[34]

Robert Pinkerton was solicitous and concerned: "You have a very trying time before you in connection with the trials in Idaho," he wrote, "and I am aware that you would have to be in the best of health to contend against the forces that you will find arrayed against you."[35] Even from afar, Pinkerton had hit the mark about the brutal confrontation that lay ahead.

One year after the assassination of Frank Steunenberg the strategy of the prosecution shifted to convicting Adams of the murder of Fred Tyler in the backwoods of northern Idaho. This would allow the State to hold out the promise of a pardon or commutation in exchange for his testimony against the inner circle.

Adams's trial was also important as a dress rehearsal for the upcoming trials of the WFM leaders. The prosecution gained hope for internal dissension among the defense when, in early January, McParland reported that "there seems to be some trouble between Mr Richardson and Mr Darrow as to who will be the leading counsel in the Moyer, Haywood and Pettibone cases.... [I]f Mr Richardson does not permit him [Darrow] to assume the lead in the defense, he has threatened to withdraw from the case entirely."[36]

However, when jury selection began in Wallace on February 11, both Richardson and Darrow were there, and Richardson would serve as the primary counsel throughout the trial. Meanwhile, Hawley was joined by special prosecutor Henry P. Knight, with assistance from the recently elected Shoshone County prosecutor Walter H. Hanson and the county's former prosecutor, James E. Gyde. Thus, of the major legal figures, only Borah, who on January 15 had been elected to the U.S. Senate, was not available.[37]

To McParland's chagrin, *he* was not there for jury selection either. Two days before, he, Siringo, Whitney, and the detective's new stenographer, Robert Shollenberger, left Boise for Wallace.[38] It transpired to be an unusually long and frustrating journey, as heavy snow, thick ice, washed-out tracks, and freight wrecks delayed them at every turn. With some tracks closed for up to ten days, they were forced to take an old cargo boat up the Columbia River to Portland, followed by a nightmarish, thirty-nine-hour train ride to Spokane. They finally reached Wallace after having been en route just short of five days for what normally would have taken less than one.

If the journey were not hellish enough, there were problems with the accommodation. McParland had asked Sutherland—recently replaced as sheriff—to book rooms for his party, as Wallace did not have much in the way of lodging.[39] When he arrived, McParland had a room, but, he wrote unhappily to Bangs, it was only "8 x 8 without any stove or heat. . . . For a place like Wallace, the county seat with some of the greatest mines on earth surrounding the town, it is a wonder to me that somebody does not build a hotel and start a dining room wherein a man could get a decent meal. . . . There is one restaurant in town and that is run just as the restaurant keeper pleases, and you must take whatever you get."[40]

McParland's mood did not improve when he discovered what had happened in court. In an area dominated by the mining industry, many potential jurors were "either members of the Western Federation or sympathizers," and the prosecution had quickly used up its peremptory challenges. Thus, he told Bangs, there were at best "nine good jurors, two very doubtful, and one we are sure will never fetch in a verdict of guilty as he is a brother-in-law of the notorious Paul Corcoran who led the attack on the Bunker Hill & Sullivan mine and mill in '99."[41]

Testimony began on Saturday, February 16, with Chris Thiele's account of a confession Adams had made to him in Whitney's office the previous April.[42] In 1904, Adams had accompanied Jack Simpkins to the latter's claim in a wild part of northern Idaho, "up on the St Joe River, above the head of navigation about fourteen miles." Once there, Simpkins offered Adams three hundred dollars to eliminate several claim jumpers who had built cabins in a heavily timbered area and were "trying to take these settlers' claims away." Adams met two rough customers—Alva Mason and Newt "Wall-Eye" Glover—who were also incensed about people without proper claims, so they decided to kill thirty-four-year-old Fred Tyler, who had moved there that spring from Michigan. Since they were so far out in the woods, they figured no one would ever know.

In August 1904, Adams, Mason, and Glover went to Tyler's place. After lying in wait until dusk, Adams ambushed Tyler. With a Winchester .25-35 pointed at him, the three "disarmed him, took him to Simpkins' cabin, stopped there until morning, had breakfast there, took him three miles out into the timber the next morning, and I killed him." Adams left the body between two logs and reported to Simpkins. Two weeks later they returned and killed Ed Boule. Tyler's body was discovered and identified a year later, and the skull was offered in evidence, with "a big bullet hole back of the left ear."[43] For most of the trial it grinned at the jury from the front of the prosecutor's table.

On the fourth day of testimony, a shabby man with long dark hair and a stubby beard suddenly stood up and proclaimed: "It is the heart that moves the hand. I am the man who killed Fred Tyler. Turn all these other fellows loose, for I am the man that done the deed."[44] In the commotion that followed, Annie Adams burst into tears, and the man—Patrick Ryan of Butte, Montana—was taken into custody. Questioned, Ryan admitted he had just finished a term in Deer Lodge penitentiary for stealing mutton. He had gone to Burke, where, he said, President Roosevelt's daughter told him to take charge of the case, because if Adams were convicted an earthquake would destroy the Coeur d'Alenes. Within days he was placed in a lunatic asylum.

That afternoon, McParland took the stand, with Richardson trying to prove that he had "obtained a confession from Adams through threats, promises and cajolery." Richardson's questions "being absolutely false," McParland noted, "my principal answer was in the negative."[45] Or, according to the Associated Press, McParland "denied that he had agreed with Governor Gooding and Warden Whitney to subject Adams to five or six days solitary confinement, that at the end of that time he would be ready to 'cough it all up' . . . denied that he had administered what is known as the 'third degree' to Adams . . . denied that he had made any arrangements by which Adams and Orchard should be locked together . . . denied that threats had been used or inducements held out, but designated the whole transaction as a 'business proposition.'"[46]

The next day McParland was back on the stand, with the defense "striving hard to prove that this confession was made under duress and that Adams was coerced by threats if he did not confess and bribed by promises of leniency and special favors if he told the story the officers desired."[47]

One thing Richardson particularly wanted to force McParland to admit to was the unsavory conditions in which Adams—and, looking ahead to later trials, Haywood, Moyer, and Pettibone—was kept in the penitentiary. However, McParland reported that, having "anticipated . . . I would be examined very closely in the matter . . . I never entered the penitentiary gate, contenting myself with never going farther than the Warden's office."[48]

Indeed, if Richardson were hoping to break someone down, McParland was the wrong target, and his methods were generally ineffective, according to the detective: "Richardson adopts a rather peculiar method of propounding questions. He propounds at least a half dozen separate questions in one. If a witness would answer the question as a whole by either yes or no, it would place him in an embarrassing position, therefore I adopted the plan of answering each question separately as though it had been propounded to me separately."[49]

At one point, having failed to force McParland to admit to any wrongdoing in obtaining the confession, Richardson pointedly asked, "You are an old hand at this kind of work, are you not?" To which McParland shot back, "I know my business."[50] Finally, "Richardson asked me if when questioning Adams I did not lead Adams in the manner that he had been trying to lead me during examination of me to which I replied not in that way as I did not assume the stagey dramatic air in talking with Adams that Mr Richardson had assumed in talking with me for the benefit of the galleries."

The mutual testiness continued even after McParland was excused.[51] Richardson had referred several times to McParland's work in Parsons, Kansas, which the detective had simply brushed off. As he was leaving the witness stand, Richardson said: "I have the affidavits relative to the Parsons, Kansas, affair."

McParland retorted: "From what I know of you you can get affidavits on anything but the time will come when you will have to produce them and the parties who made them."

A bit taken aback, Richardson said he did not want an altercation with McParland, who promptly spat back, "I didn't think so."

"I am not afraid of you," Richardson said, to which McParland responded, "Well that is the way I feel in regard to you."

The next day, the Associated Press report—picked up via *The Spokesman-Review* of Spokane—stated: "This caused a scene in court. The spectators cheered Richardson and hissed McPartland."[52] This quote—later used to suggest a negative general feeling about the detective[53]—did not fairly represent the situation. A few days later, a young reporter for *The Spokesman-Review* apologized to McParland, stating he had left court early, and the comment had been added to his story by another newspaperman, who had since been discharged due to its inaccuracy. A disgusted McParland reported, "There is no doubt [the other journalist] was paid but just how much he got I don't know. However, it has been given to the public and the old saying is a lie travels with lightening [*sic*] speed but the truth travels like a turtle. While I am well aware that the defense would resort to nearly all manner of dirt, I did not hardly expect they would resort to a low trick as this. I am not at all disconcerted about this matter, but merely wish to draw your attention to what we may expect during the trials of Moyer, Haywood and Pettibone."[54]

Soon thereafter, McParland was called back to the stand to produce Adams's confession, the relevant parts of which were introduced into evidence.[55]

The judge told the jury that they could decide whether it had been given freely and voluntarily. McParland again faced off with Richardson, who, "for the last hour of my cross-examination . . . either seemed to be out of ammunition or nonplussed as to what to ask me and looked appealingly from time to time to Darrow to prompt him."[56]

Adams's own testimony came on the last two days of February, and he carefully followed the defense line that "a deliberate conspiracy was formed among the officers of the penitentiary and the detectives to implicate the leaders of the Western Federation of Miners in the assassination of ex-Governor Steunenberg, and that this conspiracy was to be backed by false evidence, obtained by threats and bribes."[57]

On March 1, final arguments began, and Darrow ensured that McParland was part of them. After insisting Adams had confessed under duress and "that every line of that confession is a fraud," he turned on the detective. "This McParland, what is his trade?" he asked, continuing:

> Is there any worse trade than the one that man follows? Can you imagine a man being a detective until every other means of livelihood is exhausted? Watching and snaring his fellow-men. Is there any other calling in life can sink to that? But yet we have been told it is an honorable profession. Well, that depends on how you look at it. . . . It is honorable compared with some things the State has done in this case. But it is not honorable in any old-fashioned sense of that word. McParland told the jury that this confession was given freely, voluntarily. Did he lie? Is he a liar? . . . [C]an you believe a detective at all? What is he? A detective is not a liar, he is a living lie. His whole profession is that, openly and notoriously.[58]

After five seemingly endless days of summations, the case went to the jury. For two days more everyone waited, until it was decided that, "[I]t might be dangerous to keep the jury together any longer. They had divided in two parties and had ceased to speak to each other. . . . [O]ne of the jurors . . . had taken a very decided stand for conviction and told those that differed with him they were simply murderers at heart or otherwise they would look at the evidence in the proper light and convict Adams whom they knew to be a hired assassin."[59]

On the night of March 7, with six votes for conviction and six for acquittal, the judge determined that the jurors were hopelessly deadlocked, and discharged them. McParland was not surprised, as from the beginning the jurors had been a concern, and he had conducted investigations suggesting several of them had been bribed.[60] The defense was equally suspicious of foul play. In a book that was hurriedly produced in order to besmirch Pinkerton's and McParland prior to Haywood's trial, Morris Friedman, a socialist and former Pinkerton's stenographer, included an attack on the legal system, stating that Adams "very clearly proved his innocence of the murder of Fred Tyler. Strangely enough, however, his jury disagreed, and he will probably be tried again."[61]

McParland did find some positive elements to take from the trial. Not only did the judge continue the case until September—meaning Adams would remain in custody—but Adams had "in his cross-examination admitted every word to be true in his written confession except the fact that when he said he murdered Tyler and Boule he lied." This meant, McParland noted hopefully, that "if he should come back to the state he has not in reality injured himself as a witness in the Moyer, Haywood and Pettibone cases."[62]

Before long, McParland had again started working on returning Adams to the fold. With Siringo, Thiele, Whitney, and Shollenberger, he left Wallace on the afternoon of March 8. On the train he met former sheriff Harvey Brown, who recently had started working as a freelance detective. The two dined together in Spokane, then talked late into the night, during which McParland proposed to pay Brown's per diem and expenses if he would visit Lillard and convince him that it was best for both him and Adams to have Adams testify for the prosecution. "It is well worth the trying even if we are put to considerable expense," McParland reported, having already noted somberly: "This is the only chance we have got."[63]

CHAPTER 23

THE HAYWOOD TRIAL

O n Tuesday, March 12—as McParland reached Boise—events that would have an overriding influence on the upcoming trials were made public. It was the first day of the judicial term, and the incoming judge for the Seventh Judicial District was Edward L. Bryan, who had defeated Judge Smith in the November election due to union opposition to the incumbent.[1] From the start, McParland did not trust Bryan: "I am very doubtful as to whether Bryan, the Judge-Elect, can be depended upon or not. He was elected by Western Federation money."[2]

More relevant than Bryan's electoral support was that before the arrival of Miller the previous January he had been appointed to represent Orchard temporarily. Acknowledging this was a conflict of interest should Orchard appear as the primary witness, Bryan consulted Fremont Wood, the newly elected judge for the Third Judicial District—Ada and Boise Counties. Wood later wrote that Bryan "inquired if I would be willing to assume the burden of the trials if he disqualified himself and called upon me to try the cases. . . . I immediately advised Judge Bryan that I was not seeking the laborious task of trying these cases but neither was I running away from or seeking to avoid any necessary responsibility."[3] Bryan and Wood agreed that no mention of their accord would be made in advance. Thus, it was a surprise that when Moyer, Haywood, and Pettibone appeared before Bryan for setting their trial dates, he withdrew in favor of Wood.[4]

Wood was to prove an inspired choice.[5] A fifty-year-old native of Maine and the son of an abolitionist legislator, he had attended Bates College before reading law. He moved to Boise and started his law practice at the age of twenty-five, eventually becoming both the city attorney and an assistant U.S. attorney. In 1889, he succeeded Hawley as the last U.S. attorney for the Territory of Idaho, and the next year he became the first U.S. attorney for the new state. In that role, in 1892 he prosecuted the miners from the Coeur d'Alenes, convicting seventeen, including Pettibone. In more recent years he had concentrated on his private practice.

Wood was generally welcomed by both sides as a man already proven to be fair, honest, and open-minded. "We think that Judge Wood will try this case impartially," McParland reported. "He is a man of strong character and will show no favors."[6] Wood demonstrated his impartiality immediately, ruling both against and in favor of defense motions.[7] When Richardson asked that the defendants be discharged due to how long the case had taken to come to trial, Wood refused, on the ground that the defense's filings "in the habeas corpus cases had automatically deprived the Court of the power to proceed." But he did agree to a change of venue from Canyon County to his own District Court in Boise, where he announced jury selection would commence on May 9, 1907. The three men were being tried separately, and Haywood—whose vehemence, violence, and socialism made him the prosecution's primary target—would be first in the dock.

Although most labor leaders and press were content with Wood, they were less so with another public figure—Theodore Roosevelt, the president of the United States. For some time Roosevelt had had a private but ongoing dispute with E. H. Harriman, the head of the Union Pacific and several other railroads, over whether the president had made unfulfilled promises in exchange for Harriman raising much needed funds during Roosevelt's reelection campaign.[8] The same week in October 1906 that the Supreme Court ruled on the habeas corpus appeals, Roosevelt—goaded by comments reputedly made by Harriman to New York congressman James Sherman that he "could buy Congress [and] buy the judiciary"—dictated what was effectively a memo in the form of a letter addressed to Sherman. In it he stated: "But it shows a cynicism and deep-seated corruption which makes the man uttering such sentiments, and boasting, no matter how falsely, of his power to perform such crimes, at least as undesirable a citizen as Debs, or Moyer, or Haywood."[9]

Filed away, this document did not see the light of day until early April 1907, after a copy of a letter from Harriman—claiming Roosevelt had pressured him for campaign contributions and then renounced his part of the bargain—found its way into Joseph Pulitzer's New York newspaper, *The World*.[10] In response, Roosevelt ill-advisedly released his earlier letter to the Washington press to show that Harriman's version was "a deliberate and willful untruth."[11]

The result of this mudslinging was not what Roosevelt expected, as he was soon widely condemned—particularly by socialists and labor groups—for trying to prejudice the upcoming trials in Boise. In short order, national demonstrations and parades took place throughout the country, with the slogan "I am an undesirable citizen" worn on badges by those expressing their displeasure with the president. Roosevelt thereafter released letters he had written to show that he was not antiunion, had not expressed an opinion on the prisoners' guilt, and had even written to the U.S. attorney general to prevent any miscarriages of justice in the Haywood case.[12] It was to no avail, as the issue was neither quickly forgotten nor forgiven, and demonstrations were held up to the week before the trial, showing a groundswell of support for Haywood.

Meanwhile, in the final two months prior to the trial, both the prosecution and the defense flooded Idaho with undercover spies, hoping to glean anything that might give them an edge. It was virtually impossible for McParland even to keep up with every aspect of the investigation, much less run the entire Western Division. That is perhaps why, not long after the Adams trial, the Western Division was split in half, with a new Pacific Division—consisting of the San Francisco, Los Angeles, Seattle, and Portland offices—being placed under the direction of McParland's old assistant and close friend John C. Fraser, who now became one of an inner circle of eight running the agency.[13] McParland's Western Division was decreased to Denver, Kansas City, Omaha, and Spokane, but this was in no way viewed within the agency as a demotion or downgrading.

For the time being, McParland's attention was on the upcoming trial, and his greatest hope remained "turning" Adams. For almost six weeks he waited impatiently to hear if Brown had any success with Lillard.[14] But on April 17, he received word that the "old man says he would rather see Steve hung than return to that McParland gang."[15]

McParland immediately devised a new tactic. Through his friend Thomas McCabe, a deputy sheriff in Shoshone County, McParland suggested that another deputy, Carson C. Hicks, try to influence Adams. He knew that Annie had more influence over her husband than anyone else, so McParland suggested Hicks "throw himself in the way of Mrs Adams" and counsel her that "the State is the only one that can befriend Steve now, neither his uncle nor his array of counsel can do it." He laid out in great detail the conversation Hicks should conduct, how he should bring his own wife into the meeting, and that he should supply Adams cigars or a pipe.[16]

It did not take long for that plan to go awry, as only six days later Hicks was involved in a barroom brawl in which he shot Billie Quinn, a former miner and a member of the WFM, in the chest, fatally wounding him.[17] Miraculously, a form of McParland's plan still went ahead when Hicks was placed in Adams's jail cell. Shortly thereafter, McParland wrote to Hicks's lawyer, the former Adams prosecutor Henry Knight: "I have taken the matter of Mr Hicks' trouble up with Mr Hawley and Governor Gooding, and both desire me to say that while they would do everything in their power for Mr Hicks, if he succeeds in getting Adams again on the right track, he can depend upon it an extra effort will be made on part of the state to see him through this trouble."[18] He then again detailed the ways Hicks might "work on Adams." Within a week McParland heard from Hicks: "Steve is on the fence and don't know which way to 'Jump.' "[19] McParland responded, "[Y]ou know what is wanted and just keep along the lines as you are doing, and I think you will eventually be successful, however your time is short."[20] Too short, it turned out, for as the trial began, Adams had still not "jumped the right way." Nevertheless, it appears that someone let Hicks know that his efforts were appreciated, because when he went to trial in September, he did not show the slightest remorse or even any particular interest in the proceedings. Despite what the prosecutor described as "overwhelming evidence," the jury found Hicks not guilty in less than five minutes.

Hicks was not the only one facing trial. In mid-April, new senator and associate prosecutor William E. Borah found his preparations interrupted when a federal grand jury meeting in Boise returned an indictment against a number of individuals associated with the Barber Lumber Company for fraud in the acquisition of timber claims. Having served as a company attorney, Borah was among those indicted. The charges must have affected his performance in the trial, as they disturbed him enough to consider resigning his new office. McParland immediately proclaimed it "simply the work of the Western Federation."[21]

Of course, McParland saw unionists and socialists behind all sorts of nefarious behavior. One thing that annoyed him no end was that "Shoaf either through malice or to mislead the public always reports my name as McPartland. In talking with these gentlemen I wish Mr Borah, Mr Hawley, and yourself would impress upon them that the proper way to spell my name is McParland."[22] More important, he was certain prosecution secrets were being divulged to the defense by spies. And if there was one thing he understood, it was how to play spymaster.

One of McParland's most successful spies was Arthur C. Cole, referred to as Operative 28. Cole had been the secretary of the Citizens' Alliance in Cripple Creek in 1904 and, while serving in the Colorado National Guard, had ordered the troops to fire on the union hall in Victor after the miners refused to leave.[23] In 1905, he started working for Pinkerton's, and not long after Steunenberg's assassination, he investigated Orchard's Colorado background. McParland then turned him into a double agent, sending him to Darrow to volunteer to testify about a series of intended outrages by mine owners, including blowing up the Independence depot, which the owners planned to blame on the WFM.[24] McParland's goal was to convince Darrow to call him as a witness, so he could testify that Darrow had paid him to perjure himself.

McParland also had plans for numerous other operatives mentioned only by number,[25] as well as having at his fingertips vast amounts of information the prosecution hoped to use. As far back as March 1906, he had recognized Moyer as the weak link of the trio and had suggested visiting him "with a view of breaking him down."[26] The idea resurfaced in December, when Hawley learned "that Moyer and Pettibone are not on speaking terms with Haywood at the present time." McParland thereupon developed an elaborate plan to convince Moyer how Haywood and Pettibone "wanted Orchard and Adams . . . to kill you after your release from Telluride jail giving as a reason that if you had not squealed you would surely do so. Then . . . your murder would be blamed on the Mine Owners."[27]

Nothing came of these plans, but as the trial approached, McParland still hoped to find a way to take advantage of the situation. He was also waiting hopefully for the antipathy between Darrow and Richardson to escalate. "[T]here is a great deal of discord existing between [them]," he wrote after the Adams trial, continuing, "Richardson has assumed full charge of the Adams case, much to the disgust of Darrow. Darrow told my informant . . . that Richardson's cross-examination of me injured their case and that Richardson knew in advance how the testimony was procured and that being the case he should have known in cross-examining me in the manner which he did he would draw out matters that should not have been placed before the jury."[28]

At the same time, McParland had other revelations about Darrow that he wished to exploit, although he never did. "In addition to Darrow being a Socialist, both he and his wife are free lovers," he reported. "Darrow said . . . a man had a right to leave his wife if she didn't suit him."[29] Even worse was the attorney's attitude about McParland himself: "Darrow considers me not only his enemy but the enemy of everything that is good and virtuous. My informant told him this evening that he agreed with Mr Gowan [sic] in his

memorable speech on the Mollie Maguires, that if there was a man in the
country who deserved a monument erected it was me. . . . Darrow said, 'Well,
if any other man had done that work I think a monument should be built for
him, but a double-dyed villain like McParland should not be recognized by
decent people.' "

When the trial finally began, McParland and Darrow found themselves closer
in their accommodation than either wished. Both had chosen to stay in the
Idanha, the fine, French château–style hotel—complete with four turrets, a
crenellated roof, and dormer windows on the top floor—that, at six stories,
towered over Boise. Just as it dominated the city physically, the Idanha's magnificent, marble-floored lobby and ornate public rooms were the scene of most
social, political, or cultural events of note.[30]

It was on May 4, 1907—a little more than a week after Darrow, his wife,
and his stenographer took residence there—that McParland again settled into
the Idanha, which had been his base in Boise since he had taken over the investigation sixteen months before.[31] The prosecution team claimed a sizable
part of the third floor—with suites for the governor (who moved his family in
due to threats made against them) and the Great Detective and rooms for
Thiele, Siringo, and Shollenberger. Armed Pinkerton's agents made certain
that no undesirables—socialists, union men, photographers, or reporters[32]—
found their way into that wing. In fact, the hotel had such an overwhelming
number of operatives that Richardson and Miller were rumored to have
moved out, because they found the corridors "patrolled at all hours by rubber-
heeled sentinels."[33]

McParland soon could be found accompanied constantly by Siringo, now
fifty-two years old but still in fine shape and as dangerous as ever, with his
Colt .45 and a walking stick holding a hidden twenty-inch blade that he could
wield as effectively as he had his Bowie knife a decade before.[34] A strategic
decision had been made that McParland should not attend the trial, as he
made too obvious a lightning rod for verbal attacks by the defense that might
distract the jury from its "true purpose." But he was still visible, taking daily
walks with his bodyguard[35] and presiding over a horde of journalists—the "war
correspondents of the capitalist press" as Shoaf called them[36]—well-wishers,
and idle gawkers. "Here he sits and smokes and receives homage," Her-
mon Titus of *The Socialist* wrote. "Most pass by with awed looks, while some
few are proud to be seen sitting alongside and basking in the great man's
halo."[37]

McParland could also be found at breakfast time in the hotel café, where—photos suggest—he had done a sterling job in replacing the pounds he had lost during his illness the previous autumn. The socialist editor Ida Crouch-Hazlett noted that when he drank his coffee, "He sucks it up so that you can hear it all over the room."[38] Most important, a significant part of McParland's time was spent conferring with Gooding, Hawley, Borah, or his operatives. And it was these meetings that showed he was still the leader of the prosecution, for, as Titus wrote, "when McParland speaks, all civil officialdom in the capital of Idaho listens and quakes."[39]

About half a mile away from the Idanha, a square, brick building with a wooden cupola stood amid lawns lined by trees.[40] Much of the Ada County Courthouse had been left shabby by a quarter century of rough winters and housing the county jail in its basement. This was certainly the case for the third-floor courtroom that was the domain of Judge Fremont Wood.[41] The room measured about 70 feet by 45 feet, and had bare plaster walls and long, hard, uncomfortable benches that provided space for 250 people. Acknowledging the significance of the upcoming trial, Wood had ordered fifty chairs added "inside the rail," meaning that spectators were sitting virtually knee-to-knee with the attorneys and jury.

The judge's chair was in an elevated position at the east end of the room, with the jury directly in front of and below him. Although the juror's backs were normally to the judge, their chairs pivoted so that they could see him when he spoke. A raised witness box faced the judge and jury, with the prosecution and defense at tables on opposite sides of it. The court stenographers sat directly in front of the witness, and reporters filled the chairs behind the lawyers, making what was an extremely small space even more confined. Compared to four prosecutors—Hawley, Borah, Canyon County district attorney Owen Van Duyn, and William Stone representing the Steunenberg family—there were eleven defense attorneys, although all were rarely present at any one time. Haywood sat at the end of his attorneys' table, virtually within arm's reach of one of the jurors, and no more than seven or eight feet from the witness stand.

This was the setting on May 9, when jury selection began, a complicated, all-male process that entailed extensive questioning of the potential jurors (or "talesmen"), by first the prosecution and then the defense. Either side could challenge the talesman "for cause," that is, prior knowledge of or bias about the case, victim, defendant, or primary witness; holding a position that could not be changed by evidence; or for specific views about all manner of related issues. The judge then either sustained the challenge, thereby excusing the talesman, or not, in which case the man continued in the process. Each side also had ten peremptory challenges that could be used to eliminate anyone for whom the judge had not sustained the challenge for cause.

Long before they met in court, however, both sides began canvassing potential jurors—sending out agents to chat with unsuspecting men who might eventually be jury candidates. Posing as salesmen, customers, or migrant workers, the canvassers attempted to discover their targets' political and social views, opinions about the labor struggle, and thoughts about the case, the defendants, and Orchard. They then recommended which men their side should accept, reject, or examine further. If by this process one side could stack the jury, it could determine the verdict before testimony ever started. Thus, such information was considered as valuable as gold dust.

It was in this task that one of McParland's most successful agents—C. A. Johnson of the Seattle office, known as Operative 21—was engaged.[42] He had been sent to Caldwell following Steunenberg's assassination and, posing as a miner from the Coeur d'Alenes, had slowly wormed his way into the socialist community to such an extent that in the summer of 1906 he was elected to the Socialist Party's six-man Canyon County central committee. More important, he was chosen to lead the defense's canvassing efforts in the county. When the trial was moved to Ada County, Operative 21's controllers on the defense moved him—much to McParland's joy[43]—to head the canvassing operation there. Thus, as jury selection began, the prosecution knew exactly what the defense knew and how they likely would proceed, enabling the prosecution to get rid of the most dangerous potential jurors.

Unfortunately for the prosecution, in April or May the defense identified Operative 21 as "a detective who was in the employ of the other side," and, according to Gooding, he "was warned to leave the state or suffer the death penalty."[44] Gooding blamed the state auditor—who had demanded to see the detailed expense claims from Pinkerton's—for the leak that allowed the defense to uncover "every secret service agent in the state."[45] This included Cole, who in June was "shown the door and told not to come back."[46] But McParland believed there was a more nefarious reason for the exposure of his agents, and he intensified his search for moles. In so doing he discovered two defense operatives—a Boise policeman and a detective—who had infiltrated the prosecution.[47] But somewhere, he believed, there was a more subversive turncoat.

The uncovering of Operative 21 made the defense team even more wary in jury selection—as they could no longer fully believe their reports—and the questioning process dragged on day after day, until approximately 250 talesmen had been considered.[48] Finally the jury was filled, although only after each side had used its peremptory challenges. The dozen men selected formed a remarkably uniform group.[49] Nine were farmers, one a real-estate agent, one a carpenter, and one a foreman for a fence-building company. Nine were native born, two came from Scotland, and one from Canada. Only one had belonged to a union, and that was fourteen years before. Only one was less than fifty years old. Judge Wood approved the selections and scheduled testimony for the next day.

At 9:30 on the morning of June 4, the formidable, six-foot-four-inch James H. Hawley began the prosecution's opening statement in the most widely covered trial in Idaho history. To reporters from the eastern United States—and there were many, including Oscar King Davis of *The New York Times* and John Carberry of *The Boston Daily Globe*—Hawley's phrasing, verbosity, and lack of Eastern-style eloquence must have made them think he was some rustic bumpkin who would quickly be out of his depth. But the "old sagebrush lawyer" knew exactly what he was doing—he understood the mentality of Idaho jurors and how to communicate with them.

Nevertheless, within minutes Darrow interrupted Hawley, supposedly questioning the form and purpose of an opening statement.[50] It was the beginning of a pattern followed throughout the trial, as Darrow picked at Hawley with sarcastic and belittling comments. This was a tactic Darrow used throughout his career—attacking an opposition attorney in continuous and malicious ways to throw him off stride. It would work for many years, and it would work on Hawley, making him just that much less effective.[51]

Hawley promised that the State would prove that the inner circle of the WFM was responsible for the murder of Steunenberg, that they "traded in blood" and "employed hired assassins to take life and destroy property." This would be proven by the appearance on the stand of both Orchard and "James McParland, the terror of the evil doers throughout the west and whose very presence in any community is security for the good order of that community."[52]

The rest of the day was spent with a series of witnesses establishing the events surrounding Steunenberg's death. Then the next morning, around 10:30, Orchard—the monster the nation had read about but few had actually seen—was called to the stand. One of those escorting him was Siringo, who, bored of being assigned to the Idanha-bound McParland, had volunteered to be a bodyguard for Orchard.[53] Like two of the other special bodyguards, Bob Meldrum and Rudie Barthell, Siringo made no bones about coming into the courtroom heavily armed.

But no one paid attention to Siringo—all eyes were on the witness. George Kibbe Turner of *McClure's Magazine* described the fascination in finally seeing the man: "The first emotion on seeing Harry Orchard is invariably astonishment. This is the confessed assassin of eighteen men. In appearance he is like nothing so much as your milkman—the round-headed, ruddy-faced, sandy-mustached milkman, with his good-natured diffidence, breaking easily into an ingenuous smile. A year and a half ago, when he was first arrested, this man was clearly one of the most dangerous characters our civilization can produce. His face . . . possessed the characteristics of a clearly developed type—the nervous eyes, the compressed lips, and the hardened face muscles of the hunted beast we call the criminal."[54]

Other accounts also pointed out contrasts between Orchard when he was arrested and his appearance on the stand. "Orchard the criminal wore a badly fitting coat, no natty collar, no well-tied scarf, no jaunty negligee shirt. His hair was hacked, not trimmed. He was unshaven, not well-groomed. . . . The eyes were shifty and watery. . . . This man might be guilty of anything," John Nevins wrote in *The Milwaukee Journal*. But, he continued, "Orchard the witness might be a Sunday school superintendent. He is carefully attired—collar, cuffs, scarf, even to the quietly displayed watch chain, which lies across his benevolent breast. He affects dark colors, as becomes one contrite and oppressed with a sense of his own wickedness. His hair is cut in the mode, well-trimmed. The mustache is carefully arranged. His hands are perfectly kept, his nails manicured."[55]

Equally amazing as this transformation was Orchard's testimony, starting with the admission that his real name was Albert E. Horsley, a fact that in the past year Darrow's investigators had failed to uncover.[56] For the next day and a half Hawley carefully took the confessed killer from his birth in Ontario, Canada, through his string of atrocities, starting with the explosion in the Vindicator mine.[57] He detailed an attempt on the life of Colorado governor Peabody, the murder of detective Lyte Gregory, and the Independence depot bombing, all done, he said, in the company of Adams. He then described how he made two attempts on the life of former Bunker Hill and Sullivan president Fred Bradley in San Francisco, tried again to kill Peabody, planned the murder of former Colorado adjutant general Sherman Bell, and set bombs intended to eliminate state Supreme Court justices Goddard and Gabbert, the latter of which killed a passerby instead. Finally, he recounted the harrowing story of Steunenberg's assassination.

Now came the defense's chance to break Orchard's testimony and the State's case. Richardson and Darrow both wanted to conduct the cross-examination, but ultimately it went to the stern, reserved, schoolmasterly Richardson, who for a full week—twenty-six hours in court—grilled, badgered, intimidated, inveigled, and tried to outwit Orchard. He sought to portray the witness as not only a murderer but also a womanizing bigamist, a heavy drinker and obsessive gambler, a thief and swindler, an arsonist, a cheat, a braggart, and a liar. Yet, although he drew out admissions of even more crimes than those to which Orchard had already confessed, he was unable to make Orchard contradict himself, or to shake his testimony. It was a major defeat for the defense and left many newspapermen convinced of Orchard's honesty and religious conversion.

"Orchard is now the stronger moral force of the two," Davis wrote in *The New York Times*, continuing: "His self-possession is undisturbed and unshakable. His equipoise is amazing. Self-reliant, calm, steady, and alert, he meets and repulses assault after assault that would crumble and break down the sturdiest resistance based upon any other foundation than his. Richardson has planned a campaign against a house of cards. He finds a fortress built of granite, and without the wit or willingness to admit his error, batters his head against it in the vain attempt to force his faulty tactics to succeed."[58]

One of Richardson's tactics was to try to show McParland as the man behind the scenes pulling the strings; the man who had forced the confession and regularly prepped Orchard for his testimony; the driving force behind the prosecution. Day after day Richardson tried to force Orchard to admit collusion with the detective, but each time, Orchard denied it.[59] On June 13, as Orchard's time on the stand neared its conclusion, Richardson

commenced to bore in hard in the apparent effort to show that Orchard had been induced to make his confession by the promises of Detective McPartland and others, and in the hope of securing immunity from punishment for himself. Every resource at the lawyer's command was used in that effort.

His voice boomed out its loudest, and he employed with utmost vigor the tactics of blustering, bullyragging, and browbeating which had not succeeded at any point before. Then he lowered his tones and tried the other sort of attack with wheedling insinuation. He sneered and scoffed.

He distorted answers and tried the old method of testifying to his own deductions, putting them into the form of statement-questions, acting as if he expected Orchard to agree to them at once. But Orchard resisted every attack. . . . He denied from first to last that he had been promised immunity by McPartland to confess, declaring that he had had it in mind to do so before he ever saw the detective.[60]

Finally, Richardson gave up. He was beaten. Most of those who had heard Orchard's testimony agreed with the assessment of C. P. Connolly of *Collier's* that he was "the most remarkable witness that has ever appeared in an American court of justice."[61] Darrow, however, was not so sure, thinking that his success could be attributed to Richardson's lack of ability, for, as Darrow later told a reporter, Orchard could think four times while Richardson did so once.[62]

Without Adams to testify, it was now incumbent upon the prosecution to corroborate the different elements of Orchard's testimony, and for the next eight days a series of witnesses attempted to do so. Incident by incident, they elicited information that confirmed various details of Orchard's story, proved some of his movements, and attempted to show a motive. But many of the connections were tenuous, and when Hawley and Borah concluded their case on June 21, they could not have been truly confident. Certainly a great deal of evidence pointed at Haywood and the WFM—but most of it had come from Orchard. Would it be enough?

The defense did not think so, and when Borah announced that the State rested, Richardson presented a motion—speaking for two and a half hours—for a directed verdict of acquittal; he was followed by Borah and Darrow.[63] Expecting Judge Wood to take some time to determine his ruling, the attorneys were stunned when he spoke immediately. "Gentleman, the court is clearly satisfied that this case should be submitted to the jury," Wood stated, adding that although "[o]rdinarily it would be the duty of the court to give its reasons," he would not do so, as there were three others indicted on the same charges, and thus "the court will refrain from . . . pointing out the reasons for overruling the motion."[64]

If Wood's timing and decision were surprising, his reasoning was even more so. However, it would be a quarter of a century before he finally disclosed it.[65] Shortly before jury selection, Darrow, feeling the need for a local lawyer on the team, invited the prominent Ada County attorney Edgar Wilson to join the defense. Wilson had been a partner in a legal practice with Wood before entering Congress in 1895. Wood thought that "our previous association could in no way affect my ability to try the cases and to exact justice," so Wilson joined the defense. However, when Richardson asked for a directed verdict, Wood was in a quandary. He believed that "there was very little legal corroboration upon which a verdict of guilty could be justified," yet he was concerned about the way it might look should he grant the motion to his old partner's side. Therefore, he ruled that the trial should proceed.

On the morning of Monday, June 24, McParland was sitting in the lobby of the Idanha when a touring acting company arrived to check into the hotel. Remembering almost half a century later the strange atmosphere and the vast number of armed men loitering throughout the hotel, the troupe's lead actress wrote: "A big man came over to me and asked me if I was Ethel Barrymore, and when I said yes, he said, 'I was a great friend of your father's. My name is McFarland. I'm a Pinkerton man.'" Although the twenty-seven-year-old Barrymore did not remember the Great Detective's name correctly, she certainly recalled the experience. When she asked McParland what was going on, he told her that because of the trial, the whole town was like a fort. He then invited her to a room upstairs and lifted up a mattress so she could see a collection of Winchester rifles. "He said there were rifles under every mattress in the hotel."[66]

At the very moment McParland was chatting to the actress, Clarence Darrow was in Judge Wood's courtroom making the defense's opening speech—which had been postponed from the beginning of the trial. With this speech he set the pattern and tone for the defense for the rest of the trial.[67] First, Darrow hoped to convince the jury that the mine owners, their political allies, and their operatives—particularly Pinkerton's—had conspired to destroy the WFM through their creature, Harry Orchard. Second, he hoped to impeach Orchard's testimony at so many points that his entire confession would be shown to be a "great fabric of untruths." And third, through sarcasm and innuendo, Darrow hoped to implant in the minds of the jury that the man at the center of this diabolical web was James McParland.

In the next three weeks the defense called more than eighty witnesses. Some testified that they had seen Orchard when he claimed he was elsewhere. Some raised the idea that he had a vendetta against Steunenberg due to financial losses he suffered in 1899. W. F. Davis, whom Orchard had said was in charge of dynamiting the Bunker Hill and Sullivan concentrator, denied his involvement. It was suggested that the explosion in the Vindicator mine had been an accident. And it was offered that the explosion at Fred Bradley's house had been caused not by a bomb but by an exploding gas main.[68]

For two days bridging June and July, Morris Friedman, a socialist who had worked as a stenographer in Pinkerton's Denver office, created an uproar by unveiling documents that he had smuggled out. Having recently published a book entitled *The Pinkerton Labor Spy*, his testimony repeated what he had written, identifying by name agents who had infiltrated labor unions and describing the operations overseen by McParland during the Colorado Labor Wars.[69] Although sensational, his testimony was not generally considered significant, as he admitted on cross-examination that the Idaho Mine Owners' Association had not been a major client of Pinkerton's, nor did any of his documents actually have a bearing on the case.[70]

Darrow and Richardson, however, considered Friedman's testimony a major triumph, as they had not expected it to be admitted at all—and it brought with it the implication that Orchard might be yet another Pinkerton's operative. Others responded to it by publicly throwing support behind Friedman's betrayed employers. The former U.S. marshal turned sports journalist Bat Masterson—who had had a run-in with Siringo in Dodge City in 1877—stated that "the defense will not be able to involve Captain James McParland in anything discreditable" and proclaimed him "one of the shrewdest and most capable detectives that has ever handled a case in this or any other country."[71]

After Friedman, an even more shocking defense witness was called—McParland's brother Edward. Described as a "funny little bald headed shoemaker, with brogue as thick as peat,"[72] Edward told of his experiences in 1904 when he was hauled out of his shop in Victor, thrown in the bull pen, and shown over the Kansas border.[73] Although the brief statement had no relevance to the murder, it allowed the defense to portray McParland—with whom Edward claimed to have not had contact for more than six years[74]—as a heartless, soulless spy and mercenary.

In fact, even while his brother was testifying, McParland was again playing spymaster, making a last effort to separate Moyer from Haywood and Pettibone and get him to turn state's evidence. In May he had encouraged two deputies, who watched over the prisoners at the jail, to convince Moyer to work with the prosecution.[75] When this failed he devised a plan similar to the one he had developed for Hicks to talk to Annie Adams—in this case turning to Fannie Cobb, the wife of the proprietor of *The Idaho Daily Statesman*, to put pressure on Bertha Moyer. Somehow the press got hold of the story, and Mrs. Cobb hurriedly denied any involvement.[76] Moyer eventually took the stand on behalf of the defense.

When the defense completed its case on Saturday, July 13, many thought the efforts had done more harm than good. In trying to portray Orchard as a liar, witnesses had confirmed his story as often as they disproved it. And although serious questions had been raised about his involvement in some of the crimes he claimed—particularly the attempted murder of Bradley and the bomb in the Vindicator mine—the alternatives were unproven theories. Moreover, the different reasons given for Orchard's involvement—personal hatred for Steunenberg, a role as a Pinkerton's operative, serving as a double agent for the mine owners—showed the defense's arguments were riddled with internal contradictions.

Even the gains made by the defense were diluted in the following rebuttal phase, as much of the testimony disputing Orchard was drawn into question.[77] Judge Wood later noted the benefits that accrued to the prosecution during the period after he had let the trial continue: "The principal portion of the corroboration in the Haywood case was developed through the witnesses of the defendants when making their defense and while there was little or no corroboration against Haywood in the original presentation by the State, it was my opinion that the corroboration was ample when the case against Haywood was submitted [to the jury]."[78]

Wood's view was widely supported, including by C. P. Connolly of *Collier's*—a lawyer himself—who noted: "There is no escape from the conclusion that at the close of the case for the defense, a much stronger chain of evidence had been forged against Haywood than the prosecution had succeeded in welding. And the credit for laying the State's well-concealed traps for the defense to stumble into must be given to the detective McParland, an old-fashioned man in appearance and habit, who works silently and seriously, and with a passion for winning."[79]

As James Hawley began the first of four closing arguments on a sultry afternoon on Friday, July 19, he glanced at the front row of spectators, toward where sat two men who had thus far assiduously avoided making an appearance. But McParland and Gooding were both there now—it was McParland's only appearance—and their support comforted Hawley. He had been ill—due to stress—in the preceding days, but his summation was masterful. For two hours that afternoon Hawley seemed to chat informally to his fellow Idahoans on the jury. At times he leaned on the table, at others he sat on it with his feet on a chair, and at still others he sat close to the twelve men, his legs swinging free. Saturday he was back, finishing, he noted, "after occupying only eight hours."[80]

Hawley's primary task was to give a blow-by-blow account of Orchard's violent acts, of the actions taken by the WFM after the Steunenberg assassination, and of the reasons for believing Orchard's testimony. He addressed each of the alternative theories that the defense had propagated. By the time he finished, Hawley had made "one of the most masterful and forceful addresses that has perhaps ever been made to a jury in a murder case in the history of this country. It was an address that will go down in the history of court proceedings as one of the greatest efforts of its kind."[81]

When the trial paused on Sunday, Judge Wood disappeared, as was his wont, to relax in his avid pursuit of trout fishing. As he had a couple times before, Oscar King Davis accompanied him. That afternoon, for the only time on their ventures, the trial was mentioned. "Well . . . it will soon be over," Davis later recalled Wood had said. "It ought to go to the jury next week. Haywood is guilty and has been convicted. I believe he will be hanged, for I don't see how it can be upset."[82]

The next day, with the temperature soaring to 90 degrees Fahrenheit (32 degrees Celsius)—so hot that Wood announced the second daily session would be held from 6:00 to 8:30 P.M. to avoid the heat—Richardson did his best to thwart this inevitability. Wearing a three-piece suit with a formal wing collar that some thought out of place in a Boise courtroom, he spoke rapidly but distinctly in "a great, big voice," using a series of jerky arm and leg movements that made him even hotter, so he frequently had to wipe his face and balding pate. Having had the table moved "to give him a good space to walk about in as he talked," he would move as far from the jury as possible and then, "crouching down, to approach stealthily, speaking softly until he got fairly in front of the first row of jurors, and then booming out his point at the top of his voice and with explosive emphasis," he would throw his shoulders back and gesture with his fingers spread far apart.[83]

Richardson gathered steam as he described the events in the Coeur d'Alenes in 1899. This was why, he argued, Orchard had murdered Steunenberg—because the governor's actions had led him to sell his share in a mine that later became wildly successful. On and on Richardson went, building this notion, until suddenly, as his second day began, everything changed. "And when Mr Richardson had blown this bubble-theory of the personal grudge and had filled it and had it floating before the jurors and they were looking at its beauty," *The Idaho Daily Statesman* commented in derision, "the Denver attorney petulantly thrust out his finger, poked it through his own creation and the bubble broke. He had another idea. . . . [H]e spread before the jury the startling theory that the Steunenberg murder was all a plot of the Pinkerton detective agency."[84]

In actuality, Richardson had targets beyond the Pinkerton's. "You have been fooled in this case largely by the State of Colorado," he told the jurors. "She has sent up here all her dirty linen in order to have you gentlemen wash it."[85] And there was no doubt who was doing that dirty work for Colorado and Idaho: the Pinkerton's, with "the express purpose of destroying the Western Federation of Miners, the only organization that has ever had the power or the courage to raise its hand against the mining interests of the country." And so he built the argument that Orchard had been working against the WFM— had perhaps even murdered Steunenberg—on the orders of McParland, who "has been held up in a sort of nebulous atmosphere as 'the great I am' . . . and that back of it somewhere he was going to produce evidence that would astound the world. What is the evidence here that has been produced by this man? The seas have been combed, the land has been raked . . . and when we come to this trial there is not a single scintilla of evidence that has been gotten to sustain Mr Orchard's original statement."[86]

Thus, as he neared the end of his ten-hour summation, Richardson followed a strategy that had been used against McParland many years before in the Molly Maguire trials by Martin L'Velle and John Ryon. By trying to fix the blame for the assassination on McParland, not only did he hope to give the jury an alternative theory that might influence their reasonable doubt of Haywood's guilt, but he also hoped to shift the blame for Steunenberg's grisly murder from Haywood onto McParland. It was a time-tested method, so powerful, in fact, that it was used again during the next two days—by Clarence Darrow.

Darrow's closing argument—which lasted four sessions and totaled eleven hours and fifteen minutes—was one of the greatest plays on the emotions of a jury in American legal history. This consummate orator and rhetorician had a deep understanding of human nature, and he used sarcasm, indignation, pathos, invective, sorrow, humor, vituperation, and outrage to appeal to the sentiments of the jurors. His goal was to attack Orchard, Hawley, and McParland so viciously—while presenting Bill Haywood and the WFM in a positive light—that the jury would not want to convict the defendant but rather to blame those who had brought the charges.

Throughout his two-day speech—much of it in weather so hot he took off his coat and talked to the jury in shirtsleeves, with one thumb crooked behind his suspenders—he paced continuously. Sometimes he faced the gallery, sometimes he was so close to the jurors—seemingly addressing each individually—that one of them asked "that he stand further away, as it gave some of the jurors a headache to have him stand so close to them and talk so loud."[87]

Just as he wandered back and forth through the courtroom, so his impassioned speech wound around and around but always returned to the same themes. Orchard was a liar, and Hawley was even worse, "bughouse" for believing a word the man said. He again mentioned Orchard's theoretical financial motive for murdering Steunenberg. But none of the tales was worse than Orchard's supposed religious conversion—a fabrication and irrelevancy brought about by "Father McParland." Treading a dangerous line with a strongly Christian jury, Darrow cried:

> [H]ere is a piece of work, gentlemen of the jury, that will last as long as the ages last—McPartland's conversion of Orchard! . . . From the beginning of the world was ever any miracle like this performed before? Lo, and behold! A man who has spent his life as a Pinkerton—isn't a preacher—he has never been ordained except in the Pinkerton office. . . . [A]nd he [Orchard] meets this Pinkerton detective who never did anything in his life but lie and cheat and scheme, for the life of a detective is a living lie, that is his business; he lives one from the time he gets up in the morning until he goes to bed; he is deceiving people, and trapping people and lying to people . . . and Harry Orchard is caught, and he meets this famous detective who speaks to him familiarly about David and St Paul and Kelly the Bum. . . . And then he holds out the hope of life and all that life could offer to Harry Orchard, and lo and behold, he soon becomes a Christian. Now, gentlemen, Savonarola, who was a great preacher, and a mighty man in his day is dead. . . . John Wesley is dead. Cranmer is dead. Moody is dead. Pretty much all of them are gone. What is the matter with McPartland changing the sign on his office, and going into the business of saving souls instead of snaring bodies? If he could convert a man like Orchard in a twinkling of an eye, I submit he is too valuable a

man to waste his time in a Pinkerton detective office trying to catch men. . . . A man who could wash Harry Orchard's soul as white as wool need not hesitate at tackling any sort of a job that came his way. He is a wonderful detective, but his fame as a detective would be eclipsed in a moment if he would go into the business of saving souls instead of catching men.[88]

Darrow also claimed time and again that there was a plot by the mine owners to kill Bill Haywood, the WFM, and the labor movement. And he vehemently insisted that violence on behalf of labor was justified. "I don't care how many wrongs they committed," he said. "I don't care how many crimes these weak, rough, rugged, unlettered men, who often know no other power but the brute force of their strong right arm . . . how many brutalities they are guilty of. I know their cause is just."[89]

But somehow, Darrow always made his way back to the same person:

I might suggest to Mr. McPartland, the wise and the good, who quotes the Bible in one moment and then tries to impose upon some victim in the next, who quotes Scripture in one sentence and then lies in the next, who utters blessing with one word and curses with the next, I might suggest to this good man that William Haywood has a soul, Moyer has a soul, Pettibone has a soul. . . . Do you suppose McPartland is interested in Haywood's soul? Do you suppose he is interested in Moyer's? Do you suppose he is interested in Harry Orchard's? Do you suppose he is interested in his own? Do you suppose he is interested in anything except weaving a web around these men so that he may be able to hang them by the neck until dead? And to do it, like the devil, he quotes Scripture. To do it, there isn't a scheme or a plan or a device of his wily, crooked brain that he won't bring into action, whether it is the Bible or detective yarns—there is none too good for McPartland.[90]

Darrow was still at it late in his closing statement. "McPartland is not under indictment. Mac is too slick," he said. "He is the head and the front of this prosecution. He is the father confessor of the greatest criminal of modern times. He is the man who has brought every witness into this court room. He is the man who knows whether Harry Orchard was promised immunity. . . . He has been connected with this case from a time long before the case arose.... Why does he sit around the lobbies of the hotels ... and weave his webs everywhere between here and Colorado? Why ... not dare to come on the witness stand? He isn't indicted, although he ought to be."[91]

Perhaps any other speaker would have been intimidated by following the magnificent addresses of Hawley, Richardson, and Darrow. But not the senator from Idaho. When court reconvened that evening, Borah began gently, eloquently, making clear the true point of the trial. "There is here no fight on organized labor," he said. "This is simply a trial for murder. Frank Steunenberg has been murdered, and we want to know. A crime has been committed, and the integrity and the manhood of Idaho wants to know. An offense which shocked the civilized world has taken place within our borders, and unless we went about it earnestly and determinedly to know, we would [be] unfit to be called a commonwealth."[92]

He then quietly chastised the emotive methods of Richardson and Darrow. "If I were fighting for the cause of labor I wouldn't seek to engender hatred and ill will, faction against faction, or class against class; I would not inveigh against law; I wouldn't inveigh against society; I wouldn't inveigh against every man who owned his farm or his home; I wouldn't inveigh against Christianity, because without those things the laboring man goes down into slavery and dirt."[93]

During that evening and throughout the next day, Borah logically addressed the salient points of the case: He indicated that there was a conspiracy of an inner circle to kill Steunenberg, and he argued that Orchard was part of that conspiracy, stating his belief that Orchard was telling the truth and suggesting there was sufficient corroboration to connect Haywood to the crime, quite apart from Orchard's confession. The next evening, having spoken for nearly six hours, he concluded his address. "I have heard the best of them all over the country," said Haywood, "but Borah beats them all."[94]

What would prove to be the key point in the entire trial came the next morning, when Judge Wood spent about an hour giving the jury their instructions, a list of sixty-five points of law, the majority of which dealt with presumption of innocence, burden of proof, the need for corroboration, reasonable doubt, and circumstantial evidence.[95] The most important of these was Instruction 34, which in part stated: "[A] person cannot be convicted of a crime upon the testimony of an accomplice unless such accomplice is corroborated by other evidence which of itself, and without the aid of the testimony of the accomplice, tends to connect the defendant with the commission of the offense charged."[96] By his restrictive instructions, Wood had, many would later say, effectively eliminated any possibility of a guilty verdict.[97]

That, however, is not the way it seemed on Saturday, July 27, while the jury debated behind closed doors. At that point, the prosecution, the majority of the reporters, and apparently most of the locals thought a guilty verdict was on the way. Even Darrow believed so. When a reporter said to him, "Well, it takes twelve," he responded, "No, it only takes one"—showing that he held out a forlorn hope that one man would vote for acquittal, thereby creating a hung jury.[98]

Darrow did not have long to agonize. Early Sunday morning, after about twenty hours together—all in all, a relatively short time by the standards of such an important trial—the jury reported that a verdict had been reached. When the hastily summoned judge, attorneys, reporters, and others were assembled, the jury foreman, Thomas Gess, passed Wood an envelope. The judge opened it, looked at it incredulously, and said, "There's nothing here! You gave me the wrong envelope, Mr Gess?" The embarrassed Gess took another from his inside breast pocket, and passed it to the judge. Wood glanced at it and handed it to the clerk, who read aloud: "We the jury, in the above-named case, find the defendant, William D. Haywood, not guilty."[99]

Immediately after the trial, reporters mobbed the jurors wanting to know how they could have arrived at such an unexpected verdict. It boiled down to one thing: According to the instructions given by Wood, the State had not produced sufficient corroboration for Orchard's testimony. Like Wood and most of the press, many jurors believed Orchard's testimony and that Haywood was guilty—but that did not mean such a verdict could be rendered.[100]

An original eight votes for acquittal had eventually risen to eleven. "I believed that he was guilty and I still believe he is guilty, and I want the world to know it," Samuel Gilman, the last man to vote for acquittal, said afterward. "I simply acquiesced in the verdict of acquittal because I felt that I could not do otherwise after I found the entire 11 other jurors consenting to the verdict, but not because I was convinced that it was right."[101]

That comment was echoed by George Powell, the eleventh juror to vote for acquittal. "The jurors all thought Haywood guilty," he overstated, "but some of them said the state under the instructions had not made out a case against the prisoner. . . . I did not feel that it would be right to hang the jury when a majority was for acquittal."[102] Similarly, juror A. P. Burns told the press, "I was firmly convinced, when we left the courtroom, that the first ballot would show a vote for conviction. I still retain the belief that Haywood was guilty, and only changed my vote because it struck me that if the evidence presented left eight men unconvinced of the guilt of the defendant, it would be impossible to get 12 men in another trial, and that it would be better to settle the question by acquiescing in their decision."[103]

Juror O. V. Sebern thought the verdict to be "a grave miscarriage of justice—and many of the jurors concurred in this opinion. There was little or no doubt of the guilt of the defendant, but . . . the final instructions of the presiding Judge to the jury were such that . . . the resulting verdict was the only one that could be rendered."[104]

Is it possible that Wood's instructions were the lone reason for acquittal? Although nine of the jurors mentioned their significance after the trial, this is unlikely. Gilman explained this difficulty: "I cannot point out any particular instruction that seemed to decide the boys on a verdict of not guilty. . . . I believe it was the instructions generally. They couldn't seem to make head or tail of them, but were convinced that the general tone indicated that the defendant should be freed. Some of them seemed to think the instructions were very strong regarding corroborative testimony and some said that they could not be clear as to the reasonable doubt."[105]

On the other hand, jurors Sam Russell and J. A. Robertson stated they had been swayed by Darrow's remarkable closing speech, an intriguing contrast to Richardson, who condemned it as "rank. It was enough to hang any man regardless of his innocence or guilt."[106] Some, such as Russell, found Orchard's testimony untrustworthy, although the majority accepted it as honest. And that fact, more than any other, shows what was truly the masterstroke of the defense—convincing Steve Adams to recant his confession, the act that William Pinkerton said "pulled the plug on the state's case."[107] For, based on the statements of the jurors, had Adams testified in support of Orchard, there seems little doubt that Haywood would have been convicted.

Of course, there were numerous other theories thrown around to explain the prosecution's failure. Davis of *The New York Times* heard afterward "that the jury had been bought."[108] Siringo wrote that the jurors were worried about their safety and that of their families due to threats made by a fellow juror employed by the WFM.[109] And the labor supporters—well, they just crowed that Haywood was innocent.

Meanwhile, the normally loquacious McParland was notably silent. He had spent a year and a half of his life on a case that had once again thrust him back into the national spotlight, a position he clearly felt he deserved. And he had believed when he gained Adams's confession that he would finally triumph totally over what had become his archenemy: the WFM. To see Haywood, whom McParland considered the worst of that bunch, walk free must have been devastatingly disappointing. For once the newspapers did not carry his crowing reports, as McParland steadfastly refused comment on the case. Instead he turned his eyes to the future and the trials of Adams, Moyer, and Pettibone, each of whom, he agreed with Hawley and Borah, could still be successfully prosecuted. Justice could still be his.

✦

CHAPTER 24

FOUR TRIALS

W hile Orchard was on the stand in the second of week of June 1907, new Shoshone County sheriff William Bailey brought Adams to Boise, where he was put into the Ada County jail, directly below Judge Wood's courtroom. McParland had hoped that hearing about Orchard's testimony might convince Adams to follow suit, or that the defense might make the mistake of calling him to impeach Orchard, in which case Adams's confession could be introduced.[1] But Richardson and Darrow were having none of this ploy. So there Adams remained, until Bailey took him back to Wallace two days after the verdict to again stand trial for the murder of Fred Tyler.[2]

Meanwhile, in the mountains of southwest Colorado, another alleged murder victim made the news when Bulkeley Wells led a party to where Adams had previously carried out the search for William Barney's body. A dozen men digging found the bones of a man approximately Barney's size. The *Daily Journal* of Telluride—a staunch supporter of the mine owners—promptly proclaimed them Barney's bones and pointed the finger at St. John.[3] Though a local dentist could not confirm that the remains were Barney's, the claim received wide coverage.[4]

The approaching trial of Adams took on even greater significance in light of these events. Not only might a conviction persuade Adams to rejoin the prosecution for the trial of Pettibone for Steunenberg's murder, it could mean he would testify against St. John for Barney's murder.

Hot on the heels of the news from Colorado, McParland received the distressing report that Robert A. Pinkerton had died on August 12 on the steamer *Bremen*. Pinkerton had been crossing the Atlantic en route to Bad Nauheim, Germany, where he had hoped to receive treatment for the heart problem that resulted in his death.[5] He was succeeded as the principal in New York by his son Allan, who had been the agency's assistant general manager.

On September 23, about a month before Adams's second trial was scheduled, Borah's trial for land fraud got under way. As the government blew
through forty witnesses, Hawley, representing Borah, cross-examined only
two, while letting it be known that he considered the charges ridiculous.
When the time came for the defense to make its case, Borah was the only witness called. He proved that he had never had a financial stake in the Barber
Lumber Company, was retained solely as an attorney on a fixed salary, had no
knowledge of any fraudulent activities, and had no responsibility for actions
taken by the leadership of the company. On cross-examination, the prosecution could not discredit him in any way, and immediately thereafter, Hawley
rested the defense's case. The judge needed more time to prepare his instructions to the jury than they did to reach a conclusion. After only fourteen minutes, the jury returned a verdict of not guilty.[6]

Meanwhile, on many newspapers' front pages, next to the account about
the Borah trial, was a grisly story. On September 30, when ex-sheriff Harvey
Brown opened the gate to his house a dynamite bomb, similar to that which
killed Steunenberg, exploded, shredding Brown's left arm and leg, burning his
face excruciatingly, and mortally wounding him. It was immediately suspected that the attack was both in retaliation for his arrest of Adams and a
warning to those thinking of testifying in the upcoming trial.[7] As a response,
some prosecution witnesses soon disappeared—including a man named Ar-
chie Phillips, who reported that "he found a bag containing ten pounds of
dynamite back of his house" before making tracks for British Columbia, and
one William Chandler, who "fled to Butte, Mont, fearing that he will meet
with foul play should he testify."[8]

As the days grew shorter in October, some not-so-friendly rivals descended
upon Rathdrum in Kootenai County—a town of seven hundred inhabitants
about sixty-five miles west-northwest of Wallace. Nestled in a primarily agri-
cultural area, Rathdrum had been selected as a change of venue because the
prosecution hoped a jury consisting of farmers and lumbermen would give
them a better chance of conviction than one in a mining center like Wallace.
Jury selection began on October 25, with Henry Knight and Shoshone
County prosecutor Walter Hanson leading the prosecution and Charles
Heitman—who was originally from North Carolina but had practiced law in
Rathdrum for nearly two decades—the defense, because Richardson had de-
cided never to work with Darrow again. A few days later the heavyweights—
Darrow and Hawley—arrived.[9]

In constant agony due to a virulent case of mastoiditis—an infection of the mastoid bone of the skull, located just behind the ear—Darrow had been told by specialists that he was risking his life by going to Rathdrum, where there was no hospital.[10] However, Darrow felt compelled to go, as "Adams had turned his back on the State largely through his confidence in me. I had told him I would try his case; it was set, and I could not leave him."[11]

Once again, jury selection proved extremely lengthy, so it was not until the afternoon of November 5 that the prosecution made its opening address. For several days the testimony plodded along, until Chris Thiele mentioned Adams's confession. Darrow objected on the grounds that it had been obtained by threats and promises of immunity. Excluding the jury, Judge W. W. Woods (not to be confused with Judge Fremont Wood in Boise) allowed Darrow to examine McParland, in order to determine if the confession was admissible. The detective acknowledged that he had told Adams: "[H]e owed to himself and the community to expose the crimes that he had been implicated in, and who instigated him to commit them. I told him that he was simply a tool for other parties . . . and told him that there was such a thing as even a man that had committed the crimes that he had committed, that he might become penitent and would be forgiven his sins."

"Forgiven his sins?" Darrow asked.

"Yes sir."

"Did you tell him by whom?"

"By God, of course."

"You did not tell him by you? . . ."

"I haven't the power of absolution."

"We thought you had."[12]

As the interchange continued, Darrow elicited that McParland had told Adams the story from the Bible of David and Uriah—how "David never thought he had committed a crime until his attention was called to it by the prophet Nathan. . . . David became a penitent and wrote the Penitential Psalms, confessed his crime."

"You did not tell him he got hung by the neck until dead for killing Uriah?"

"No, I have never read any record of that."[13]

To some it seemed that Darrow won the confrontation, yet that afternoon Woods ruled that Adams's confession was admissible. Late the next day McParland was back on the stand to read the confession into the record and testify as to how he had obtained it. The following morning, Darrow and the detective continued their wrestling match. Early on, Darrow pressed McParland about his methods for obtaining confessions:

> Q: Can you tell about how many confessions you have obtained in your
>   business?
> A: I could not.
> Q: Went up into the hundreds?
> A: I dont hardly think so.
> Q: Ever fail to get one when you went after it?
> A: Not if the party was guilty, I never failed that I know of.
> Q: Ever fail when they were innocent?
> A: Invariably.
> Q: You have failed, then, when you have tried to get it? . . .
> A: Yes, when I tried to get a confession from an innocent man.
> Q: You have tried that?
> A: I have, considered that he was guilty until I talked to him. . . .
> Q: And you say you never failed to get one from a guilty man?
> A: Never.
> Q: And the fact that a man gave you a confession was proof to you that
>   he was guilty?
> A: Very conclusive proof.[14]

As Darrow hammered at the detective about his background, his time with the Molly Maguires, and how his involvement with the Steunenberg case began, McParland made several errors of fact in his answers. He said he was born in 1839 (five years too early), that he came to the United States in 1857 (ten years too early), that he joined Pinkerton's in 1869 (three years too early), and that he became involved in the Steunenberg murder in 1896 (ten years too early).[15] Were the mistakes caused by a failing memory? Were they a form of bragging, by making it look like he "had been around"? Was he having a subconscious laugh at Darrow by not telling the truth? Any of these seem possible—but what is certain is that no one picked up on the errors other than the date he claimed to have become involved in the Steunenberg case.

Darrow then returned to how McParland obtained Adams's confession. He drew out the story of the detective speaking of Kelly the Bum, little Jimmy Kerrigan, and "Patsy" Butler, all of whom turned state's evidence.[16] Darrow tried to catch McParland on conflicting comments between his testimony in the current trial and the previous Adams trial, and then he suddenly shifted back to the confession. In a mocking manner he asked McParland about his stories of David and St. Paul. "You told him David was a murderer and Paul was a murderer?"

A: No question about that.

Q: And David had become a man after God's own heart, in spite of that?

A: He had done penance, yes.

Q: Paul had become a mighty man in the Christian Faith?

A: Yes, sir. . . .

Q: Did you have any purpose in it? . . .

A: I had the purpose to show that his soul might be saved. . . .

Q: And did you have any purpose in relating to him about "Kelly the Bum," and telling him the State always treated its witnesses fairly, if they treated it fairly?

A: Certainly; that was stated for the purpose of leading him up to a confession.[17]

Darrow spent most of the morning grilling McParland in a fashion so sneeringly unpleasant that Hawley frequently objected, finally exclaiming that such tactics would simply not be tolerated. "Do you mean to say that my life is in danger?" shouted Darrow in a display of histrionics. Before tempers escalated further, the judge interrupted and forced the two to settle down.[18] At the lunch break, Darrow left for Spokane to see an ear specialist,[19] having asked to recall McParland upon his return, and in the meantime leaving his associates to continue.

Late on the morning of November 14, McParland again took the stand, but it was not until midafternoon that he made one of his most telling statements—although neither the defense nor the prosecution realized it. On redirect examination, inquiring about his investigations when he first met Adams, Hawley asked: "State whether or not you were investigating affairs in northern Idaho, or the killing of Tyler and Bouley?"

"I never heard of them until Adams told me about it," McParland responded.

"I was about to ask you whether you knew about Tyler and Bouley, or knew anything about these men prior to that time?"

"I never did," assured McParland.

Moments later, on re–cross-examination, Darrow returned to the topic: "Do you swear that Harry Orchard told you nothing about any killing of claim jumpers up on the St. Joe River in north Idaho?"

"He didnt tell me of any claim jumpers in Idaho."[20]

And thus, as he had many years before, McParland perjured himself on the stand about a key aspect of his knowledge of a relevant crime. On January 27, 1906—the first day of his confession—Orchard had told McParland how Adams, Mason, and Glover had killed Tyler.[21] It is clear from the transcript of the confession that this—and Orchard subsequently tying him to other crimes—is what made Adams a figure of interest. This was such a fundamental part of the sequence of events that it is impossible it could have been a mistake or have slipped McParland's mind.

McParland had also lied about his own background in his testimony the previous day, when he told Darrow that he had spent thirteen years at sea before coming to the United States.[22] This draws into question the inaccurate dates he gave during that same exchange, and suggests that they were *not* mistakes, but more intentional lies. These falsehoods from the previous day are truly unfathomable. One can comprehend McParland lying about the material in Orchard's confession because it made a stronger case for the prosecution—a case he had worked on for a year and a half—and because McParland's ethics, even under oath, seem to have allowed this as they evolved over many years spent trying "to do good by doing bad—preventing crime or apprehending criminals by resorting to lies, deceit, trickery."[23] This lie about Orchard's confession fits this category perfectly: The end justifies the means.

But the statements about his past were simply gratuitous falsehoods under oath that accomplished no known purpose—making them inexplicable. Was Darrow right? Had McParland lived with lies so long that he could not distinguish them from the truth? Had he become so influential a figure in his own circle—and his own mind—that he felt he could do as he pleased, say as he pleased, and truth be damned? Or was he simply willing to do anything, say anything, to "win"? That these are even possibilities leaves a large question mark over the rest of his testimony and many of his actions at this stage of his career.

After McParland's testimony, the State rested. For the next week the defense presented alibis for Adams, and then called the defendant to the stand, where he remained two days, being "subjected to a most rigid cross-examination" by Hawley.[24] Then, after Annie Adams testified, the defense rested.

The prosecution and defense had agreed that the closing arguments would be limited to a total of seven hours per side, and when these were completed on the evening of November 23, Judge Woods gave the jury their instructions, which were considered to be "in favor of the State in that it is stated, should it be shown that special inducements had been offered Adams by Detective McParland of the Pinkertons, they must be disregarded and a verdict of guilty found. But not unless some worldly promise had been given Adams should the jury regard the plea of the defense that Adams has been influenced. The judge further instructed the jury that if the confession as to the killing of Tyler had been made as incidental to the Steunenberg confession, the verdict should be accordingly found for conviction."[25]

The following evening the jury announced that it was unable to agree on a verdict. The vote of eight to four for acquittal had stood with no change since the first ballot. Woods released Adams, but once again he had no time for celebration, as Sheriff Bailey arrested him for the murder of Ed Boule.[26]

Both Darrow and Hawley promptly left Rathdrum—Darrow went to San Francisco to consult specialist doctors, and Hawley to Boise, where the trial of George Pettibone, delayed while Adams's trial was completed, moved ahead. Darrow tried to force a postponement, as his doctor "thought it might be fatal to me if I went, but Pettibone thought it might be fatal to him if I stayed."[27] His plea was unsuccessful, so he resignedly boarded a train back to Idaho despite his unceasing pain.

On November 27, jury selection began. It proved the same slow plod as in Haywood's trial, and it was not until December 10 that Hawley made the opening argument, in which he called Pettibone "the most guilty of all those accused of causing the death of former Governor Frank Steunenberg."[28] Giving a brief history of the WFM, he stated that "about eight years ago a conspiracy was formed by what is known as the 'inner circle,' the purpose of which was the murder of those who in public life refused to obey the dictates of the 'inner circle.'" Pettibone, he said, "was the paymaster into whose hands was passed the money given to the actual murderers."[29]

When court convened for the first witnesses in its afternoon session, there to question them was Borah, who had just arrived. Orchard was called to the stand the next day, where he remained for four days, carefully guided by Hawley through his maze of murders, bombings, and attempted killings. He then faced Darrow, who approached Orchard differently than Richardson. First he tried to show contradictions between his statements in the Haywood testimony and those he had just made. As in the earlier trial, however, Orchard proved a resolute witness with a remarkable memory, and he held his own; in fact, at one point it was Darrow who "was forced to admit that he was mistaken in regard to the former testimony of the witness."[30]

Unsuccessful in this approach, Darrow changed tactics and forced Orchard to elaborate on some of his most heinous crimes. For example, referring to a child that Orchard had intended to kidnap and hold for ransom, Darrow "had him carefully describe Paulson's little boy and their playing together on the floor." He also asked for specific details about a bomb Orchard had taken into the Idanha to plant in a suite that Steunenberg used, knowing it would also kill dozens of other people. Darrow later wrote about the confrontation: "As I went along, one could see the jury drawing from him in horror and disgust. . . . I did not try to contradict him. I treated him with what seemed kindness and consideration and pity. . . . [H]e no longer looked at the jury, and they avoided him. I felt quite certain that every one of the jury looked upon him with distrust, hatred, and contempt."[31]

Shortly thereafter, Darrow became seriously ill. He missed several days of cross-examination and, after making the defense's opening argument on December 26, he left for Los Angeles, where he was eventually operated upon and his "freak mastoid" condition resolved, although it took weeks for him to recover. Meanwhile, Orrin Hilton was summoned from Colorado to take over. On December 31, his first full day in Boise, Hilton stunningly announced that the defense was resting its case, as he believed the State had not proved its charges.[32]

At 8:50 P.M. on the night of January 3, 1908, the jury left to deliberate, and the next afternoon returned a verdict of not guilty. Hawley, on behalf of the State, thereupon dismissed the charges against Moyer.[33] Strangely, the case's primary loser was Pettibone, who contracted consumption while in jail. It contributed mightily to his death the next autumn following an operation for cancer.[34]

It was not only the trial results that seemed to turn against McParland at this stage. Even something as simple as fulfilling his charitable duties as a Christian proved problematic for him. For example, in February 1908, Pat Crowe— a former train robber and kidnapper who had once made threats against William Pinkerton—came to see him and spun a tale of how difficult life had been since his release from prison. McParland wrote to Bangs that, "He wanted to know if I could not loan him $5.00, so he could get something to eat and a bed. . . . I told him that I was not allowed to use the Agency's money in that way ... [but] no matter what his previous character was, or what it might be now, I did not like to see a man go hungry, or be without a place to sleep, therefore, I would give him $5.00 from my own pocket, and desired that he would pay me at his earliest convenience. ... I don't suppose I will ever see the $5.00, nor do I believe that he has reformed."[35]

Pinkerton was at times a soft touch himself, but not for Crowe. When he heard what McParland had done, he exploded: "Of all the low down, dirty deadbeats and contemptible no-account thieves I ever knew, Pat Crowe is the worst. He always was a four flusher and a bluffer and got himself a reputation by giving out stories about himself. He is the biggest liar and blowhard in the United States and I am surprised that Mr McParland would even give him an audience, let alone loan him $5." After all, Pinkerton continued, the man was "nothing more than a dime novel desperado and I would not give him 50¢ to save him from drowning or being hung."[36] McParland's charitable act kept him in hot water with Pinkerton until Bangs pointed out that the money was McParland's own, not the agency's, and eventually Pinkerton calmed down enough to tell him to charge it to Denver expenses as charity. "He need not be afraid of Crowe paying it back again. Crowe never paid anything to anybody in his life."[37]

Another bad piece of news for McParland came the next month, when his special colleague, Siringo, finally left the agency. He had resigned after the Haywood trial to get married for the third time and move to his ranch in New Mexico, but McParland talked him into coming back for an assignment in the Badlands of South Dakota. But that was the last time. Despite being offered a position as a superintendent, he again retired—this time for good.[38]

Around the same time, Harry Orchard, the one man left to stand trial for the murder of Steunenberg, was brought before Judge Fremont Wood. He stated that, against the advice of his attorney, he wished to withdraw the not-guilty plea and enter one of guilty. After being assured that Orchard understood the consequences, Wood allowed the change of plea.[39] On March 18, Orchard's forty-second birthday, Wood, with no legal leeway, sentenced him to death but, indicating that he fully believed Orchard's testimony in both the Haywood and Pettibone trials, recommended that the Idaho Board of Pardons commute the sentence to life in prison.[40]

"On the first trial he was subjected to the most critical cross-examination by very able counsel for six days, and I do not now recall that at any time he contradicted himself on any material matter," Wood stated, continuing:

Upon the second trial referred to, the same testimony was given, and a thorough and critical cross-examination followed. In no particular was there any discrepancy in material matters between the testimony given upon the latter trial, and that given by the same witness on the former trial. . . . A man of mature years may be able to frame his story and testify falsely to a brief statement of facts involving a transaction and maintain himself on cross-examination. But I cannot conceive of a case where even the greatest intellect can conceive a story of crime, covering years of duration with constantly shifting scenes and changing characters, and maintain that story with circumstantial detail as to times, places, persons and particular circumstances, and under as merciless a cross-examination as was ever given a witness in an American court, unless the witness thus testifying was speaking truthfully and without any attempt to misrepresent or conceal.[41]

McParland was more prosaic when asked his views. "I know nothing about what will be done with Orchard," he said. "He was never promised immunity, and never asked any. I do not know whether his sentence will be commuted or not. He is guilty and he has confessed his guilt."[42] Orchard subsequently told Chris Thiele that he should not be reprieved, because he was "trying to atone for his past [and] thought this course the proper one" and "does not believe he could render the State of Idaho a greater service than by going on the scaffold and meeting his just fate."[43] McParland was impressed with his conviction but still thought it a deception:

I have seen and read of many penitent sinners who were fully prepared to die, admitting the justice of the court's sentence of death, but all of such people would have much rather lived if that was possible. Even the saviour of mankind, as holy writ informs us, requested of the Father in heaven that if in his wisdom he could do so that the cup, meaning the crucifixion, should be passed away. From this it will be seen that Orchard's stand is the first of the kind that has ever come under my notice, and while I think that he is a true penitent, and that I am satisfied he would go to the gallows without flinching, something tells me that inwardly he has an idea that . . . his sentence will be commuted.[44]

If so, Orchard was correct. On July 1, the Idaho Board of Pardons commuted his sentence to life imprisonment. "I am not at all pleased," Orchard stated. "I would rather die on Friday than spend the rest of my life in prison."[45] The latter, however, is exactly what he did, in so doing discovering that life still had much to offer. He became a model prisoner, helped convert others to the Seventh-day Adventist Church, lived in his own small cottage on penitentiary grounds, became a woodworker, raised chickens, and grew berries. He died at the age of eighty-eight in 1954, having late in life republished his story as the record of a man transformed by Christ.[46]

Adams's case was now the only one left unresolved. Even before his second trial, the authorities in Colorado had determined that he had not provided enough evidence to tie St. John to the murder of either William Barney or Arthur Collins.[47] But Adams *had* confessed to killing Collins, so the State of Colorado—and more particularly Bulkeley Wells—could still gain satisfaction by putting *him* on trial. Therefore, on December 27, 1907, Sheriff Charles Fitzpatrick of San Miguel County, Colorado, was on hand in Rathdrum when Adams was discharged for the murder of Boule, and promptly rearrested him for the murder of Collins.[48] Within a few days, Fitzpatrick and his deputy C. C. Hicks—who having been cleared of murder charges in Wallace was now serving in Telluride—took Adams to Colorado.[49]

Not surprisingly, the WFM gave its full financial support to Adams, hiring Orrin Hilton for the case. District Attorney Hugo Selig and former congressman Herschel M. Hogg headed the prosecution. The trial was scheduled for June 22, with a change of venue to Grand Junction in Mesa County. Yet again, jury selection was a major battle, and it was not until July 6 that opening arguments were made before Judge Sprigg Shackleford.[50] Early the next afternoon Hilton objected to a reference made to Adams's confession, on the grounds that "it was extorted from him the defendant by McPharland [*sic*] by the grossest intimidation and threats of punishment and promises of reward."[51] Most of the afternoon was thereafter consumed with legal bickering.

The next day, with the jury excluded, Shackleford heard testimony to determine whether to admit Adams's confession. The first witness was McParland, who explained that he had told Adams: "I knew pretty well what he had done, but that it would be better for him to come through with a full confession. I told him we knew who had been hiring the assassins, and that it would be to his interest to make a clean breast of it. I quoted some Scripture to him and advised him in a spiritual way, telling him that there was salvation even for a murderer." At this point, McParland said, Adams agreed to give his full confession the next day.[52] As the confession was made, it was recorded in shorthand, following which it was transcribed, typed up, and taken to Adams for his approval. "Adams made several interlineations in his own handwriting," the press reported, "and had the chief clerk of the penitentiary . . . correct other typographical errors. After the paper was completed to the satisfaction of Adams, . . . it was signed by him."[53]

Most important, McParland noted that the confession was given voluntarily. "Was there any promise of immunity?" asked Hogg.

"None."

"Were there any threats made?"

"None. . . . I told him I had no authority to make promises, and if I did I couldn't carry them out. I told him that the state generally acted fairly with those who acted fairly with it."[54]

Things were not so comfortable for McParland when Hilton took over the questioning. Armed with a transcript from one of the Idaho trials, he tried to catch the detective in inconsistencies, and also to show that McParland's Bible stories and references to those of the Molly Maguires who turned state's evidence were designed to imply—even if not precisely stating—that Adams would receive immunity.

"Did you tell him there was a chance for him to be forgiven?" asked Hilton.

"I did."

"Did you tell him by whom he would be forgiven?"

"I was speaking from the spiritual end at that time."

"Did you tell him you had assurance that the Almighty would forgive him?"

"I object," burst in Hogg. "Some people might call this blasphemy."[55]

Remaining calm, Hilton continued to grill McParland: "Did you tell him that [Tom] Horn's life would have been saved if he had confessed?"

"I did."

"Did you tell him that you were going to hang the instigators of the crime, but not the tools?"

"I did."

"Did you advise him to seek a clergyman or a lawyer?"

"I did not."[56]

McParland's testimony was followed by more closed evidence from the two men who had recorded the confession: Wellington B. Hopkins and George Huebener. Hopkins stated that "he heard no threats from McParland and that Adams made his own answers," and he then produced the notes that he had taken. Huebener stated that the confession was Adams's "own free and voluntary act," and that he had made some "corrections in the copy after it had been typewritten, at the insistence of Adams, who claimed that he was not accustomed to writing." Further, he said that the claim that McParland had stopped the stenographers from recording at points was true, but it had been done to "discuss points with Adams . . . in order that a clear statement of all facts could be made directly by Adams after deliberation."[57]

Wells then testified that Adams returned with him to Telluride "for the purpose of exhuming a body, and the men who went with him were for protection against violence at the hands of the Western Federation of Miners." It "was at [Adams's] express wish and desire" that he helped in the discovery of Barney's remains, Wells said, in order "to prove that his confession was true."[58]

When the arguments about the confession continued the next morning, Hilton censured McParland as "a pirate, cut throat, a man who should be put behind the bars for criminal method in securing the Adams confession."[59] Despite the rhetoric, however, the prosecution felt confident, as the confession had twice been admitted on the same evidence. Their surprise can therefore only be imagined when that afternoon Judge Shackleford unleashed a bolt from the blue, ruling that: "the method by which Detective James McParland secured a confession from Steve Adams in the penitentiary at Boise, Idaho, rendered the confession inadmissible as evidence."[60]

"A smile played about the mouth of Steve Adams when he heard the words of the court," a far cry from the response of McParland, who was in the witness room when told. "Leaping from the chair he shouted, 'What! Not admissible?' When informed such was the case he resumed his seat, wiped the perspiration from his brow, but said nothing further."[61]

McParland knew, the prosecution knew, the defense knew, and all the reporters knew that the trial was now, for all intents and purposes, over. What had been a weak case *with* the confession had no chance without it. Nevertheless, the prosecution proceeded, with Wells, Marshal Willard Runnels of Telluride, and Mills, the deputy warden of the Idaho penitentiary, testifying.[62] When the prosecution rested on Friday, Shackleford, sympathetic to a juror who said that his religion prevented him doing any work on Saturday, adjourned until Monday, July 13.[63]

Once back in court, Hilton quickly produced eight alibis for Adams on the night of the murder and, resting the case the following day, in his closing argument turned his not inconsiderable skills of denunciation upon Wells, Mills,

McParland, Pinkerton's, Hogg, and even Senator Borah.[64] Late the night of July 14, "McParland and six assistants arrived here in company of Warden Whitney . . . It is reported that they are here to re-arrest Adams in case of his acquittal."[65] It was only a façade, however, for the next day, when Adams was acquitted, he was discharged, and no move was made against him. He boarded a train to Oregon, disappearing back to where he had been picked up almost two and a half years before.

The ramifications of the Steunenberg murder and its investigations and trials had not yet completely played out, however. McParland had long believed there was a traitor who supplied the defense with information, particularly considering that ever since Adams recanted his confession, "every secret operative that we had from time to time had been uncovered."[66] He had routed out two spies, "but there were others." Further, Haywood had once told operative J. N. Londoner "that he could get any information he wanted from the Denver office; that he got his information from one of the highest officials of that office and one that would never be suspected."

McParland therefore launched a secret investigation, code-named Vatwood. What he discovered was that large deposits had been made to a certain bank account, commencing in September 1906, just as Adams "had gone over to the Defense" and McParland "had left for Idaho to try and get him to come back to the State." There was also a deposit made around the time that Operative 21 was uncovered, and still more prior to each of the trials, at points when the defense was desperate to discover the prosecution's plans. The holder of the account into which these funds had been paid was Denver superintendent H. Frank Cary.

Cary had first been employed by Pinkerton's in 1899 to investigate pilfering in Denver's Brown Palace Hotel. He performed well, and was hired as a full-time operative.[67] Two years later, in a surprisingly swift ascent, he was promoted to assistant superintendent,[68] and in 1905, when Fraser moved to San Francisco, Cary took over the Denver office.

On December 4, 1908, McParland called Cary into his office. He first raised the question of several fraudulent expense bills that Cary had submitted—Cary had claimed payment for expenses not incurred and for money owed to other operatives. He also asked about charges that Cary had submitted for train travel that the railroad company had provided for free. Demanding to see Cary's bankbook, McParland confirmed the information he had received about the deposits. "I asked him how much of this he had done," McParland reported, "and he said, well, he would admit what I could prove and that was all."

When Cary refused to comment on a deposit of $594 made when Operative 21 was exposed, McParland "told him I was satisfied that he was loyal to the Agency up to the time he was approached in Sept, 1906 . . . from that time he had been loyal neither to the Agency, nor myself."

"Well, so far as regards that $594.00 . . . that did not come from the funds of the Western Federation, but it came about in a way which I could never discuss while I am in the Agency," Cary said.

"Well, you are no longer in the Agency," McParland replied, "you are discharged and I wish you right now to deliver up to me your keys."

"What! Am I discharged?" said Cary, shocked. "Won't you allow me to resign?"

McParland looked coldly through his thick glasses. "No, I do not allow a man to resign who has admitted himself to be a thief and a forger and when conclusive evidence proves him to be a traitor. You are not fit for the company of a dog. A man of your character should be killed and your carcass thrown to the dogs and if I killed you, Mr Cary, in this room this minute I would not consider I would have to ask the forgiveness of God Almighty for doing so."

Cary handed over his keys, but "swore by high and low that, while he was guilty of everything else of which I had accused him, he was not guilty of giving away secrets to the Western Federation and never received a dollar from them. I told him I would not believe him under oath, or otherwise, that his bank book gave the lie to what he said." When Cary returned a short while later and asked for his salary for the first four days of the month, McParland "told him I was not surprised at his request because a man who was such an infernal scoundrel as he had admitted himself to be was capable of making such a request as he had made. I told him . . . to get out of my office and never show his face here again."

CHAPTER 25

THE LONG GOOD-BYE

T he failure to convict Haywood, Pettibone, or Adams had little impact on McParland's public reputation, and he was still deeply admired by many and detested by others. In the short term, he remained not far from the public eye—even his minor cases were mentioned in the press simply because of his participation.

On May 22, 1909, in a tip of the hat to the tactics of the Wild Bunch, five bandits held up the Union Pacific Overland Limited in the outskirts of Omaha.' Two men already on the train came over the tender and, pointing pistols at the conductor, ordered him to stop in an area known as the Mud Cut, which was hidden by high embankments. Ignoring the passenger compartments, they shot out a window of the mail car, forcing its clerks to open the door. Firing more shots to keep crew and passengers cowed, the robbers took seven mailbags and disappeared. Within hours, local police and county sheriffs, U.S. marshals, postal agents, and "Pinkerton's shrewdest operatives" were on the case,² the last of these under the charge of McParland. The major break in what became known as the Mud Cut case, however, was not due to detection but to happenstance—some schoolboys found the guns, hats, and handkerchiefs used as masks by the robbers. Within days, three of the robbers had been arrested, and the other two were caught not long thereafter. All five were convicted and sentenced to prison.

Not all McParland's cases ended with a guilty verdict. The next year he oversaw a sensational investigation that began after pretty seventeen-year-old Gladys Whitney induced traveling salesman J. D. Diehl to go to the Metropole Hotel in Salt Lake City with her. There she served him a drugged drink and made off with an estimated $10,500 worth of uncut diamonds.³ Superintendent W. I. Willsie of Pinkerton's Salt Lake City office—which had opened under McParland's auspices only five months before⁴—was contacted.

It quickly became apparent that Whitney had an accomplice named

Walter Perry, who had disappeared at the same time. Willsie and McParland oversaw a search that led operatives from Idaho to Nevada to California before, in mid-October, the couple was discovered at Hot Springs, Arkansas. The local authorities attempted to make the arrest before the Pinkertons could, and getting wind of the plan, Perry and Whitney skipped south. A week and a half later they were arrested in Huntsville, Texas, but again disappeared after "something happened which no one could fully understand and since then the police of Huntsville have been held under suspicion."[5] Finally, in mid-December, Whitney gave herself up in Memphis, and several days later Perry was taken in Pueblo, Colorado.[6]

Suspecting the pair had not operated alone, McParland hunted down W. C. Douglas, "said to have a bad record as a confidence man and gambler all over the United States."[7] Douglas admitted during an interrogation in Denver that he had received some of the diamonds and sold them. In March, McParland took him to Salt Lake City, where he testified at the preliminary hearing for Whitney and Perry. Released on bond, Douglas promptly disappeared.[8] Without his testimony, and with his wife claiming the couple had never come to their house—for which she was later prosecuted for perjury—Whitney was acquitted on June 9, following which Perry was released.[9]

McParland had no more success in a concurrent case. On January 2, 1911, the Overland Limited was robbed near Rees, Utah; one porter was killed, another wounded, and two thousand dollars taken from passengers.[10] McParland's investigation identified Bryan O'Hara as "the tall man" in the holdup, and Victor Clore as "the short man." McParland sent agents to Michigan, where O'Hara was visiting his mother, and they were put under surveillance. Satisfied that these were the culprits, McParland ordered them arrested and returned to Ogden, Utah, for trial. However, the magistrate dismissed the case at a preliminary hearing, leading law enforcement officers to complain bitterly. The press reported, "Evidence of a convincing nature which the Pinkerton detectives led local officers to believe was in their possession, failed to materialize at the preliminary hearing, and after the two men were brought back to Ogden the Pinkerton detectives effaced themselves from the case, . . . leaving all of the responsibility of gathering evidence and prosecuting the case to the local officers."[11]

Yet McParland's reputation remained intact, and was even enhanced in his later years by publications such as a book about famous criminal cases by the captain of the San Francisco police. Six photographs in that volume—of the greatest detectives in history—featured McParland along with Allan and William Pinkerton.[12] But the greatest paean to McParland and his career came in 1914, when Sir Arthur Conan Doyle published *The Valley of Fear*, a tale based on the Molly Maguires, in which detective Birdy Edwards, going under the name John McMurdo, infiltrates the Scowrers, a violent group that has been terrorizing the coal fields for years. After bringing down the Scowrers and their leader, Jack McGinty—based on Kehoe—Edwards is forced to flee for his life under another name, and it is only after a mysterious murder in England that Sherlock Holmes discovers that his fellow detective is still alive.[13]

Virtually no one in America needed to be told that Birdy Edwards was McParland. Yet although the novel portrayed him as a hero, it nevertheless created great ill feeling between the agency's management and the author. Conan Doyle was reportedly first told the tale of the Molly Maguires by William Pinkerton in the smoking lounge of an ocean liner during a transAtlantic crossing. Fascinated, Conan Doyle spun his own version, which infuriated Pinkerton, because Conan Doyle had not shown the courtesy of asking his permission to use a confidential discussion for his work, even in a fictional account. The two men had previously been on friendly terms, but their relationship thereafter was not particularly warm.[14]

At the same time, Pinkerton and McParland were promoting their own—and thus the agency's—public image. In late 1911, *The Washington Herald* ran a series of seven lengthy articles that, the newspaper claimed, "without adornment . . . relate experiences that dim the most imaginative fiction, including the inside history of the great Molly Maguire case." Told in theory by Pinkerton and McParland, the stories were, according to the principal, "the last of this class of publications that will ever come from our agency."[15] Three of the articles recounted McParland's investigations into the Molly Maguires and were subsequently republished in other papers across the country, producing a remarkable amount of free publicity and advertising and reintroducing McParland to a whole new generation of hero worshippers.[16]

Alternatively, McParland could be downright hostile about publications that did not mesh with his memories or follow his agenda. Referring to an article about Harvey Logan in 1910, he wrote: "[T]he article in the Wide World Magazine referred to is simply a fake written up from extracts gleaned from time to time from newspaper stories to which is added the imagination of the writer." He pointed out several inaccuracies, but was particularly annoyed that it seemed to be "an advertisement for Mr Swain," who, "I have concluded [is] the real power behind this article. Swain is now running a Private Detective Agency on his own hook in Spokane, and at no time was he ever employed to effect the arrest of any of the 'Wild Bunch.'"[17]

Four years later, McParland was still vehemently criticizing viewpoints that did not conform to his own. "Would say that I have concluded that the Menace is well named," he wrote to Bangs. "As a publication it is indeed a menace to good citizenship and common decency, but to cover up the falsehoods that it sets forth it states a few facts which are true, but leaves out the main facts in each case."[18]

That said, McParland made his own errors in the same letter—confusing his "facts" about his greatest investigation: "One of the reasons why the Ancient Order of Hibernians did not defend themselves or show to the public that they had no connection with the Molly Maguires, was the fact that there was no evidence during the trial of these defendants which in any way connected the Ancient Order of Hibernians with the Molly Maguires. . . . During the first trials . . . Mr Gowen asked me a question, namely: if I had investigated, or knew to my own knowledge as to whether or not the Molly Maguires were a branch of the Ancient Order of Hibernians, or had any affiliation with that Order. My reply was that I had fully investigated that part of the case and was prepared to swear that the Ancient Order of Hibernians had no affiliation, pro or con, with the Molly Maguires."[19] It is a stunning statement from a man who had said repeatedly during the trials, "the Ancient Order of Hibernians, more commonly called the Molly Maguires."[20] Moreover, it was not the only time he "misremembered" what he had so staunchly claimed over and over years before.[21]

Was he going senile, was he just forgetful, was he lying yet again, or did he have some other agenda? With McParland's increasing age and subtle makeup, one cannot discount any of those options.

As much as McParland could be an implacable opponent, he could be an equally generous benefactor, particularly to the Denver Catholic community. "The ball to be given Monday evening, January 3, at Knights of Columbus hall for the benefit of St Vincent's orphanage, promises to be, as usual, the most brilliant event of the year in Catholic society," a newspaper stated. "It will be given under the auspices of St Vincent's Aid society," it continued, noting that the five-man arrangements committee included McParland, as did the committee in charge of the supper.[22] McParland was also noted for donations of money and time to the Cathedral and the Knights of Columbus, including organizing a benefit play for an Italian orphanage.[23]

McParland also had a tender spot for loyal employees. One of these was Philip McMahon, who had joined the agency's New York bureau at age fifteen as an office boy and worked his way up to stenographer, and then to Robert Pinkerton's personal clerk.[24] He resigned after ten years due to ill health, but later returned to the Boston and Montreal offices, before being committed to a sanitarium with tuberculosis. In 1915, he sought a job in a healthier environment, and Allan Pinkerton asked McParland to provide him with a position. Despite balking initially, McParland took McMahon under his wing, personally escorted him to a lung specialist and paid his bill, and then gave him a position as a clerk. When McMahon again became ill, McParland spent time with him and his wife, and also reprimanded E. E. Prettyman—Cary's replacement as Denver superintendent—for working McMahon too hard when he wasn't healthy.[25] He continued to look out for the frail younger man for the rest of his career.

In a letter about McMahon to Allan Pinkerton, McParland revisited an issue that had long annoyed him. "I see that our New York office from time to time spells my name McPartland," he wrote. "I have called the attention of the New York office and some of our other offices to the fact that the name McPartland was given to me in derision by the Appeal to Reason and I do not take very kindly to having my name spelled in that way . . . and would respectfully request that addressing me as McPartland be discontinued."[26] An embarrassed Allan Pinkerton wrote back that "the error of incorrectly addressing you is mine and entirely unintentional."[27]

Such issues paled, however, compared to his growing health concerns. As he approached seventy, McParland's eyesight became poorer than ever, and his excess weight was even more problematic. In the middle of an exceedingly hot summer in 1916, he was temporarily out of commission following complications due to the extraction of a wisdom tooth. He bled profusely, and the doctors were unable to stop it for five hours.[28] He thereafter returned to work too quickly, and as a result his "entire nervous system has sustained a severe shock. He was unable to eat or sleep for several days and nights." His wife told Prettyman that "his heart is very weak and that his legs do not appear to be able to carry his weight—that today he walked to the barber shop, only a block away, and when he returned he was exhausted."[29]

In the following days, Mary McParland continued to express her concerns, but her husband refused to listen. Two days after Prettyman urged her "to prevent his coming to the office until he is stronger and [hopefully] for a week or ten days,"[30] he was back. "She realizes that his age makes it impossible for him to recover quickly," Prettyman reported to Bangs, "but he thinks he is just as strong and well as he was when a young man."[31]

Even when he *was* in the office, McParland could not accomplish as much as he once had. The last case in which he was heavily involved was in March 1914, when Milton Joseph, a Salt Lake City stockbroker, disappeared from Ogden, Utah, with about $54,000 from a stock transaction.[32] Joseph was charged with embezzling, and McParland took over the investigation, but despite a nationwide search, the broker could not be found. It was not until 1922—after McParland's death—that Joseph was finally arrested in Miami, tried, and convicted.[33]

In September 1916, William Pinkerton raised an uncomfortable subject with his nephew, writing, "McParland has been an old and faithful servant, at all times loyal and trustworthy, but he has become old and, in a way, a little superannuated. I realize we must make the change, still in view of past services I would like to be as liberal with him as possible and would like to have your ideas as to what amount of pension we allow him during his life time. . . . I would not object if you decide to pay him his salary in full. As you know, I am very much attached to the old fellow and it is going to be a painful task to sit down on him, no matter what we do for him."[34]

McParland did not want to give up his lifetime's occupation, but he had slowly become aware that he no longer had the energy and vigor to continue the job full time. The Pinkertons were extremely accommodating, and within a short while he was able to take what was in effect a retirement, although he was given the title of assistant to the general manager, was allowed to maintain an office at the Denver headquarters, and remained on a generous salary of two thousand dollars per year.[35] He continued to do enough to feel that he was still a part of the organization, but he gracefully kept out of local decision making and spent more and more time at home with Mary, his beloved bulldogs,[36] and part of the time, his niece Kittie.

Unfortunately, the added rest did not help him to regain his health. By early 1918, he was suffering from diabetes and kidney troubles.[37] In 1919, he faced new problems with his feet, and in March a seriously ingrown toenail was removed, but the infection it caused was accompanied by the onset of gangrene.[38] On April 30, at Mercy Hospital, the big toe on his left foot was amputated, but doctors soon discovered that the gangrene "had set in further and that it is now necessary to amputate the second toe and possibly the foot."[39]

Shortly after the operation, McParland suffered a stroke. On May 14, it was noted that he "is apparently sinking rapidly. He has absolutely no control of himself whatever, and the physicians are under the impression that he had another stroke last Sunday, and it is possible that he may pass away at any time."[40]

That time came at 6:20 A.M. on Sunday, May 18, 1919, when McParland slipped away "after extreme suffering during the entire night," dying from what was officially diagnosed as "apoplexy."[41] On his death certificate, Mary listed his date of birth as the same highly uncertain date on his tombstone: March 22, 1844. Where it came from no one knows, but it did allow McParland to go out just as he would have liked—a man of mystery, first, last, and forever.

At nine o'clock on the morning of Tuesday, May 20, a Solemn Requiem Mass for James McParland was held at the Cathedral of the Immaculate Conception in Denver, where, years before, "No man bore a more radiant smile than he at the dedication ceremonies."[42] According to press accounts, "the Cathedral was crowded to capacity with friends and acquaintances of the widely-known detective, and the Elks and fourth degree Knights of Columbus . . . were present in a body."[43] He was then buried at Mount Olivet Cemetery, immediately adjacent to the grave of his beloved nephew Eneas.

In the following days, messages of condolence poured in to Mary, a High Mass was held in McParland's honor at the Annunciation Church in Denver, and the Pinkertons and Bangs agreed that the agency would pay the funeral expenses and medical bills of their "faithful employe [sic] and friend," as well as give his widow a handsome pension of one thousand dollars per year.[44]

At the same time, the process of hagiography—long before started by the press and Allan Pinkerton—moved full speed ahead. McParland "performed one of the greatest services that has ever been rendered to the Catholic Church in America," the *Denver Catholic Register* claimed.[45] "Once on the trail he never gave up," an editorial in *The Rocky Mountain News* stated. "He would disappear for weeks at a time, lost to his agency, winding after his man thru city street and mountain trail. . . . By nature he was endowed with an instinctive knowledge of human nature, particularly where it fell into the crooked path."[46]

Another source that gave generous praise to the man it called "the most picturesque and one of the ablest detectives in the history of wholesale American crime" was *The Minneapolis Journal*: "James McParland's methods were his own. So successful were they that heads of foreign government's detective bureaus studied them constantly and often conferred with him."[47] According to both friends and enemies, it declared, McParland "understood the psychology of the wholesale slayer better than any man of his time. His ability to size up the hunted man's mind and thoughts was almost uncanny. Today, in many a big case, the methods of McParland are being used. They were not then particularly new methods, but the Irishman had developed them to a degree of fineness that was almost perfection."

McParland had paid a heavy price for his services to law and order, the Minneapolis newspaper continued, noting that "the McParland of the Colorado trials was a man with gray hair and heavy glasses," but was truly a man's man. "A miner's bullet had ripped off half the right ear. . . . In his body were 38 bullet and knife wounds, each one of which had been given him by a miner in his long life fight against murder and terrorism," proving that he had long lived "in greater danger of assassination, probably, than any man hunter of his time."

This effusive praise was widespread. His life was eulogized throughout the country, his virtues extolled. And although there were publications that disagreed, many Americans went to bed just a little less comfortably, knowing that the Great Detective was no longer there to protect them.

Most of those who had known McParland best—his friends, family, professional colleagues, and enemies—did not last many more years themselves. William Pinkerton died of a heart attack on December 11, 1923, in a hotel room in Los Angeles, where he had gone to preside over a series of law-enforcement conferences.[48]

Five years later, on October 18, 1928, McParland's closest colleague, Charlie Siringo, died of a coronary at his son Lee Roy's house in Altadena, California. Snappish and cantankerous until the end, Siringo had for years waged legal battles with Pinkerton's over three books that he wrote about his detective career.[49] Siringo's old pal and a man McParland trusted as much as any—Doc Shores—died where he had lived for so long, in Gunnison, Colorado, in October 1934, just short of his ninetieth birthday.[50]

The members of McParland's family with whom he had been closest all passed away in the decade following his death. Edward, a bitter man who had never come to terms with living in the shadow of his older brother, died on July 3, 1926, in Manitou Springs, Colorado, where he had served for a number of years as a justice of the peace, and had told many stories about how he and his brother were responsible for breaking up the Molly Maguires.[51]

Not long after her husband's death, Mary moved back to Chicago to be close to her sisters. She died in November 1928, and was buried with McParland at Mount Olivet Cemetery. As a seemingly fitting tribute to the mystery about her husband's date of birth, her inscription on their joint tombstone reads "Died Nov. 20, 1928," despite the fact that her death certificate showed the date to be November 19.[52]

McParland's brother Charles, long his dearest sibling, had flourished, and in 1911 was elected an Illinois state representative. Later a successful real-estate agent, he died on December 15, 1928, in Chicago, where he had come decades before at his brother's recommendation.[53]

Meanwhile, Big Bill Haywood succeeded Vincent St. John as the head of the Industrial Workers of the World in 1915. Three years later he was convicted of violating the Espionage Act of 1917—which had been passed with the U.S. entry into World War I—and was sentenced to prison. While out on appeal in 1921, he fled to the Soviet Union, where he remained until his death from a stroke on May 18, 1928.[54]

Five weeks later—June 24, 1928—Frank Gooding, who in 1921 had joined Borah as a U.S. senator, died in office.[55] And a little more than a year after that, on August 3, 1929, James Hawley, who had served as the ninth governor of Idaho from 1911 through 1913 before returning to his law practice, died in his beloved Boise. William E. Borah was reelected to the U.S. Senate five times, serving on numerous committees before dying in office on January 19, 1940.[56]

The lead attorney on the opposing side of the Haywood trial is not remembered nearly as well as the other major players, because his career was tragically cut short. In May 1911, Edmund Richardson was killed at the age of forty-eight when a car in which he was a passenger plunged down an embankment near Louisville Junction, Colorado.[57]

McParland's greatest adversary—Clarence Darrow—went on to conduct some of the most famous defense efforts in U.S. legal history, including the Leopold and Loeb "thrill kill" trial, the "Scopes Monkey Trial," and the murder trial of Ossian Sweet.[58] He died in Chicago on March 13, 1938—two years after historian J. Walter Coleman inaccurately used him to "prove" his points about McParland's role in the Molly Maguire trials, thus starting a revisionist interpretation of McParland that has influenced opinion about him through the present day.[59]

So was James McParland one of America's greatest heroes: a man who liberated the anthracite fields from a reign of terror; who hunted down robbers, murderers, and bad men wherever they dared to attack civilized society; and

who was "the most resourceful and dare-devil product of the American system
of developing men to cope with the wit and daring of super-criminals"?[60] Or
was he "the rottenest sonafabitch America ever produced, not barring Sacco
and Vanzetti's Judge Thayer or Joe McCarthy"?[61]

Not surprisingly, he was, in reality, something in between. Many mine
owners, bank tellers, directors of big businesses, shopkeepers, and state and
local officials thought he left America a better place because of his life's work.
But thousands of mine workers, union organizers, and labor leaders disagreed
wholeheartedly. And it is safe to say that even today McParland and Pinkerton's are still very much symbolic of the mistrust, hatred, and violence between owners and workers during the growth of labor unions.

On a more personal level, McParland served as a model and inspiration for
subsequent generations of undercover detectives and other law-enforcement
officers. He was long remembered as a larger-than-life link to the past, an icon
of a previous rough and rowdy age, and a grand old man telling tall tales—
some probably too tall—of events that could no longer happen in the modern
world. The statue Gowen spoke of so glowingly might not have existed, but
the memory of the Great Detective served the same purpose.

Yet others remembered or learned of him as the epitome of evil, a man who
did more damage to labor than any other non–mine owner ever had. This
image is certainly what Darrow focused on when he attacked McParland, portraying him, Pinkerton's, and the entire detective profession as unethical, immoral, and unworthy of trust or belief. But in assessing Darrow's arguments,
it should be remembered that the task of trial lawyers is to convince and influence the jury by any means available, whether accurate, honest, or not. McParland provided a focus by which Darrow could divert the jury from weaknesses
in the defense's case—as a recent biographer noted: "With a target like McParland at hand, Darrow would not neglect one of his guiding dictums: the jury
needs a villain."[62]

Darrow further argued that McParland was not just a liar, but a man who
had lived with lies so long that he could not distinguish them from the truth.
This was a brilliant strategy, because McParland's frequent shadowy role—
hunting for the truth while living a lie—made it easy to see in him a man for
whom the truth and lies were so closely intertwined that they became indis-
tinct. And thus it was a manufactured image of McParland's acts, rather than
any true behavior, that helped dictate how he has since been viewed.

Similarly, many assessments of McParland have been based on his *perceived*
role in the Molly Maguire investigation and trials. But such one-dimensional

caricatures—whether positive or negative—cannot convincingly produce a true portrait of any man. McParland's actions have been interpreted in so many different ways that most appraisals are tainted with suspicion. For example, McParland has often, with more bias than calm evaluation, been taken to task as an agent provocateur. Yet, as the classic article on the subject stated: "It is impossible to conclusively determine whether McParlan's role was either that of an agent provocateur or that of a passive collector of information."[63]

McParland has also been damned as being "an informer" who testified against men with whom he had broken bread and in whose homes he had stayed. But if those convicted *were* guilty, should McParland *not* have testified? Have not the critics who claim that murder, attempted murder, and assault are not as wicked as being an informer simply lost their perspective, just as the defense lawyers did when they suggested that McParland's failure to prevent the murders made him worse than the killers? Thus, as with those who have criticized McParland for his role in the Haywood trial, most of those who have evaluated his character based on what he did in relation to the Molly Maguires have not truly produced assessments that withstand impartial analysis of the full facts.

If one begins with a belief that James McParland was a noble hero on the side of the angels, a man who fought for right, one can find "facts" to support the notion. Similarly, if one begins with a belief that McParland was a villain lacking a conscience, and that time and again his testimony was a pack of lies, one can find "evidence" to support that, too.

However, no one can ever truly know what was in the mind or heart of a man a century ago—particularly one as complex and mysterious as McParland. The reality is that we will never know for certain what he believed, what he felt, why he acted as he did. He was certainly not a saint. He probably betrayed his sister-in-law in order to gain financially, he certainly perjured himself on the witness stand more than once, and he used dubious means to force Adams to support Orchard's confession. But he was human, too—he took pity on a destitute ex-convict looking for help, he was appalled by the vigilante killing of Ellen McAllister at Wiggans Patch, he was frightened and unsteady in the most hair-raising parts of his undercover work with the Molly Maguires, and he was generous to his church. He was also extremely loyal, as proven in many instances.

So what does all this say about James McParland? He did seem to have his own moral code, which allowed him to do anything, say anything, go to any extreme, to "get his man." When that objective was to secure a conviction, this made him dissimilar only in scale to other law-enforcement agents of his time, or, in some respects, to the police today, who are confined to much narrower legal and ethical limits than McParland was. He was willing to lie, even when under oath, to secure a conviction, and his letters and reports show an unattractive certainty of his own rectitude that at times verged on the fanatical.[64]

There was also a streak of contempt and vicious retribution that differentiated him from many other law-enforcement officers. This came out at times such as when he gleefully gloated that "it will cost Moyer, Haywood and Pettibone and as many more their lives."[65] It is hard to know if he believed they had done what they were accused of, or if his dealings with union men had convinced him that even if they weren't guilty of the crimes for which they were charged, they were guilty of others, and the country would be better off without them.

Perhaps the development of such an attitude was inevitable, as many of the men whom he dealt with *were* brutal, contemptible characters. Killing, beating, robbing, blowing up buildings and people—these were things McParland investigated on a regular basis. Moreover, he worked in places where life was cheap, and in a rough, violent society in which poverty, drink, and the wretched conditions of the mines were unlikely to bring out the best in anyone. So it should not be unexpected that he became as tough, as determined, as merciless as the men he faced. Perhaps it was those precise attributes that made him so very good at his job.

His success rate was also enhanced by the fact that he was extremely self-confident, could bluff like a professional card player, and had an innate sense of what buttons to push in verbal jousts, whether with men he was interrogating or when the role was reversed in court. However, this attitude seems to have reached the point of arrogance late in his career—he sometimes seemed to feel that he didn't just represent Pinkerton's, but that he *was* Pinkerton's— and some of his self-serving responses might well have hurt the prosecution's case. Was McParland's ego so inflated because he had earned such fame so early? Because he truly never did miss getting a confession? Or was he just naturally pompous? Whichever, such smug self-satisfaction cannot have made him easy to work for or with, and it would not have always endeared him to juries, or others.

In many biographies, the subject's true character can be glimpsed from his private life, but this is impossible with McParland. No personal letters, diaries, or written confidences with friends or family are known to exist. Records show he was generous to his Church, but none show if he was really just "buying off" God for his bad acts. Did he believe he could do that? Did his generosity give him a confidence in his standing in Heaven, so much so that he was serious when he said, "[I]f I killed you, Mr Cary, in this room this minute I would not consider I would have to ask the forgiveness of God Almighty for doing so,"[66] or was it just a figure of speech? We simply don't know.

There is also no proof of what McParland was like as a husband, a father, a brother, or a son. There are no emotionally charged documents illustrating how he reacted to the tragic loss of two young daughters or how he felt about the premature death of his first wife. Did he ever become truly close to anyone—even Mary—after that? Did he ever write a "love letter"? Was he a delight—or a misery—at a dinner party?

As always with James McParland, there are more questions than answers. It is just this elusiveness that is the essence of the Great Detective, who was, is, and will forever remain, an enigma.

ACKNOWLEDGMENTS

In the research, writing, and other preparations of this book, I received generous assistance from numerous individuals and organizations. My thanks are first due to my wife, Dr. Elizabeth Cruwys, who served at different times as research assistant, adviser, and copyeditor, as well as providing encouragement, enthusiasm, and critical assessment.

This story would not have been told without the efforts of Bill Hamilton of A.M. Heath, George Lucas of InkWell Management, and Maggie Riggs and Joshua Kendall of Penguin Group USA. To each of them I am profoundly grateful. I am also most appreciative of the help of Charles Brotherstone of A.M. Heath and Wendy Wolf of Penguin Group USA.

Several other individuals deserve particular mention for special contributions to this project: Professor David H. Grover; John Horneber, my research assistant in Colorado; Jan Kinzer of the Pennsylvania State Archives; Carolyn Lord; and Sarah Tischer Scully of the Jones Media Center, Dartmouth College Library. I would also like to express my thanks to Professor Julian Dowdeswell, Heather Lane, and Georgina Cronin of the Scott Polar Research Institute at the University of Cambridge.

For their willingness to share their specialist knowledge and opinions relating to the Molly Maguires, the investigations and trials following the Steunenberg assassination, and other historical material pertinent to McParland's life, I thank Professor Eugenio Biagini of the Faculty of History, University of Cambridge; Patrick Campbell; Howard Crown; Professor David H. Grover; MaryJoy Martin; Dennis McCann; Martin McParland; Stu Richards; Frank Taaffe; Chris and Annie Wilson; and Dr. Peter Yasenchak of the Schuylkill County Historical Society.

For access to documents and other holdings, I would like to express my appreciation to the staffs of the Albert and Shirley Small Special Collections Library at the University of Virginia; the Bancroft Library of the University of California at Berkeley; the Beinecke Rare Book and Manuscript Library of Yale University; the British Library; the Cambridge University Library of the University of Cambridge; the Church of St. James Tandragee parish; the Colorado State Archives; the Denver Public Library; the Georgetown University Library; the Gotlieb Archival Research Center at Boston University; the Hagley Museum and Library; the Historical Society of Pennsylvania; History Colorado; the Huntington Library; the Idaho State Archives; the Illinois State Archives; the Jones Media Center of the Dartmouth College Library; the Kansas Historical Society; Library and Archives Canada; the Library of Congress; the National Library of Ireland; the Newberry Library of Chicago; the New Mexico State Records Center and Archives; the Pennsylvania State Archives; the Philadelphia Archdiocesan Historical Research Center; the Pottsville Free Public Library; the Public Record Office of Northern Ireland; the Robert E. Smylie Archives of the College of Idaho; the Schuylkill County Historical Society; the Scott Polar Research Institute Library; the U.S. National Archives and Records Administration; the University of Colorado at Boulder Libraries Archives; the University of Minnesota Law Library; the University of Wisconsin–Madison Libraries; the Western History Collections of the University of Oklahoma; and the Wyoming State Archives, Department of State Parks and Cultural Resources.

For their individual help with access to holdings, I am very grateful for the kindness of Jan Boles of the College of Idaho; Lynn Catanese and Marge McNinch of the Hagley Museum and Library; Dave Derbes and Dr. Peter Yasenchak of the Schuylkill County Historical Society; Barry Drucker of the New Mexico State Records Center and Archives; Elizabeth Falk, Carolyn Ruby, and John Yandell of the Idaho State Archives; Darrell Garwood of the Kansas Historical Society; Sarah Ash Georgi of the Huntington Library; Carl Hallberg of the Wyoming State Archives; Michael J. Hannon of the University of Minnesota Law Library; Shane Harper of DartDoc at Dartmouth College; David M. Hayes, archivist at the University of Colorado at Boulder Libraries; Margaret Hrabe of the Albert and Shirley Small Special Collections Library at the University of Virginia; John C. Johnson of the Gotlieb Archival Research Center at Boston University; the Kaercher descendants; Jan Kinzer of the Pennsylvania State Archives; Carolyn Lord; Jeremy D. Popkin of the University of Kentucky; Sarah Tischer Scully of the Jones Media Center, Dartmouth College Library; and Steven Smith of the Historical Society of Pennsylvania.

For help with photographs, I thank George Bacon; Annette Fugita of the Archdiocese of Denver Mortuary; the Kaercher descendants; Carolyn Lord;

Martin McParland; and Barbara Natanson of the Library of Congress, Prints & Photographs Division.

I would also like to thank those others who kindly aided my research, including Susan H. Brosnan and Sean Esby of the Knights of Columbus; James Campbell of Selinsgrove, Pennsylvania; Professor Michael Churgin of the University of Texas School of Law; Elena Cline of the Colorado Department of Personnel & Administration, Colorado State Archives; Carol Ressler Lockman of the Hagley Museum and Library; David W. Mattox of Parsons, Kansas; Consuelo Piñeda of the New Mexico State Records Center and Archives; and Dr. Ralph S. Riffenburgh of the Doheny Eye Institute.

I am grateful to the following for permission to use copyrighted or privately held material: the Albert and Shirley Small Special Collections Library at the University of Virginia, for the correspondence of Robert A. Pinkerton; the American Academy of Political and Social Science, for a quotation from the book *Private Police*, by Jeremiah P. Shalloo; Tyler Anbinder, for a quotation from his book *Five Points*; Harold Aurand, for quotations from his book *From the Molly Maguires to the United Mine Workers* and his article "The Myth of Molly Maguire"; the Bancroft Library of the University of California at Berkeley, for the papers of Charles Erskine Scott Wood; Patrick Campbell, for quotations from his book *A Molly Maguire Story*; Caxton Printers, for quotations from the monograph *The Introductory Chapter to the History of the Trials of Moyer, Haywood, and Pettibone, and Harry Orchard*, by Fremont Wood; Geoffrey Cowan, for quotations from his book *The People v. Clarence Darrow*; John A. Farrell, for a quotation from his book *Clarence Darrow*; David H. Grover, for quotations from his book *Debaters and Dynamiters*; the Hagley Museum and Library, for the Molly Maguire Papers of the Reading Company Law Department Records; Linda Healey, for quotations from the book *Big Trouble*, by J. Anthony Lukas; the Historical Society of Pennsylvania, for the Molly Maguire Reports, Society Small Collection (0022B); the Idaho State Archives, for the Pinkerton Papers of the James H. Hawley Papers, as well as the James Henry Hawley Papers; Elizabeth Jameson, for quotations from her book *All That Glitters*; the Kaercher descendants, for the Kaercher MSS; Kevin Kenny, for quotations from his book *Making Sense of the Molly Maguires* and his article "The Molly Maguires in Popular Culture"; John P. Lavelle, for quotations from his book *The Hard Coal Docket*; the Library of Congress, for the Pinkerton's National Detective Agency Records and numerous unprocessed visual materials from those holdings; Alan Marshall, for quotations from his book *Intelligence and Espionage in the Reign of Charles II, 1660–1685*; MaryJoy

Martin, for quotations from her book *The Corpse on Boomerang Road*; Gary T. Marx, for a quotation from his book *Undercover: Police Surveillance in America*; the New Mexico State Records Center and Archives for the Governor L. Bradford Prince Papers of the Territorial Archives of New Mexico; Richard Patterson, for quotations from his book *Butch Cassidy*; the Pennsylvania State Archives for the transcripts of the trials of Alexander Campbell, John Donahue, Michael J. Doyle, Thomas P. Fisher and Patrick McKenna, Edward Kelly, and Patrick Hester, Peter McHugh, and Patrick Tully; the Philadelphia Archdiocesan Historical Research Center, for the Molly Maguire Manuscript Collection of the American Catholic Historical Society Manuscript Collections and the Archbishop James Wood Papers; Random House Bertelsmann for quotations from the book *Red Harvest*, by Dashiell Hammett; Dan Rockwell, for quotations from the book his father, Wilson Rockwell, edited, *Memoirs of a Lawman* by Cyrus Wells Shores; Clancy Sigal, for quotations from his book *Going Away*; the Robert E. Smylie Archives of the College of Idaho for the GL Crookham Jr. Papers; Southern Methodist University Press, for a quotation from the book *Guide to Life and Literature of the Southwest*, by J. Frank Dobie; Texas A&M University Press, for quotations from Ben Pingenot's book *Siringo*; the University of Colorado at Boulder Libraries Archives for Edmund Richardson's Notes, Affidavits, and Related Material produced for the first trial of Steve Adams and the transcripts for the second trial of Steve Adams and the trial of Bill Haywood; the University of Minnesota Press, for a quotation from the book *The Welsh in America*, edited by Alan Conway; the University of Oklahoma, for the Frank M. Canton Collection, Western History Collections; Hedy Weinberg, for quotations from the book *Attorney for the Damned*, edited by Arthur Weinberg; Robert P. Weiss, for a quotation from his article "Private Detective Agencies and Labour Discipline in the United States"; and the Wyoming State Archives, Department of State Parks and Cultural Resources, for the correspondence and papers of Sheriff Frank A. Hadsell. If I have overlooked anybody, or failed to trace the correct copyright holders, I hope they will forgive me. Acknowledgment of help does not imply endorsement of the views or interpretations expressed in this book about a most controversial figure.

As always, I would like to express my gratitude and love to my parents, Ralph and Angelyn Riffenburgh, for their ongoing patience, encouragement, and support. And I am grateful for the day-to-day cheer given by Ma, Gertrude, and Ethel while I was writing the manuscript.

INDEX